The Provisional Pulpit

Joseph V. Hughes Jr. and Holly O. Hughes
Series on the Presidency and Leadership

A list of all titles in this series is available at the end of the book.

The Provisional Pulpit

MODERN PRESIDENTIAL LEADERSHIP OF PUBLIC OPINION

Brandon Rottinghaus

TEXAS A&M UNIVERSITY PRESS • COLLEGE STATION

First edition

This paper meets the requirements
of ANSI/NISO Z39.48-1992 (Permanence of Paper).
Binding materials have been chosen for durability.

∞

Library of Congress Cataloging-in-Publication Data

Rottinghaus, Brandon, 1977
The provisional pulpit : modern presidential leadership of public opinion / Brandon Rottinghaus.—1st ed.
p. cm.—(Joseph V. Hughes Jr. and Holly O. Hughes series on the presidency and leadership)
Includes bibliographical references and index.
ISBN 978-1-60344-187-2 (hardback : alk. paper)
ISBN 978-1-60344-195-7 (pbk. : alk. paper)
1. Presidents—United States—Public opinion—Case studies. 2. Political leadership—United States—Case studies. 3. Communication in politics—United States—Case studies. 4. Persuasion (Rhetoric)—Political aspects—United States—Case studies. 5. United States—Politics and government—20th century. 6. United States—Politics and government—21st century. I. Title. II. Series: Presidency and leadership (Unnumbered)
JK516.R67 2010
352.23'60973—dc22
2009036379

To my parents,
who took me to my first presidential library

Contents

List of Illustrations

Figures

Tables

Preface

In this book I pose a simple but critical question that is at the core of modern presidential politics: when and under what conditions do presidents find success at leading public opinion? To address this question and begin this investigation, in this preface I make an informal (but instructional) survey of three moments of attempted presidential leadership. In assessing the interaction of period, president, and policy, we hope to uncover which factors helped produce successful leadership of public opinion. Or, if leadership was not successful, we want to know which factors are to blame. This is a difficult task because there are countless factors that could be considered and only sparse notions of the predictable conditions under which we might expect presidential success. In the three vignettes that follow, I examine President Franklin Roosevelt's rhetoric and the steady entry of the United States into World War II, President Ronald Reagan's solutions to the budget issues of the 1980s, and President George W. Bush's race to "save" Social Security at the onset of his second term.

Franklin Roosevelt and the Onset of War

Longstanding historical impressions suggest that President Franklin Roosevelt could lead public opinion with the click of a radio dial.[1] The president, elected in tumultuous times, seemed to have an uncommon bond with the American people, due in part to his popular position as the "savior" of the country in dire economic times. This perception was also due to his techniques. A pioneer in the use of radio to communicate his (often complicated or controversial) message to the voters across the country, President Roosevelt is often viewed as a successful leader of public opinion. In some instances this was accurate, but in leading the public into World War II, the president faced a reluctant public and Congress. His growing concerns about the threat posed by Nazi Germany and a widening of the war in Europe were not shared by an isolationist public.[2]

In a true test of presidential leadership, President Roosevelt, still relatively popular after an unprecedented reelection to a third term in 1940, had to convince a recalcitrant American public to accept the potential international German threat and get the public to embrace his plans for U.S. economic intervention in the conflict.[3] As the European conflict heated up in the summer of 1941, President Roosevelt utilized a "fireside chat" in May to attempt to move public opinion to accept an "unlimited national emergency." President Roosevelt argued, "The first and fundamental fact is that what started as a European war has developed, as the Nazis always intended it should develop, into a world war for world domination. Adolf Hitler never considered the domination of Europe as an end in itself. European conquest was but a step toward ultimate goals in all the other continents. It is unmistakably apparent to all of us that, unless the advance of Hitlerism is forcibly checked now, the Western Hemisphere will be within range of the Nazi weapons of destruction." The president's message was clear: the world must fear and prepare for German aggression, and the United States must do its part.

What was the effect of the president's leadership efforts? His intent was to gain additional public approval to supply Great Britain with the economic and military tools to continue to fight the war against Germany herself. Even though Roosevelt exhaustively catalogued the growing threat of conflict on the seas and the country's strategic security vulnerabilities, the president's pollster, Hadley Cantril, found no significant movement after the president's speech in terms of the percentages of the public approving of continued assistance to England in fighting the war. On the justification for the war, Cantril argued that "there have been no significant shifts in percentages" where, after the president's speech, only 37% of the public agreed England is fighting for democracy (compared to 31% arguing that she was fighting to "keep her power and wealth").[4] The president's rhetoric clearly failed to move public opinion.

Why didn't the public follow the president? Cantril noted that "I believe the main reason [the speech] had comparatively little effect was that [Roosevelt] failed to indicate any new, overt policy that people could readily conceptualize, and that the 'national emergency' meant little when it required no change whatever in daily life."[5] Even more specific references, though, Cantril argued, would not necessarily have hastened any movement in the percentage of the public feeling that the president's assistance of Britain was "about right" (a figure that stood at 53% in July of 1941), since that figure had not budged for months.[6] Similarly exposing the leaning isolationist sentiments steering the public, by the end of 1941 (in a poll taken two days before the attack on Pearl Harbor) only

51% of the public agreed that "the United States will go to war against Japan some time in the near future."[7] The public had made up their minds against involvement. Not surprisingly, public mobilization for war in the wake of Pearl Harbor would be unquestioned, but before that time, the White House was unable to move public opinion in its direction.

Ronald Reagan and Budget "Fitness"

President Reagan campaigned in 1980 on improving the nation's struggling economy by reducing government spending and reducing taxes. A landslide victory in 1984 (sweeping every state except Minnesota and the District of Columbia) framed Reagan's second term in office. The president's "coattails" also ushered in significant gains (sixteen seats) for Republicans in the House. Although the Republicans lost two seats in the Senate, they still retained control of the body while the House was controlled by the Democrats. Because the Iran-Contra scandal that damaged the president's reputation did not break until November of 1986, he retained relatively high approval ratings, with 64% of the public expressing approval of his performance in January of 1986. The White House therefore had a popular issue, a persuasive speaker, and a popular president with which to sell its policy ideas to the public in the upcoming State of the Union address.

In preparation for the 1986 State of the Union speech, Dick Wirthlin (the president's pollster) conducted a survey on the themes and strategies of the speech related to the 1987 budget. The primary objective (and most salient theme) was budgetary "fitness." Polling results indicated, "'*Fitness*'—making the federal government (and budget) fit for the future is a *very well received theme.* This should be our emphasis for selling off government assets (making the government 'fit' by selling off its extra poundage)."[8] In particular, there was "virtual unanimous agreement that the '*federal deficit remains the last obstacle to launching a national era of prosperity.*' This sets up the President's objective of achieving a balanced budget under Gramm-Rudman-Hollings."[9] Balancing the budget was a policy that could persuade the public; however, in the face of persistent poverty and unemployment in the United States, one significant failing of this policy was the public perception that the president was not compassionate. Polling data revealed that this perceived lack was his "weakest" attribute and that "the President needs to identify with the public's concern for fairness and compassion."[10]

The president's speech, delivered from the well of the House chamber, reflected these themes from the polling data when he declared:

> The detailed budget that we will submit will meet the Gramm-Rudman-Hollings target for deficit reductions, meet our commitment to ensure a strong national defense, meet our commitment to protect Social Security and the truly less fortunate, and, yes, meet our commitment to not raise taxes. How should we accomplish this? Well, not by taking from those in need. As families take care of their own, government must provide shelter and nourishment for those who cannot provide for themselves. But we must revise or replace programs enacted in the name of compassion that degrade the moral worth of work, encourage family breakups, and drive entire communities into a bleak and heartless dependency. Gramm-Rudman-Hollings can mark a dramatic improvement.[11]

The speech worked in moving public opinion. Post-speech polling results indicated that the percentage of the public who approved of the president's handling of the economy rose from 52% before the speech to 72% after the speech.[12] In addition, support for the Gramm-Rudman legislation increased from 26% in December of 1986 to 47% in February of 1987.[13]

George W. Bush and the Salvation of Social Security

President Bush met his second term with a decidedly divided public. His reelection in 2004 was slim (51% of the popular vote and 286 votes in the Electoral College, compared to Senator John Kerry's 251 Electoral College votes) and his popularity hovered at around 50%. Both measures reflected political majorities, albeit modest majorities. The election was largely fought over the state of the conflict in Iraq and issues of national security, rather than domestic political issues. However, at the outset of his second term, President Bush sought to invigorate his domestic political agenda within a healthy but precariously balanced economy by using supportive GOP majorities in both houses of Congress. In his first public statement after being reelected, he argued that he "earned capital in this campaign, political capital, and now I intend to spend it."[14]

The first domestic policy item on his list was privatizing Social Security by utilizing personal, private accounts. The president embarked on a tour of sixty cities in sixty days in an attempt to lead public opinion to support his policy, a domestic "barnstorming" tactic many presidents employ. Bush faced an uphill battle, as most Americans wanted a guaranteed monthly benefit from Social Security, and the percentage of the public identifying personal Social Security accounts as a "bad idea" was around 50%.[15] Even with the full attention of the White House, and with the president out conversing with America, there was little support generated. After the president spent a week on the road stumping for the plan, a *Washington Post*/ ABC News survey suggested that a majority of the public did not agree with him. The poll found that 56% of the public believed the president's plan would cut overall payments to seniors, 63% indicated that the plan would not fix long-term financial problems in the stability of Social Security, and the percentage of the public rejecting private investment accounts declined five percentage points from before the president's trip.[16]

Even with significant interest-group mobilization opposing his policy and little movement of the public to his preferred policy position, President Bush was not deterred. He noted, "I'm going to head back out again, and I'm going to spend time talking about Social Security every week until something gets done—because that's my job."[17] A few days later, at a speech to members of the Associated Builders and Contractors Trade Association, the president said, "My strategy is pretty simple: explain the problem to the American people, and keep explaining it and explaining it, and assuring seniors that you're going to get your check."[18] In the end, after significant presidential talking and White House attention, Congress did not consider the president's legislation, and the policy faded over the course of the president's second term.

What We Know (and Don't Know) about Presidential Leadership

What factors facilitate successful presidential leadership of public opinion? Clearly, each of these three presidents faced different domestic and international circumstances when they attempted to foster support for their policies. A popular President Roosevelt encountered a reluctant and isolationist public, and only through attempts at gradual leadership and the disaster at Pearl Harbor was he able to gain public approval to enter World War II. President Reagan operated from a position of strength at the height of his popularity and attempted to lead a nation under a divided government in economic trouble—attempts that were largely successful. A moderately popular President Bush, having been reelected by a small margin, faced significant opposition from several groups (seniors and Democrats) and was unable to rally mass support for privatization of Social Security. But which were the salient features that allowed for President Reagan to succeed but caused Presidents Roosevelt and Bush to fail? Was it popularity, divided government, public knowledge, the issue itself, or the state of the economy that facilitated this success? Or did the delivery of the president's messages (radio, television or domestic travel) make the crucial difference?

Although their circumstances were different and their success was mixed, these presidents share a particularly important characteristic: they all possessed the "bully pulpit" and the persuasive power of the presidency. However, that all presidents have the power to "go public" (and frequently do) does not a sufficiently explain why certain presidents succeed and others do not.[19] Scholars, as routine observers of the presidency, often have only anecdotal evidence for how and when presidents are most likely to succeed at leading public opinion. This lack of clear understanding, which would substantiate the theoretical arguments at the core of the public presidency, limits our ability to explain the function of the modern presidency. If presidential leadership of public opinion is a critical component of contemporary White House tactics, scholars should seek, with some urgency, missing evidence for how and when presidents succeed at leading public opinion.

Indeed, without an understanding of the roles presidents play in leading public opinion, there may also be an undercounting of the role of presidential power in effective governance. For instance, crucial to the establishment (or perhaps maintenance) of public policy is an understanding of the central role that public opinion (and presidents as facilitators of that opinion) plays in explaining how and why certain public policies exist. Whether legislation is ultimately accepted or rejected, it is important to understand the role of each actor involved, and without a full comprehension of the role of the president as guide of public opinion, success or failure may be erroneously attributed to other individuals or institutions, obscuring democratic accountability. Similarly, insufficient understanding of leadership success may underestimate the damage presidents can do to a system designed to run on shared powers, as their rhetoric slips into demagoguery. Certain policies or issues may be truncated or stalled by such presidential efforts. Understanding the role presidents play in managing public preferences is important to understanding the ritual of policy streams in government.

All modern presidents clearly attempt to lead public opinion. Often, due to factors outside their control, they fail. This book is an exploration into how and when they succeed. In the chapters that follow, a simple theory of presidential leadership is developed that argues that presidential messages are more likely to be received if there are fewer countervailing agents or messages to counter the president's message. Based upon the findings in this book, the "bully pulpit" is largely *provisional* for modern presidents. Presidents are successful at leading opinion when they continuously push the issue in public, when their approval rating is higher (also invoking several additional moments of success), when they deliver speeches on television from the seat of presidential power, and when the public is persuadable, as well as under several other contingencies. The implication is that presidential strategies and the political environment matter more than institutional settings or rhetorical skill in leading public opinion. These conclusions add to an understanding of how and under what conditions presidents lead public opinion. The findings here support and complement several theories in the literature. However, these findings also challenge several existing findings or recast assumptions pertaining to presidential behavior regarding public opinion.

Acknowledgments

In writing this book, many colleagues and friends along the way gave helpful comments for improving the manuscript, working through methodological issues, and sharpening my focus on the key arguments. These include Jeff Cohen, Dan Wood, Matt Eshbaugh-Soha, Lori Cox Han, Jamie Druckman, Nick Jorgensen, Dan Bergan, Justin Vaughn, Elvin Lim, Noah Kaplan, John Sloan, Scott Basinger, Harrell Rodgers, Kent Tedin, Diane Heith, and Bill Cunion. Earlier versions of this manuscript were also thoughtfully read by Dennis Chong and Brandice Canes-Wrone, both of whom seemed preternaturally able to critique the work with an anticipation of what I wanted to say but didn't. My colleagues at the University of Houston have also provided their sage advice, listened to me opine about presidential leadership, and a generally made Houston a wonderful place to work. But perhaps more than their intellectual abilities, I value their friendship.

Texas A&M University Press Editor-in-Chief Mary Lenn Dixon and series editor Jim Pfiffner were both helpful and enthusiastic in ushering this project to completion. In particular, Jim's comments on the earliest drafts (along with an anonymous reviewer) significantly helped to press me to explore the main contribution of the book and clarify my contribution to the field. I cannot imagine working with a kinder or more efficient group.

Several organizations and institutions have been immensely supportive financially of this project from the beginning. Thanks are due to (in order of award) an Albert M. Greenfield Research Grant from the Franklin and Eleanor Roosevelt Institute, a Moody Research Grant from the Lyndon B. Johnson Foundation, a Theodore Sorenson Research Grant from the John F. Kennedy Library, a travel grant from the Gerald R. Ford Library, and a grant from the Scowcroft Institute at the George Bush School of Government and Public Service. Also making this research possible was the assistance of the White House Historical Association, which provided a substantial research grant for a visit to several presidential libraries. Dennis Chong (who holds the John D. and Catherine T. MacArthur Endowed Chair at Northwestern University) also provided research funds for travel. Support from the University of Idaho and the University of Houston (especially a sabbatical in the spring of 2009) also provided much-needed assistance to complete the book.

Thanks are also due to several research assistants who assisted in data collection over the life of this project, including Terry Starkey, Josh Harman, Jill Dawson, Chris Nicholson, and Alan Steinberg.

I also owe a special debt to several specific individuals whom I am fortunate to call friends and colleagues. Jay McCann went above and beyond his duty in providing early comments on the book and made many excellent suggestions about how to proceed when I was stumped by a problem. From my days as an undergraduate, he has been an unflappable mentor and friend.

My most significant intellectual debt goes to my graduate school adviser at Northwestern, Benjamin I. Page. His measured and methodical approach to crafting a project of this magnitude helped keep me on track and guided me through the rough patches. He is the perfect "leader by example," and I feel very privileged to have studied with him and learned from him about the academic world.

To my mentor and friend Martha Joynt Kumar I also offer a few grateful words of thanks. Martha was always quick with an encouraging e-mail and good-natured about my anxiety about finishing the book. Her perspectives on framing the questions and thoughts on the scope of the topic were most helpful in shaping my arguments. Her terrific insight into the connection between politics and scholarship made this book better.

Without question, this book would not exist without the insight, ideas, guidance, and support of George Edwards, who was generous with his time and sharp with his critiques. His savvy and good humor helped me clarify the arguments and finish the book.

Finally, to B. J., I apologize for irritability and preoccupation taking away from the joy it is to be your father. Perhaps most importantly, to Tracy, who has been with this project from the start, mere thanks are not enough. This is all because of you.

—Brandon Rottinghaus
Humble, Texas

The Provisional Pulpit

CHAPTER 1

Questions and Quandaries of Presidential Leadership

We see presidents talking all the time, but what effect does this rhetoric have on the public's policy preferences? All modern presidents spend time attempting to lead public opinion by speaking to groups, doing Saturday radio addresses, holding press conferences, giving speeches from the Oval Office, and more. Given an expansive executive office to help shape and control their message, an army of political surrogates to carry out their message, and a fully focused cadre of press devoted to their every word, presidents should see a significant amount of leadership success, and we should know much about how they accomplish this persuasion. Yet after decades of study on all of this presidential talking and public attention, we still do not have a full and systematic understanding of when and under what conditions modern presidents are successful at leading public opinion. Indeed, there has been significant debate about whether or not a president can lead public opinion and which factors enhance or detract from this prospect.

This presents a challenging puzzle: if the president is constantly talking, why is there (it is argued) so little movement in public opinion? To address this puzzle, in this book I investigate modern presidential leadership of public opinion on public policy. Specifically, I investigate how, when, and under what conditions presidents succeed at leading public opinion on public policy. Although much has been written about presidential leadership of opinion (broadly construed) and recent scholarship has significantly advanced our understanding of the conditions and obstacles involved, there are still many questions pertaining to the success of presidential efforts to lead opinion throughout the modern presidency. For instance, how is presidential leadership systematically affected by soaring or souring approval ratings, midterm or presidential elections, high or low salience of an issue, presidential term, high or low public knowledge, presidential speechmaking in the nation or via television?

Although others have addressed the subject, surprisingly little is known about the conditions of leadership success, either in terms of political conditions or presidential strategies.[1]

It is a simple but important inquiry, yet only a handful of studies examine the effect of presidential leadership of public opinion using a comparative, systematic study across several administrations. For instance Benjamin Page, Robert Shapiro, and Glenn Dempsey make use of news coverage of presidential statements to determine the probable effect of presidential leadership on public opinion.[2] Elsewhere, Page and Shapiro examine matched public opinion before and after presidential policy statements as sources in newspaper coverage.[3] In both cases, small effects are found, but there were too few cases to generalize across issues and conditions. Further, several authors explore presidential leadership in a broad sense but only measure one aspect of the idea. For instance, scholarly works have addressed leadership as movement of congressional opinion, leadership as "responsiveness," leadership as "anticipation" of public opinion, leadership as issue framing, and presidential preference signaling.[4]

Similarly, many studies do not expand beyond a specific president or type of leadership strategy. For instance, George Edwards's influential work on this subject is the most direct and comprehensive to date, yet the measures of public opinion leadership are largely confined to recent presidents (Reagan, Bush, and Clinton) and only on selected issues.[5] Several other works also only focus on one president, one issue, or one time period.[6] An analysis of leadership must look past the nexus of individual president and impressionistic assumptions about what makes presidents "great" leaders to a more sustainable sense of how and when presidents are able to lead public opinion. Other studies address only presidential statements made on television or in State of the Union speeches, rather than all presidential speeches.[7] These limitations also make for a less-than-complete view of the multiple interactive conditions that might help or hinder presidential leadership strategies.

What is still missing is a systematic, sequential, and direct approach to describing empirical trends in presidential leadership of public opinion (as positive opinion movement based on presidential influence). Such an approach would expand on important scholarly queries, establish a baseline figure against which to judge successful or unsuccessful leadership of opinion, resolve empirical disputes in the literature, and check the accuracy of conventional political wisdom on how, when, and why presidents lead public opinion. With the right approach, several improvements can be made in weaving a comprehensive story about presidential leadership that builds on previous findings. We can be more precise in identifying which presidents are effective leaders, which are not, and which circumstances assist or restrict them in this process. The systematic statistical and historical archival data that I draw on in this book deliver a more well-rounded and comprehensive perspective and advance our collective understanding of presidential leadership.

To address the critical questions posed here, I develop a simple theory of presidential leadership that argues that presidential messages are more likely to be received if there are fewer countervailing agents or messages to counter the president's message. To test this theory, I examine a comparative series of matched presidential statements and opinion data from 1953 to 2001 (the Eisenhower to Clinton administrations) to ascertain under what conditions, which leadership tactics, and during which time periods presidents successfully lead public opinion. With a guiding theory, these data are able to determine successful and unsuccessful conditions and tactics affecting presidential leadership and are able to connect with previous scholarly discussion on divided government, public knowledge, presidential popularity, electoral status, and more. In addition to these aggregate data, documentation from presidential archives supplements and enliven the statistical findings. Analysis of internal presidential decision-making significantly illuminates presidential leadership success in ways that volumes of statistical data cannot. With empirical answers directly from inside the White House, the integrated approach in this book will significantly advance our collective understanding of how and why presidents lead public opinion.

Do Presidents Find Success in Leading Public Opinion?

It is clear that presidents have the tools, the intent, and the desire to lead public opinion, but are these quests successful? Presidential rhetoric itself can have an effect on many elements of public policy, even if public preferences are not moved.[8] Presidential speech can help a president in crafting a public image of sympathy, toughness, or humanity. Image-based politics are now the norm, supplanting policy substance with personal, political representations of leadership.[9] Indeed, scholars studying the growth of public opinion polls have found that polling now focuses less on policy and more on the personal or political, creating the "second face" of presidential polling and possibly posing a threat to deliberative communication.[10] Corey Rosen also finds that respondents are less willing to disagree with a position if that position is associated with the president, granting credibility to presidential image as a prima facie persuasive effect.[11] Ultimately, Roderick Hart argues that speech is not simply an empty exercise, it is governance.[12]

Although several definitions of "leadership" and "leader" are explored in the literature (from the vantage point of rhetorical criticism, internal institutional leadership, or classic "exchange-based" leadership), in order to answer the critical questions posed here, a firm and clear definition is needed that relates to the public's policy preferences. As defined in this book, successful leadership of public opinion requires positive movement of public opinion, as registered by public opinion polls, from before a presidential statement on that policy to after that statement (more on this measure in chapter 3 and appendix A). This process of moving public opinion necessitates that presidents have something to say, that a president's policy statement appeals to citizens, that citizens are receptive and attentive, and that citizens are willing to potentially alter their previous perception of the policy. Persuasion, therefore, is a causal element in leadership of opinion. Following the theory outlined in chapter 2, persuasion, no matter how critical to presidential governance, is difficult for presidents to accomplish because of multiple competing factors, distractions, and disturbances surrounding political messages.

This definition of successful leadership of public opinion distinguishes between types of leadership to more carefully examine the success presidents find. For instance, several studies examine *agenda setting* as leadership or the moving of *approval ratings* as leadership. The relevant findings in the literature on these subjects are also inconsistent, varying between success and failure across several time periods, issues, and actors. Scholars have found presidents to be effective agenda setters while others have found presidents less effective (or ineffective) at agenda setting.[13] Similarly, on the movement of approval ratings, some scholars have found presidents effective at motivating popular perceptions of themselves while others dispute this notion.[14] Both concepts (agenda setting and approval) are important to presidential political success but do not speak directly to the degree to which presidents inform and move public preferences on public policy, which is the central concern here.

Indeed, little comparative study (by time period or presidential administration) exists on the extent to which presidents are empirically able to accomplish the task of moving public opinion on *policy matters* to the president's preferred position. We therefore have an opportunity to build on existing findings to develop a broader understanding of the parameters of leadership on these matters. Taken as a whole, the scholarly assessment of presidential ability to move substantive public opinion on policy matters with their rhetoric is rather grim. Most prominent studies find little success for presidents in moving public opinion to the president's preferred policy outcome. As a classic representative of "nonfindings" of presidential leadership, many often refer to Woodrow Wilson's exasperating (and eventually fatal) trip across the nation to drum up support for the League of Nations.[15] In individual case studies, Robert Finbow similarly finds that President Carter's efforts at convincing the public to reform the nation's health-care system fell short, primarily in concert with other political problems such as lack of support in Congress and internal White House disorganization.[16] In an analysis of President Clinton's first years in office, Lawrence Jacobs and Robert Shapiro find that the president was a responsive (but not effective) leader on health-care policy and was not successful on issues of foreign policy (especially on the Bosnian war).[17]

Perhaps the most significant "nonfindings" work to date is George Edwards's *On Deaf Ears,* which establishes a compelling argument for presidential ineffectiveness in leading public opinion.[18] He argues, "Very little work has focused on systematically examining the president's ability to influence the public."[19] In this important book, he examines public approval of a handful of policies pursued by Presidents Reagan, Bush, and Clinton. In examining Ronald Reagan, Edwards peers behind the "Great Communicator" label to determine whether or not Reagan was as skilled as advertised. Readjusting this image, Edwards pinpoints several leadership failures, including funding to the Contras in Nicaragua, the Strategic Defense Initiative (SDI), and support for increased government spending. Edwards also analyzes Bill Clinton on several issues, including his economic package, health-care reform, crime policy, and interventions in Haiti, Bosnia, and Kosovo. Edwards concludes, "Despite his [Clinton's] impressive political and communications skills, the evidence is clear that the president typically failed to obtain public support."[20]

One of the most important contributions of *On Deaf Ears* is the discussion of the political environment surrounding presidential leadership. Its value emanates from a transmission model where Edwards examines the communicator (the president), the message (presidential rhetoric), and the audience (the public). In this model, several variables must be included to justifiably understand presidential leadership. Presidential credibility, popularity, and charisma are important. Audience participation, attention, and conversion are critical. Not surprisingly, these elements are disconnected at several points, complicating the process of presidential leadership and leaving it largely defunct.[21] Of course, there are other instances of presidential success at leadership (Edwards labels this "facilitating"), including leading Congress, elite debate, or particular segments of the public, but Edwards argues that attempts at leadership of mass opinion characteristically fail.

Yet presidents may succeed more than we know, and either because we assume they will fail (and a research design is modeled on this assumption) or because their failures are often more public (and therefore easier to see and measure), we may underestimate the effect of presidential leadership. Interestingly, despite recent studies indicating less than significant public opinion movement after policy speeches, there are many documented instances where presidents do successfully lead public opinion. Many texts are filled with dramatic and subtle "findings" of successful leadership of public opinion, both specified and unspecified as opinion "leadership."[22] If one includes all works in history, communications, sociology, public policy, and other related fields, there are more instances than a single scholar could ever catalogue. Indeed, it is because so many case studies describe how presidents can lead public opinion in particular circumstances that we need a comprehensive study of the multiple conditions of successful presidential leadership.

In fact, there are several moments when presidents are successful at leading public opinion. Andreas Wenger and Marcel Gerber find that President Kennedy, while less than successful during the Bay of Pigs invasion, was very successful in negotiating the Limited Test Ban Treaty in 1963 and securing public support, especially considering tough international circumstances.[23] John Sloan argues that President Reagan used his pragmatic tenacity to successfully lead public opinion on several economic policy issues and return economic growth to the U.S. economy.[24] President Clinton has also been a favorite recent source of descriptions of successful political leadership. Jacobs and Shapiro found, despite the examples of Clinton's nonleadership in the same chapter, that President Clinton was able to lead the public on welfare reform, gun control, drug crime enforcement, and campaign finance reform.[25] Michael Bailey, Lee Sigelman, and Clyde Wilcox similarly argue that President Clinton was able to positively affect the public's judgments about his "don't ask, don't tell" policy.[26] In another Clinton example, Jeffrey Koch finds evidence of increased support for national health insurance subsequent to presidential activity, although he is hesitant to definitively suggest that presidential leadership occurred.[27] Other important qualitative work has also advanced our historical understanding of individual presidents through descriptions of presidential leadership as successful, successful but gradual and with mixed success.[28]

Interestingly, scholars have also shown that presidents are successful at motivating positive perceptions of the economy, a potentially powerful tool in dour economic times. Dan Wood argues that presidents attempt to project an image of economic leadership regardless of negative economic news or economic evaluations.[29] Presidents, as stewards of the economy, consistently speak optimistically and positively about the economy. In these cases, the effect of presidential shaping of economic circumstances is indirect: presidential optimism affects news coverage of the economy, which affects economic approval. This "economic leadership" trend also appears to be amplified when presidents are making foreign policy speeches and are more personally popular.[30] The prospect that the president's rhetoric could influence public policy (budget packages, tax increases or cuts) is therefore real.

In addition, although there is no consensus on when presidents are able to lead opinion on domestic policy, there is consensus that presidents can generally lead public opinion successfully on matters of foreign policy or military intervention.[31] Findings of presidential leadership of foreign policy on both approval and substantive policy have been consistent over time, partially as a result of the White House's cultivation of this support. For instance, Sigelman found that President Reagan's endorsement of the Intermediate-Range Nuclear Forces (INF) Treaty had a modest impact on individuals who perceived the Soviets as "relatively nonthreatening" while the endorsement had a much larger impact on those who viewed the Soviets as threatening.[32] Alan Rosenblatt found that individuals exposed to President Reagan's speech committing military personnel to Lebanon and Grenada demonstrated that their support for the policy (rather than their approval of the president) rose as a result of exposure to presidential persuasion.[33] In his book *Going Public,* Samuel Kernell also identified several incidents of foreign policy leadership, including President Bush on Desert Storm and President Truman on aid to Greece under the Truman Doctrine.[34]

A Fragmented Story

What, then, is the effect of presidential rhetoric on public opinion? On this question, Edwards contends, "What is missing is an understanding of the linkage between what the president says and does and the public's response."[35] In *The Strategic President,* he further argues, "We would benefit from work that explores systematically the contribution of presidential energy, perseverance, and resiliency to presidential success."[36] Similarly, the 2008 *Report of the National Task Force on the Presidency and Public Opinion* suggests that an important avenue for research is the question, "What are the effects of presidential rhetoric on public opinion, and what are the limitations or constraints on the president's ability to rally the public behind his agenda?"[37] The report concludes, "We need to illuminate more precisely the circumstances under which presidents lead or follow public opinion and investigate the implications of that relationship for the business of governing."[38]

Each of these suggestions, along with the empirical gaps identified above and the ongoing debate about the effectiveness of presidential leadership, indicate that more needs to be done on the study of presidential leadership of public opinion. It is undeniable that presidents are more "public" now and that the leadership expectations of the modern presidency are elevated, but what is less clearly understood is the success presidents *systematically* obtain when attempting to lead public opinion and the conditions that aid that success. Investigations of the thousands of speeches made by presidents would likely yield as many incidents of failure as success in leading public opinion. However, if one were to sum the findings from recent research in presidential leadership, one would come away with the idea that presidents are *rarely if ever* effective at leading public opinion to support policy proposals. Conventional wisdom of presidential inability to lead public opinion has hardened with time, but it is a claim that can be nuanced.

Of course, as discussed above, there are incidents of success, even if these are scattered, momentary, and unpredictable. On this point, what we have is a fragmented story on the indicators of success, often specific to certain presidents, linked inseparably to political or international events, limited to specific media or to a too-narrow time frame. Several works explore similar dimensions qualitatively and quantitatively,[39] but few explore these approaches together and none provides a systematic study of modern presidential leadership. This book builds on findings from these works and attempts a comprehensive understanding, using both qualitative and quantitative data, of presidential leadership tactics and conditional success across the modern presidency. Thus, I hope to advance the discussion of presidential leadership strategies and success by identifying situations in the political environment that condition success or failure and the degree to which presidents can themselves effect these changes.

A Provisional Pulpit

As I noted above, several recent studies have suggested that presidential leadership of opinion is an unsound strategy. It generally fails, challenging the notion that presidents effectively employ the "bully pulpit" to lead the public. Scholars point out that presidents struggle with opinion leadership in a dense political environment, crowded with a truculent media, a narrowing public, and partisanship from both political parties.[40] Yet opinion leadership is not a bankrupt strategy—quite the contrary. In the pages that follow, I analyze presidential leadership of public opinion and the president as public agent for the nuances that reveal when leadership might be effective. Opinion leadership is simply poor as a *general* strategy but excellent as a *specific* strategy. The findings in this book establish that the "bully pulpit" is largely *provisional* for modern presidents. Presidents are successful at leading opinion when they continuously push the issue in public, when their approval rating is higher (also invoking several additional moments of success), while delivering speeches on television from the seat of presidential power, and when the public is persuadable, as well as under several other contingencies. Thus, the White House *does* succeed at leading public opinion, but not in every circumstance and certainly not simply because they address the public.

The findings in this book amend and add to the literature on the public presidency by examining its most simple, basic questions: does presidential leadership of public opinion work, and if so, under what circumstances? The core finding is that presidents are constrained in leading public opinion *except under particular circumstances.* This line of inquiry also provides perspective on several relevant questions connecting the president and the public, including presidential leadership of foreign policy, the effect of presidential approval rating on public acceptance of public policy, management of the president's political agenda (in the public and in Congress), the effect of divided government in executive-legislative negotiations, the role and utility of various presidential speech strategies, political framing (the use of language to shape political reality), and leadership by group coalition. I also hope to illuminate the prospect of the modern president as a rhetorical demagogue and the potential of the president to short-circuit the process of shared legislative powers, as the focus on stagecraft over practical governance may limit effective governance.

My conclusions also ultimately speak to the concerns people have about the role of public opinion in furthering or limiting public policy, especially the degree to which political actors can manipulate public opinion to their own political ends. Is the public persuaded by the grandiose spectacle of presidential stagecraft or are efforts to persuade them futile? Public opinion sets the broad parameters of the policy-making environment, but if those "dikes" (to borrow a phrase from V. O. Key) that shape and restrain public opinion are movable, the role of public opinion in the process is compromised and must be rethought.[41] Conversely, if public opinion becomes more informed about political matters as a result of such leadership efforts, the public's role in democratic governance will become more potent. To recognize the nature of presidential leadership efforts on public opinion is to comprehend the foundation of democratic authority itself.

Plan of the Book

The aim of this book is to define and isolate *conditions* of successful and unsuccessful presidential leadership. Gaining perspective on the nature and degree of presidential success in leading public opinion will provide a window into the goals, tribulations, and strategy of the modern presidency. It will also establish a benchmark for the rate at which presidents succeed at leading public opinion and will build the overall argument that presidential leadership is "provisional" by time periods, political conditions, and presidential tactics.

In chapter 2, I discuss the importance of presidential leadership, introduce a theory of when presidents are most likely to lead public opinion, and identify specific hypotheses correlated to that theory.

In chapter 3, I describe the comparative series of matched presidential statements and opinion data from 1953 to 2001 (the Eisenhower to Clinton administrations) to ascertain the percentage of time presidents successfully lead public opinion. The data reveal that presidents are only modestly able to motivate public opinion to more favorable positions—in only 49% of the cases did presidents succeed at leading opinion at all times and in only 23% of the cases when considering "significant" opinion change (greater than 5%). When presidents are able to move opinion, they generally succeed in small increments. Interestingly, even "skilled" presidents (such as Kennedy, Reagan, and Clinton) do not fare better than their colleagues in leading public opinion. These conclusions suggest that presidential strategies and the political environment matter more than institutional settings or rhetorical flourish in leading public opinion. Also, chapter 3 sets the stage for the statistical inquiry in the subsequent chapters.

Using the data outlined in chapter 3 along with several multivariate statistical models, in chapter 4 I directly test the hypotheses described in chapter 2. I find that presidents are most successful in moving public opinion when their popularity is higher (especially combined with a high-salience issue), when they talk about the issue publicly for multiple days, and when the public grows more knowledgeable or certain as a result of persuasion. Presidents who served earlier (Eisenhower to Ford) also have more success at leading public opinion than later-serving presidents under several conditions, especially in televised addresses. Foreign policy issues, separated in several of the models, produce similar results but also enhance positive leadership success when the president is deploying troops into harm's way and when the president is using certain communications tactics. These findings alter our understanding of presidential leadership by enhancing previous scholarly findings and by challenging conventional and scholarly wisdom.

Modern presidents, replete with the luxury of technology of communications and travel, are constantly speaking to the public—but which of these activities pay off in leadership success? In chapter 4, I also identify four distinct communications approaches to presidential opinion leadership ("barnstorming" the country, major televised speeches, press conferences, and speaking outside the country) and examine the effectiveness of these strategies in several political contexts. Ultimately, the strategies involving domestic travel and televised addresses are most effective, and when the issue is foreign policy, a strategy where presidents "go public" on television is even more effective. Press conferences never positively affect leadership success. These findings amend previous interpretations of the presumed noneffects of television in leading public opinion but confirm previous assessments of the difficulty of relying on the mass media to lead public opinion.

In order to amplify the statistical findings from chapters 3 and 4, I illustrate three instances of successful or unsuccessful opinion leadership in each of chapters 5 through 8. Each illustration describes the conditions that the aggregate statistical models argue will affect leadership success. In addition to giving qualitative weight to the quantitative arguments, these chapters draw on archival data from inside the White House on the subject of presidential leadership of public opinion. In chapter 5, I describe three instances of successful leadership on domestic policy and in chapter 7 three instances of successful leadership on foreign policy. Then, to illustrate the political or temporal conditions described in chapter 4 where presidents find leading public opinion more difficult, in chapter 6, I identify three case studies where presidential leadership fails in domestic policy and in chapter 8 three case studies where presidential leadership fails in foreign policy.

CHAPTER 2

The Constrained Presidency

A Conditional Theory of Presidential Leadership

In the previous chapter I introduced a puzzle about presidential leadership: if the president is constantly talking and is consistently visible, why is there so little movement in public opinion? My goal in this book is to understand when presidents succeed at leading public opinion. To take the next step in addressing this puzzle, I offer a theory of conditional presidential success of leadership and pose several hypotheses that magnify this theory. Thus, in this chapter, specific variables of interest are isolated, while the hypothesized effects of each condition on leadership success are determined in the following two chapters. Here, I generally outline when presidents should be successful at leading public opinion, with the assumption that these effects are conditional and contingent upon the interactions with the rest of the political environment. The end result is a theme that guides the analysis in the following two chapters through statistical investigation (chapters 3 and 4) and is illustrated in the case study chapters that follow (chapters 5 through 8).

How Should a President Interact with Public Opinion?

The framers of the Constitution knew public opinion to be a powerful (but uncontrollable) force, and they did not trust it alone to govern the nation. The "general mass" of the public was not thought to be adequate enough in its reasoning, understanding, or consistency to be entrusted with such an important job, and the framers desired to limit that voice. With this in mind, Alexander Hamilton sketched his vision for the "presidential term" in Federalist 71:

> There are some who would be inclined to regard the servile pliancy of the Executive to a prevailing current, either in the community or in the legislature, as its best recommendation. But

> such men entertain very crude notions, as well of the purposes for which government is instituted, as of the true means by which the public happiness may be promoted. The republican principle demands that the deliberate sense of the community should govern the conduct of those to whom they intrust the management of their affairs; but it does not require an unqualified complaisance to every sudden breeze of passion, or to every transient impulse which the people may receive from the arts of men, who flatter their prejudices to betray their interests.[1]

Complete compliance to public opinion, according to Hamilton, defeats the purpose of representative government, but some clear accounting of public preferences is justified and required.[2] Hamilton also took for granted the need for an "energetic" executive because "a feeble Executive implies a feeble execution of the government." Still, closely connected to executing this "energy" was "due dependence on the people." Yet Hamilton only hints at how presidents lead or follow public opinion. For him, presidents operate somewhere *in between* the "deliberate sense of community" and "every sudden breeze of passion" and *in between* an "energetic" execution of office and "due dependence on the people."

Modern presidential leadership departs significantly from the old constitutional order in the method by which presidents exercise this "energy" within a responsive democratic system. Jeffrey Tulis argues that the emergence of the "rhetorical presidency," and the tension between it and the statutory presidency (as derived from the Constitution), can be traced to the ambiguity of the president's constitutional station.[3] This ambiguity is reflected in Hamilton's contradictory claims that the president is both leader and follower. Tulis notes that Woodrow Wilson (both as a scholar and as president) promoted a different reading of the Constitution and presided over his terms in office as a practitioner of this new theory. Wilson thought that the executive's power should be expanded to encompass leading Congress, and the method he used to do so was to take his message to the people to pressure Congress.[4] Merging Hamilton's dichotomy of "energy" and "dependence on the people," Wilson argued that "interpretation" of public preferences is critical to presidential leadership. Wilson wrote, "Leadership, for the statesman, is interpretation. He must read the common thought: he must calculate very circumspectly the preparation of the nation for the next move in the progress of politics."[5] Wilson continued, "That general sense of the community may wait to be aroused, and the statesman must arouse it; [it] may be inchoate and vague, and the statesman must formulate and make it explicit."[6]

Why Presidents Try to Lead Public Opinion

After Woodrow Wilson, the importance of public opinion and the practice of presidential leadership in political life intersected and became the cornerstone of modern presidential politics. According to Wilson, there is "but one national voice in the country and that is the voice of the President."[7] Presidents, adhering to Wilson's approach, have endorsed the position that public opinion matters a great deal for governing and that ignoring it means they may face their own political demise. What's more, presidents recognize that diverse actors, such as the media or interest groups as siphons of public opinion, serve as inputs and outputs to the policy-making process and attempt to harness these factors to their advantage. Not surprisingly, presidents seek to operate within a political environment with the hopes of securing reelection or a grander place in the annals of history. Of course, *only* being responsive to public opinion is not necessarily a recipe for advancing a successful policy agenda. Leadership of public opinion is now an accepted strategy to accomplish political goals, even if this approach can sometimes preclude political success with presidential "overpromises" or friction between the branches.[8]

According to the tension in democratic theory as outlined above, presidents do not *have* to lead public opinion to be strong public advocates. They could take the "delegate" position and be a responsive vessel of the public's will. However, Wilson's transition from a presidency dependent on constitutionally proscribed powers to a presidency free to advocate policies to the public requires a closer connection between the public and the president and the concurrent expansion of power. In particular, Theodore Lowi presciently argued that the plebiscitary presidency (as part of the personal presidency) emerged from the expanded role presidents themselves play in courting the nomination of their party and the larger political consistency of the modern president.[9] The spread of direct primaries and the weakening of the party system encourage presidents to act as independent agents rather than team players.[10] As part of this emerging national democratic character, the public also expects presidents to lead.[11] Presidents use leadership to close the gap between their ability to affect their political world (which can be limited) and the expectations placed on them. And, in a real sense, presidents are forced to engage in this "hyper-rhetorical" presidency because the availability of presidential communications creates the opportunities to do so, and a crowded media environment creates a de facto requirement to do so.[12]

Thus, the desire and need for presidential administrations to shape and lead public opinion has, over time, grown into paramount importance, especially as policy agendas proliferate and congressional acquiescence becomes more difficult to secure. To this end, Elmer Cornwell argued that presidents *must* lead public opinion in order for the Republic to function and noted that "above all [the president] must win and channel public support."[13] Similarly, eminent leadership historian James MacGregor Burns expressly links democracy and presidential governance, establishing a requirement that presidents use the "bully pulpit" to motivate and inspire the public.[14] With Americans expecting more from their president than ever before, Burns later argued that this public leadership is key to efficient government and to empowering policy action.[15] Bert Rockman also implies that leadership is indispensable and a critical factor in what makes a good president.[16]

The theoretical lynchpin of this approach to public leadership is Kernell's "going public" argument, a conceptualization of presidential leadership that supplants traditional institutional political bargaining arrangements and relies instead on active and energetic public leadership of opinion.[17] Kernell argues that presidents do not "go public" to lead public opinion as an end goal—rather, presidents lead public opinion with the hopes of influencing members of Congress. Kernell notes, "Political Washington has come to look less like institutionalized pluralism (which is conducive to bargaining) and more like individualized pluralism (which is conducive to going public). Presidents more freely go public nowadays because it is a strategy better adapted to modern politics."[18] By going "over the heads" of Congress to the root of the representative public, presidents are able to pressure the legislative branch to pursue their agenda.[19] Mel Laracey argues that presidents have long employed this tactic as a way to expand their limited constitutional power.[20] As a theoretical investigation, "going public" is also a powerful tool to explain presidential behavior and agenda setting. Indeed, Brandice Canes-Wrone demonstrates formally that presidents can obtain influence from not only the act of agenda setting but also the threat of agenda setting (although presidents do not always have incentives to do so).[21]

Presidents have not casually undertaken these developments; rather, they have developed internal mechanisms to assess, predict, shape, and control public opinion.[22] Inherent in this strategy is the need to understand public preferences in order to manage opinion, and presidents have formalized these informational patterns in the White House through the "public opinion apparatus."[23] Accurate data on public preferences has ushered in an era where presidents are able to understand public preferences with more certainty, thus establishing an expectation that presidents can lead public opinion at will. To this end, presidents since Franklin Roosevelt have solicited and utilized public opinion polling (and other data) to assess the public mood and make policy decisions. The White House worked to internalize, centralize, and strengthen their access to the public (in this case, with information) independent of Congress or the media.[24] More recently, presidents have employed focus groups to test public support of arguments for policies with select members of the public.[25]

A Constrained President

That the structural opportunity, and perhaps requirement, exists for a president to lead public opinion does not mean that the conditions will always be favorable for the president to do so. Many of the factors that create the impetus for presidential leadership also limit his ability to communicate with the public. For instance, the formation of direct primaries created an environment where the public's voice (both the general public and the partisan public) matters more but also requires that the president now emphasize a message that appeals to the public and competes with other political voices for public attention. The message must be clear, direct, specifically related to a policy, and easily digestible. The birth of the modern media engendered presidential ability to communicate with millions of people instantly, yet this filtering system inherently limits which messages get through and how presidential image is portrayed. Divided government, more frequently occurring than unified government, creates the incentive for presidents to "go public," but the opposition has similar communications tools, limiting the president's ability to clearly convey his message.

Taken together, the president's ability to lead public opinion is constrained for many of the same reasons it is required. Presidents operate within a hostile and crowded political environment, limiting their opportunities to effectively convey their message to the public and thus persuade the public on the president's preferred policy.[26] Not surprisingly, scholars have found presidential ability to lead difficult in these settings, as presidents (to varying degrees) all face obstacles during their terms in office. Yet, as illustrated in the three vignettes in the preface, presidents all face *different* types of obstacles, be they economic, political, or social. Those presidents who face more constraints are less likely to lead while those that face fewer constraints are more likely to lead. In short, a constrained president is not necessarily an ineffective leader. Presidents will find instances where they are able to break free of these constraints and effectively lead the public. The degree and nature of the constraints on the president are the critical components.

A Theory of Conditional Presidential Leadership of Public Opinion

To advance this constraint theme, I offer here a theory of presidential leadership of public opinion. Generally, presidents should succeed at leading public opinion when they make consistent, solid, and unwavering attempts to do so. Much anecdotal and historical evidence suggests that this is the case: modern presidents who devote considerable attention and focus to leading public opinion, with the full resources of the White House, over a short time period, and on one issue at a time, will be able to move public opinion. For instance, Kernell argues that a presidential appeal to the public will work if the president "accurately communicates his preferences to the citizenry" and citizens respond with favorable changes in public opinion.[27] Hart argues that "presidents are now extraordinarily active players in the game of public opinion, and all of their policy statements—even the most casual—are strategically designed to position the president for the next one in an endless series of moves and countermoves."[28] Presidents often utilize this continual approach across multiple communications avenues.[29] The White House must aggressively push its agenda. John Anthony Maltese, describing the development of the White House Office of Communications under President Nixon, notes, "To maintain control of the public agenda, then, the White House must not only minimize exposure of internal conflict but also aggressively promote the messages that it wants conveyed to the American people."[30]

The "one issue at time" rule is important because it allows for the condition of clarity and unity of presidential purpose. Presidential messages will be lost if they are obscured by too many competing messages.[31] The president possesses the tools to conduct such persuasion, including nationally televised speeches, access to the media at virtually all times, an apparatus designed to craft and disseminate his message, and the ability to travel across the nation and globe to "sell" his policies. Other scholarship on message transmission has demonstrated that if individuals are exposed to consistent and strong arguments (and fewer counterarguments), they will be more likely to accept a particular opinion frame.[32] Indeed, the media are more likely to report presidential messages if those messages are considered important to the president.[33] Of course, the demands of governing, bargaining, and international diplomacy often preclude such actions as persuading the public, which is yet another hurdle presidents face in achieving leadership success.

Although difficult to measure, given that one cannot know for certain the myriad of issues on which the White House is *trying* to lead public opinion or when it has other goals in mind, a president's continual rhetorical mentions of an issue objectively suggest that he is attempting to lead public opinion on that issue.[34] The theory of conditional presidential leadership acknowledges that presidents are strategic with their communication and covetous of the national spotlight to advance their political agenda. Therefore, presidential mentions of an issue (1) during the State of the Union message to Congress and (2) in the two days prior to the day the president gave the speech reflect presidential "attempts" to lead public opinion. This reflects their "core" agenda.[35] And if the theory is correct, presidents will be more successful in their attempts under these two conditions.

Of course, the president's leadership ability does not exist in a vacuum. Presidents must operate within the boundary of their political, economic, and partisan reality. Therefore, part of the explanation of presidential leadership must include particular events or conditions that limit the president's ability to communicate. These limits include *constraining elements* and *constraining agents.* Constraining elements are those events or conditions that are beyond the president's control and that disrupt the president's ability to convey his message credibly or truthfully. These elements include low popularity (or low credibility), economic troubles (perhaps also signaling low credibility and encouraging dissent), or "lame duck" status that manifests in second terms. Constraining agents are those individuals or groups that intentionally challenge the president's message or actively discount what he is saying so that the president's message retains less credibility. Examples include an unpersuadable public or group (such minority partisans or others that traditionally ally with the opposition party), divided government (where the president's political opponents obscure the strength or veracity of the president's message), or the media that challenge the president's message.[36]

The greater the number or impact of these countervailing elements, the less likely that presidents are to lead public opinion. Not surprisingly, presidents are significantly disadvantaged by the presence of one (but often more) of these countervailing elements. There are simply so many different ways in which presidential messages will be obscured and comparatively few times when they will be adequately and completely received by the public. As a result, scholars generally find few moments where presidents are able to lead public opinion.[37] The conditions shaping presidential difficulty in leading public opinion are both internal and external; therefore, it is understandable that presidents generally fail at leading public opinion. But when such contrary voices are more silent or the president's voice is more resonant, the opportunities for presidential leadership will be greater.

The theory of conditional presidential leadership of public opinion builds on previous work, as other scholars have identified the transmission and reception of presidential messages as important elements in presidential leadership.[38] Indeed, Edwards argues that the "president transmits his messages in an environment clogged with competing communications from a wide variety of sources," thereby limiting the influence the president might have in leading public opinion.[39] These "competitors for attention" congest the political environment with multiple competing messages.[40] The reception component is also difficult in that many in the public may not listen to or understand what the president says.[41] I expand this line of investigation by pulling these themes together into a testable theory and offering conditional explanations of which constraining elements or constraining agents most impede presidential leadership, in addition to those that buttress presidential leadership.

Specific Conditional Expectations

To further amplify and qualify the theory of conditional presidential leadership, in this section I outline the specific literature that informs our understanding of the political circumstances, time periods, tactics, and levels of public interest that enhance or detract from a constrained president's ability to lead public opinion. I argued above that presidents who were aggressive with their message and who constantly pressed it in public would succeed, yet external political factors would intentionally or unintentionally limit this ability. To extend this general theory, I develop eleven conditional expectations that suggest when and under what specific conditions presidents might find success in leading public opinion.[42] These hypotheses will serve as useful barometers for guiding the discussion of conditional presidential leadership success and for shaping the discussion of the conditional nature of opinion leadership.

Conditional Expectation 1:
Presidents who served in the era of ubiquitous polling in the White House (post-Carter) will lead public opinion more successfully.

Since the Eisenhower administration, the dramatic systemic, institutional, and political changes witnessed by the White House have perpetually shaped and reshaped the role of the president in the political system.[43] Understanding these developing trends, presidents have adapted internal and external tools to meet their ongoing political and policy needs.[44] This grand shift in obtaining greater information "certainty" occurs in the transition from the pre-poll to post-poll era, a span of time that is captured in the data used in this book.[45] Even if later-serving presidents are not more skilled rhetoricians, better and more complete information on public preferences will yield presidential rhetorical techniques that are more easily able to lead public opinion. Thus, an expanded capacity to understand the public and create more direct communications will yield expanded opportunity and success for presidential leadership.

Specifically, observers have suggested that the expanded operation within the White House to gauge opinion creates conditions where contemporary presidents are more likely to be able to lead public preferences.[46] During the modern era, a sophisticated process of gauging public opinion was created. The advent of this public opinion polling apparatus led to the use of the power and prestige of the presidency to promote public relations goals, a use that is now more institutionalized.[47] However, until President Carter provided space in the West Wing for his pollster, Patrick Caddell, the process of getting information from pollsters was largely an external one. Paul Light notes that the use of surveys reached its peak in the Carter administration when the White House "elevated polling to a new plane."[48] Because of the ability and necessity of establishing a close proximity between presidents and public concerns and the concomitant heightened responsibility of gauging the public's mood, later-serving presidents are theoretically better equipped to lead public opinion.

The practice of "going public," that is, attempting to persuade the public, reaches back to the early days of the presidency.[49] However, the modern use of new public relations tools to frame public opinion (and thereby lead it) has given rise to what Jacobs and Shapiro dub "crafted talk."[50] Jacobs and Shapiro claim that politicians using "crafted talk" are "intent on lowering the potential electoral costs of subordinating voters' preferences to their policy goals," and that they "use polls and focus groups not to move their positions closer to the public's but just the opposite: to find the most effective means *to move public opinion closer to their own desired policies.*"[51] By using public opinion polling and focus groups, presidents locate the preferences of most Americans (that is, "centrist opinion") and attempt to *move* majority public opinion to their own preferred location by framing the issue in favorable terms. Later-serving presidents, with these new tools and the accumulated knowledge of their use, will succeed more at leading opinion as a result.

Conditional Expectation 2:
Presidents will have an easier time leading public opinion when the public is (or grows) less informed or less certain about an issue.

Most scholars of the modern presidency argue that presidents must be effective teachers to achieve their policy preferences in a system that shares political power among three branches. Indeed, underlying opinion leadership is the president's ability to clearly and accurately provide information to the public. For instance, Erwin Hargrove argues that presidents can lead public opinion by "teaching" constituents about reality.[52] Richard Neustadt also identifies the phenomenon of "president-as-teacher" (as a resource in the "power to persuade") and explains that "a president concerned for leeway inside government must try to shape the thoughts of men outside. If he would be effective as a guardian of public standing, he must be effective as a teacher to the public."[53] Neustadt acknowledges that this process is difficult but that self-constructed events "create his opportunities to teach."[54] The presence of these "teaching" effects reinforces the argument that presidents are the central player in the political system, and as such, the media centralize him as the protagonist or antagonist in news concerning that policy issue.

Related to the "president as teacher" claim, the level of political information possessed by the public is therefore important when evaluating policy leadership.[55] Specifically, when many in the public already hold an opinion (a lower percentage registers "don't know" in the polls), the opportunities for leadership are minimal, yet when fewer hold an opinion, the opportunities for presidential leadership will be greater.[56] Simply put, another way in which to view leadership as conditional is the amount of information the public has before and after the president's speech. This is what John Geer terms "Wilsonian" leadership: if the public does not have strongly held preferences on policy issues, "politicians attempt to move and to shape the distribution of public policy towards their stated position."[57] In this scenario, presidents "create" attitudes where none existed before.

Related scholarship on the individual roots of mass opinion change is deep. Individuals who are less informed about politics are more likely to respond "don't know" to survey questions.[58] Converse argues that those individuals with more political information are less likely to be able to be persuaded by elites due to "large storage of political lore."[59] John Zaller similarly finds that those with less political information are more likely to be persuadable because they will have conflicting political considerations making them susceptible to elite influence.[60] For individuals, reception of the president's message should theoretically be limited if the individual has firm beliefs in place (less likely to respond "don't know" to survey questions). That is, those with more political information know which messages to resist because they are able to "counterargue" against messages aimed at changing their preferences. Indeed, Zaller finds that as political awareness increases, the ratio of consistent-to-inconsistent considerations decreases, or put another way, those with more political knowledge are more consistent in their preferences than those who have lower awareness.[61] Therefore, in the models presented in chapter 4, the change (decrease) in the percentage of the public responding "don't know" to the survey questions is included to model this arrangement.[62]

Conditional Expectation 3:
Presidents will have a more difficult time leading on salient political issues (issues registered by the public as more important).

It makes sense to think that presidents would be interested in publicly addressing the most "talked about" issues of the day. Appearing active and engaged with current public events is critical to serving as president of the United States. Of course, the president cannot spend time on every compelling public issue; the White House must make careful decisions as to which issues to speak about openly. Nothing mandates that presidents pay attention to any particular issue, Light argues. However, concerns about the passage of legislation, reelection, historical achievement, and enactment of good policy often force the president's hand.[63] This observation is most accurate when issues are at their most salient. Not surprisingly, scholars have found presidents to be responsive on salient policy issues. Canes-Wrone and Kenneth Shotts find that presidents are more likely to take popular positions on issues that are "highly familiar" to voters while presidents appear to be less responsive on less familiar issues, such as defense and foreign aid.[64] Presidential rhetoric has also been shown to be effective in directing issue salience.[65] Jeffrey Cohen similarly finds a short-term impact of presidential rhetoric on moving salient policy issues (economic and foreign policy and civil rights) in the public's mind.[66] Similar research has shown that on some issues, but not all, presidents have a "one-way" influence on public attention, especially in the area of civil rights.[67]

Yet when the issue is highly salient (measured by pollsters' "most important problem" question) it is expected that presidents will be less consistently able to use their persuasive powers to *lead* public opinion.[68] E. E. Schattschneider argues that when issue visibility is low, and the "scope of conflict" is limited (that is, the public is not paying attention), the president has more ability to activate his own policy preferences.[69] However, the greater the importance of the issue to the public—that is, the greater the "scope of conflict"—the more likely that other groups are to make a claim on that issue, crowding the number of political voices present in the system and challenging the president's message.[70] So, the president talking about salient issues may activate the voices of opposition groups to challenge the president's message, a prospect that limits leadership. Therefore, the more the president directs his attention to issues that are more important to the public, the less likely that the president can lead effectively with less interference.[71]

Conditional Expectation 4:
The closer presidential elections are, the greater the president's ability to lead public opinion.

The importance of elections in driving public presidential rhetorical behavior has been widely established. If presidents are interested in securing reelection, they must take policy positions that are likely to be supported by a majority of the public. Specifically, James Stimson, Michael MacKuen, and Robert Erikson argue that elections have a strong shaping effect on presidential behavior.[72] Scholars have found presidents to be responsive to public preferences when an election is imminent or when a policy position is seen to be favorable in terms of leadership image.[73] Jacobs and Shapiro also suggest that politicians facing an imminent election should be more responsive to the median voter's preferences.[74] Indeed, presidents have been shown to respond to the public's ideological leanings particularly when elections are close.[75] Light similarly notes that "every first term President is interested in reelection" and that the goal of electoral success does not "abate with the first inaugural."[76]

Conditional Expectation 4 argues that this expanded capacity to court the voters and the increased visibility of an election should yield leadership success. First, there is more media attention to the president's day-to-day activities leading up to elections than when the election is farther away.[77] Savvy presidents should take advantage of this development and use their position to push for their policy agenda. Second, as a resource capacity, the dual White House and presidential campaign public relations apparatuses should significantly enhance the power of the president to get his message to the public.[78] This theory of election proximity also corresponds with the conditional theory of presidential leadership: the more presidents attempt to lead and the more people who hear his message, the more likely he will successfully lead public opinion. Third, related to the nature of campaigning, presidents will travel more during the campaign than they are able to do when there is no campaign.[79] This expanded exposure will assist presidents in getting their message to the public.

Conditional Expectation 5:
Popularity will have a positive effect on the White House's ability to lead public opinion, especially during a president's honeymoon year.

Popular presidents are theoretically more likely to find support in the media and the public (in the form of less critical evaluations). Therefore, concurrent with the conditional theory of presidential leadership, the presence of fewer constraining agents will assist popular presidents in leading public opinion.[80] Simply stated, the more popular the president is, the more muted his critics will be, providing the president with fewer critical voices against which he must present his message. Neustadt's recommendations about maintaining a positive reputation with those who "share in governing" in an "incestuous community" suggest that popularity can be effective in inducing positive perceptions of the president's actions and it may mute disagreements.[81] Indeed, Bruce Buchanan finds that higher popularity can lead to better media coverage, a phenomenon that reinforces the above theory about countervailing influences.[82] Other scholars find empirically that presidents who are more popular are able to move pubic opinion in small amounts.[83]

Presidential popularity can also be represented as a function of the year a president is in office. Specifically, the "honeymoon" period (coded as a president's first year in office) is argued to have a unique role in fostering presidential leadership. It is argued that in their first year, presidents generally have higher popularity since the media run fewer critical stories and the public softens their generally high expectations.[84] If the expectation about the connection between presidential popularity and leading public opinion is correct, then one can expect leadership success to be more pronounced in the president's first year because fewer constraining agents are given voices (or are simply naturally quiet during these times).

Conditional Expectation 6:
By virtue of being commander-in-chief, presidents will have an easier time leading on issues of foreign policy than on domestic policy.

Discussion of foreign policy issues augments presidential leadership ability. Aaron Wildavsky argued that "two presidencies" exist: one president who was successful in getting policies passed through Congress on foreign policy and one president who was less successful in getting domestic policies passed through Congress.[85] Wildavsky, writing in the post–World War II era but before Vietnam, discovered empirically that on diverse foreign policy matters of military funding, national defense, and allocation and deployment of service personnel, presidents held a significant advantage.[86] Similarly, debate on domestic policy is contentious and is influenced by groups both inside and outside government, while foreign policy, whose governance is largely set in the confines of the White House, allows for the president to manage and lead public opinion more expeditiously.[87] Discussion of domestic policy, therefore, hosts several countervailing influences while foreign policy allows for fewer countervailing influences. Presidents can rhetorically construct an environment for "crisis," which the public, the media, nor Congress tends to challenge.[88] The broad implication is that the president has expanded credibility on foreign policy matters, providing him with advantages in public persuasion.

One important concept related to presidential success at leading public opinion is the "rally around the flag" effect, where the president's job approval ratings increase during a crisis of foreign policy, international or military. Richard Brody suggests that this effect occurs frequently enough to consider it a fact of presidential leadership.[89] Because presidents can generally count on a "rally" effect, they can be reasonably assured that the public will support their leadership actions.[90] The theory behind a rally is twofold: (1) that patriotic sentiment emerges in the public and the media and (2) that all groups are less willing to criticize or challenge the president on these matters.[91] These two factors help to explain both the impact and duration of rally events and reflect the argument about countervailing agents in the theory of conditional presidential leadership.

Scholarship in other contexts has demonstrated that presidents are able to move public opinion on foreign policy matters more readily than domestic policy. Cohen and John Hamman argue that foreign policy speeches (because of their unifying and symbolic nature) will have stronger impacts on the public's future orientation than other types of speeches.[92] Cohen also found that presidential influence over public opinion on issues of foreign policy was persistent and strong (a result that did not hold for domestic policy issues).[93] And, when special rhetorical attention is marshaled by the White House to a particular agenda in foreign policy, presidents have been shown to be effective at engendering support for that agenda.[94] Overall, then, issues of foreign policy will significantly enhance leadership success.

Conditional Expectation 7: Divided government will limit presidential ability to lead public opinion.

Presidents are hypothesized to be less likely to lead public opinion when fewer members of Congress share his party affiliation. Kernell's classic tradeoff is that presidents can either bargain with the Congress (institutionalized pluralism) or "go public" to persuade the public over the heads of Congress (individualized pluralism).[95] Therefore, when a president does not have a majority of his party in one or both houses, or when he faces significant opposition, a president may resort to populist leadership in an attempt to lobby his legislative agenda through Congress.[96] Specifically, Hart finds that presidents make more national speeches when the opposition party controls Congress or when the president is "frustrated by congressional behavior," but this expanding of the scope of conflict does not guarantee success.[97] In fact, if the conditional theory about presidential leadership is accurate, this tactic will be less effective because there are functionally more diverse issues on the table, and as a result, more voices competing with the president's voice.

Indeed, during these times, the theory of countervailing influences (in this case the constraining agent of Congress) suggests that there will be more voices critical of the president which will therefore limit the clear reception of the president's message. The White House needs to work with Congress to obtain positive legislative outcomes to enact its policy agenda.[98] Presidential support from party loyalists in both chambers is the determining factor predicting presidential success in Congress.[99] The president's legislative role, therefore, is intimately linked to the number of "copartisans" the president has in the House and Senate. Fewer copartisans generally mean more opponents in Congress. Therefore, presidents will be less able to lead public opinion when government is divided because the expanded number of voices in the political system contradict or counterweigh the message of the president and limits the effective reach of his full message (and therefore limits the public's unconditional acceptance of the policy message).

Which Leadership Tactics Are Most Successful in Leading Opinion?

Presidential politics do not exist in a bubble. Presidents must actively get their message to the people. Indeed, this finding is a critical component of the theory of conditional leadership. Presidents since Woodrow Wilson have seen public persuasion as a critical part of modern politics and have capitalized on their position as leader of the country to ensure that the other political actors in the system hear their message loudly and clearly. This approach may involve travel, technology, or talking (often all three), but it certainly requires an active and involved president and a strategic White House.[100] This practice is in harmony with the theoretical expectation of an active president. The end result perpetuates the presidency as the center of American governance and facilitates the "permanent campaign" in the White House.[101]

Again confronting the puzzle presented in chapter 1 and above, we may ask *which* communications tactics systematically affect presidential leadership of public opinion? Presidents are continuously utilizing their bully pulpit in its various incarnations to communicate with the nation, but the leadership effects of these strategies are not well understood. Specifically, which strategic communications activities are more likely to produce leadership success (holding all the other factors constant)? Has the advent of television (both network and cable) facilitated or hindered the dissemination of presidential messages? Does presidential travel around the country or abroad have a consistent effect on the movement of public opinion to the president's position? Do press conferences ,where the president spars with the "fourth branch of government," have a negative effect on presidential communications? Ultimately, to capture the effects of these strategies is to fully understand leadership in the modern presidency. Four hypotheses related to four communications tactics are presented below.

Conditional Expectation 8:
A presidential "barnstorm" will be a successful tool in leading public opinion.

Akin to Kernell's "going public" theory, the barnstorm strategy captures a president making a speech outside Washington, D.C., not on television and to a broad audience (that is, not a private fundraiser or party event).[102] This measure evaluates the president's communication to the public during moments when they were out in the nation speaking directly to the public.[103] Presidents continually engage in these kinds of events in order to explain or build support for policies, consistent with the theory of presidents actively getting their message to the people. This kind of communication tactic is possible because technology allows modern presidents to travel and stay connected to the apparatus of governing. A good example of this tactic was discussed in the preface—President Bush's "sixty cities in sixty days" tour to privatize Social Security in 2005, in which he went on the road to multiple states and was covered by the newspapers and local television in those states.

With modern presidents logging more miles to communicate directly with the public, it is expected that this strategy of presidential leadership will yield success.[104] Indeed, the ability of the White House to communicate directly with the American public is critical to modern presidential leadership. Once the utility of public opinion became central in governing, presidents began to try to corral public opinion directly by talking to the American public.[105] Kernell notes that "the president who rests his leadership on going public will be tempted to travel frequently, in search of sympathetic audiences and 'presidential images.'"[106] Woodrow Wilson's infamous tour to drum up support for the League of Nations in 1919 was undertaken partly due to Wilson's "faith in the power of his own oratory to influence public opinion" and he assumed that, through his public mandate, "in the end, public opinion would force the Senate to surrender to his uncompromising position."[107]

This strategic tactic has grown from presidential prerogative to presidential necessity as the modern media and contemporary political message strategies require sure-handed, direct guidance of the White House's message by the president. The evidence suggests that presidents are taking the cue. Presidents have increasingly been taking more trips per year in their first year in office, and Brendan Doherty argues that presidents are more likely to travel to larger, more competitive states.[108] The overall rate has been also increasing over the modern presidency. Kernell substantiates these findings and discovers that domestic travel has significantly increased in the past half century to the point where President Clinton was traveling "every fourth day or so during his first three years in office," demonstrating the effect of the emergence of "barnstorming" as a consistent communications strategy.[109] Scholars have found that this strategy has the effect of producing favorable outcomes for presidents (although not necessarily in moving public policy preferences). Domestic political travel (outside Washington, D.C.) has been demonstrated to have a modest impact on presidential electoral success and presidential legislative success.[110] Such travel has also been demonstrated to have a modest impact on state-level presidential approval, although the effect is limited to nonelection years and larger states.[111] Charles Ostrom and Dennis Simon find that President Reagan's domestic travel did have a small positive effect on his popularity.[112] These findings suggest that presidential travel is linked to campaigning and governing, a potent combination for a president on the move. In addition, presidents can also use the barnstorming technique to influence local media outlets who may be less critical of presidential policy, more willing to provide extended airtime to the president (and concurrently his message) and more supportive of presidential policy.[113] Theoretically, this strategy affords the president more chances to get his message directly to the public with less interference from reporters asking tough questions and the limitations on the amount of news coverage provided. These efforts have grown in popularity with the White House because of the advantages it provides to persuasive efforts.

Conditional Expectation 9: A presidential "major address" strategy will be a successful tool in leading public opinion.

A strategy that makes use of a "major address" encompasses speeches that were delivered on television (either live or taped) from Washington, D.C. (including State of the Union, inaugural addresses, and Oval Office speeches).[114] In using this strategy, the White House seeks to harness the image and prestige of the presidency by using the White House and its trappings to communicate with the American public. These speeches are designed to capture the president's ability to focus the attention of the entire nation on his words and cultivate significant national public persuasion on the issues he will discuss. Given the pomp and circumstance surrounding these events, Lori Cox Han adeptly labels this "governing from center stage."[115] These speeches allow the president to bypass the media and Congress and speak directly to the American people, and to "operate in a setting where he is unhindered by rival decision makers or aggressive reporters."[116]

The advent of television as a medium of mass communication has advanced presidential ability to connect with the public. The communication revolution ushered in by the advent of television clearly changed the way that presidents communicate.[117] Indeed, given that these presentations are on the national stage, several studies point to these addresses as critical elements in presidential leadership.[118] Paul Brace and Barbara Hinckley find that presidents use these major addresses strategically, especially in relation to economic decline and reductions in presidential approval, and especially during presidential reelection years.[119] Cox Han argues that "starting with Johnson, a trend emerges for presidents to increasingly rely on major addresses as a means of communicating their policy goals," and for recent presidents such as Reagan, Bush, and Clinton, changes in communications strategies "require each president to go public even more frequently" on television.[120] Scholars have also given empirical weight to these trends in presidential communications. Cohen finds that presidential mentions of issues in State of the Union addresses increased the public's perception of that issue as important.[121] In moving popularity, Ostrom and Simon find that President Reagan's major speeches had a modest effect on his short-term popularity, but this effect was generally smaller than the events taking place in the political and economic environment.[122] Simon and Ostrom also find that these speeches are most effective in buttressing public support when they are accompanied with a trip and an "approval-enhancing" event.[123]

However, as a strategy, leadership of public opinion on television is difficult to manage in the age of the modern media. Presidents fail for a number of reasons, generally in combination, such as shrinking audiences, media message screeners, political partisanship, and a lack of public cognition.[124] The audience that is paying attention is more partisan than before, ensuring that only some of those who receive the president's message are going to be remotely receptive to it.[125] On this point, Neustadt argued that as "teacher," a president's pupils (the public) are habitually inattentive to his message.[126] The emergence of divided government and strong party leadership complicate the conduct of successful presidential leadership.[127] These factors are beyond the control of the White House but ultimately complicate the president's ability to chart a successful course for moving public opinion.[128]

Part of the cause of the difficulty in leading public opinion has been the presence of television as, ironically, a barrier to communication. Although television allows the president to speak to more citizens than any other medium, television-viewing habits limit whom the president can reach. The amount of exposure and education individuals have is important in determining whether or not they are receptive and can receive the message.[129] Nationally televised presidential addresses are often too broad (that is, covering too many issues) to do much good in influencing mass public opinion.[130] Similarly, the audience that is paying attention on television is more partisan than before, ensuring that only some of those who receive the president's message are going to be remotely receptive to it.[131] Televised speeches thus may actually decrease approval ratings, particularly if the post-speech news stories were negative.[132] Cable television is also referenced as a culprit in ending the "golden age" of presidential communication, where the proliferation of channels has decreased the impact of presidential rhetoric by reducing the viewing audience.[133]

However, despite the difficulties, there are moments where presidents are able to successfully communicate with the public through television. For instance, prime-time addresses have been shown to be particularly beneficial in boosting presidential popularity among middle- and upper-income people.[134] Others have found that President Reagan, in particular, was successful at communicating his message through nationally televised speeches to those who were educated and male; however, his speeches often had a negative effect on overall presidential approval.[135] Generally, greater exposure to the content of the speech did engender more positive movement of approval of the president, although these results were contingent upon actual viewership (rather than indirect information on the speech), and if the speech was a foreign policy speech (instead of an economic speech).[136] And, indirectly connecting to the public, attention to media coverage of the State of the Union is also found to increase public knowledge of presidential policy initiatives.[137]

Presidents typically use these strategies sparingly, saving them for important or emergent situations. Matthew Baum and Kernell find that with the reduction in the ratings for the president's televised addresses, presidents began to use this medium less frequently.[138] Reed Welch argues that presidents must carefully choose moments to deliver nationally televised addresses to maximize viewership and minimize inattentiveness—this can be done with the timing and the issues chosen.[139] Full network television coverage of these kinds of speeches (with the notable exception of the State of the Union) is more rare than in years past, contributing to lean presidential reliance on these speeches for public communication. Specifically, William Lammers finds that the preemption of national television on the major networks for a major television address does not occur with great regularity.[140] Andrew Barrett finds that presidential appeals on specific legislation are more likely to be done in front of small audiences than on television (although the State of the Union did produce 31.8% of all of the proposal appeals from Carter to George H. W. Bush).[141]

Conditional Expectation 10: A presidential press conference will not be a successful tool in leading public opinion.

The relationship between the press and the president is largely symbiotic, with each needing the other to engage in their jobs. The press conference is but one way in which this relationship manifests itself, and news organizations often prefer this format (even if the White House does not) because it allows for direct media access to the president with little interference from the White House staff.[142] Ironically, press conferences were originally televised by the White House because of a fear that the reporters were not fully reporting the president's message and because of the hope that the president as messenger could more readily and persuasively convey his thoughts to the public.[143] As press conferences became routinely televised, they were transformed into "high-risk performances" and the White House attempted to find ways to "meet the press" without holding a press conference. This is not surprising because, over time, the media has been found to be less deferential to the president in their questions during press conferences while directness by the press has gradually increased over time.[144]

As a result of this typically combative relationship, presidents have made press conferences more formal events (rather than informal in the early years of press conferences) and attempted to find alternative venues for engaging the press "without the risks posed by long news conferences in formal settings."[145] Kernell argues that the adversarial nature of press conferences led presidents to place additional rules on them, including hosting impromptu press conferences (Johnson), limiting questions to specific policy areas (Nixon), and scheduling the events later in the day to allow less time for editing of the president's remarks.[146] Jeremy Mayer and Mark Rozell point out that George W. Bush, furthering this avoidance trend, held "fewer press conferences than any president since William Howard Taft" in his first six months in office, and by 2002 he had held only seven solo press conferences.[147] Press conferences held in prime time have also become rarer with the advent of television.[148] These findings link nicely with the conditional theory of presidential leadership: the presence of more countervailing agents to limit the president's message, the less likely presidents are to lead public opinion.

Despite the potential to communicate with the larger political crowd both inside and outside the Beltway, most scholars argue that press conferences are net negatives for presidential communications. Consequently, televised presidential press conferences are expected to not have a positive effect on presidential leadership. Consistent with the theory outlined above, the media act as a countervailing agent and limit the pure reception of the president's message. The media typically interpret or filter the president's message, so by limiting a fuller reception or challenging the veracity of the president's message, the media act as a constraining force. Specifically, as others have found, press conferences are difficult venues in which to attempt to lead public opinion because presidents are less likely to be able to control the specific trajectory of the discussion and more likely to be boxed into answering a question on issues they may not prefer to discuss.[149] Presidents are also constrained by their political circumstances in these instances, making these events largely reactive instead of proactive.[150]

Conditional Expectation 11:
A presidential trip abroad ("going international") will be a successful tool in leading public opinion.

The availability of rapid air travel (beginning with Truman and Eisenhower in the 1950s) has hastened the president's role as "leader of the free world" by allowing the president to step foot on foreign soil in a matter of hours. This strategy, referred to as "going international," is a companion approach to "going public." It is similar to barnstorming except the location from which the president speaks is *outside* the United States. The conditions are the same: delivering the speech to a broad audience and not on television. Lyndon Johnson's trip to Vietnam in 1967, Richard Nixon's visit to China in 1972, and George W. Bush's many surprise trips to Iraq (such as the Thanksgiving Day visit in 2003) are excellent examples of this strategy. These examples emphasize both the drama and symbolism of the American presidency.

Indeed, international travel affords presidents the opportunity to ceremonially function as the head of state, a potentially strong signal to the public about the power of the presidency. Kernell notes that when presidents travel abroad "they frequently do so in search of special opportunities to appear presidential. Meetings abroad with other heads of state are especially valuable in reminding the electorate of the weighty responsibilities of office and the president's diligence in attending to them."[151] Events that allow for "high-level" diplomacy are likely to enhance this effect.[152] These international events are not, however, simply comprised of foreign policy issues. Presidents often encounter questions about domestic politics while traveling abroad or when meeting with foreign leaders. Contemporary presidents have utilized this strategy more, with Presidents Nixon, Ford, and Carter taking an average of more than one day of international travel per month and all presidents taking between two and three trips per year.[153] This number is also greater for later-serving presidents (especially Reagan, Bush, and Clinton) than earlier presidents.[154] Most of these trips are taken in presidential election years (but not midterm election years).[155] Theoretically, presidents who are acting presidential in this capacity, similar to their image on foreign policy issues, expect fewer sources of dissent among the media and public, and, consistent with the theory of presidential leadership, are more likely to lead public opinion.

Although there is little work on presidential international travel and leadership of public opinion, several scholars address it as an important part of presidential communications. Hart argues that President Kennedy ushered in an "international style" by beginning the trend of speaking internationally.[156] Brace and Hinckley find trips abroad to be strategic, wherein presidents reactively attempt to buttress approval with international travel.[157] These trips may be undertaken to attract attention away from potentially damaging domestic events. Indeed, Kernell notes that presidents may travel for strategic avoidance of domestic events.[158] These findings also comport with the observation that presidents strategically use international trips as "representatives of the nation" and can be used to evoke "common unity and patriotic support."[159] This subtle reminder to the public may be significant enough to give a president an effective tool in motivating domestic opinion while abroad.

Conclusion

Constitutional design limits the president as a "popular politician" (since the Electoral College is not a "popular" medium). Yet, ironically, the Constitution also requires "energetic" leadership by presidents as the ceremonial head of state. This narrow passageway, along with the political developments that limit the president's ability to control the political system, leaves little room for the expanded needs of modern presidents to lead public opinion based upon strategic necessity. As such, presidents are constrained. But in the modern evolution of the office, presidents have traversed this legal and statutory restriction and have expanded the power of the presidency with their words. Woodrow Wilson's arguments about educating the people and serving their will in office are predicated on direct and clear presidential communications. Wilson argued in *Congressional Government* that "there is no trouble now about getting the president's speeches printed and read, every word" as a means for the public to understand the president's position.[160] Of course, this is mitigated by a reluctant, uninformed, or polarized public, and by the ability of the president to communicate his message and the circumstances that limit the clear reception of the president's messages. Thus, a constrained presidency emerges and effective leaders must navigate these choppy waters. The degree to which presidents succeed at this is explored in the remaining chapters.

CHAPTER 3

Presidential (Non-)Leadership of Public Opinion

In the previous two chapters I outlined several important works in the study of presidential leadership of public opinion and introduced a theory pertaining to when presidents should successfully lead public opinion. I argued that presidents are more likely to lead when fewer countervailing agents limit the reach of the president's message. In addition, I posed several hypotheses that are necessary to address in order to further the study of presidential leadership of the public's policy preferences. With these in mind, my goal in this chapter is to introduce a definition of leadership of opinion, to outline the data used, and to offer some "big picture" summaries of the success (or lack of success) presidents have in leading public opinion. These simple summaries inform our understanding of the plebiscitary presidency, and these trends also help set the stage for more thorough statistical investigations in chapter 4.

How frequently do presidents lead public opinion? In part, this depends on how one conceptualizes "leadership." Clearly, presidents "lead" government in many instances and their actions both large and small can have a significant impact on the direction and scope of government.[1] Leadership can be a rhetorical construction that is initiated by the White House to control an issue, a tangible movement of congressional voting patterns, attention to an issue designed to signal the intentions of the White House, or improvement in the image of the president as the nation's chief executive. This book focuses on how presidents manage to successfully lead mass public opinion on preferences of public policy, a keystone modern presidential strategy according to many observers. To that end, this chapter explores the connections between presidential policy action (in the form of policy statements) and the public's policy preferences. Therefore, the baseline condition is an instance when presidents have made a statement on an issue (as they do on most issues in the public domain).

It is therefore necessary to construct a workable and durable measure of leadership by ability to change opinion. In particular, in this book I am interested in a firm numerical conclusion about how frequently presidents lead public opinion given the sample of speeches collected here. And, importantly, the analysis is concerned with the president's ability to move public opinion on matters of *public policy* with his rhetoric, rather than changing his personal approval ratings or his party's approval ratings, his anticipation of future opinion, his framing of opinion yet to be formed, or leading Congress to endorse his policy proposals. Simply put, this chapter matches a president's statement with public opinion polling on that statement before and after the date of the statement to determine the degree of opinion movement.

Measuring Short-term Presidential Leadership

In order to construct workable and manageable observations to match presidential policy statements to public opinion, I obtained a random sample of 4% of the total pages from the *Public Papers of the President* from Presidents Eisenhower to Clinton (see appendix A for a full accounting of the procedures). These statements reflect a number of characteristics (or absence of certain characteristics), but in general the statement recorded a specific policy issue. Because the *Public Papers* includes a massive number of statements, several criteria were created for what constituted a valid policy statement on each page. An item was considered valid if it came from the president (not subordinates or other actors) and advocated a position on a specific policy issue.[2] The online polling archive at the Roper Center for Public Opinion Research was used to search for public polling data that could be matched up with the randomly selected policy statements.[3] Polling data was searched for one year before the statement on the assumption that the White House may require time to digest public opinion results, and the pre-poll closest to the statement was coded.[4] The average distance between the first poll and the president's statement was one hundred days. In addition, at multiple points in the analysis, this post-statement window is narrowed (to one month and three months after the statement) to improve the causal certainty.

The dependent variable of opinion movement is defined by the change in opinion in favor of the president's policy after the president's statement (when public opinion polling with the same question wording was found both before and after the president's statement).[5] *Positive* movement signifies *successful* leadership, but in the continuous dependent variable used in chapter 4, both no change and negative changes are included. The matching of the before- and after-statement poll is important because we can then judge the changes without interference from question wording.[6] This matching process permits the construction of a simple pre- and post-statement design to model the possibility of presidential leadership. To reference a specific example from the data of successful leadership of opinion, on February 10, 1995, President Clinton announced a nationwide ban on assault rifles as part of his crime package. On January 3, 67% of the public supported the ban, and on February 25, 69% of the public supported the ban (see appendix A for additional examples available).[7]

This statement-poll matching process resulted in 665 cases where an opinion poll was found both before and after the president's statement, allowing presidential leadership to be measured.[8] This total (665) of matched statements encompasses approximately one-third of the total data (1,976 randomly selected statements), an impressive statistic considering that the range of topics presidents talk about fluctuates from the major (foreign conflicts) to the minor (specific education initiatives) to the obscure (specific goods under import and export policy).

The analysis focuses on short-term leadership in that there are several advantages to examining this type of opinion movement. First, this conceptualization and definition of opinion leadership closely mirrors how other prominent scholars have conceptualized opinion leadership. For instance, this pays thematic homage to Edwards's conceptualization of the president as "director" of public opinion where presidents move an existing shape of mass opinion distribution closer to their ideal point.[9] Second, this method is consistent with how presidents view their ability to move public opinion.[10] It is apparent from the case studies in chapters 5 and 7 that presidents use their speeches to try to pressure congressional deliberations, swing key legislative votes, and gain public attention. Third, the literature on presidential communications success suggests that presidents find the most public attention soon after they make a speech on a topic, but the effect is temporary.[11] Indeed, given the "stickiness" of public opinion, temporarily moving public opinion may be the best presidents can hope for.[12] Fourth, this approach is methodologically proper because extending the randomly sampled policy statements to beyond a single data point would mean extending the time period of the post-poll for a year or longer, obstructing the causal arguments.[13] This is therefore a more causally secure approach, even if it is biased toward finding leadership effects.

Do Speeches Move Public Opinion?

There are several reasons why causal claims are offered in this research design. First, presidents as national figures play a significant role in public politics, such that much of the opinion movement found results from presidential policy pronouncements.[14] Indeed, Genovese argues that, in media coverage, the "president is the nation's center of political attention."[15] Presidents also play the role of facilitator in moving opinion into policy by being the educator of public opinion and by structuring policy choices by framing the discussion of issues.[16] Further, on most major policy issues of the day, presidents continually attempt (with mixed success) to gain support for themselves and their programs—this is a consistent leadership effect used by presidents and can be measured with the repeated-statements design.[17] All eyes gravitate to the president on policy issues, a fact that allows the president's position to be a major part of the national discussion.

In addition, even though other factors intervene in the pre- and post-statement measure of opinion, the measure still captures presidents as agenda setters and policy framers. Specifically, the president's support for an issue quickly becomes categorized and crystallized into opposition or support for a policy. This is especially true given the routines of journalists in working with the White House and presidential success at defining political "reality" through language.[18] Similarly, on major issues, presidential policy pronouncements become "indexed" into the media's reporting of the issue.[19] The president's policy preferences are included in the discussion and analysis of the issue in the media, and as a result, the president's role in the process is an important point of public reference. Thus, the opinion movement measured represents a tacit referendum on the president's policy since the president plays a major role in directing the policy environment.[20] Therefore, although presidential position taking is measured specific to an individual speech, the probable reach of the president's speech is broader.

Even smaller and local speeches like some of those measured here (those not on television or to a major audience, for instance) still find their way to the mass public. This media "trickle-up" effect happens regularly when the president makes a local speech and national media organizations cover it.[21] This trickle-up effect is especially apparent because local news organizations are often the target of presidential speeches, and the twenty-four-hour news networks use this information as "filler" in their political discussions around the clock.[22] These local speeches are often covered by national news organizations since, as with many other events, all eyes are focused on the president.[23] Ultimately, although their overall coverage is understandably less extensive, local media outlets also frequently cover presidential activities.[24] In this sense, smaller and more focused speeches will reach the American public in both national and local settings, even if the initial speech was not broadly heard.

Further, this "sequential" approach to understanding the president's role in the process of leading public opinion is used by several scholars, both quantitative and qualitative, to estimate the political environment with the president at the epicenter of policy activity.[25] Such studies examine a simple pre- and post-opinion dynamic (with the president's statement or action in between) and infer a quasi-experimental design (with the assumption the president's statement moved public opinion) to demonstrate causality, even though there is no definitive means to prove presidents "move" policy preferences. The analysis in this book simply aggregates the methods of previous scholars across several presidents and extrapolates conclusions accordingly.

In addition, because I am interested in the effect of the president's speech on public opinion, it makes sense to consider individual cases (speeches) aggregated across time. Sigelman and Rosenblatt note that a simple "before-and-after" design (comparable to the methods employed here) may have trouble with causal inferences and inevitably may explain all, some, or none of the effect of the president's statement on public opinion![26] However, they likewise acknowledge that such a design has merit and that multivariate designs with a before-and-after component that employ several cases across time solve several of these inference problems. Sigelman argues that such before-and-after tests are "weak" because of the problem of controlling for sampling error, history, or the presence of events; however, both of his concerns are addressed in the aggregate models presented in this book by including variables that control for the effect of exogenous events in moving public preferences.[27]

Presidential Leadership of Opinion, 1953–2001

Presidents try mightily to influence public opinion, due to conventional wisdom and a sincere belief that they can motivate public opinion to support their policies.[28] But, despite all this effort, presidents are only modestly strong at facilitating positive movement of public opinion, an interesting finding given both the mythology of the bully pulpit and the fact that the White House consistently pursues a strategy that attempts to utilize the grand stage. As shown in table 3.1, in 49% of the cases where valid opinion data was found both before and after the president's statement, opinion moved in a positive direction (toward the president's position) up to one year after the president's statement.[29] Thus, this finding is a reasonable, if not overwhelming, batting average for presidents. These findings compliment conclusions from Edwards and Cohen, who argue that presidential leadership is difficult to achieve because of the growing disconnect between speaker and audience.[30]

However, it is difficult to definitively interpret these data as opinion *leadership.* Assuming some indeterminable number of the cases of opinion leadership in the 1% to 5% opinion category is due to sampling error, removing these cases depresses the opinion movement figure. With these cases removed from the sample, only 23% of the cases reveal positive opinion movement ($n = 141$). This is a more humble record for presidents, especially contrasting these trends to the White House's faith in a strategy that presidential rhetoric can lead opinion. If these modest movements are momentary, the White House would need to keep up its rhetoric to continue these positive trends. Although these opinion-movement figures are only a sample of moments of leadership collected from individual speeches, they provide a baseline set of figures to more concretely identify presidential leadership of opinion. Even if not perfect, these data offer a more definitive sense of the frequency with which modern presidents are able to lead public opinion, an empirical investigation missing from the current discussion of the public presidency.

To further examine presidential leadership, table 3.1 analyzes opinion movement by delineating the percentage change by the category in which presidents are able to lead public opinion. It is clear that when public opinion moves, it primarily moves in small increments. Most of the positive opinion changes are in the 1% to 5% range (25%), underscoring the modest ability of presidents to move public opinion. Still, Geer suggests that small movement by the public toward a politician's

TABLE 3.1
Percentage Change in Leading Public Opinion

Percentage change	Percentage of data (n)	
−100% to −41%	0% (5)	**Negative change**
−40 to −21	3 (17)	**51% (318)**
−20 to −1	8 (50)	
−10 to −6	13 (89)	
−5 to −1	24 (157)	
0 (No change)	**6 (42)**	
1 to 5	25 (164)	
6 to 10	12 (79)	
11 to 20	7 (49)	
21 to 40	2 (12)	**Positive change**
41 to 100	0 (1)	**49% (305)**

Note: These percentages are calculated from the total number of instances where valid opinion data was found (n = 665). The total n of the data set is 1,976. The total cases that exhibit some opinion change are 623 (which is used to calculate the percentage changes in the far right column). The percentages are rounded up. The "no change" totals are left out of the figures for positive and negative change in the far right column.

preference counts as leadership.[31] Yet, as noted above, considering some of the changes in this 1%–5% category may be due to sampling error, the figure may be even slighter. Presidents are rarely able to move public opinion by larger amounts, but it does happen, at a rate of 12% in the 6% to 10% range and at a rate of 7% in the 11% to 20% range. Considering the many factors that limit attention to presidential messages, leadership of opinion in small increments may be the only viable option. In contrast, the negative-change portion of table 3.1 acknowledges that in 51% of the cases (n = 318) where there was opinion change, opinion moved *away from* the president's position. Therefore, the evaluation of presidents as opinion motivators has to be tempered considering that opinion moves away from the president's position almost as frequently, and in similar segments, as often as it moves toward the president's position.

Table 3.1 reports data for a matched poll and statement up to one year after the president's statement. Obviously, this time lag allows for a number of political, international, or economic circumstances to alter public

TABLE 3.2
Shorter Windows on Opinion Leadership

	Post Poll Window Percent (total n)		
Opinion Movement	One Month	Three Months	Six Months
1%–5%	61% (70)	57% (99)	54% (128)
6–10	17 (19)	19 (33)	23 (53)
11–20	18 (21)	21 (37)	20 (46)
41–21	3 (3)	3 (5)	3 (7)
100–41	1 (1)	1 (1)	0 (1)
Total	114	175	235

Note: Only successful leadership movement data are shown. All three measures retain statistical significance at $p > .05$ for gamma but not the chi square statistics.

opinion after the president's statement without direct impact from the president's statement. To examine a narrower window of time following the president's statement, the results in table 3.2 narrow down the post-poll data to one month, three months, and six months following the president's statement.[32] The results suggest that, if the poll was taken within a month of the president's speech (the most restrictive window), the percentage movement of opinion in the 1%–5% category was greatest. Following that category row across the three columns suggests that a president's power to move public opinion is generally limited to the short term since the percentage of movement of opinion in the three-month and six-month windows progressively declines. These findings correspond with previous findings suggesting the impact of presidential speeches is ephemeral.[33] On the other hand, opinion leadership percentages progressively rise in the 6%–10% and 11%–20% category over the same time period, suggesting that leadership in larger amounts is possible but takes longer to achieve. However, since these data are not consecutive (that is, not following the same issue across several points in time) we cannot be determine for certain the lasting impact of a specific presidential speech.

Examining individual presidents will also help to explain the important juxtaposition between presidential skill, circumstance, and history.[34] Individual presidents rarely broke the 50% leadership threshold (that is, opinion moved toward the president's position 50% of the time).[35] As seen in the left-hand bar in figure 3.1 (measuring all cases of opinion movement), after rising to a historical peak of 60% in President Eisenhower's second term, three major dips in leadership are present. First, there is a brief but substantial decline in President Nixon's second term (rebounding during the Ford administration). Genovese explains this by arguing that leadership during this time was "impossible" and labels this as a "presidency-bashing era."[36] Second, there is similar dip during the presidency of Jimmy Carter (rebounding during the Reagan administration). Third, there is a final dip in leadership during the presidency of George H. W. Bush, rebounding somewhat during the first Clinton administration. Interestingly, change in political party (Presidents Reagan and Clinton) and the transition from the Nixon to Ford administrations punctuate these effects, implying that the public may refresh their endorsement of presidents with a "changing of the guard."

Significant opinion change is also registered in figure 3.1 in the right-hand bar (in these cases, presidential leadership by term was not disaggregated due to the small number of cases). As noted above, the overall percentage of leadership (when cases were present) was 21%, a much smaller percentage than the grouping of all cases (left-hand bar). Because the issues on which the president is likely to lead public opinion in greater numbers are rare, the overall small percentage seen in figure 3.1 is logical. As for the trends in significant opinion change, we see a steady and gradual decline in the percentage of significant leadership success from the Johnson administration (33%) to the Nixon administration (23%) to the Ford administration (30%) to the Carter administration (26%) to the Reagan administration (19%) to the Bush administration (11%). Again, the erosion of trust inflicted on these presidents caused by Vietnam and Watergate took a lasting toll on White House leadership efforts. Similarly, the media grew more aggressive over this time period, complicating the ability of presidents to more clearly convey their messages. These trends are discussed further below and in chapter 4. There is a modest rebound beginning with the Clinton administration (19%), but the overall average for presidents in leading public opinion beyond 5% is not very high.

Evaluating this progression, presidents who served earlier in the twentieth century were thought to be less adept at changing public opinion than their later counterparts (as argued in Conditional Expectation 1 in chapter 2). The institutionalization of public opinion pollsters in the White House (beginning with pollster Patrick Caddell receiving office space in the West Wing under President Carter) and the more aggressive

Presidential Leadership of Public Opinion, 1953–2001

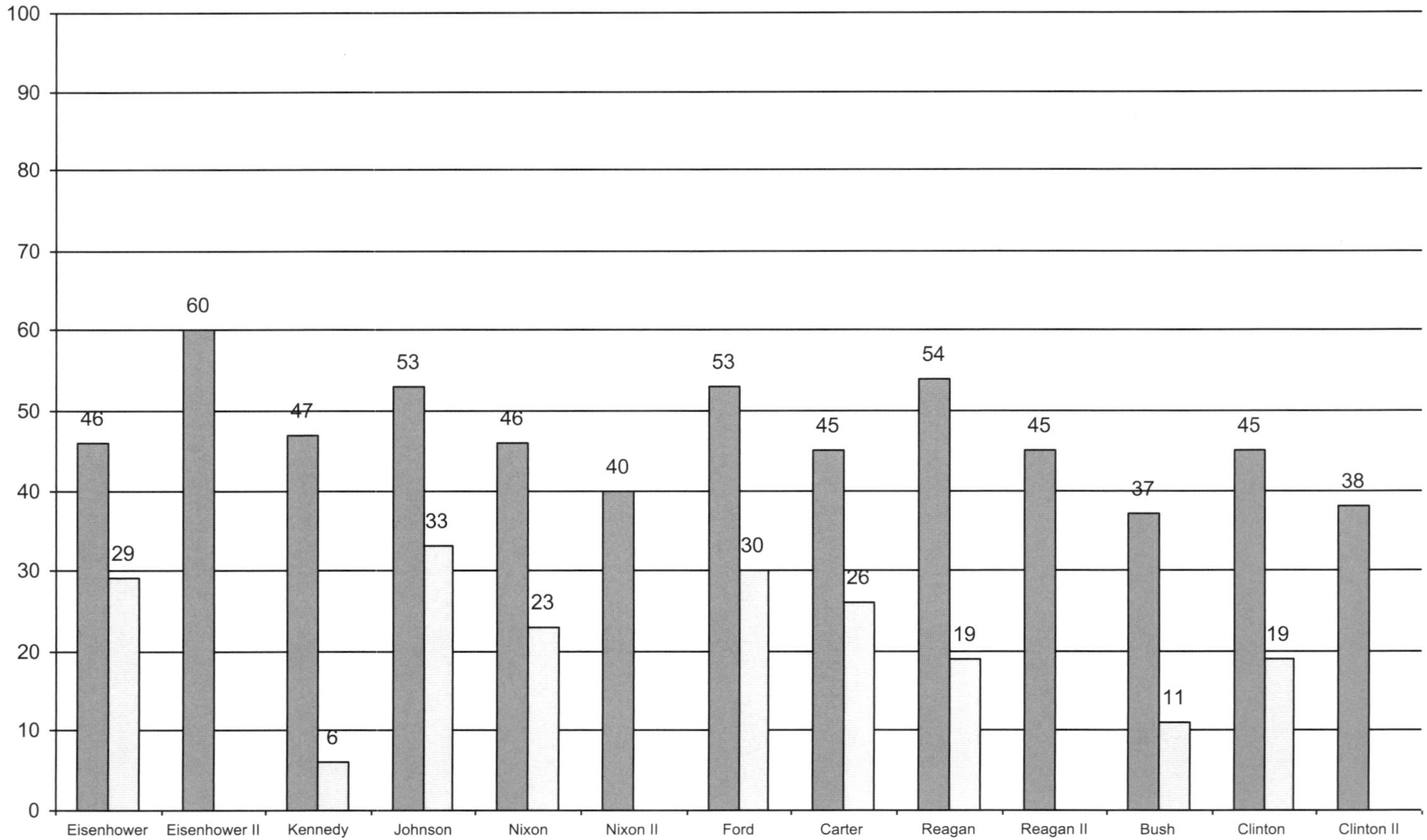

use of polling during the Reagan and Clinton administrations did not significantly improve prospects for successful leadership of opinion as gauged by the bivariate evidence in figure 3.1.[37] Indeed, dividing the data by early (Eisenhower to Ford) and late (Carter to Clinton) administrations reveals that presidents who served earlier were not able to lead public opinion more successfully than later-serving presidents. As a group, presidents in both time periods led public opinion in similar segments. Grouped together, Presidents Eisenhower to Ford led public opinion 49% of the time while Presidents Carter to Clinton led public opinion 45% of the time.[38] Considering significant opinion change, early presidents led in this category 28% of the time while later presidents lead 25% of the time.[39]

What explains this counterintuitive finding? First, presidents who served earlier did not face the contentious and crowded political environment that later presidents faced. The rise of interest groups, the growth of the size of government, and the growing role of congressional power created more actors on the government stage and contributed to the president's voice being often crowded out.[40] This explanation is consistent with the theory of conditional presidential leadership presented in chapter 2. Second, once the complementary tools of public opinion polling, advanced public relations, and continuous communication became routine and acceptable in the White House (beginning with Franklin Roosevelt and expanding during the Kennedy, Johnson, and Nixon administrations), the ability of presidents to gauge public opinion (if not necessarily lead) seems to have equalized.[41]

Ironically, for all cases of opinion movement, President Eisenhower was the most effective at leading public opinion in his second administration (60%) but was average at leading public opinion in his first administration (46%). Contrary to the conventional wisdom of "dynamic" presidents leading public opinion most frequently, the relatively staid (but forthright) President Eisenhower was the most successful leader of public opinion. Others have reached similar conclusions regarding Eisen-

Fig. 3.1. (opposite). Presidential leadership of public opinion, 1953–2001. The number on the top of the bar is the percentage of successful movement of public opinion obtained by dividing the total number of instances of opinion movement by those that were positive. The bar on the left represents all leadership success while the bar on the right represents significant leadership attempts (opinion movement greater than 5%). Data compiled by the author.

hower's leadership. William Cunion also finds that President Eisenhower was successful at leading public opinion, and my assertions here mirror his results in that Eisenhower was even more successful in his second term. These findings also underscore that the political environment and individual presidential tactics significantly shape leadership success.[42]

For several terms following the Johnson administration, the percentage of time presidents led public opinion was on average lower for the two categories "all opinion change" and "significant change." The declining public trust in government and President Nixon's continuous decline in credibility associated with the protracted media coverage of Watergate is primarily to blame. Indeed, low levels of trust in government have been shown to make it more difficult for presidents to lead.[43] No amount of spin could prepare the administration for the fallout of public preferences on wage and price controls (see case study in chapter 5), the backlash over Vietnam (see case study in chapter 8), and the loss of public credibility over Watergate. Indeed, President Nixon's second term, from January 1973 until April 1974, was bogged down with trying to convince the public (to no avail) about the necessity for escalation in Vietnam, the reinstitution of wage and price controls, and the unimportance of Watergate. The administration was fighting too many political battles on too many fronts, and messages from challengers were drowning out the White House.

Ironically, this historic decline in leadership comes at a time when the White House was as well prepared as any in American history to navigate the treacherous waters of the modern media. Before the sudden decline began, President Nixon's White House well understood that the power over information and the ability of the White House to control the public presentation of the presidency was critical to maintaining support. The creation of the White House Office of Communications and related public relations strategies during this time are a direct outgrowth of this realization.[44] The fact that the Nixon White House, possessing some of the most advanced thinking and creative tools to manage their image and manipulate the media, was unable to counteract negative publicity suggests the supreme difficulty that modern presidents face in trying to lead public opinion. The case of the Nixon White House emphasizes the constrained nature of presidential leadership and that presidential *capacity* to lead is not sufficient for modern presidents.

President Clinton's two terms in the White House are a tale of two presidencies. Similar to Ronald Reagan, President Clinton had higher leadership ratings in his first term than in his second. In his first term, Clinton was average at leading public opinion (45%). His initiatives such as "don't ask, don't tell" for homosexual military service personnel, lack of success at reducing unemployment, and declining public support for his health-care plan all damaged his leadership score. But on the positive side, in matters of foreign policy his efforts to remain engaged internationally without committing serious resources or using troops were successful, such as air strikes against Iraq and efforts at brokering peace in the Middle East. In addition, President Clinton's success in handling matters of the deficit and economic prosperity began to pay off for him as more of the public began to agree with his policies on the economy.[45] In fact, these leadership efforts allowed him to gain the upper hand in bargaining with Congress in 1995 and 1996 when he and the Republican-led Congress sparred over balancing the budget (see case study in chapter 5).[46] However, in his second term, his leadership rate dropped considerably (38% for all cases), partly because he did not unveil any new major policy initiatives and partly because of the crowding out of his policy messages by the Lewinsky scandal.

What about second-term presidents? Interestingly, at the aggregate level there appears to be little difference between first- and second-term presidents. The data show that first-term presidents successfully led public opinion 45% of the time while second-term presidents successfully led public opinion 47% of the time.[47] Similarly, examining only significant opinion change, the differences are slight and insignificant as well: 22% in first terms and 20% in second terms.[48] The differences between each set of variables are not statistically significant, underscoring the muted differences between presidential terms.[49] Still, some individual presidents do better in second terms (Eisenhower) than others (Reagan, Clinton). Again, it appears that the political environment and the tactics used by these presidents is as important in explaining presidential leadership as institutional settings. This reinforces the general point made in chapters 1 and 2 that presidents are not always disadvantaged in persuading the public simply by virtue of their institutional or political circumstances.

Presidential Skill?

Much of the discussion of presidential leadership hinges on the activities of "skilled" presidents. In Richard Neustadt's interpretation of presidential "skill," presidents must be aware of their political surroundings, educated as to alternatives, able to gather and process information, solicitous of expert advice, and ultimately, able to tactfully use these resources to persuade and induce Congress and the public to believe that the president's way is the "right" way. Indeed, Neustadt argued that "the essence of a President's persuasive task, with congressmen and everybody else, is to induce them to believe that what he wants of them is what their own appraisal of their own responsibilities requires them to do in their interest, not his."[50] To be successful, presidents cannot simply rely on their official power to command, they must expand these sources of authority to include elements of personal persuasion to actors inside government.

However, in the modern era of presidential governance, the ability to bargain internally within the executive branch or externally with the legislative branch is as important as bargaining for (in Neustadt's phrase) "prestige." Kernell argues that presidents are not merely leaders within government but also conduits between the government and the public.[51] As a result, presidents must use their persuasive skills to create a more favorable environment to accomplish their goals. Kathleen Jamieson suggests that certain presidents, prominently Ronald Reagan, were more skilled public rhetoricians than others, based upon their use of stories and catchy phrasings to manipulate public preferences.[52] Other observers point to Bill Clinton as another "natural" politician with inherent persuasive talents.[53] However, challenging these assumptions, Edwards suggests "charisma" is a post hoc attribution and finds no systematic evidence that it assists presidential effectiveness.[54]

Fortunately, the data in this book can address the question, "How important is presidential 'skill'?" In particular, the three presidents who are most often thought of as skilled at communicating with the public and possessing a commanding personal image are John Kennedy, Ronald Reagan, and Bill Clinton. Each deserves attention in this context. From an early point, President Kennedy recognized that "public communication—educating, persuading and mobilizing that opinion" was critical to his presidency.[55] The charm of "Camelot" was not lost on most reporters as the Kennedy administration cultivated its relationship with the press far more energetically than its predecessors.[56] President Kennedy enjoyed relatively high approval ratings during his tenure in office related to the image his presidency cultivated in the American public and resulting from several international events that galvanized the public behind the president.

In addition, President Reagan and his advisers similarly sought to promote a patriotic and straightforward presidential image.[57] President Reagan's reputation as the "Great Communicator" emerged from his ability to distill issues down into digestible bites for the American public.[58] Sloan argued that President Reagan's stage presence and experience as an actor enabled him to offer simple and direct arguments.[59] Other observers have pointed to President Reagan's "personal magic" in describing his ability to connect with the public.[60] President Reagan also enjoyed relatively high popularity (primarily in the first term), yet these ratings would tumble in his second term at the onset and gradual exposure of the Iran-Contra scandal.

The same is true for President Bill Clinton, whom many consider to be an eloquent and effective communicator. Contemporary observers have argued that Clinton's presidency was significantly shaped by public opinion polling, almost to the point of "corruption" of the office with "quantitative thinking."[61] The president's avid consumption of polls and the inclusion of public opinion polling into most decisions in the White House gave rise to criticism that Clinton governed exclusively by polls.[62] The White House's spending on polling was upwards of $2 million in his first three years in office and it averaged $1.5 million each year.[63] Clinton's ability to read an audience and effectively phrase an argument using his natural instinctual empathy as well as opinion polling data established his reputation as a skilled leader.

However, these presidents' reputations as skilled communicators with the public seem to be largely unwarranted. Rather, each of these "skilled" leaders exhibit similar patterns of leadership of public opinion. Specifically, the data reveal that neither Kennedy nor Reagan was overwhelmingly successful at leading public opinion, at least not enough to justify their laudatory reputations (although President Reagan fares better on both scores than does President Kennedy). Specifically, Kennedy was successful 47% of the time for all cases and 6% for significant change, while Reagan was successful 54% of the time in his first term and 45% of the time in his second term for all cases and 19% for significant change. President Kennedy was unable to convince the public that he was successful on controlling the proliferation of nuclear weapons, on implementing Medicare (see case study in chapter 6), and on reforming tax policy. President Reagan was unable to convince the public to endorse the presence of troops in Beirut and to support anti-Communist forces in Central America (see case study in chapter 8). Similarly, in President Clinton's first term, he was successful at moving opinion in 45% of the cases, but in his second term, this statistic fell to 38%, as discussed above. He was modestly effective (but still below average) at leading significant opinion change (19% successful), comporting with similarly low numbers for his later-serving colleagues.

Although contemporary accounts praised the "skill" of these presidents, the historical legacy of Kennedy, Reagan, and Clinton is overstated if one considers only their ability to motivate the public. Of course, these findings do mask other manifestations of presidential skill, such as improving the vibrancy of the image of the president, engendering courage in the American public, or assuaging the public in times of crisis. But on the core effect—their leadership of the public's policy preferences—none of these presidents fared remarkably better than their predecessors or successors, whose record was also modest. It is a combination of presidential strategies and the political environment that matters most in explaining leadership of public opinion, not necessarily the eloquence of the president or the quality of delivery.

Conclusion

This chapter began the empirical investigation into the success (or lack of success) presidents find when leading public opinion. The most important finding here is that presidents as a whole are not especially good leaders of public opinion in the long term. Indeed, presidents move public opinion in the direction of their preferred policy position as frequently as opinion moves *away* from them. This finding comports with what scholars have typically discovered when investigating the success presidents have in their attempts to lead public opinion.[64] Their leadership tends to affect public opinion in small increments, perhaps enough to encourage temporary approval of their policy position but not necessarily igniting a broad-scale change of the public's policy preferences. And although some presidents did comparatively better than their colleagues at leading public opinion, few presidents did better than average in leading public opinion.

The lack of leadership of public opinion is not absolute, however. Amending the prominent "non-findings" literature, there are moments when presidents do lead public opinion effectively. As I argue in this book, presidential public opinion leadership is provisional. The conditional nature of public leadership manifests itself in several ways. There is a fair amount of variation by president and time period, suggesting that the political environment has much to do with the conditions factoring into successful leadership. Moreover, individual speeches appear to move public opinion modestly in the president's direction but can just as easily move against the president's position. A president's best strategy, it seems, is to attempt to lead the public when political conditions are favorable, so that his message can get through. Certain kinds of issues, certain moments in time, and certain political conditions likely all have some effect in mitigating the reception of the president's message. Therefore, presidents must be strategic about how and when they attempt to lead public opinion.[65] This point underscores the argument made in chapter 2 that presidents must navigate through a complex political environment to successfully lead public opinion.

Of course, it is highly likely that these conditions are all interrelated. In the following chapters I disentangle how each of these political, temporal, economic, and social circumstances interacts with one another in a complicated environment to facilitate or restrict presidential leadership of public opinion.

CHAPTER 4

Successful Presidential Leadership of Public Opinion

Presidents have not been shy about using the bully pulpit to carry their messages to the American public, believing it to be important to their policy success while in office and to their political legacy after they leave office.[1] It is surprising to learn, however, that despite lofty expectations and requisite tools, presidents are generally unsuccessful at leading opinion as a way to advance their policy agenda.[2] Scholars argue that presidents fail at moving public preferences for a number of reasons, typically in combination with each other, such as shrinking audiences, media message screeners, political partisanship, and a lack of public cognition.[3] In the previous chapter we saw that leadership of public opinion is difficult to manage, a finding that is consistent with recent scholarship.[4] Many of these reasons for failure are beyond the control of the White House.

This chapter takes aim at the specific time periods, political conditions, communication tactics, and levels of public information that enhance or detract from the president's ability to lead public opinion. The explanation takes as a starting point that presidential persuasion is difficult, yet, consistent with the theory outlined in chapter 2, the more the president can get his message out to the public and the more clearly that message is received, the more effective presidents can be in leading public opinion. In the analysis that follows, I utilize the data outlined in the previous chapter in several multivariate statistical models. The results provide perspective on the degree to which each conditional expectation outlined in chapter 2 enhances or detracts from presidential leadership efforts.

Model Specification

To analyze which factors enhance or detract from the president's ability to lead public opinion, I used several multivariate ordinary least squares

(OLS) models. These models allow us to determine the probable effect of the independent variables on the continuous dependent variable (that is, the amount of opinion change from pre-statement to post-statement).[5] In essence, the OLS model allows for an interpretation of the percentage of opinion movement (the dependent variable) resulting from a 1% change in the independent variable (the conditions in the far left column).[6] The assumption here is that the president is speaking on almost every issue of the day. The baseline (constant) in the model is a presidential speech with no special conditions (e.g., speeches that do not have the characteristics of any of the independent variables being measured), so that the control is the source of the information and the nature of the speech rather than whether or not the president made a speech on that issue. In effect, the question to be addressed is, when the president speaks on an issue, which conditions enhance his ability to lead public opinion?

The models also explore variants on specific time periods, specific political circumstances, and specific issues by isolating the cases used for analysis that will help provide additional perspective. To enhance causal certainty, the models are split between a one-month and a three-month post-poll window (limiting the cases to those time periods after the president's statement) so that we can examine changes in opinion as close in time to the president's statement as possible. The sample of presidents is periodically divided by early and late presidents to capture any changes in modern political communications tactics or the emergence of an aggressive media beginning in the 1970s.[7] To determine whether presidents take advantage of information asymmetries to lead public opinion, the percentage change in "don't know" responses to survey questions is also included in the models, both by itself and in combination with each of the communications strategies outlined in chapter 2.[8] Overall, each of the models below explains a relatively high percentage of the variance (adjusted for the number of variables).[9] Tests for multicollinearity (high correlations between the variables) reveal no significant problems.[10] In addition, several measures have been taken to control for the fact that presidents may discuss particular issues at particular times (for example, speeches on popular issues or ones made during an election year)—a detailed discussion of the treatment of such endogeneity issues is included in appendix C. In appendix C, I also discuss supplemental and alternative model specifications.[11]

When Presidents Lead Public Opinion

The conditions outlined in chapter 2 have been segmented in each table below by category for ease of reference. To begin, the "two days before" variable in table 4.1 captures whether or not the president made the same argument to the public in each of the two days prior to the date of the president's selected statement. This coefficient suggests that presidents are more likely to lead public opinion when actively pushing their agenda in public (about 5% in column 1 of table 4.1). It implies, as suggested in the theory of opinion leadership in chapter 2, that presidents who continually press an issue in public and who use the "bully pulpit" to buttress their larger political agenda can find success at leading public opinion. It confirms Edwards's arguments that presidents must repeat their messages to the public "so that they will break through the public's disinterest in politics and the countless distractions from it."[12] However, these trends are temporary, as the significance of the coefficient dissipates after the one-month window. Similarly, presidents who reference arguments from their past State of the Union messages are more likely to lead public opinion, especially the later presidents (column 2) and all presidents at the three-month window (columns 3 and 4). Again, presidential efforts to heavily publicize a core issue pay leadership dividends, as I argued in chapter 2. This finding is also confirmed in other selection models in appendix C.

Interestingly, the information theory outlined in chapter 2 is not fully confirmed in table 4.1, which shows that a decrease in the percentage of the public registering "don't know" to a policy question *assists* presidential leadership. According to Conditional Expectation 2, the opposite was expected.[13] This anomaly suggests that the more the public learns about a topic or the more certain they become about an issue, the more easily (but modestly) the president is able to lead them. In effect, this phenomenon is the golden apple of presidential communications. Presidents are teaching and leading—the public hears and understands the president's policy message and alters their opinion on that policy accordingly. However, when interacted with the specific strategies, the coefficients, in contrast to stand-alone coefficients of each strategy, are smaller or do not retain significance, suggesting that more public certainty on an issue may minimize the president's ability to persuade with these specific tactics.

The single communications tactic involving television ("major address") demonstrates success in leading public opinion. In table 4.1, column 1 (one month), all presidents taken together find success at leading public opinion with a "major address" tactic (where presidents deliver televised addresses from Washington, D.C.), comporting with Conditional Expectation 9. The effect is an impressive 8% change in opinion on average. Generally, that the "major address" tactic is significant for all presidents at the one-month window suggests that White House–driven presentations (where the White House has more control over the format and message) are more suitable venues for successful presidential leadership than those events where the president must react to questions or explain a policy through other kinds of individual speeches. But, when interacted with a decrease in the percentage of the public responding "don't know," the effect lowers to about a 1% movement of opinion. It is therefore possible, but more difficult, for presidents to persuade *and* educate the public in a single national address.

An example of this effect helps illustrate how it can be effective for presidential leadership. By the time Jimmy Carter was elected president, the energy crisis was at its apex. President Carter argued that the need to conserve energy was the "moral equivalent of war."[14] One of President Carter's major programs was the creation of a national energy policy—a proposal that initially received only modest support in Congress. Early in his administration, President Carter pressed the issue, but other concerns, specifically the economy, began to crowd out energy policy discussions, a limiting factor in the explanation of successful leadership. Subsequently, Rick Hutcheson (special assistant to the president) summarized his concerns to the president on June 10, 1977, by arguing, "Communication with the public on energy has now stalled badly; the momentum of public support needs to be built up again; your speeches caught the public's attention and started a dialogue, but the communication process now seems arrested in mid air."[15] He continued, suggesting that the president "make monthly progress reports to the Nation, responding to questions which have been raised, entering into a true dialogue with the public."[16] Heeding this advice, President Carter took to the airwaves several more times on this issue. The tactic worked: those supporting the president's energy plans rose from 21% to 33% in October of 1977 to 37% in early November of 1977.[17]

Yet, the coefficient for the major address strategy is less strong for later presidents (Carter to Clinton) in both the one-month and three-month windows (columns 2 and 4) or in the one-month window when interacted with a decrease in "don't know" (also columns 2 and 4). In examining

TABLE 4.1
Opinion Movement at One and Three Months

	One Month		Three Months	
Variable *q*	Eisenhower to Clinton	Carter to Clinton	Eisenhower to Clinton	Carter to Clinton
Political Conditions				
Divided government	.116	–.742	–1.19	–2.97
	(2.58)	(.307)	(2.85)	(3.66)
Honeymoon	–4.63	–13.1**	–3.17	–19.2***
	(4.39)	(6.40)	(4.56)	(6.49)
Second term	3.07	–.121	1.49	–2.37
	(3.19)	(3.32)	(3.33)	(3.59)
Presidential approval	–.053	–.021	.041	.091
	(.123)	(.154)	(.131)	(.176)
"Rally"	–2.92	–5.81**	1.60	–1.38
	(2.63)	(2.63)	(2.76)	(2.90)
Presidential election	–5.52*	–7.77**	–1.26	–3.20
	(2.95)	(3.45)	(3.24)	(3.70)
Carter–Clinton	3.73	—	1.02	—
	(3.58)		(3.71)	
Public information				
Issue salience	.098	–.144	–.035	–.335*
	(.119)	(.164)	(.124)	(.189)
Decrease in "don't know"	.726***	.802***	.617***	.755***
	(.145)	(.132)	(.168)	(.160)
Communications tactics				
Two days before	5.18*	4.02	1.08	–1.29
	(3.12)	(3.21)	(3.22)	(3.16)
"Barnstorm"	3.73	–1.60	5.39*	–.249
	(2.99)	(3.24)	(3.31)	(3.66)
Major address	8.13**	5.22	4.48	4.64
	(3.49)	(4.14)	(4.03)	(5.05)

TABLE 4.1
Continued

	One Month		Three Months	
Variable *q*	Eisenhower to Clinton	Carter to Clinton	Eisenhower to Clinton	Carter to Clinton
Press conference	−2.03	−.201	−2.59	.520
	(2.16)	(2.41)	(2.41)	(2.78)
Going international	9.63	9.96	14.6	15.7
	(10.2)	(9.35)	(12.0)	(11.0)
Communications tactics (interacted with decrease in "don't know")				
"Barnstorm"	−.446	−.463	−.723	−.891
	(.416)	(.408)	(.491)	(.486)
Major address	.919	2.12*	1.13	1.88
	(.721)	(1.17)	(.853)	(1.41)
Press conference	−.018	−.142	.624	.597
	(.450)	(.475)	(.498)	(.549)
Control variables				
Popular before statement	−.039	−.016	.002	.073
	(.072)	(.075)	(.072)	(.078)
State of the Union promise	1.87	4.90*	4.95*	8.22***
	(2.57)	(2.72)	(2.75)	(3.08)
Constant	−4.09	3.96	−9.13	−8.90
	(10.8)	(8.71)	(12.2)	(9.81)
N	82	61	101	72
Probability > F	.000	.000	.003	.000
Adjusted R^2	.386	.480	.209	.377

Note: Dependent variable: continuous variable indicating movement of public opinion from before presidential statement to after (post-statement poll minus pre-statement poll). One- and three-month columns capture the outer time boundary of survey dates for those data. Standard errors in parentheses. Dashes denote variables removed because the data overlapped. Statistical significance: $^{***}p < .01$; $^{**}p < .05$; $^{*}p < .10$.

the interaction with a decrease in "don't know" for later presidents (column 2), these results imply that these presidents, when they can educate the public, have the potential to lead public opinion with a televised address. But the effect is smaller here than for all presidents without the interaction (column 1), with a 2% change in public opinion, which is well within the margin of error. Therefore, later-serving presidents *are* able to lead with major addresses if the public's knowledge increases, although less so than all presidents grouped together with no interacted conditions. When the public has firmer opinions on a policy, later presidents *can* lead public opinion, but it is more challenging because later presidents face a more crowded message environment.

However, although a televised address generally enhances leadership in formal settings like speeches from the Oval Office or the State of the Union, press conferences do not, despite the existence of a national stage and wide public exposure (as expected by Conditional Expectation 10). Indeed, the coefficients capturing statements in press conferences are generally negative and never statistically significant, as predicted.[18] The national stage (and concurrent exposure to the public) magnifies the aggressive questions from the national press corps and makes the president's message more difficult to categorically explain.[19] As counterweights to the president's clear and focused messages emerge, it becomes more difficult for the president to maintain cohesion in his messages and easier for opponents to follow the lead of the press in finding fault with the president's policies. Acknowledging this difficulty with communicating through the media as a conduit, recent presidents are less likely to schedule press conferences as a primary means to communicate with the public. Indeed, press conferences held in prime time have also become rarer with the advent of television and for recent presidents.[20]

These results amend previous findings indicating that television does not necessarily buttress leadership. Several authors claim that the rise of television (and the rise in the diversity of viewers) challenges presidential ability to lead public opinion.[21] In fact, television can help presidents to lead public opinion, but the White House must more tightly control the setting and presentation of these events and understand the nature of public opinion for these to have a positive effect. Although the timing and setting of press conferences are controlled by the White House, the content can drift away from the president's preferred issue, especially in times of conflict or scandal.[22] In televised addresses, on the other hand, the White House has the potential to dictate the timing, setting, and content, facilitating a greater chance that the president's message will be transmitted in full either directly or indirectly through a media "echo" effect for subsequent days after these addresses.[23]

Surprisingly, the "barnstorm" tactic is ineffective in the short term (at the one-month window in column 1) yet is positive and significant for all presidents at the three-month window (column 3), where a presidential barnstorm can create about a 5% movement of opinion.[24] Why is the barnstorm tactic not more quickly successful when Conditional Expectation 8 predicted it would be? In mobilizing the whole of the public with an event-by-event strategy (visiting several cities or states consecutively), the effect of moving national public opinion is glacial. Further, the feedback loop inherent in this "going public" strategy may take time to mature. It takes longer to build support for an issue on a visit-by-visit basis to cities and states compared to a more broad nationally televised message (the "echo" of which will be disseminated nationwide). If the president is successful in altering public preferences while visiting a state (which is not measured here at the state level) then it will take time for that opinion to manifest itself into national public opinion polls. Likewise, when the barnstorm coefficient is interacted with a decrease in "don't know," the coefficient loses significance. Educating and leading the public with this tactic is clearly more difficult than with a national address. The president must assuage local concerns and may find that pockets of the public in places he is visiting are less receptive to his message. President George W. Bush found this out when attempting to stimulate support for his Social Security reforms (see the preface and epilogue).

Similarly, in none of the four models in table 4.1 does the "going international" strategy have any effect in leading public opinion, demonstrating no support for Conditional Expectation 11. Several factors may limit the president's ability to reach his domestic audience with international speeches. First, the content of the president's speech may not trickle down to the domestic media. Second, even if the effect does trickle down, the White House is still faced with a reluctant public and narrowing communication avenues at home, making it difficult to get their messages through to the public. Third, findings of success may very likely be conditioned by positive media coverage of the president's trip, consistent with the argument in chapter 2.[25] Findings from Brace and Hinckley also agree with these findings in that they discover foreign travel makes no overall difference in presidential approval ratings.[26] Yet, despite the non-effect found here, Brace and Hinckley advocate trips abroad as "low risk" propositions where there is "no imminent thread of a decline in public standing," as they find that such travel is most effective when combined with other approval enhancing effects.[27]

In Conditional Expectation 5, it is argued that presidents would have an easier time leading public opinion on foreign policy than domestic policy, especially in moments where the public "rallied" around the president in national or international crises (see chapter 2 for definition and details). Yet the results from table 4.1 (all four models) reveal that this assumption on "rally" moments is not accurate—in fact, the effect is consistently negative.[28] There may be several causes for this. First, rally effects may be contingent on the makeup of the public. Specifically, scholars have found that the effect of events in which force is used may be more pronounced for self-identified presidential partisans.[29] Thus, the overall effect of a rally event may also be very small at the national level.[30] Second, media stories are significantly linked to rally effects, in that the public must be aware of the events associated with the rally. When all rally events are included (specifically, the lesser known events included in the present data), then the public may not know enough to change their policy preferences.[31] Also, Baum and Groeling find that more recent rally effects are significantly hampered by negative news stories, a condition limiting the rally and explaining the negative findings here.[32] Third, simply put, any sustained effect from military events may be only related to the *popularity* of the president, as scholars found in the case of President Bush and the events of 9/11, rather than substantive policy change.[33]

The coefficient for presidential election year is also negative and significant in the two one-month models in table 4.1 (columns 1 and 2) with opinion moving away from the president's position on average from 6% to 8%, contradicting Conditional Expectation 4. Why do election years limit leadership success? First, elections are not fought alone, and presidents have an opponent against which they must compete for space in the public spotlight. This election-year finding challenges the assumption in chapter 2 that elections would provide for a larger spotlight to the president. Over time, as elections grow more competitive, as partisanship becomes more intense, and as the election "year" begins earlier, the White House's clear message is muted by a flock of opponents who challenge this message. The president's ability to more directly communicate his message to the public is key to his ability to move public preferences; therefore, when the president confronts significant opposition, his ability to lead public opinion is concurrently diminished.

Similar to the noneffect of elections in helping presidents lead public opinion, presidential popularity *by itself* is not a condition that favors presidents in moving public preferences on a policy, contrary to what was predicted in Conditional Expectation 5. In none of the models in table 4.1 is the coefficient for the Gallup-measured approval significant, possibly because many scholars find that presidential popularity has little direct independent effect on presidential success in policy making. Canes-Wrone finds that public appeals are profitable for popular and unpopular presidents alike, mooting the observed differences between the two.[34] Popularity *can* be effective in moving public opinion, but it has been found to be minimally effective or effective only in combination with other factors, such as repeated appeals, supermajority presidential approval, and positive media coverage.[35] Some of these interconnected findings are confirmed below.

As a subset of instances of presumed presidential popularity (also argued in Conditional Expectation 5), the results reveal that a president's "honeymoon" is not necessarily a happy one, as the coefficient is negative for all presidents and negative and significant for later-serving presidents (columns 2 and 4).[36] Although it was presumed in chapter 2 that presidents could more easily lead during honeymoons because the criticism of the president would be lower, recent history indicates that presidents' first year in office is too short a time when they are not receiving criticism from the media or opponents. Indeed, the findings here suggest that this affects later presidents more severely. Brody similarly argues the honeymoon effect is lessened for later presidents because of higher expectations and less "friendly" coverage by the media, two factors that would otherwise theoretically advantage presidents in their first year.[37]

In summarizing these results, we find that several of the effects in table 4.1 are time (or era) dependent. If we examine differences between presidents who served earlier (Eisenhower to Ford, columns 1 and 3) with those who served later (Carter to Clinton, columns 2 and 4), several of the effects are conditional based upon *when* the president served. Indeed, when the dependent variable in table 4.1 is censored by era, later presidents are afflicted with several more negative conditions than are earlier presidents. To some degree, this time-dependent effect contradicts the hypothesis in Conditional Expectation 1, which suggested that later-serving presidents would be better equipped to lead public opinion because of better information, more savvy political advisers, and more stored political wisdom. More specifically, there are three important differences between early-serving presidents and later-serving presidents that seemingly advantage earlier presidents. First, as noted, later-serving presidents find significantly less support during their "honeymoon" year in office (columns 2 and 4). Second, table 4.1 reveals that "major addresses" and the "two days before" strategies are less effective for later presidents. Third, the election effect is more damaging to later presidents. It is consistently negative for all presidents in table 4.1, but the effect is *more* negative for later presidents (about 8% less likely; column 2) than for earlier presidents (about 5% less likely; column 1) at the one-month window.

Although there are likely several explanations for these differences, one of the most prominent is the emergence of a more aggressive and combative media that is willing to challenge the authority and veracity of the president's message. Each of these effects are predicated to some degree on the nature of the media coverage. Earlier-serving presidents had more cordial relations with the news media and could rely on the media to cooperate with their need to distribute political information with less probing.[38] But later-serving presidents (especially since the Watergate scandal) face a more hostile and challenging media that is less willing to provide a "free pass" to the president to use the media as a vehicle for the dissemination of his political messages.[39] The march of modern politics to greater polarization and alienation (or outright hostility) between the White House and the media has limited the president's rhetorical reach.[40]

To illustrate this phenomenon, table 4.2 presents an association between the ability of early and late presidents to lead public opinion when considering the tone of coverage from the day before the president's speech. Specifically, the data were coded from the abstracts of the *ABC Nightly News* (which was selected at random among the three major networks), housed in the Vanderbilt Television News Archive, on a scale of negative, neutral, or positive.[41] The results suggest that for early presidents the association between coverage content and presidential leadership success was not significantly different from chance (because the measures of association do not rise to statistical significance). But for later presidents, measures of association are statistically significant, such that, when the tone of coverage is negative, presidents lead public opinion 15% of the time but when the tone of coverage is positive, presidents lead public opinion 20% of the time. Most of the cases of leadership for later presidents come when the coverage of the issue is neutral (65%). These results are limited because they only span 1969 to 2001 (the duration of the Vanderbilt database) and the number of cases is small (too small to include in the regression models). Yet these findings provide a flavor for

TABLE 4.2
Media Coverage and Leadership Success

	Media coverage tone		
	Negative	Neutral	Positive
Early presidents			
Unsuccessful leadership	0% (0)	86% (6)	14% (1)
Successful leadership	20% (1)	80% (4)	0% (0)
Late presidents			
Unsuccessful leadership	6% (3)	79% (41)	15% (8)
Successful leadership	15% (7)	65% (30)	20% (9)

Note: Data compiled and coded from the Vanderbilt Television News Archive. Percentages listed are row percentages. *N* in parentheses. The chi square statistic is not significant for either model but the Kendall's tau-b is statistically significant at $p > .10$ for the late presidents cross-tabulation (−0.04).

the changing nature of news coverage and the president's constraints in leading public opinion.

The interactions between key variables are also important to understanding the combined effects of the specific conditions. Table 4.3 includes three alternative models (with the other variables the same as in column 1 of table 4.1) to capture possible trends where two specific conditions occur together: Model 1 includes an interacted condition where the president retains above-average popularity and the issue is of above-average salience; Model 2 includes an interacted condition where the president retains above-average popularity and the issue is popular; Model 3 includes a model where the issue is popular and the issue is of above-average salience.[42] The results suggest that the only interacted specification that is statistically significant is when the president is popular and is talking about a high-salience issue (column 1)—in these circumstances presidents are more likely to lead public opinion by about 10% points on average. The other variables in the model are approximately the same as in table 4.1 (column 1). This interaction combines two potent effects that are individually less powerful. Taken together, on higher-salience issues where the president is popular, the president is better situated because of the dual power of the increased visibility of the issue and the president.

Interestingly, these findings imply that presidents are most able to lead public opinion when they already have a high degree of public support.

TABLE 4.3

Opinion Movement at One Month (Alternate Specifications)

	Model specification		
Variable	1	2	3
Political conditions			
Divided government	−2.74	−3.77	−2.31
	(2.80)	(2.74)	(2.75)
Honeymoon	−7.11	−5.86	−4.60
	(4.73)	(4.20)	(4.63)
Second term	4.47	4.52	4.89
	(3.43)	(3.19)	(3.49)
Presidential approval	−.174	−.339	−.095
	(.213)	(.205)	(.133)
"Rally"	−5.48*	−3.65	−3.40
	(2.69)	(2.48)	(2.67)
Presidential election	−7.38**	−8.39**	−7.87**
	(3.13)	(2.94)	(3.16)
Carter–Clinton	5.08	3.13	2.60
	(3.89)	(3.64)	(3.94)
Above-average salience	−.648	—	.828
	(4.95)		(5.66)
Popular issue	—	−13.1***	−10.9**
		(5.46)	(5.41)
Popular president	.801	4.67***	—
	(4.71)	(4.75)	
Public information			
Issue salience	−.014	.083	.044
	(.179)	(.118)	(.191)
Decrease in "don't know"	.739***	.734***	.735***
	(.130)	(.122)	(.130)
Communications tactics			
Two days before	4.84	7.04*	7.21**
	(3.28)	(3.07)	(3.20)
"Barnstorm"	4.27	3.32	4.30
	(3.06)	(2.90)	(3.02)

TABLE 4.3
Continued

	Model specification		
Variable	1	2	3
Major address	11.1***	9.82***	9.28***
	(3.47)	(3.32)	(3.43)
Press conference	−2.56	−3.06	−3.39
	(2.31)	(2.17)	(2.35)
Going international	11.4	9.27	7.60
	(10.6)	(10.2)	(10.4)
Interacted variables			
Popular president × High salience	10.1**	—	—
	(5.32)		
Popular president × Popular issue	—	4.11	—
		(4.60)	
Popular issue × High salience	—	—	.623
			(5.62)
Control variables			
State of the Union promise	.665	−1.36	−.569
	(2.65)	(2.62)	(2.83)
Popular before statement	−.056	.207	.189
	(.073)	(.134)	(.140)
Constant	4.74	8.26	−2.88
	(13.9)	(12.6)	(11.8)
N	79	82	79
Probability > F	.000	.000	.000
Adjusted R^2	.337	.414	.335

Note: Dependent variable: continuous variable indicating movement of public opinion from before presidential statement to after (post-statement poll minus pre-statement poll). The models are all truncated to the one-month post-statement window. Standard errors in parentheses. Dashes denote variables removed because the data overlapped. Statistical significance: ***$p < .01$; **$p < .05$; *$p < .10$.

Again, underscoring the conditional nature of presidential leadership, presidents are likely to effectively lead public opinion when external conditions favor them, making their dominant strategy to only attempt to lead public opinion when the conditions are right. This supports the theory in Chapter 2 but pokes a hole in Kernell's thinking about the necessity of presidents persistently "going public" to persuade Congress—the data here caution that such a strategy is not likely to not be effective and may risk alienating Congress during times where conditions are not extraordinary. Yet, when the issue and president are popular and the public is persuadable but Congress is reluctant to act, these results suggest that strategic presidents are wise to take their case to the public.

Popular Presidents

Conventional wisdom (and Conditional Hypothesis 5) suggests that being popular helps presidents lead public opinion, whereas the findings in the literature often point in the opposite direction (as found above). To address this debate, table 4.4 identifies only cases where the president retains above-average popularity (greater than 54%), a condition that does not occur with great frequency. This approach is distinct from the one taken in table 4.1 because, instead of using popularity as a single continuous variable, the cases have been truncated to where the president sustains a high level of popularity.[43] The results reveal that being significantly popular makes several conditions helpful in leading public opinion when they were not before, including leadership in the second term (all presidents, column 1) and on higher-salience issues (only significant for later presidents, column 2). First, although second-term presidents are typically less likely to exercise political muscle (and often all but ignored by Congress and the media), being popular provides a political "fountain of youth" for successful leadership during these times. Second, for later-serving presidents, the negative effect of a higher-salience issue is reversed, making more attention to an issue when presidents are popular a positive harbinger for leadership (by a modest amount). This trend mirrors the interaction finding of popularity and salience in table 4.3. Similarly, other effects that significantly disadvantaged presidential ability to lead public opinion are *less* significantly damaging when presidents are popular (compared to table 4.1)—including election years and "rally" moments—in that both are not significantly negative in this specification.

So, although the political environment flatlines presidential persuasive power during these time periods, sustained high popularity can revive them or mitigate otherwise negative impacts. Explaining this, public attention to the president is key in these circumstances. If the public perceives the president as a more important figure in the political system because of his popularity, their desire to understand and be attentive to the president's message may be more pronounced. Similarly, the tone of media coverage may be more favorable for a popular president, giving the White House an enhanced platform from which to communicate their policies more easily and clearly. The president's role as centerpiece of the government is therefore enhanced when they are more popular, making their actions especially relevant and of political consequence in the case of second terms and on more contentious issues.

In considering individual communications strategies, the "barnstorm" leadership strategy (column 1) is the only strategy that finds greater and quicker success during moments of above-average presidential popularity (with about 5% movement of opinion with such efforts). The effect occurs more quickly than demonstrated in table 4.1 (column 3) where the "barnstorm" tactic was effective at the three-month window but not the one-month window. Again, the success of this strategy establishes that a *direct* and *domestic* strategy is best for communicating with the public when presidents are enjoying greater-than-average approval of the public but that this is a much riskier strategy when presidents are less popular. This strategy smartly bypasses the national media in favor of the local media, which may tend to be more sympathetic, deferential, and accommodating to the president than the national media—especially to a popular president.

There are several cases where presidents have exploited these situations, one of which is taking advantage of an election-year post-convention "bounce." For example, in September 2004, after the Republican National Convention nominated him as their party's choice for the presidency, a popular George W. Bush hit the road to stump for support for the policies he articulated in his acceptance speech. He traveled to Wisconsin, Pennsylvania, Iowa and Ohio in the days following the convention. As a core agenda item, the President's stumping across the nation did have the immediate effect of leading public opinion on his handling of the Iraq War. The percentages of the public revealed in table 4.5 moved gradually from 45% to closer to 50% within the month. Of course, this effect is short-lived—as the president's popularity declines and other actors (especially Democratic presidential nominee John Kerry) begin to

TABLE 4.4
Popular Presidents at One Month

Variable	Eisenhower to Clinton	Carter to Clinton
Political conditions		
Divided government	2.79	—
	(6.41)	
Honeymoon	−5.07	−17.2**
	(3.32)	(3.28)
Second term	5.48*	3.00
	(2.78)	(1.79)
Presidential approval	.219	.148
	(.236)	(.138)
"Rally"	3.95	−.524
	(2.80)	(1.95)
Presidential election	1.24	−3.34
	(3.13)	(2.15)
Carter–Clinton	6.52	—
	(3.96)	
Public information		
Issue salience	.136	.118*
	(.141)	(.055)
Decrease in "don't know"	1.65***	.887***
	(.325)	(.244)
Communications tactics		
Two days before	1.78	−1.61
	(2.96)	(1.15)
"Barnstorm"	5.25*	2.46
	(2.77)	(1.52)
Major address	7.37*	—
	(4.13)	

TABLE 4.4
Continued

Variable	Eisenhower to Clinton	Carter to Clinton
Press conference	−3.76*	−2.42*
	(2.18)	(1.01)
Control variables		
State of the Union promise	7.95***	.218
	(2.27)	(1.77)
Popular before statement	−.060	.000
	(.072)	(.033)
Constant	−25.9	−9.50
	(16.0)	(8.66)
N	34	18
Probability > F	.000	.000
Adjusted R^2	.735	.949

Note: Dependent variable: continuous variable indicating movement of public opinion from before presidential statement to after (post-statement poll minus pre-statement poll). Above-average popularity in the sample was popularity above 54%. Going international was dropped from the models. Standard errors in parentheses. Dashes denote variables removed because the data overlapped. Statistical significance: ***$p < .01$; **$p < .05$; *$p < .10$.

TABLE 4.5
Barnstorming for Iraq after the Convention

	9/8‡	9/14†	9/16‡	9/19*	9/22‡	9/26*	10/3‡
Approve	45	47	46	51	45	48	45
Disapprove	48	45	49	48	50	49	51
Don't know	7	8	5	1	5	3	4

Note: The question was "Do you approve or disapprove of the way George W. Bush is handling the situation in Iraq?" ‡CBS News/*New York Times* Poll.*Gallup Organization Poll. †Princeton Survey Research Associates International Poll.

weigh in on the issue, the support for the President's policy began to slip by early October.

Foreign Policy

As discussed in chapter 2 (Conditional Expectation 6), several scholars have outlined why presidents are more easily able to lead public opinion on foreign policy. The inherent and delegated powers possessed by the president give the White House added stature during times where the public is looking for leadership on international issues.[44] The "inherent drama" in situations of foreign policy can often evoke a "presidential hero" who is glorified as the nation's leader.[45] Primarily, the degree of public ignorance of the particulars of foreign policy and the public trust in the president to engage foreign policy decisions assist them in leading public opinion.[46] This has been a prominent explanation for presidential advantage in policy success.[47] Indeed, the public follows the president's lead in part because the president is signaling the importance of the issue and his command of the situation. In short, in situations where the president can be an effective teacher, and that message can be clearly transferred by the White House, the president should be able to lead public opinion on foreign policy.

This also extends to minor foreign policy issues.[48] The public has less knowledge of minor foreign policy issues and therefore, because of an information advantage, the president should be able to lead more effectively.[49] Yet, many studies do not include "routine" foreign policy issues where we might expect to see leadership on foreign policy. Several studies focus excessively on military actions or on budget data related to foreign policy, each of which may over or underestimate presidential effectiveness at persuading the public.[50] Many excluded issues are statements of friendship or trade with economic partners, commitments to or denouncing of international organizations, dispensation of foreign aid or United States' participation in ceremonial matters of state—issues not of particular importance to the public and therefore issues on which the president might retain an information advantage. This is not to imply that these "less important issues" are not discussed. In fact, Peake finds that presidential ability to set the public agenda with less-important foreign policy issues buttresses his ability to lead opinion on foreign policy.[51] And, many seemingly innocuous issues, such as the state of arms sales, the proliferation of weapons or violence across state lines, the interventions of other countries in each others' affairs, statements defending U.S. allies, are all significant enough to encourage the White House to discuss the matters in public.

The analysis in table 4.6 distinguishes cases where the president's statement dealt with (1) all foreign policy issues and (2) only minor foreign policy issues (as defined above).[52] Indeed, Conditional Expectation 6 argued that presidents should generally do better on leading the public on matters of foreign policy by virtue of almost unilateral and all-encompassing powers to design, promote, and execute foreign policy. Comparing the success at leading public opinion found in table 4.1, several findings from table 4.6 suggest that discussing foreign policy issues makes it easier for presidents to lead in certain conditions, specifically the "two days before" and "major address" tactics. This comports with the arguments from chapter 2 that presidents can move public opinion more easily on foreign policy issues.

These communications tactics are important to examine individually. First, the effect of the president "stumping" on an issue for two consecutive days (the "two days before" tactic) did have a significant leadership-enhancing effect for all grouped foreign policy events: approximately 8% opinion movement (column 1), suggesting leadership can work on foreign policy by bringing the issue up more frequently. This result comports with other findings that imply aggressive marketing from the president on matters of foreign policy works to motivate the public on foreign policy.[53] Yet the result did not hold for modern presidents (column 2) or occasions when the president was discussing minor issues (columns 3 and 4), as such minor issues are rarely discussed by the president for multiple days and are not generally in the public eye as much as other foreign policy issues.

Second, the "major addresses" tactic is strong and significant for all presidents and all foreign policy issues (amounting to about a 12% movement of public opinion; column 1), but for modern presidents the effect, at 9% (column 2), is weaker.[54] Nevertheless, there is an effect for later presidents where there was none in table 4.1. These findings generally underscore the relative ease presidents have in leading public opinion on matters of foreign policy. The unique position of the issue (foreign policy) and the president (as commander-in-chief) brings a greater focus on the message and messenger and consequently gives the president a leg up when attempting to lead public opinion. Further, given the national security nature of foreign policy topics, the president's speeches

TABLE 4.6

Opinion Movement on Major and Minor Foreign Policy Issues Within One Month

	All Foreign Policy Issues		Minor Foreign Policy Issues	
Variable	Eisenhower to Clinton	Carter to Clinton	Eisenhower to Clinton	Carter to Clinton
Political Conditions				
Divided government	−2.15	−3.65	−.043	−2.62
	(3.17)	(3.69)	(2.12)	(2.64)
Honeymoon	−7.49*	−14.4*	−.738	−1.88
	(4.84)	(8.27)	(2.36)	(2.63)
Presidential election	−5.69**	−9.49***	.824	.245
	(2.94)	(3.57)	(1.92)	(2.19)
Second term	3.26	−.152	.493	1.70
	(3.78)	(4.28)	(2.04)	(2.25)
Presidential approval	.004	−.013	−.131*	−.091
	(.137)	(.183)	(.079)	(.098)
Public attention issues				
Issue salience	−.025	−.416**	−.138**	−.170***
	(.122)	(.191)	(.057)	(.064)
Decrease in "don't know"	.734***	.725***	.707***	.746***
	(.135)	(.136)	(.111)	(.116)
Foreign policy variables				
Deployment of troops	9.66*	11.9*	—	—
	(5.28)	(5.27)		
Airstrikes	−4.05	−5.15	—	—
	(4.28)	(3.96)		
Congressional authorization	−2.61	−3.60	—	—
	(5.18)	(5.48)		
Specific issues	**Data included in appendix C**			

TABLE 4.6
Continued

Variable	All Foreign Policy Issues: Eisenhower to Clinton	All Foreign Policy Issues: Carter to Clinton	Minor Foreign Policy Issues: Eisenhower to Clinton	Minor Foreign Policy Issues: Carter to Clinton
Communications tactics				
Two days before	7.97***	4.30	1.60	2.07
	(3.14)	(3.39)	(1.85)	(1.95)
"Barnstorm"	2.47	−2.42	.097	−.459
	(3.18)	(3.70)	(1.84)	(1.99)
Major address	12.7***	9.41*	5.17	6.74
	(3.85)	(4.97)	(4.31)	(4.90)
Press conference	−2.22	−1.36	−2.98*	−3.26*
	(2.22)	(2.57)	(1.78)	(1.96)
Going international	2.72	5.92	.774	−.164
	(10.8)	(10.2)	(6.77)	(6.93)
Control variables				
State of the Union	.880	4.47	2.40	2.36
	(2.71)	(2.99)	(2.10)	(2.28)
Popular before statement	−.106**	−.141	−.179***	−.209***
	(.092)	(.110)	(.046)	(.050)
Constant	−4.00	9.85	16.5**	16.2***
	(13.3)	(10.6)	(7.61)	(6.40)
N	82	61	145	127
Probability > F	.000	.000	.000	.000
Adjusted R^2	.359	.459	.328	.367

Note: Dependent variable: continuous variable indicating movement of public opinion from before presidential statement to after (post-statement poll minus pre-statement poll). Standard errors in parentheses. Dashes denote variables removed because the data overlapped. Statistical significance: ***$p < .01$; **$p < .05$. *$p < .10$.

are generally afforded airtime by the networks, as opposed to domestic policy speeches that might be considered discretionary political opportunities and might not be provided airtime. Televised speeches also play on the White House's image as the center of government. Television, as the "official" and symbolic means of presidential communication, also gives presidents an advantage in leading public opinion on foreign policy because, even if the viewing audience is fragmented or disinterested, it provides an image of the president fulfilling his constitutional role. The president's performative role as national leader in times of crisis clearly gives the president an edge when leading public opinion.

For example, President Reagan found success in appealing to the public on foreign policy through televised addresses. Communications director David Gergen, in a review of President Reagan's "Record of Communications" from 1981 to 1983, noted that "over the course of the first three years, Ronald Reagan has been speaking directly to the American people through prime-time television more frequently and more effectively than any previous president." He suggested that "there is also evidence that Ronald Reagan's prime-time speeches have been particularly effective in moving public opinion" and pointed to the "Grenada/Lebanon speech of 1983" as a "conspicuous" example.[55] The effect of this speech on substantive public opinion is argued to have increased support for the president's policies (especially for sending troops to Grenada).[56]

Likewise, considering political information, for both all foreign policy issues (columns 1 and 2) and "minor" foreign policy issues (columns 3 and 4), a decrease in those responding "don't know" heightens presidential ability to lead public opinion. That is, during these moments when the percentage of the public who are certain or informed about a situation or issue decreases, the president is more able to lead public opinion.[57] In effect, the public is being educated or is becoming more certain, and when this occurs, the findings here suggest the public most often sides with the president's position following the president's speech. Even on issues typically under the radar of the media (minor foreign policy issues), when the president talks about them and public knowledge increases, the president can more easily lead the public. This is not surprising since the public treats the president as a credible and informed source on foreign policy issues.

Yet, again underscoring the provisional nature of leadership, several negative effects retain their significance but are not significantly different from the conditions presented in table 4.1. First, again contradicting expectations, during presidential election years, presidents are still less likely to lead public opinion (column 1). The coefficient strength corresponds to about a 5% to 9% *negative* movement of public opinion if the president makes a statement in an election year. The effect does not hold for minor foreign policy issues (columns 3 and 4).[58] Although scholars have suggested that presidential incumbents may use foreign policy events to precipitate greater probability of reelection under particular conditions, elections have a similarly negative effect in all cases together and in all foreign policy cases.[59] Second, presidential honeymoon years are difficult for presidents to lead public opinion on foreign policy, similar to the findings in table 4.1. Both temporal conditions still disadvantage the president's efforts to lead public opinion, even on issues where the president is theorized to have an advantage.

Likewise, as expected in chapter 2 (Conditional Expectation 3), when the issue grows in importance, the president is less able to lead public opinion. The coefficient for issue salience is significant and negative across each model (with the exception of the full model in column 1), although the overall effect is small. Again it seems clear that when the issue grows in importance, the president is no longer the central (or only) political actor and the president's voice can be crowded out. The information advantage described at the beginning of this section implies that presidents should lead on lower-salience issues because the public is presumed to care less about these issues, but when the issue grows more in salience, the public will care more about the issue, causing the president's information asymmetry to diminish. These trends clearly affect later presidents more acutely since the coefficient is larger for them than for all presidents (column 2). These trends also hold for minor issues considering the significant negative coefficients for minor issues (columns 3 and 4).

The results in table 4.6 also reveal mixed success for the measure of presidential use of force, which are included as control variables.[60] Only the deployment of troops (columns 1 and 2) is a significant enhancer of presidential leadership of public opinion for all foreign policy issues.[61] Airstrikes and congressional authorization of force are consistently negatively related to leadership success but never statistically significant in any of the model categories for grouped presidents (columns 1 and 2). Explaining this, scholars have found that rally effects diminish when presidents use force and that support for conflict declines when cumulative actions escalate a conflict without solving it.[62] There is evidence of this in the case studies concerning the conflict in Vietnam during the Nixon administration and in the conflict in Somalia during the Clinton administration (both described in chapter 8). Overall, these findings suggest that other issues, especially public attention and presidential communication issues, are more important to explaining presidential leadership success than specific events.

It is also ironic that the "going international" tactic does not have a significant effect on leading public opinion on foreign policy, since, under Conditional Expectation 11, presidents' acting in the role of the leader of the United States purportedly provides an advantage in moving public opinion. In none of the models in table 4.6 does the president giving a speech on a foreign policy issue abroad play positively to his domestic audience. Given the ceremonial roles of the president in leading the nation, it was expected that leading public opinion while abroad would be a successful strategy. Yet the public views presidential speeches from abroad in much the same way other speeches—these speeches are subject to the same problems of issue salience and partisan attentiveness under which all speeches fall. For instance, David Gergen in the Reagan White House argued that the president's speeches "even in foreign policy" have been some of his greatest successes. Gergen suggests the speech from Europe be televised: "While [President Reagan] will be speaking primarily to a European audience, this would be an excellent opportunity to speak to the U.S., too. One obvious need at that point is to defuse as much of the anti-nuclear movement as possible (in addition to the European protesters), it appears there may be a large demonstration in the U.S. on June 12, just after RR returns."[63] A political dispute surrounding an issue generates a lack of successful leadership in the same way that these kinds of disputes do when the president is at home. Critical voices have a way of limiting the president's message wherever he is.

Conclusion

Revising previous interpretations of consistent presidential leadership failure, the results from this chapter demonstrate that presidents can succeed at leading public opinion. Of course, emphasizing the theme of this book, there are specific conditions governing that success, making the bully pulpit provisional. These findings provide a more global perspective on the conditional likelihood of presidential success in moving public opinion. And, furthering the theoretical analysis offered in chapter 2, presidents are constrained in their leadership success by the cacophonous political environment that can, at times, outshout the president's generally loud voice. The conditional hypotheses offered in chapter 2 and tested in this chapter frame the context of president as messenger and help to clarify the expectations about when presidents find success in moving public opinion.

Indeed, as the data suggest, there are several factors that work with the president to assist him in leading public opinion, amending recent scholarship describing the difficulties presidents have in leading public opinion. In particular, the most significant enhancer of presidential leadership of public opinion is when presidents actively try to lead public opinion. Consistent with the broad argument of this book, presidents must press their messages constantly to ensure that they get through. These successful leadership findings are most prominent for all issues when presidents talk about the issue for consecutive days and provide a consistent message and theme for the public and media. Speeches from the Oval Office are also effective for all presidents when examining all issues and are more pronounced for both early- and later-serving presidents on foreign policy issues. The barnstorm tactic is effective in the medium term (three months) if the president is not highly popular but works immediately if the president is highly popular. Similar positive effects are present for sustained presidential popularity, especially in the second term and when interacted with higher-salience issues.

Although many of the conditions found are positive, several negative conditions also produce moments where presidents are not likely or less likely to lead public opinion, consistent with the theory of countervailing elements and agents. First, the "going international" and press conference communication strategies do not enhance a president's ability to move public preferences, especially on foreign policy issues where the effect is more negative. Second, presidential election years and honeymoons, thought to be moments when presidents would have the ear of the public, turn out to be times when the president is not the only voice. This competition limits the ability of the president to get his message through to the public. Third, "rally" moments are negative predictors of political leadership success because the media are growing more critical during these periods over time, and the public's views are consequently more difficult to change. Finally, the greater the saliences of an issue, especially on foreign policy, the less likely presidents are to lead on that issue. The sum of these results implies that presidents can move public opinion, although modern political communications circumstances and countervailing forces often prevent the message from getting through.[64]

Interestingly, later-serving presidents possess several disadvantages over their earlier-serving colleagues. The analysis suggests that Presidents Carter to Clinton were less able to lead the public than earlier presidents with several tactics and in several political conditions. Attempts by later-serving presidents to persuade the public through national addresses and the media find limited success compared to earlier presidents, a finding that affirms presidents' recent alternative strategies to "go local" in persuading the public and to host fewer press conferences.[65] Similar findings were discovered for presidential honeymoon years, election years, and in second terms. Indeed, the emergence of a more aggressive media, the proliferation of interest groups, and rising partisanship each partially explain why messages from modern presidents are less likely to get through to the public than those of earlier presidents.

All told, it is clear that events or political institutions do not alone drive presidential leadership of the public's policy preferences; rather, it appears that the role of the public (especially their certainty or knowledge), the importance of the issue to the public, and the president's communications tactics are as important as political circumstances or the control of political institutions. Ultimately, presidential success is conditional on several factors, but some of these factors are within the control of the White House, including the communications tactics used and the timing of the speech in the political cycle.[66] Indeed, Neustadt, in discussing prospects for leadership, argues that the president's ability to control his power is in his hands and "regulated (insofar as he controls them) by his choices of objectives, and of timing, and of instruments, and by his choice of choices to avoid."[67] Presidents can best motivate public attitudes on policy issues with their capacity to strategically time and deliver policy speeches to amplify attention paid, their ability to select the medium of delivery (through major addresses), the frequency of the discussion of the issue, their ability to select the issue (foreign policy or higher-salience issues), and their ability to strategically time the address during particular conditions (higher popularity). These findings suggest presidents can strategically lead public opinion and presidents have some capacity to facilitate their own leadership success, but this success is conditioned by the degree of public information, the prominence of the issue, the time period, and the tactic used.

CHAPTER 5

Successful Leadership in Domestic Policy

The previous two chapters outlined the broad statistical trends in presidential leadership of public opinion. However, since those data amalgamate several presidents, we might be missing important historical points about presidential leadership. Therefore, it is instructive to decouple these findings by looking at individual periods of time, confronting particular presidents at key moments in their administrations. In disaggregating and examining several individual leadership moments we can learn about some of the assumptions made by presidents at the time of their leadership (or nonleadership) and determine what questions or notions guided their strategy and their impressions about their strategic choices. This focus on individual moments lets us put a face on presidential leadership efforts and helps to bind together the conditional leadership theory presented in chapter 2. It can also help us determine, in a more intimate and immediate sense, whether or not the aggregate findings are accurate in predicting the conditions of presidential leadership success.

Thus, in order to illustrate and amplify the statistical inquiry from the previous two chapters, this chapter charts three instances of policy leadership that meet the conditions I argued in chapter 4 enhance leadership success. The conditions enhancing or detracting from leadership success culled from these findings are summarized in table 5.1. In addition to giving qualitative weight to the quantitative arguments, in this chapter (and the following three), I draw on often unexplored archival data that concern presidential leadership of public opinion from inside the White House. First, I explore the impact of the wage and price freeze during the Nixon administration (during his first term). Second, I examine President Reagan's leadership of the public on his economic policies in his first year in office (primarily concerning tax and budget policies). Third, I analyze President Clinton's conflict (and eventual victory) with

TABLE 5.1
Successful and Unsuccessful Leadership Conditions

	All Issues	Popular Presidents	All Foreign Policy
Successful leadership			
All presidents	Decrease in “don’t know” Two days before Major address Barnstorm* Popular president × High-salience issue	Decrease in “don’t know” Barnstorm Major address State of the Union promise Second term	Decrease in “don’t know” Troops deployed Two days before Major address
Late presidents	State of the Union promise* Decrease in “don’t know” Two days before Major address†	High-salience issue Decrease in “don’t know”	Decrease in “don’t know” Troops deployed Major address
Unsuccessful leadership			
All presidents	Election year	Press conference	Presidential election
Late presidents	Honeymoon “Rally” Election year High-salience issue*	Honeymoon Press conference	Honeymoon Presidential election High-salience issue

Note: Variables are compiled from data in chapter 4 and are all at the one-month window unless otherwise noted. *Significance at the three-month mark. †Significance interacted with decrease in “don’t know.”

Congress during the budget negotiations (related to funding battles over several key government programs) in 1995 and 1996. In each case we find the president not only leading public opinion but also, partly as a result, gaining traction on legislation in Congress.

A Quick Note on Case Studies

A case study approach is an informative way to analyze presidential history. And, when these historical interpretations are combined with archival data from inside the White House, the result is an elegant and direct way to test the theoretical and empirical assumptions I have laid out in this book. This approach to studying presidential leadership can also tease out nuances missed in the aggregate data. As Page notes, untangling the connection between policy making and opinion may be best conducted by a case study method since it provides a relatively clear and valid explanation of the players' thoughts and arguments.[1] For instance, in this analysis, we can examine which conditions were foremost on the minds of the participants and which factors were believed to have the most significant impact on presidential success or failure at leadership. Others have successfully applied these techniques to the study of mid-twentieth-century presidents.[2] We can therefore identify important timing sequences to investigate how public opinion had an effect on decision making and on the strategies the White House considered, which is key information needed for testing the hypotheses from chapter 2.

Of course, it is often difficult to treat archival data of this sort in a systematic manner. For this reason, as with most scholarship based on case studies, my analysis is unable to definitively *prove* the assertions. Considering that the cases are hand-picked intentionally to illustrate broad empirical findings, it cannot be claimed that these case studies represent all types of leadership or can be generalized beyond their own political and temporal arrangements. Rather than attempt to explain the process of leadership through randomly selected cases, I picked these cases through an inductive assumption because the outcome of the case was known. Case studies on their own are limited in what they can say about presidential leadership, but when they are combined with the aggregate data, we can then consider the weight of all the evidence. In case studies, evidentiary proof lies in the preponderance of documentation all pointing in the same direction.[3] Also, the longitudinal nature of the data allows for appropriate time-ordered causal claims. Ultimately, the approach here remedies the selection problem by relying on a wide range of available documents (both primary and secondary) to explain the positions and evaluate the key arguments.

Fortunately, given that the range of cases spans several time periods and presidents and that the case studies are patterned on the aggregate results found in chapters 3 and 4, it can be said with some certainty that the assertions in the case studies are representative (more on the case selection process and archival records search in appendix B). The diversity of cases also adds certainty to the conclusions. To that end, the case studies in this chapter and the following three examine a range of cases: early- and late-serving presidents, first- and second-term presidents, high- and low-popularity presidents, and presidents with differing levels of implied political "skill." Several kinds of issues are also examined, including both foreign and domestic policies. Domestic policy cases include economic policy, budget politics, and the politics of social welfare programs. Foreign policy cases include relations with superpowers, short military conflicts, long military conflicts, and key moments of international diplomacy.

Nixon Implements Wage and Price Controls

President Nixon's road to the White House was a long and circuitous one, but after the turmoil of the late 1960s, the nation turned to the former congressman, senator, and vice president to put the country's fiscal and international house in order. Complicating this return to "law and order" was a presidency beleaguered with public anger toward the ongoing war in Vietnam and a souring economy. And, unfortunately for the Nixon White House, the president became the first "since 1853 to assume office without his party's having a majority in at least one house of Congress."[4] The president, however, had been relatively popular during the course of his term and was enjoying above-average popularity in the summer and fall of 1971, a condition found to help presidential leadership. However, in his first two years in office (and after several policies), "Nixonomics" had failed to improve either the inflation or unemployment situation.[5] Drastic measures were to come.

Just before the president announced the wage and price freeze in August of 1971, the administration was looking for a way to improve public perception of his leadership, especially on "holding down" inflation and unemployment, according to Tom Benham's Opinion Research Corporation poll from June of 1971. Benham, one of the White House's outside pollsters, wrote, "Right now the Administration gets a high 'poor' rating on most of these [economic measures]." Benham suggested that the president build on the public's view of him as a good "family man": "Without resorting to sloganizing, the kind of concept that the average person needs to have about the President and his Administration is 'dedicated and working hard to improve my future and my family's well-being.' This type of concept (or some such) could unify programs and aims in such diverse areas as fighting inflation, combating unemployment, striving for world peace, improving the environment, providing better health care, introducing greater efficiently and lowering the cost of government, and so on and so on."[6]

A similar poll done by another of the White House's external pollsters, David Derge (of Indiana University) in July of 1971, found that although the public viewed the president as hardworking, "the Nixon Administration is not seen as a dramatic or innovative force. Any Administration action which can be cast in these terms might help offset that problem."[7] Others observed that voluntary measures would not have gone far enough—"the situation in the summer of 1971 seemed to require bolder measures in both political and economic terms."[8]

Benham's polling analysis indicated that economic issues are those that "seem obvious to us to require action or communication on the part of the Administration." In particular, he wrote, "The Nixon Administration needs to identify more with people who see themselves as victims of inflation." As the most important issue of the day and with the president as central figure in the economic situation, Benham argued, the president must exercise leadership:

> This is the number one domestic problem and, also, one on which a large percentage say not enough progress is being made. When the Nixon Administration took office in 1969, it clearly got across its point that action needed to be taken on inflation; and many steps were taken to deal with the problem. However, the progress that has been made to date has not been clearly evidence[d] to the average man who sees prices going up, and large wage demands being granted every time he reads about negotiations. The public needs reassurance that at some point this process will slow down

> and they will be able to resume their personal financial progress, that seems to have been slowed coincident with a Republican Administration.[9]

The administration, therefore, needed a policy to shore up the economic troubles of the nation and claim credit for doing so, especially with the president at the helm. John Whitaker (principle domestic policy adviser on the environment) forcefully argued that the problem was "the public perception of the President not being personally involved in domestic issues" and that without the president's involvement, "its [*sic*] like a plane radio controlled but no pilot in the cockpit." Guiding the president's scheduling, Whitaker suggested that "*never a week goes by* that the President doesn't *himself* get on the tube—not Mitchell or Richardson on drugs; not Train, Morton or Ruckelshaus on pollution; not Shultz, McCracken on the economy; *but the President.*"[10] The combination of the bully pulpit, a vocal president, and a successful policy was sorely needed by the White House, and an arrangement like this was argued in the conditional theory of leadership to engender leadership success.

On August 15, 1971, President Nixon instituted "Phase I" (the New Economic Policy), a ninety-day freeze on wages, prices, rents, and profit margins, which also lifted the excise tax from automobiles, announced spending cuts, and reinstated the investment tax credit.[11] The economy (especially inflation) was, according the president's polling data, the most important issue of the day.[12] Beyond the economic reasons, Arnold Weber observed, "the freeze may serve to dissipate political pressures and to restore some latitude to the national leadership."[13] The president's boastful claim that "I am now a Keynesian" demonstrated a major shift in economic policy toward centralized government regulation of the economy and signaled a fear about having economic trouble in the year of an election.[14] Thus, politics (and political motives) were now driving economic policy in the United States.

The president was on firm ground in asking for the freeze. Weber notes that in the summer of 1971 there was "considerable evidence that a broad consensus for controls did exist."[15] Benham wrote of his polling data, "In other surveys, we have observed a majority who favor price control, and majorities who feel the government 'should put pressure on unions to hold down their wage demands.' More forceful intervention by the Administration—even if not necessarily successful—would at least establish identity with the goals of the average citizen in fighting inflation."[16] It seems Benham was correct—in a memorandum relaying a private discussion between Dwight Chapin (deputy assistant to the president) and George Gallup Jr., in which Gallup shared early polling results that revealed the president's plan met with "strong approval" from 46% of the public and "mild approval" from 22%, while 38% thought the president's plan would "help," 14% said it would "hurt," and 32% said it would make "no difference." Chapin further noted, "George Gallup Junior pointed out that the breakdown is very interesting. For example, of the people that said they would be hurt, nearly 50% expressed approval of the President's action in the interest of stabilizing the economy."[17]

The president followed the advice from his pollsters and aides to take a firm stand. He addressed the nation on television on August 15, 1971. Richard Reeves adeptly noted that, in ushering in a successful policy during Nixon's price and wage freeze, "the speechwriter was as important as the economists."[18] The president, using the "gutsy rhetoric" he asked for from his speechwriters, spoke from the Oval Office that evening: "We are going to take that action—not timidly, not half-heartedly, and not in piecemeal fashion. We are going to move forward to the new prosperity without war as befits a great people—all together, and along a broad front. The time has come for a new economic policy for the United States. Its targets are unemployment, inflation, and international speculation."[19]

In the next five days, President Nixon traveled to several states, including New York, Illinois, Idaho, Texas, and California. Comporting with expectations about successful tactics of leadership (i.e., a "barnstorm" around the nation), the president continued to push his case with the public. For instance, in an address to the Knights of Columbus in New York City, he said, "I would like to address this organization tonight on America's problems, and particularly one which I addressed myself to just two nights ago. . . . Now, these are all Government actions. There is a need for these actions, because only by coming to grips with all of our problems can we expect to solve any of them. And there is a need for bold, decisive action, because a nation can remain great only if it acts with a sure sense of destiny."[20]

To keep the pressure on the public and Congress, the president followed up his initial speech and trip around the country with another prime-time address to Congress, "Stabilization of the Economy" on September 9, 1971. In sketching a vision for a world without "war or inflation," the president noted, "The reaction of the American people to the new economic policy has been unselfish and courageous. The reaction of our trading partners abroad has been measured and constructive. I ask the Congress to respond in a similar spirit, as the Congress has to so many other great challenges in the past. This is a time to set aside partisanship. Let us join together in placing the national interest above special interests in America."[21] Chief of staff H. R. Haldeman reported in his diary that although the Nixon privately indicated that "it was a damn dull subject," the president "did a superb job on the speech to Congress, and all the reactions were very good, especially on his presentation and delivery."[22] In chapter 4 both this major address tactic and the barnstorm tactic (for popular presidents) were found to be successful, and both paid off for the president here.

Although the policy was unconventional (even radical considering a Republican president and a country in peacetime), the president's efforts were instantly economically successful. The program improved inflation in the short run by leading to a reduction in wholesale prices.[23] The popularity of the freeze itself was also instantly apparent. Table 5.2 demonstrates the arc of this trend. Indeed, during the August, September, and October polling waves, the public's response to the president's handling of the economy was significantly more positive than before the institution of the wage-price freeze. In a memorandum to Patrick Buchanan (consultant to the president for media analysis and speech writing), Haldeman wrote, "Overwhelming public endorsement of the President's economic proposals is clearly indicated by the attached poll done by Opinion Research Corporation. In particular, the results show that: 1. On every specific action taken by the President—a majority of the public approved. 2. Contrary to the opposition of some union leaders, *America's union families overwhelmingly support the President's new economic program.* 3. People are now more confident about their future."[24] These full findings are reported in table 5.3.

As expected, the public was persuaded by the president's policy push. In a memorandum from Donald Rumsfeld to Chuck Colson (both special counsel to the president), Rumsfeld concluded that the president's leadership worked: "Most Americans approved of the 90-day freeze. On August 22, 1971, 68% of those polled indicated strong or mild approval of the freeze, and on August 28, 73% of those polled stated that their overall reaction to the President's new economic program was favorable."[25] Those responding "no opinion" declined modestly from 12% to 10%, an occurrence that reflected more effective leadership and suggested that the public was growing more certain about the president's plan. This growing

TABLE 5.2
Approval of Nixon's Handling of the Economy, 1971 and 1972

Polling date	Pollster	Approve	Disapprove
February 19–21 (1971)	Harris	37	48
August 21–22	ORC	59	31
September 7–8	ORC	56	31
October 9–10	ORC	57	35
November 19–20	ORC	48	39
January 3–20 (1972)	MOR	49	38
January 26–27	ORC	46	45
June 16–26	MOR	39	45

Note: Data reproduced from the Richard Nixon Materials Project, National Archives II, H. R. Haldeman Files, Spending Poll, "Polling Summary," Box 19. The original memorandum included reference to "H" (Harris Poll), "O" (Opinion Research Poll), and "T" ("Teeter" poll done by Bob Teeter at MOR). "No opinion" results are not shown. The question was "Do you approve or disapprove of the way President Nixon is dealing with the economic conditions in this country?"

certainty was combined with an increase in the percentage of the public who felt the president's program did more "good than harm." Rumsfeld noted, "In five surveys taken since the inception of the New Economic Policy (Phase I) in August, 1971, approximately half of those polled have stated that the President's economic policies were doing more good than harm, as contrasted to the roughly one-third who so believed during the first eight months of 1971."[26] President Nixon noted in his memoirs that public reaction to his speech was "overwhelmingly positive" and it received favorable news coverage as well.[27] Benham noted that from June to August of 1971, approval of the president was at its highest point. The polls following the price and wage freeze announcement in August were met with significant bumps in approval (rising from 54% to 56% in the "Wage-Price Freeze Survey" conducted August 23–24, and maintaining at 56% in the "Catch-Up Survey" conducted August 30–31).[28]

Congress had previously given the president the authority to "stabilize prices, rents, wages, and salaries," which allowed the president to take his unprecedented action.[29] Congress stayed out of the president's way and, despite ideological objections from within his own party, did not attempt to restrict the president's ability to carry out his far-reaching economic

TABLE 5.3
Approval of Phase I Programs, August 1971

1. Do you think President Nixon's decision to take action against unemployment, inflation, and to protest the stability of the dollar is the right thing or the wrong thing to do at this time?

	Right	Wrong	No opinion
Total public	77	10	13
Union	71	15	14
Non-Union	79	9	12

2. I am going to read a number of the measures that President Nixon ordered or proposed relating to the economy. For each one, I would like you to tell me whether you approve or disapprove of that measure:

A. The President ordered a 90-day freeze on wages, prices, and rents. Do you approve or disapprove?

	Approve	Disapprove	No opinion
Total public	77	20	3
Union	68	29	3
Non-Union	80	16	4

B. The President asked Congress to repeal the 7% excise tax on automobiles. Do you approve or disapprove?

	Approve	Disapprove	No opinion
Total public	75	16	9
Union	76	17	7
Non-Union	75	16	9

Note: Sample table reproduced from the Richard Nixon Materials Project, National Archives II, Patrick Buchanan Files, Haldeman 1971 (2 of 2), "Haldeman to Buchanan," August 26, 1971, Box 3.

plans. "Outmaneuvered by the President, Congress was afraid to challenge the political popularity of the freeze," Reeves notes.[30] The implication is that the president was able to convince Congress *not* to act rather than to act, as the popularity of the program and his ability to motivate the public behind his policies created an environment where Congress was hesitant to work against the president. The president's ability to lead the public, therefore, has a close relationship to the degree of policy success achieved.

As with most moments of leadership success discussed in chapter 3, this one would be short-lived. Indeed, President Nixon himself noted the short-term popularity of the freeze.[31] By the time Phase II (a six-month extension of Phase I) ended in April of 1972, the public had not seen the progress it wanted from the program and began to disapprove of it. "The public strongly supports the objectives of the price-wage control program but clearly feels performance has not measured up to objectives," wrote Peter Peterson a year after the initial wage-price freeze was imposed.[32] Peterson, the assistant to the president for international economic affairs, noted that the president had not taken the message to the people in a while and urged Nixon to "put a great deal more emphasis on getting the recovery and the anti-inflation story across in much more vivid and human terms (i.e., market basket in relation to paychecks, rather than just in statistical terms). You would know best how to do this."[33] Without constant pressure, as argued in the theory from chapter 2, the movement of opinion would naturally truncate.

Part of the problem was the concurrent increase in spending during 1972. This spending, done with the hope of lowering the unemployment rate, led to significant increases in inflation.[34] Unfortunately for the administration, by October of 1972 (a month before the election) the public perceived that "federal spending remains the number one cause of inflation in the public mind."[35] And although the early anti-inflation efforts were met with success, by the time a year had passed, "the substantial majority feel there has been either no improvement or that economic conditions are worse."[36] The economic damage of the Phase II period had largely undone the gains from Phase I.[37] Given the lack of success in fighting inflation in the long run (even though the freeze worked in the short run), the White House was unable to lead the public on these issues for as long as it needed.

The price controls, which had not been adequately enforced, also led to public panic during which "many stories reported a run on goods, purchased by people who did not know what to expect from their president next."[38] In a memorandum to Charles Colson, Rumsfeld argued, "While favorable responses to the overall effect of Nixon's economic policies continue to be higher than they were during the twelve months preceding the announcement of the New Economic Policy [Phase I price controls], they have declined slightly from the last three months of 1971. Public confidence peaked during the period of transition from the freeze to Phase II [November 1971], and since that time it appears to have been gradually eroding."[39] He argued that this erosion was fast because "the public tends very quickly to become disenchanted with the ways in which controls are administered and the effects on the economy they seem to have."[40]

Reagan and the Negotiation over the Budget

The focus of this case study is on President Reagan's first year in office and the gradual success he had in passing his economic programs. By the end of the Carter administration and the 1980 election, the economy was in dire straits. As a result, several of President Reagan's economic campaign themes resonated with his party and the public, especially the themes of less government, a balanced budget, and lower taxes.[41] The election of 1980 was heralded as a sea change in American politics, in particular on the issue of the economy, but Republican party chairman Bill Brock put Ronald Reagan's landslide victory in the clearest perspective: "We've got to act with some urgency to deal with the problems on which people voted—unemployment and inflation."[42] Ensuring economic stimulus and long-term growth of the economy were critical to the success of the White House and the furtherance of the "Reagan Revolution." Reagan's election in 1980 after four "failed" presidencies allowed for large-scale changes, especially in social and economic issues.[43] The president's economic plan was the administration's first step in affecting economic recovery.

This case study is viable because, according to the findings in chapters 3 and 4, the Reagan White House should have found leadership success with his policies during this time period. For instance, it was found that popular presidents did better at leading public opinion in several instances. The president retained high levels of popularity, especially from March to June of 1981 when his popularity was in the high sixties.[44] Robert Dallek similarly claimed that the president's popularity (in the wake of an attempted assassination in March) assisted the White House in pushing their proposals through Congress.[45] Second, the president made this policy the cornerstone of his economic renewal, suggesting that it was a core part of his agenda, generally a positive harbinger of leadership of public opinion for later presidents. Third, the findings from chapter 4 revealed that the interaction between a popular president and a highly salient issue was a powerful sponsor of presidential leadership, combining a higher degree of attention to the president and his issues.

In a concerted push to garner public support for the president's economic policies beginning in the summer of 1981, the administration undertook communications planning in "Phases I and II" between January 1981 and July 1981. Special assistant to the president Richard Beal noted, "In essence, Phase I strategies called for strong Presidential leadership by restricting the focus to a short-list of objectives, being consistent, guarding against foolish errors, undertaking the difficult early, and demonstrating that the President is in charge. It was essential to begin the President's term by relying on his skills as *communicator-in-chief* to explain the central policy thrust of the New Administration."[46] Phase II shifted from managing public support to managing congressional support. The lynchpin of Phase I was a televised address to Congress in February of 1981 that outlined the president's economic policies.[47] Reagan himself endorsed this strategy when, in his autobiography, he reminisced that he learned as governor of California "the value of making an end run around the legislature by going directly to the people" and "as president, I intended to do the same thing."[48]

The administration's push in the spring and summer of 1981 to ensure the passage and public support of its policies was critical to the successful passage of their programs in Congress. The intense focus on reducing nondefense expenditures and cutting taxes (and no other legislative priorities) fostered a condition where the president "delivered more public remarks about his economic process than about any other topic."[49] The White House deployed the president to fifty-one congressional districts (forty-five in the south) and mobilized resources from the Republican National Committee, the National Conservative Political Action Committee, and the Moral Majority to attempt to lead public opinion.[50] The president also went on the airwaves in a nationally televised address on July 27 to push for final passage of his tax reduction policy.[51]

After addressing the nation, the president thereafter took to the road, traveling to Georgia, California, and Illinois in the following weeks, and again, he noted in his memoirs that the strategy was to put pressure on those reluctant members of Congress to side with his legislative proposals.[52] As we saw in chapter 4, a presidential barnstorm of the nation was more quickly effective when the president was popular, and with the president enjoying high popularity, it was a strategy the White House could utilize successfully. The presidential addresses and barnstorming had the effect of providing "the Republican gypsy moths and the Democratic boll weevils who constituted swing votes in Reagan's legislative coalition with a grass roots rationale for voting with him."[53] The president drew on his public support and, just days after his televised address to the nation, noted in a speech in Atlanta on July 30, "The outpouring of support from the people has been one of the most inspiring events I can remember. Since Tuesday morning, Washington has been filled with the voices of the people, the voices of democracy. They've been ringing throughout the Capitol. The Congress and the White House have been flooded with calls and telegrams from thousands and thousands of Americans in support of our economic program that crossed party lines and is truly bipartisan."[54]

Another valuable communications strategy that was found to enhance presidential leadership efforts was talking about the issue for consecutive days. During the course of the budget debate, the president was nearly constantly talking about the issue in public, discussing the issue on consecutive days twelve times between June 23 and October 1, 1981. These remarks were in diverse venues, including fundraisers, press conferences, question-and-answer sessions with the public, legislation-signing ceremonies at the White House, and several speeches throughout the country. Considering that the White House was working only on this issue in public or Congress at the time, the sharp and focused discussion allowed this communications strategy to pay off in successful leadership of public opinion.

By July of 1981, the president's cumulative efforts had paid off. Poll results from White House pollster Richard (Dick) Wirthlin indicated "a slight increase in the optimism regarding the future of the economy. In this nationwide study, respondents were asked which of these descriptions they feel will be more true of 1981: a year of economic prosperity or a year of economic difficulty. Until now, results had been holding steady at 16% aggregate response for prosperity, with 84% predicting economic difficulty. However, in the July study, prosperity had increased marginally, from 16% to 18%, while the number of people responding economic difficulty has dropped from 84% to 78%." Wirthin also noted that Reagan's core public constituencies were more likely to support him: "Most of the positive responses came from Republicans, conservatives, and Reagan voters."[55] In evaluating "Reaganomics," William Niskanen noted that Reagan's campaign generated "commitments to specific economic groups" and these economic plans were a continuation of that sentiment.[56]

To be sure, these positive shifts in opinion were modest short-term gains (to be followed by larger gains in the subsequent months, as I explain below). However, these results comport with the findings that movement of opinion on policy is generally within 1% to 5%. However, the White House, by virtue of President Reagan's positive positioning in the political environment and conditions favoring his leadership ability, needed only to patiently push the public. William Schneider argued, "The president sold his tax and budget policies as a means to an end, which was to curb inflation and restore the nation's economic stability. In the public's view, the policies worked."[57] His strategies, in particular, helped him accomplish this. In a May barnstorm speech at Notre Dame in Indiana, Reagan recalled his movie career in rallying the audience to support his policies despite a slumping economy, encouraging them to "win one for the Gipper."[58] The president joked, "Now, today I hear very often, 'Win one for the Gipper,' spoken in a humorous vein. Lately I've been hearing it by Congressmen who are supportive of the programs that I've introduced."[59]

Despite lingering pessimism about the duration of the economic recovery, there was positive movement in the percentage of the public who felt President Reagan's plans would help the economy, demonstrating leadership on the issue. Wirthlin's July analysis stated, "Aggregate results show that the number of people thinking that Reagan's economic policies will help has not recovered to its February high of 78%, but, with a reading of 68% [of the public approving of the President's plans], represents a significant positive increase over the last month."[60] Interestingly, this number was driven by liberal respondents, where the "very liberal" increased their "help rating" by twelve points and in all age categories. And because there is a likely six-month lag in economic evaluations picked up in the survey results, Wirthlin indicated that the support for the plan was growing.[61] Similarly, the White House's continual push to persuade the public worked better the longer they did it. By August of 1981, "positive perceptions of the effect of Reagan's economic program have increased significantly and unilaterally over last month's readings" where 74% of the public agreed the president's plan would "help" the economy, which "represents a six-percentage-point increase over last month, and a twelve-point jump since June."[62] The percentage of the public registering "no opinion" also fell from 11% in June of 1981 to 7% in the August of 1981 poll.

As a result, Congress willingly accepted the popular president's policies for tax cuts and reforms. The president's budget was passed in July, which cut more than $38 billion from the federal budget, and the president's tax plan (the Economic Recovery Tax Act) was also passed in July, which reduced the individual income tax rates for all taxpayers, the capital gains tax, and the "marriage penalty."[63] These objectives, including a pledge to balance the budget and increase defense spending by 1983, were a fulfillment of the president's major campaign promises.[64] These initiatives met with support from majorities of the public, in part because the public felt, according to internal White House polling, that "the current economic situation is very serious." By the time Congress voted, half (48%) of the respondents thought the plan would "make things better for the economy," 21% said it would be the same, and 16% said it would be worse), and "Americans also favor the president's planned tax rate reductions" for businesses and individuals.[65]

Although it was assumed that a Democratic House and Republican Senate would substantially alter the president's plans, the president's skill at managing public opinion "overwhelmed remaining congressional opposition to his policies."[66] The president's position was bolstered by the popularity of the issue and his ability to rally the public behind his signature campaign issue. President Reagan himself noted that the pressure he put on Congress via the public was instrumental in getting key votes from congressional Democrats.[67] The president combined a congressional lobbying strategy to persuade key members of Congress along with the televised address "prior to the House vote on the Gramm-Latta budget resolution and another two days before the House voted on the tax cut legislation"—this "well-orchestrated outpouring of public support" converted opponents and kept potential party defectors in line.[68] This support from the public and business allowed the legislation to sail through Congress.

However, although President Reagan's leadership of public opinion assisted in the passage of the legislation, this leadership from President Reagan proved to be short-lived. By October of 1981, as a harbinger of the economic woes to come in 1982, the public's support of the president's economic plan had begun to decline. In the fall of 1981, Dick Wirthlin observed, "As economic issues continue to dominate perceptions of what are the top problems in the country today, public confidence in the Reagan economic program is beginning to fade. A number of measures point to this conclusion, including the ratings for the President's actions and as well as the characteristics of the program in particular."[69] The White House attempted to focus on their base in these politically troubled times. Wirthlin noted, "Reagan voters in 1980 continue to remain loyal to the economic package as hurt ratings [the percentage responding that the Reagan Economic Package "hurts" the economy] only reach 7% in this study."[70]

It was asserted in chapters 2 and 4 that more arguments leveled against the president would have a significantly negative impact on presidential leadership. Indeed, by the end of the year, the president's ability to move policy opinion was limited by a resurgent Democratic Party in Congress. In a memorandum to Edwin Meese (counselor to the president), James Baker (chief of staff), and Michael Deaver (deputy chief of staff), Wirthlin argued that the public was reacting against Republican Party gains in 1980 (given the findings that more in the public are identifying with the Democratic Party) and wrote "what appears to be happening, therefore, is the equal but opposite reaction to the policies and performance of the Republican party. More specifically, the Republican pledge of strong, consistent leadership, leadership which asserts an ability to deal with the nation's economic problems, is under some question."[71] The key to holding the line in the 1982 elections, Wirthlin believed, was keeping the economy on the positive track.

As enough time passes and Congress weighs in on policy matters, a president's leadership advantage naturally shrinks. By the time President Reagan had gotten his way on the budget battles and on his tax cut legislation, the Democrats (and allied groups) were beginning to mount a public protest. Columnist David Broder noted in September, after the administration's message began to be significantly challenged:

> It is plain now that the opposition to President Reagan and his program is beginning to find its voice. The 260,000 people who assembled on the Mall last Saturday at the call of the AFL-CIO and some 200 other organizations to protest the Reagan economic policies was the largest such demonstration since Vietnam War days. This weekend, the Democratic Party will hold its first major training session for the 1982 campaign, in Des Moines, and on Oct. 1 it will parade a number of mayors before the microphones

> at a dinner here to describe the damage they say will be done by the Reagan budget cuts that go into effect that day. Meantime, House Democrats have recalled that the committees they control are allowed to conduct investigations, and Tip O'Neill has launched a number of them into regional hearings focused on the effects of high interest rates and scarce federal dollars. As a result of all this, the Republicans are getting shaky about their support of the new round of budget cuts.[72]

These factors (a worsening economy and rising opposition voices) converged during the midterm elections of 1982. The president's progress (both in politics and policy) was halted in the 1982 midterm elections in part because the number of unemployed reached 11.9 million people and the recession had made the economy suffer—the Democrats were easily able to use this as political fodder against the president during the midterm elections.[73]

Clinton and the Budget Debate

Most observers of the Clinton presidency in the first half of his first term would have balked at the notion that he would be included in a discussion of successful presidential leadership.[74] His efforts at leadership early in his term tended to end in policy failure (as in the defeated health-care initiative from 1993) or significant political losses (as in the midterm elections in 1994). Several have accused the Clinton White House of being too politically responsive—their use of polling to craft their political messages (and to an extent public policy) and their willingness to "triangulate" their political position brought the ire of those inside and outside the White House.[75] Of course, in retrospect, there were several definable moments of public opinion leadership during this time. The moment this case study will focus on is the budget battles with the Republican-led Congress in 1995 and 1996, an example of successful leadership of Congress via public opinion.

In the fall of 1995, the Republican-led House and Senate approved a budget for 1996 that balanced the budget in seven years, made $270 billion in cuts to Medicare, provided $245 billion in tax cuts, created large cuts in the Earned Income Tax Credit, and other cuts in domestic programs.[76] Thereafter, the president expressed his unwillingness to approve this budget, and to force a political showdown, he vetoed a continuing resolution that would have increased the debt ceiling as a stopgap remedy to fund the government until a budget agreement could be reached. As a result of no agreement on the budget, the government shut down on November 14, 1995, and again on December 16, 1995 (after a continuing resolution was signed but in the absence of a second budget agreement). Both sides believed they would win in the long run, with the Republicans (led by Newt Gingrich) viewing this fight as the fulfillment of the 1994 Republican electoral "revolution" in Congress and with the Clinton administration fighting for their constituencies and their ideological commitments to New Deal programs.

The president was encouraged by several staff members to stay the course and not give in to the Republicans' demands for more severe budget cuts. Dick Morris, the president's consultant and longtime friend, found in October of 1995 that the president was solidly backed by the public to "not cave in" and to "stay the course." Morris argued that "Americans, by 64–31 wanted Clinton to stand firm and not compromise. They wanted the Republicans to compromise and not stand firm—by 20 (stand firm) to 76 (compromise). If a breakdown in negotiations were to come, the poll reported that the public would blame the Republicans rather than Clinton, by 58–25. The agendas counseled 'tenacity, stubbornness, no concessions.'"[77] This strategy was successful, in part, because the White House had televised reelection advertisements running through all of 1995 (advertisements they had spent $4.2 million on through November 1)—Morris noted that "we are on paid media and that is doing everything to shape public attitudes" and, as a result "we can be forceful and strong in public and even err on the side of rigidity because our media is showing people why were are taking so hard a stand."[78]

The White House intelligently used the bully pulpit during this time to capitalize on the political conditions that favored them. The president used the Saturday radio address in several consecutive weeks to address the budget debate (September 30, October 7 and 28, November 4 and 11). For instance, in the November 11 address the president argued:

> At midnight this Monday night, unless Congress passes legislation to keep the Government running, the Federal Government will be required by law to begin shutting down. For months, the congressional Republicans have made a consistent threat: If I don't sign legislation cutting Medicare, education and the environment, they'll plunge the Government into default and force it to close its

> doors. I don't want to shut down basic Government services for the American people, but I can't allow that to be used to force us to accept extreme budget measures that would violate our basic values as a nation and undermine the long-term welfare of the American people.

He further argued, "The congressional Republicans propose to balance the budget in seven years, but they would get there with deep cuts in Medicare, education, protection for the environment, and by raising taxes on working people. Five full months ago, I proposed an alternative plan to balance the budget in 10 years while protecting Medicare and Medicaid, increasing our investment in education and technology, protecting the environment, without raising taxes on working families."[79] As is evident from his language, a major part of the president's plan was to "triangulate" or to create a third position independent of the two parties in Congress.[80] This allowed the president to offer his own version of a balanced budget (on his timetable) independent of what the Republicans or Democrats in Congress were offering.[81] This provided him room to pursue the marginal voter rather than only his own base.[82]

President Clinton was a frequent traveler around the nation, especially during this critical time; actions that this book finds are consistent with successful leadership. Indeed, the president "was a frequent flyer domestically and was beginning to add substantial foreign travel as well. He continued to travel at the same pace following the [1994] election, now with a determination bolstered by a threat to his political survival."[83] The president's rhetorical focus on the budget as his primary topic was part of the same strategy. He made significant use of the "two days before" strategy, speaking on the issue most every day in the days before the first government shutdown until his 1996 State of the Union message. These talks occurred on several consecutive days: November 10–13, November 16–20, December 6–10, December 18–23, January 3–6, January 9–12, and January 18–20, an impressive record especially considering the president also traveled to Paris, Belfast, and Germany in late November and early December. Although he could not engage in a traditional barnstorm of the country while the budget negotiations were ongoing with Congress (requiring multiple meetings at the White House), the president made good use of the bully pulpit to continuously press the issue in public.

Although it has been argued that presidential statements made during press conferences are less likely to lead public opinion, the president routinely spoke to the press several times over the course of the budget impasse. The theorized *cause* of the limits on leadership in press conferences was that reporters are allowed to pose critical questions of the president, thereby challenging his message. President Clinton's strategy circumvented this by briefing the press with a prepared statement before the conference began and by limiting the number of questions asked, which he accomplished by only being available for a short time. For instance, in a press conference on January 9, 1996, he opened the discussion by stating:

> Good afternoon. As you know, we have just completed another long meeting with the Republican and Democratic leaders in the Congress. We have arrived at a point where, clearly, all sides have agreed on more than enough cuts to both balance the budget in seven years, according to the Congressional Budget Office, and allow a modest tax cut. A final agreement on the balanced budget, I believe, is clearly within reach. Unfortunately, the talks have not yet succeeded because we do still disagree on the level of cuts in the programs of Medicare, Medicaid, aid to poor children, the earned-income credit, which protects the hardest pressed working families, and education and the environment. The Republicans still want cuts in Medicare and Medicaid that we believe are well beyond what is necessary to balance the budget, and cuts in the discretionary account which funds education and the environment that we believe are excessive and beyond what is needed to balance the budget or to provide a reasonable tax cut.[84]

The press were only permitted to ask four questions of the president, which he answered briefly. The White House was therefore able to control the situation more effectively by using it as a platform for delivering their message to the public with limited unfavorable response.

The president's efforts paid leadership dividends. The public endorsed the substance of his proposals. On November 1, 1995, Morris argued to the president that "the public wants a veto" and that "Republicans' only weapon is the debt limit and CR [congressional resolution] and the public will hate them for using blackmail once they start to do it even more than they hate their [budget] cuts."[85] Public polls taken over the month of November confirmed this thinking. In consecutive polls juxtaposing the president's position ("Clinton says this budget makes too many cuts in

Who Is "Really Trying" to Find a Solution?

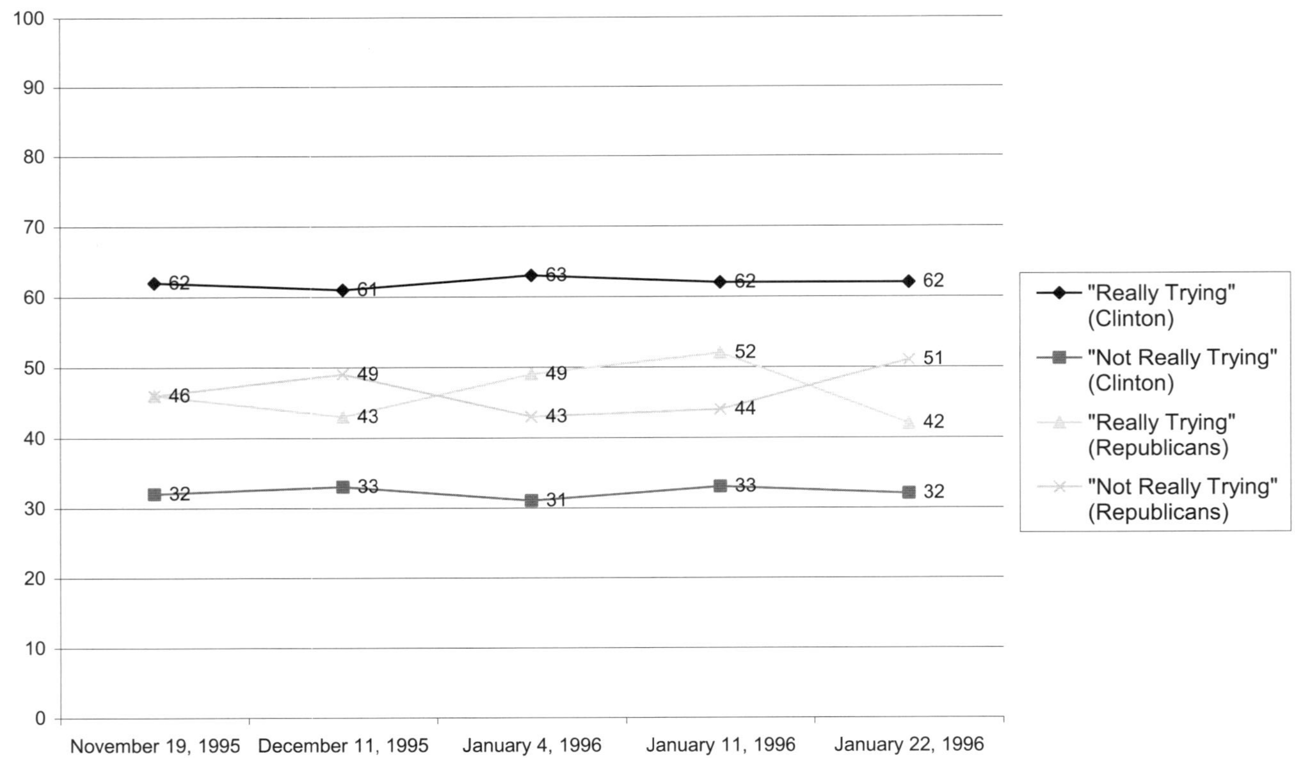

domestic programs and gives tax breaks to the wealthy") and the Republicans' position ("they say the budget will balance the federal budget in seven years and cut taxes for most Americans"), the percentage indicating Clinton was "right" rose from 54% on November 13 (before the shutdown) to 60% on November 19 (after the shutdown).[86] The percentage registering "no opinion" also fell from 7% to 3%. Sixty-one percent also favored a presidential veto of this budget (using the same question) after the government shutdown.[87] Concurrently, the percentage of the public approving of the president's handling of Medicare rose by 11% from October of 1995 to January of 1996.[88] Morris's polling from December, in the aftermath of the first shutdown, suggested to him that "the results were as predicted—a tremendous growth in Clinton's personal image and a dramatic falloff in perceptions that he was weak or wishy-washy."[89]

Figure 5.1 similarly reveals poll trends in the percentages of the public who believed that either President Clinton or the Republicans in Congress were "really trying" to find a solution to the government shutdown. From the outset, it is clear that the public tended to believe that the president was "really trying" to find a solution, thus winning the public relations battle (even if in private negotiations with Congress he was not always gaining concessions). From November 1995 until late January 1996, more than 60% of the public responded that the president was "really trying," a number that deviated little over the course of this budget battle. The Republicans were consistently thought less likely to be "really trying" to find a solution to the government shutdown, and there were times where they were *more likely* to be viewed as "not really trying," including in early December and late January.

Concurrent with these developments (on November 15) was Newt Gingrich's complaint about the lack of presidential "face time" on Air

*Fig. 5.1. (opposite). Who is "really trying" to find a solution? All polls were conducted by CBS/*New York Times. *The question referencing Bill Clinton was "Do you think President (Bill) Clinton is really trying to find a solution to the budget standoff with the Republicans in Congress, or not?" Those responding "don't know" were 6% on November 19, 7% on December 11, 6% on January 4, 5% on January 5, and 6% on January 22. The question referencing the Republicans in Congress was "Do you think the Republicans in Congress are really trying to find a solution to the budget standoff with President (Bill) Clinton, or not?" Those responding "don't know" were 8% on November 19, 8% on December 11, 8% on January 4, 4% on January 5, and 7% on January 22.*

Force One flying back from Israel for the funeral of Yitzhak Rabin and that he (along with other Republican leaders) was forced to leave the plane by the rear exit. This prompted the *New York Daily News* to print a cartoon caricature of Newt Gingrich in diapers under the headline "Cry Baby."[90] Similarly, the onset of negotiations with the White House (on December 22) did not seem to lessen the perception of Republicans as "not really trying" to come to a solution on the budget debate as compared to the president. In the waning days of the showdown, just before the State of the Union address, 51% of the public viewed the Republicans as "not really trying" to find a solution to the budget debate, an impression that was solidified by the president's message in the 1996 State of the Union speech. Ironically, the Republicans were not silent in the days following the first government shutdown—indeed, they ran television advertisements and appeared on several Sunday morning political shows to attempt to "win the propaganda war."[91] Their polling indicated that Americans opposed their budget cuts, but they were determined to attempt to sway public opinion anyway.[92] Ultimately, however, the White House's public pressure swayed public opinion in its direction.

The president's 1996 State of the Union address (delivered on January 23) was also a good example of the effective use of the bully pulpit. Using a "major address" strategy (such as in the State of the Union) is a successful portent of presidential leadership. In addition, mentioning an issue in the State of the Union speech is a positive way for presidents to lead public opinion—the visibility and prominence of the issue assisted later-serving presidents in successfully leading public opinion. Charles Jones argued that President Clinton, in delivering his 1996 State of the Union address, was "tested, rested, and with a well-worn veto pen" and "could assert a much stronger role in national policy making. The soon-to-be-familiar recital of issues was introduced: Medicare, Medicaid, education, and the environment."[93] Morris points to the president's State of the Union address as the "punch through" moment where the president took charge of the national stage.[94] The president also combined his communications efforts by barnstorming around the country by going to Ohio and Tennessee before delivering the State of the Union and to Kentucky and Illinois immediately after (then to New Hampshire in the days that followed for the 1996 New Hampshire primary).

The president also used the opportunely scheduled State of the Union to hammer his message home to the public and Congress. From the rostrum in the House, the president argued that he wanted to use the address "to reach out to the Republicans, rally the Democrats, and explain to the American people my position on the budget debate, and on the larger question that the budget battle presented."[95] Again he emphasized the "triangulation" theme as he had done throughout the budget negotiation: "As I have said before, and let me say again, many good ideas have come out of our negotiations. I have learned a lot about the way both Republicans and Democrats view the debate before us. I have learned a lot about the good ideas that each side has that we could all embrace. We ought to resolve our remaining differences. I am willing to work to resolve them. I am ready to meet tomorrow. But I ask you to consider that we should at least enact these savings that both plans have in common and give the American people their balanced budget, a tax cut, lower interest rates, and a brighter future. We should do that now and make permanent deficits yesterday's legacy."[96] Because the issue was made a core of the president's policy agenda through the State of the Union, his message was more direct and his ability to lead the public was strengthened.

Consistent with the White House's early view of the situation, with enough public pressure, President Clinton would triumph in the public debate over the budget. Figure 5.2 illustrates this phenomenon by outlining the trend in "blame" for the government shutdown during January of 1996. Negotiations continuing from the previous year resumed on January 2 and favored the Clinton administration—one White House aide noted that "we're killing them" on the issues of adequate funding for Medicare, Medicaid, education, and the environment.[97] From the start of this polling data on January 4, 1996, the Clinton administration had the upper hand in not being blamed (never more than the Republicans). In addition, the percentage of the public "blaming" the Republicans for the government shutdown increased from the mid-forties to the low-fifties, and the percentage "blaming" the Clinton White House fell at particular moments but held relatively steady in the mid-thirties.

Falling in the polls, the Republicans "paid a high price for their convictions" by agreeing to support President Clinton's plan for a balanced budget in seven years, using the White House's timetable and policy priorities.[98] Republicans in Congress had wanted sharp cuts in domestic spending, but the final submitted 1996 budget ensured the protections on which President Clinton had been talking about in public, including Medicare, Social Security, the environment, and education. The Republicans, "recognizing that the public was blaming them for the shutdown of government" and realizing the White House would not back down,

Who Is to Blame for the Government Shutdown?

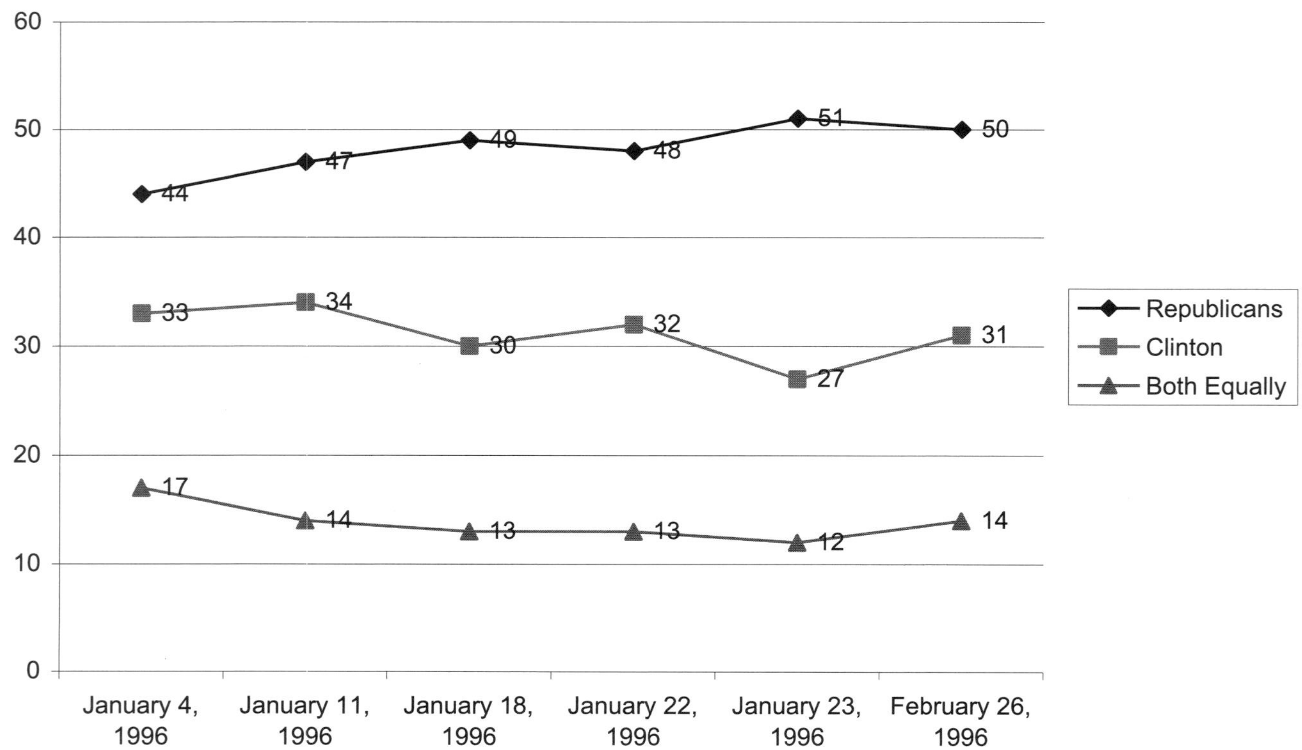

"began to cooperate with Clinton to pass FY [fiscal year] 1996 appropriations."[99] In effect, the president had won the public relations battle. This ability to persuade the public and to follow through on these policy proposals gave the president "the high ground."[100] Clinton's constant pressure on the issue during the months described here provided positive groundwork enabling him to strike the precise arguments by which the public would be persuaded. His efforts allowed him to shape the political environment in his favor and extract a legislative environment where he was able to influence Congress to accept his policy initiatives over their initial objections.

Effective in assisting the president's leadership efforts was the White House's "major address" strategy. The president's image and message combined with the right medium was a political winner for the White House. For instance, after President Clinton's televised address to the nation vetoing the first continuing resolution on November 13, political aide George Stephanopoulos reminisced, "When he appeared before the cameras to scold the 'deeply irresponsible' Republican leaders for cutting Medicare 'as a condition of keeping the government open,' the president was the picture of stern compassion, America's dad."[101] The president's appearances on nightly television news signing the Bosnian peace accords in Paris (following a televised address to the nation on the subject from the Oval Office on November 27) also likely contributed to his standing as a successful leader. These efforts, combined with a televised media blitz noted by the president in his memoirs, pressured the Congress to bow to his budget proposals.[102]

Also helping the president lead the public (and secure reelection) was a strong (and growing stronger) economy. Inflation was low during this period. Early interest rate increases had hurt the president politically by keeping unemployment high, "but by mid-1995, with inflation in sight, he [Alan Greenspan] proceeded to lower those interest rates, which helped to fuel the historic economic and stock market boom to

Fig. 5.2. (opposite). Who is to blame for the government shutdown? All polls were conducted by CBS News. The question was "President (Bill) Clinton and the Republicans in Congress are still trying to resolve their disagreements on plans to balance the federal budget by the year 2002. Who do you blame more for the budget standoff—the Republicans in Congress or Bill Clinton?" Those undecided on January 4 were 6%, 5% on January 11, 8% on January 18, 7% on January 22, 10% on January 23, and 5% on February 23.

come."[103] The gross domestic product of the nation was continuing to gain progress over this period as well, helping the president lead public opinion. President Clinton himself noted that, in November of 1995, "the economy had continued to grow, with the deficit dropping more than expected."[104] This economic progress convinced the president that a balanced budget could be reached in seven years with his desired priorities, and that as a result of this progress and public pressure which the president could marshal, he would be able to compete, proposal for proposal, with Congress.

President Clinton met several of the conditions for leading public opinion that were found to bolster his leadership, including talking about the issue on consecutive days and making the issue a core agenda item through State of the Union promises. On the latter point, in his 1995 State of the Union Address, the president outlined several budget themes that would set the stage for the debate in late 1995 and early 1996. He remarked from the well of the House chamber, "But I think we should all remember, and almost all of us would agree, that government still has important responsibilities. Our young people—we should think of this when we cut—our young people hold our future in their hands. We still owe a debt to our veterans. And our senior citizens have made us what we are. Now, my budget cuts a lot. But it protects education, veterans, Social Security, and Medicare, and I hope you will do the same thing. You should, and I hope you will."[105] Similarly, later-serving presidents did much better than their predecessors at leading public opinion when the issue involved a president's core legislative or political priority in the State of the Union. Part of this is explained by a president's greater willingness to use the bully pulpit to lead public opinion and part is due to the availability of polling data that can help to shape political messages, both of which the reelection-oriented Clinton White House possessed.

Conclusion

The three case studies in this chapter have given us additional perspective on the ways in which certain predicted political conditions assist presidential leadership of public opinion. The explication of these brief case studies advances the broad argument that leadership is provisional and highly subject to the specific political environment presidents face. Although these particular cases have been studied before (and will no doubt be studied again), the value added from this perspective is that we are able to see with more clarity the factors that helped or hindered presidential leadership in these instances. Read with the criteria from chapter 4, these case studies also help to illuminate and contextualize the broad arguments about presidential leadership of public opinion as a struggle to get the White House's messages heard through a dense fog of competing messages. The findings here largely reinforce the aggregate statistical findings from chapter 4.

Indeed, of the factors studied in these cases, perhaps the most important is the strategy employed to communicate with the public. The presidents studied here were all popular at the time of their leadership attempts, a condition that enhanced the barnstorming communications strategy. Presidents Nixon, Reagan, and Clinton each used the bully pulpit to their advantage with these strategies by traveling around the nation and taking their case directly to the public. Part of this strategy is continually pushing the White House's issues in public (where the president mentions the issue for at least two consecutive days). Each of the three presidents engaged this strategy with success. Each president described here also went public on television in these instances to make his case to the public, a tactic that often provides for presidential success in leading public opinion. Finally, each president made these issues the central part of his agenda for the time in which he was trying to lead public opinion (especially Clinton using his State of the Union message), and this assisted the president in convincing the public (and Congress) to support his agenda.

These case studies also suggest that presidents do have the ability to facilitate success in Congress using the bully pulpit. Presidents Nixon, Reagan, and Clinton each used the power of the pulpit to alter congressional opposition, diffuse congressional opposition, or create congressional acquiescence. In fact, as noted in chapter 1, presidents often find success in leading public opinion on matters of economic policy because they are able to create more positive coverage with their rhetoric.[106] This communications prowess combined with the president's ability to lead public opinion to support his economic-based policies reveals a presidency that has the capacity to alter the political environment in their favor. Of course, these circumstances are limited to cases where conditions allowed the presidents to more directly communicate their messages to the public. Such times were when economic conditions were improving, when direct appeal was possible, when the public became better informed about the policies, and when presidents were popular.

CHAPTER 6

Unsuccessful Leadership in Domestic Policy

In the previous chapter, I outlined three case studies of successful leadership of public opinion. These cases helped advance our understanding of when presidents can lead public opinion, the conditions that enhance presidential leadership, and how these moments interact with one another in real political contexts. In this chapter I examine three cases where presidents are unable to lead public opinion, due to the absence of characteristics that were argued would enhance leadership or the presence of conditions that were argued would not enhance leadership. This is a more familiar story for scholars of presidential leadership—one of presidential failure to lead public opinion in critical political moments. This inquiry is as effective and important as determining the conditions of success because it helps to qualify impressions of how presidential leadership fails so the analysis can be more precise in pinpointing the contextual factors that contribute to the lack of opinion movement.

Therefore, to explore more directly when and how presidents fail at leading public opinion, I identify three instances where presidents were *unsuccessful,* in part because the favorable political conditions discussed in chapter 4 are not met or the unfavorable conditions in chapter 4 are met. Similarly, the degree of congruence with the theoretical expectations from chapter 2 is explored to determine whether or not these expectations hold. First, I analyze President Kennedy's inability to get the public and Congress to accept his proposals for funding the Medicare program from Social Security. Second, I investigate President Ford's lack of success in leading the public on his proposals for economic reform (specifically his tax surcharge policy and "Whip Inflation Now" campaign). In the third case study I explore the Reagan administration's inept handling of their early proposals to reprioritize funds from Social Security in 1981.

Kennedy's Medicare Proposal

One of the first and most potent examples of President John F. Kennedy's "New Frontier" agenda was the expansion of health-care coverage to older Americans. In 1960, increasing medical care for the aged (Medicare) was a major campaign promise of the Kennedy campaign, when, according to chief aide and White House speechwriter Theodore "Ted" Sorensen, the president "pushed this bill hard in the campaign."[1] Passing Medicare legislation would not be easy, in part because the president would have to rely on a fragile political coalition in the Democratic Party and convince the public that paying for Medicare would not be a burdensome tax. The president himself pointed to Medicare as one of the few issues that "still roused powerful feelings among the general public."[2] Leading the public to endorse the White House's policy for the government's funding of Medicare would prove to be a tough challenge—one too difficult even for the "prince of Camelot."

Legislation to initiate the Medicare program was proposed in February of 1961, one of the first pieces of legislation the Kennedy administration sent to Congress. The Kennedy proposal "would have levied an additional 0.25 percent increase in Social Security payroll taxes to pay hospital and nursing bills of persons eligible for Social Security old-age benefits."[3] The plan would also provide for 90 days of hospital care and 180 days of nursing home care to more than 17 million elderly Americans.[4] In his letter to Congress introducing the legislation, the president argued:

> In our Social Security and Railroad Retirement systems we have the instruments which can spread the cost of health services in old age over the working years—effectively, and in a manner consistent with the dignity of the individual. By using these proved systems to provide health insurance protection, it will be possible for our older people to get the vital hospital services they need without exhausting their resources or turning to public assistance. The self-supporting insurance method of financing the cost of such health services is certainly to be preferred to an expansion of public assistance, and should reduce the number of those needing medical care under the public assistance program.

Anticipating opposition, the president concluded by noting, "This program is not a program of socialized medicine. It is a program of prepayment of health costs with absolute freedom of choice guaranteed. Every person will choose his own doctor and hospital."[5] The president was trying to make Medicare the signature issue of his administration and was attempting to balance the needs of a core Democratic constituency (the elderly) in a fragile economy.

At that time, several obstacles stood in the way of public acceptance of the plan. First, although the president argued the program was not "socialized medicine," the American Medical Association (AMA) contended that the program would implement unnecessary and burdensome government control over an area traditionally freely open to public choice. In the summer of 1962, before the debate began in Congress, the president "ridiculed the attacks of the American Medical Association as 'incomprehensible' and met with a group of leading physicians supporting his position."[6] Second, the public was growing more concerned about using federal tax dollars to fund social welfare programs. In October of 1961, 48% of the public responded that the government is "spending too much tax money for welfare programs" or "about right" compared to 35% who responded "not enough."[7] The administration, then, had to deal with widening opposition and hardening public preferences.

However, despite public opposition to social welfare spending and organized interest groups arguing against Medicare, polling done at the sixty-day mark for the administration by pollster Louis Harris (continuing his work from the 1960 election and before he went into private polling work) suggested that the public was primed for accepting expanded medical care for the elderly provided that the president utilize the "bully pulpit" effectively. Harris argued that "medical care for the aged is a veritable skyrocket among issues with the electorate. We were able to observe throughout the 1960 elections. As soon as public discussion of the issue warms, then public response is immediate and overwhelming. It is a classic case of an issue which, if handled quietly, will die aborning in the legislative chambers. But if made a dramatic and essentially human and economic issue, it will in short order overpower the special interest groups working on Capitol Hill." Harris's specific tactical recommendation was that "we would recommend that this issue be one that the president takes directly to the people" and "the fundamental way in which the president can obtain passage of his medical care legislation is to take a human, caring case to the people directly."[8]

However, the White House did not follow Harris's advice. Given that the president was highly popular at the time legislation was introduced (averaging in the mid- to upper seventies in the spring and summer of 1962), the president could have used two strategies: "barnstorming" the nation with his message and discussing the issue for consecutive days in public (both positive harbingers of leadership).[9] Yet, during no two consecutive days in 1961 (the year the White House proposed the legislation) and during no two consecutive days in 1962 (until after Congress rejected the proposals in July) did the president speak of the issue of medical funding for the aged.[10] Generally, the president was reluctant to discuss the issue publicly and only did so on a few occasions.[11] This functionally negated a successful barnstorm possibility. Ted Sorensen also noted in his biography of Kennedy that the president had forgotten that "convincing the skeptical TV viewer at home" was more difficult than rallying those already on his side.[12] Indeed, a third of the nation, when asked in polls after Congress rejected the Kennedy proposal, responded that they had "very little" information about the Medicare proposals.[13]

The president only briefly mentioned the issue in his 1961 State of the Union speech by noting, "But in matters of health, no piece of unfinished business is more important or more urgent than the enactment under the social security system of health insurance for the aged. For our older citizens have longer and more frequent illnesses, higher hospital and medical bills and too little income to pay them. Private health insurance helps very few—for its cost is high and its coverage limited. Public welfare cannot help those too proud to seek relief but hard-pressed to pay their own bills. Nor can their children or grandchildren always sacrifice their own health budgets to meet this constant drain."[14] This policy mention (lost in a bevy of other proposals) was not significant enough to persuade the public either to understand or accept the policy or to lean on Congress to pursue the policy. To this end, the White House let Medicare slip as its top priority.

In chapter 4, it was found that television is an effective medium in leading public opinion. President Kennedy, in the only other appearance on television where he mentioned the Medicare plan besides the State of the Union address, attempted to personalize the issue consistent with what Harris advised him to do in 1960. Giglio observed that in order "to dramatize and increase public pressure, Kennedy addressed a Madison Square Garden [May 20, 1962] throng of senior citizens—before a national TV audience" and that "he spoke passionately of the need for such assistance and condemned the AMA for its opposition, but to no avail."[15] At Madison Square Garden, he argued,

> He [a hypothetical citizen] owns his house. He has twenty-five hundred or three thousand dollars in the bank. And then his wife gets sick—and we're all going to be in a hospital, 9 out of 10 of us, before we finally pass away, and particularly when we're over 65—now she is sick, not just for a week but for a long time. First goes the twenty-five hundred dollars—that's gone. Next he mortgages his house, even though he may have some difficulty making the payments out of his social security. Then he goes to his children, who themselves are heavily burdened because they're paying for their houses and they are paying for their sicknesses, and they want to educate their children. Then their savings begin to go. This is not a rare case.[16]

The personal family drama described by the president was designed to appeal to a constituency that had experienced such pain with a viable remedy. But these remarks to groups of seniors (even on television) were less effective at moving public opinion than other strategies would have been. Ted Sorensen similarly suggested, "He already had support from senior citizens; he needed more support from the home viewers, and that speech did not induce it."[17] Unfortunately for the White House, the president's approach was too narrowly pitched to effectively lead mass opinion.

Without traction in the public, the Senate tabled the legislation by a vote of fifty-two to forty-eight. As soon as the measure was defeated in Congress, the president took to the airwaves to declare that this "most serious defeat for every American family" would be a major issue in the 1962 campaign.[18] By then, however, it was too late to lead public opinion or to get Congress to reconsider the proposal. In a memorandum in the aftermath of Congress not passing the Kennedy administration's Medicare legislation, Harris noted, "In my judgment, they [the causes of lack of leadership] are two-fold: one substantive and one procedural" and he reasoned, "The procedural concerns what you communicate."[19] He found that, although the leadership on foreign policy matters was better than hoped, "There has been no similar clarity of communication on the domestic economy. The long succession of economic messages you have sent up to the Hill have been essentially accompanied by messages for Congressional ears only. Fundamentally you have played the Congress 'inside' in the hope of obtaining cooperation and actual legislation passed. The general public knows your style, but not the substance of your domestic economic program. You made more dent as a Senator on unemployment insurance than you have as President with any single domestic economic program." Harris concluded by arguing, "Your fundamental constituency is the people. And when you lay it on the line to them this is that we need to move the country ahead, they will believe you and respond to it. However, Mr. President, I must remind you of a basic fact of communications you taught me in 1960: saying it once in a message or a speech, or a news conference is not enough; you must say it over and over again until you can't bear to hear yourself say it again."[20] Harris stressed to the president that the public is "aching for your leadership," and with the people on the administration's side, "I dare say you will have found the ultimate weapon."

Not surprisingly, the president did not move public opinion to accept his Medicare plan. Dallek notes that, despite President Kennedy's passionate appeals, it was "insufficient to identify a formula that would disarm conservative opponents and satisfy a majority of liberal advocates."[21] In July 1962 pollster Harris found that "much more serious is the steady downward drift in public support for your programs. We now find states where a majority oppose Medicare, contrasted to 4 to 1 support in March."[22] Similarly, the results from public polls taken both before and after the president's public discussion of the issue also reveal no movement toward the president's position on the necessity of including old-age insurance in Social Security. Figure 6.1 charts poll questions asking the public whether they favored "meeting hospital costs for older persons" by increasing Social Security taxes (the administration's plan) and covering the population with the extra revenue or voluntarily letting the elderly buy some form of private insurance. The data show a downward trend in the percentage of the public willing to endorse the Kennedy proposal. In March of 1962, 55% of the public supported the Kennedy plan, but by June this number had slipped to 48%, then to 44% in late July (and stayed steady at 44% in late August). And, also limiting the president's persuasive power, the percentages of the public who registered "don't know" rose, whereas for successful leadership, the White House would have wanted that percentage to decline, if the result were consistent with the findings in chapter 4. The implication is that the public became less certain about the viability of the Kennedy plan and the president was less able to convince them.

What caused this failure of leadership? Several political conditions limited the president's ability to lead public opinion. It seems clear from

Declining Support for Medicare Financed through Social Security

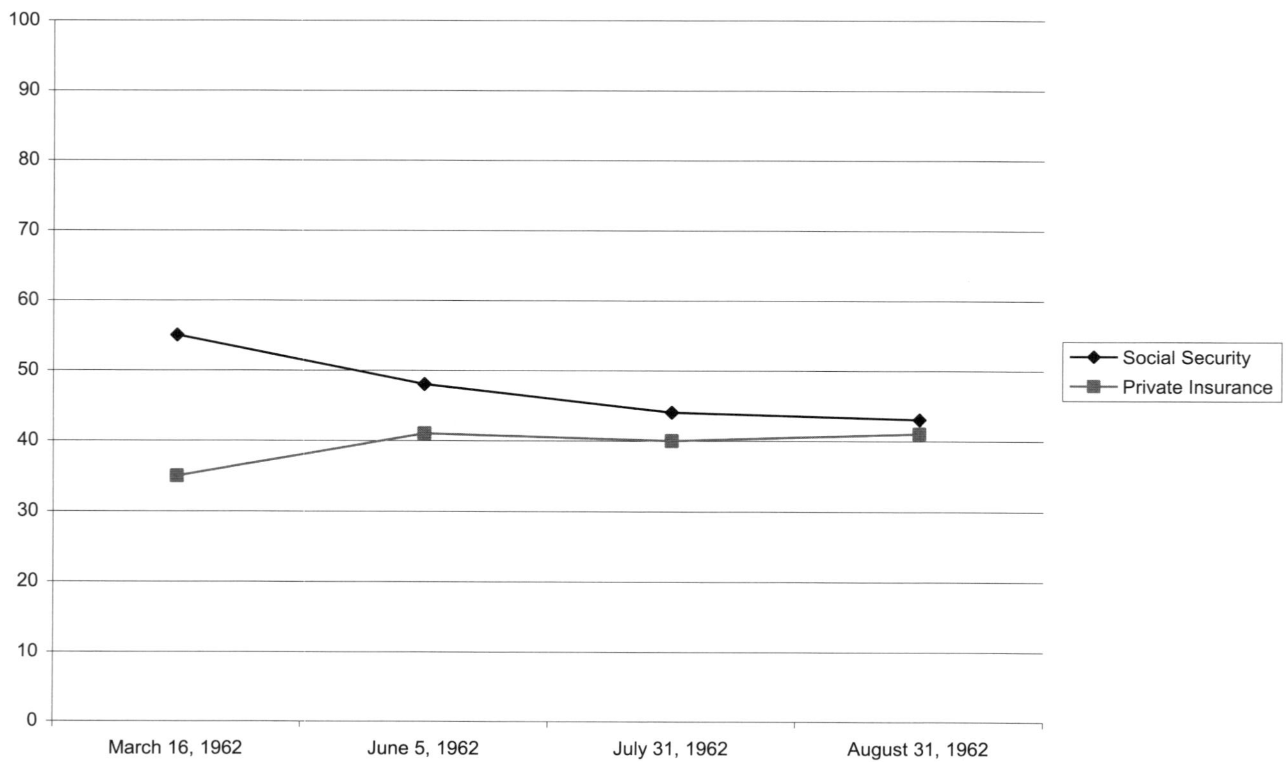

the communications critique from Harris that the White House did not execute its public relations strategy well, a critical component to leading public opinion. Also, the president, responding to "demands" from the *New York Times* to take his case to the public, effectively filtered much of his public discussion of the issue through the media. But, after recommending he take his case to the public on Medicare, the *New York Times* condemned the tactics he used, effectively scolding the administration and taking the momentum out of his public pitch.[23] This comports with the conditional leadership theory presented in chapter 2 that argued such filtered messages impede successful leadership efforts.

Another reason the president found little success in leading public opinion was that, at the time he was discussing his Medicare plan, several other issues crowded the political agenda. The effect of these other issues seems to substantiate the theorized impact of countervailing messages. The president was concurrently pursuing several issues in Congress (and in the public agenda) at the same time—too many to adequately focus on one with great attention. Specifically, in one of the few times where the president publicly mentioned his Medicare plan (coincidentally, in a

Fig. 6.1. (opposite). Declining support for Medicare financed through Social Security. The March and June Gallup polls asked, "Two different plans are being discussed in Washington for meeting hospital costs for older persons: One plan would let each individual decide whether to join Blue Cross or buy some form of voluntary health insurance. The other plan would cover persons on Social Security and would be paid by increasing the Social Security tax deducted from paychecks. Which of these two plans would you prefer?" In the March poll 10% responded "don't know" and in the June poll 11% responded "don't know." In July a Gallup poll (from the same organization but with slightly different wording) asked, "Which of these two different proposals do you prefer for meeting hospital costs for older persons: One proposal—the Medicare plan—would cover persons on Social Security and would be paid by increasing the Social Security tax deducted from everyone's paychecks. The other proposal would leave it up to each individual to decide whether to join Blue Cross or buy some other form of voluntary hospital insurance. Which of these two proposals would you prefer?" In this poll, 15% responded "don't know." In August, the Opinion Research Corporation poll asked a similar but not the same question: "(Now, I'd like your opinion on some of the things the [Kennedy] Administration may have to deal with.) . . . Which do you favor on medical insurance for older people—changing the government Social Security program to cover this, or expanding voluntary medical insurance plans to cover this?" Seventeen percent responded "don't know."

press conference, which can negatively affect leadership), the president listed *several* issues he was working on:

> Well, we are trying to do two or three things in the domestic program. We are trying to protect and provide jobs for people—that is, I think, a matter of concern to all Americans. We are committed to that goal, and the programs which we have sent up to the Hill have that object in mind. We are also trying to strengthen our educational system, which needs to be strengthened over the long period in which we are going to be tested. We are trying to provide for more orderly and effective programs of medical care for the elderly. Now, these programs, in my opinion, are in the public interest, and they are being assessed in that regard.[24]

The Kennedy administration, in pushing for so many proposals at once, may have jeopardized them all. Giglio notes that the administration did not push the Medicare issue with key House members "so as not to jeopardize other pending legislation," a move that sealed the Medicare legislation's fate.[25]

Another reason that the White House had trouble leading the public on the matter was the presence of significant opposition from several groups, chiefly the American Medical Association. The conditional theory in chapter 2 indicated that the presence of countervailing agents damages the president's ability to lead public opinion. The AMA's lobbying was "determined and expensive" in the Senate, the key point of showdown between the president and Congress.[26] Harris, in his 1960 strategy memorandum, outlined a strategy to combat the AMA's influence: "The President can make the American Medical Association—as a lobbyist group—the target, with his asking the people to help him solicit the support of Congress as the ultimate source of legislative initiative." He concluded, "One should appeal to the people to rise up against the special interest groups which are trying to hoodwink Congress in the absence of the public being on the job."[27] However, this communications effort was not undertaken. Interestingly, a similar pattern of leadership defeat occurred for President Clinton in his efforts to pass universal health-care coverage in 1993.[28]

Similarly, the nature of the ideological split in Congress meant too many critical voices to challenge the president's message. The Democratic Party, which prominently included conservative members, functioned similarly to divided government for the White House's political goals. Ted Sorensen argued that defections of key southern Democratic votes on the passage of legislation "made every vote a cliff-hanger" and that the president could not afford to antagonize the Congress too much.[29] Giglio remarked, "Chairman Wilbur Mills (D-Ark.), a long-time opponent of health benefits tied to Social Security, joined with other southern Democrats and Republicans to curb action [to pass Medicare]."[30] The problem with the Medicare bill was not the only defeat for the administration in Congress in 1962—the school funding legislation also fell victim to political failure during this same period.[31] A memorandum from pollster Harris argued that Congress has "posed in the role of a break, a conservative force, that wants less government in our lives."[32]

Ford Attempts to "Whip Inflation Now"

When President Nixon left office, he bequeathed a struggling economy to the incoming Ford administration. Rising inflation, growing unemployment, quadrupling oil prices, skyrocketing food prices, a plummeting Dow Jones, and slowing business growth all contributed to a gloomy economic outlook for the Ford White House.[33] Indeed, the Ford White House conceded that the nation was facing a recession that several economists argued was the "deepest recession in the American economy since the Depression of the 1930s."[34] During this time, the White House could do no right and had significant trouble mustering the support of the public or Congress. This case study focuses on President Ford's attempts to get the economy back on track—leadership that would prove largely unsuccessful in convincing the public to support the new administration's economic reforms.

President Ford unveiled his economic plan in a joint session of Congress on October 8, 1974, wearing a "W.I.N." button standing for "Whip Inflation Now." President Ford prefaced his specific policy remarks by stating, "My conclusions are very simply stated. There is only one point on which all advisers have agreed: We must whip inflation right now. None of the remedies proposed, great or small, compulsory or voluntary, stands a chance unless they are combined in a considered package, in a concerted effort, in a grand design."[35] Specifically, President Ford wanted Congress to pass a temporary 5% income tax surcharge on corporate and upper-level individual incomes, make cuts of $4.4 billion in federal spending, and limit overall federal spending to below $300 billion.[36] The president also announced the creation of a volunteer organization committed to keeping prices down.

After the president's address, the media and Congress were underwhelmed by his proposals. There was widespread opposition to several of Ford's economic proposals in both parties in Congress, especially on the tax surcharge. Mike Mansfield, Democrat from Montana and the Senate majority leader, rejected the Ford program as one that "bears too close a resemblance to the fiscal and monetary policies of the previous administration."[37] The media was also largely negative on the plan—both the *Wall Street Journal* and the *New York Times* interviewed business leaders who voiced doubts that the Ford program would be strong enough to make a "real impact on inflation."[38] In his autobiography, President Ford challenged the press's assertion that the speech was "weak, flaccid and disappointing" by arguing that the decision to argue for tax increases a month before the elections in 1974 was bold.[39] Challenging Congress and the media, however, was not enough to convince the public that his programs were the right option. The presence of these constraining agents limited the reach of the president's message and made it difficult to lead public opinion.

In the days following the president's announcement, Ford pollster Robert "Bob" Teeter articulated in his report "President Ford's Anti-Inflation Program: The Public Reaction" that "as a single issue that overshadows all others in the minds of the American public, concern about increasing prices now rivals anguish expressed by the electorate over the Vietnam War in the late 1960s. Therefore, it is not surprising that almost seven out of every ten registered voters said they had heard of or read about President Gerald Ford's anti-inflation program shortly after it was delivered to the nation on television."[40] And, given that President Ford had identified inflation as "domestic enemy number one," the public's desire to see it reduced was paramount. Despite the popular marks the program received, Bob Teeter was convinced that on paper the support was soft. He lamented, "The free-response comments polarized equally pro and con." In addition, he concluded, "While the approval rating seems to be very solid, it is fragile."[41]

After making his announcement in prime time, the president hit the road to sell the program. He visited Pennsylvania, Michigan, Missouri, South Dakota, Indiana, South Carolina, and Kentucky in the two weeks that followed. Unfortunately, this tactic only works quickly for popular presidents. However, a president does not necessarily have to be popular to have the barnstorm tactic succeed—the findings from chapter 4 indicated that, with enough time (three months), the barnstorm strategy begins to pay off. Had President Ford continued this practice or had he been more popular, his strategy may have worked better. However, it seemed that the president had little choice since the timing of his rise to the Oval Office coincided with the congressional midterm elections in 1974. Also, the president unwisely defended his proposals at two major points after his initial announcement: at a press conference on October 9 and in a prime-time address to the nation on October 16.[42] Televised addresses are found to be successful for presidential leadership, but other factors such as unpopularity, a sour economy, trepidation from the media, and an uncertain public were enough to outweigh any positive effects of a nationally televised address.

The president's program, while initially popular, was found to not imbue the public with confidence in the administration to stop the advance of inflation. Bob Teeter's polling indicated, "While the general rating is positive the electorate's confidence that the program will stop inflation does not wax too strongly." The results indicated that only 6% of the public were "very confident" that the president's plan would stop inflation, with 48% "somewhat confident" and 46% "not confident."[43] Bob Teeter argued that this number is "extremely fragile" and "it would seem that people are greatly sensitized and to some extent suffering from the consequences of ever-increasing prices. They want relief; they hope for relief. Hence they are willing to nod their head in approval when confronted with the Presidential package."[44]

The public was right. The economy by late 1974 and early 1975 was in recession and bordering on stagflation. Reflecting these joint problems, by the time of his 1975 State of the Union message, Ford had abandoned the tax surcharge he had argued for in his October 8 address (a policy that hurt him in the 1974 elections), and the perception grew that his economic plan had no focus.[45] An uncertain public creates fewer opportunities to lead since the public is not committed to a policy and are unlikely to change their minds pursuant to presidential persuasion.

Overall, the president was unable to move public opinion to support his economic plan. A few trends stand out. First, five months after the president unveiled his economic program (in October 1974), public opinion was split on the disposition of President Ford's economic program. On one point, Teeter claimed, "Wage and price controls, while slightly favored, are given this support with considerably less enthusiasm now than in the months just preceding the initiation of Nixon's attempt to cope with rising prices and wages through his Phases I–IV programs." Second, the percentage of those agreeing that the president had done an "excellent" or "good" job in "keeping inflation under control" declined from 18% in December 1974 to 14% in February 1975 to 13% in March 1975.[46] Third, on the specific policies outlined by the president, the percentage of those opposing the 5% surcharge increased from 52% in early December 1974 to 62% in late December 1974.[47]

Polling data from March of 1975, the next major poll taken by Bob Teeter six months after the president's announcement, found that the public's impressions of the Ford economic policy had not changed at all, again indicating lack of leadership. A major component of the program was reducing federal spending, and Teeter noted that "the public does not view federal spending as an economic panacea: a full 67% said they favored placing a lid on all federal spending except for energy programs. This level of support has not changed since February."[48] In fact, the data actually suggested that the percentage of the public supporting the policy had declined somewhat (from 68% supporting in February).[49] And, from February to March of 1975, the percentage registering "no opinion" increased from 7% to 9%. The president was, however, making gains with his core groups. Table 6.1 lists the "ratios" of support to opposition created by Bob Teeter. These reveal that while the mass public in March was not any more supportive of the policies of the Ford administration than in February, the Republicans, Ticket Splitters, Men, and Rural (among others) were more likely to support the president's plans.

Part of the problem of leadership for President Ford was that the economic problems were too widespread (including both inflation and unemployment) and the public demanded the administration's focus on both problems, which it could not do. Polling from March of 1975 indicated a ten-point dip in the public listing inflation as the "most important problem" and a two-point increase in those claiming unemployment was the "most important problem."[50] Bob Teeter found that "those with higher incomes are much more worried about inflation than the lower income recipient" along with those over age sixty-five and Republicans. Democrats were more "wary of the dangers of unemployment than inflation."[51] Other data suggested the same phenomenon. In analyzing advance Gallup poll results in August of 1975, Fred Slight wrote to Jerry Jones (both special assistants to the president) that the percentage of the public responding that inflation was the most important problem of the

TABLE 6.1

Ratios of Ford Economic Program Supporters to Nonsupporters

	February		March	
	Positive ratio	Negative ratio	Positive ratio	Negative ratio
Voter behavior				
Hardcore Republican	+5.0		+6.0	
Ticket splitter	+1.4		+2.3	
Hardcore Democrat		−0.5		−0.9
Socioeconomic status				
Affulent class	+2.4			
Upper middle class	+1.5			
Middle class	+1.3			
Lower working class	+1.1			
Poverty household		−0.7		
Sex				
Men	+1.3		+1.7	
Women	+1.1		+1.7	
Residence				
Suburban	+1.4		+1.5	
Urban	+1.1		+1.8	
Rural	+1.1		+2.0	
Geopolitical Region				
Midwest	+1.4		+1.8	
South	+1.3		+2.1	
Northeast	+1.2		+1.4	
West		−0.9	+1.3	

Note: Table reproduced from Gerald Ford Presidential Library, Robert Hartmann Files, Study of National Issues, "National Impact Study #2, March 1975," Box 32, p. 51. An explanatory note at the bottom of the original table reads: "For example, in February 50% of the hardcore Republicans rated Ford's energy program as excellent, very good, or good, and 10% rated it poor, hence the ratio of 50/10 or +5.0."

day declined from 77% in August of 1974 to 60% in February and March of 1975 to 47% in July of 1975. Those claiming unemployment was the most important issue increased slightly over this period.[52]

This change in public opinion was not necessarily in the White House's control. When the president took office in August of 1974, inflation was the most important problem and the administration offered proposals in that direction. However, a year later, the public began to focus more on unemployment as the most important problem. Bob Teeter concluded in his analysis of an early 1975 survey by noting, "Crises, be they economic or military, seldom place U.S. national leaders in favorable stead with the public. Viewed through their perspective, considerable concern now focuses on the economic twin reapers of unemployment and inflation." According to Teeter, "While inflation continues to be the dominant issue of concern, more and more Americans are now distracted by the specter of unemployment."[53] The news was bad for the Ford White House here, too. When people were asked about their feelings toward Ford's unemployment policies, only 22% of the spontaneous answers were positive, 26% were neutral, and 52% were specifically negative. As shown by Table 6.2, which summarizes the top responses, the most frequently cited concern was the lack of help for unemployment. These paradoxical results underscore that it is difficult to lead when too many issues are on the agenda, especially combined with an uncertain public.

The president was not popular when the White House took its plan to the public in late 1974, although he was popular on his ascendancy to the White House (71% on August 16, 1974). By early 1975, Bob Teeter argued that "when a President's job approval rating falls below 50% 'approval' he is considered by some observers of public attitudes as being in trouble." The president's approval rating was at 48% at the time, suggesting the president's bargaining position was less potent than before.[54] The president's popularity was also endemic of other political problems. Observers remarked, "A new Gallup poll found that his popularity had waned to an all-time low of 42 per cent—down 29 points since he took office. Fully 158 bills left by the outgoing 93rd Congress lay on his desk. He had to contend with allegations of illegal domestic spying on Americans by the CIA [from the Church Committee in the Senate]—and Ford's advisers on energy and the economy, whom he had summoned to help prepare the programs he will announce in his mid-January State of the Union speech, brought only chilling news."[55]

TABLE 6.2
Priority Summary of Feelings Toward Ford Economic Plan

Positive responses		Neutral responses		Negative responses	
1. Ford is working hard	8%	1. No opinion	13%	1. Unemployed need more help	7%
2. Generally positive	8%	2. Needs cooperative Congress	6%	2. Generally anti-Ford	6%
3. Tax rebate	2%	3. Generally neutral	5%	3. Doesn't help the poor	6%
4. Would reduce unemployment	2%	4. Too soon to know	2%	4. Generally negative	6%
5. Other positive miscellaneous	2%			5. Program not extensive enough	6%
				6. Other negative miscellaneous	21%
Totals:	22%		26%		52%

Note: Table reproduced from Gerald Ford Presidential Library, Robert Hartmann Files, DMI, "The Public Perceptions of Economic Issues," February 1975, Box 30, p. 39.

Timing was also not on the president's side. Stu Spencer (deputy chair of the president's reelection committee) and Bob Teeter wrote with concerns about the president's image to Dick Cheney (chief of staff): "Given the relatively short period of time we have to set perceptions, it would be useful if the theme of the president's program were given a name soon."[56] Unfortunately for the White House, several of the strategies they considered utilizing to lead public opinion take longer to work. For instance, in the same strategy memorandum from Spencer and Teeter, they argue that a speech to a joint session of Congress should *not* be the venue for the unveiling of the president's theme speech and that "a youthful audience somewhere outside of Washington would probably be best."[57] The barnstorming strategy described by the president's consultants takes more than three months to develop, an amount of time that the White House did not have. A major address to the public, like the rejected speech to a joint session of Congress, may have helped to lead public opinion. In addition, although the issue was foremost in the public's mind, the president's policy campaign was rushed to the media,[58] and, because it was the top issue to the public, was challenged by many competing voices.

Indeed, the negative voices within Congress significantly hurt the president's chances to lead public opinion. Also, President Ford was seriously hurt by the significant interbranch conflict that he was shackled with during his time in office. Part of the problem was the manner in which the president became president. Continuing their analysis, Spencer and Teeter argued that the president "needs to appear more presidential. While his warm friendly manner has served him well, he does not have any of the aura of being president. Also, appearing more presidential should help to improve his perception as being knowledgeable and competent."[59] Congress also was generally resistant to a tax hike, which many new members of Congress (the "Watergate babies") opposed as being "too little, too late and too uncaring to boot."[60] In addition, the administration's polling found that, over the time the president unveiled his economic program, *Congress,* not the president, was viewed as the agent most likely to make the situation better. In an early 1975 report, Teeter noted that, when asked the question, "'Who can solve the problem that you yourself are most concerned about,' twice as many Americans look toward government and Congress action generally as the number who cite the President as the action agent."[61]

Reagan "Reforms" Social Security

President Reagan made promises during his 1980 campaign not to cut Social Security, a promise he came close to breaking in his first term in office.[62] The financial situation the administration found themselves in during the creation of the first two federal budgets revealed the need for additional revenue, and several in the Reagan administration were interested in harnessing the excess funds from Social Security.[63] The promise of solving the nation's fiscal problems and meeting the White House's economic goals by reengineering Social Security proved difficult to pass up. It would, however, prove politically difficult. Social Security has long been called the "third rail" in American politics: touch it and face political demise. The president well understood this, and in the closing days of the 1980 campaign, he pledged to a group of several thousand senior citizens attending Super Senior Sunday in Philadelphia, "Now I know that lately you've been hearing what others have to say about my views on that crucial issue. I thought you'd like to hear them from me. Let me repeat, I will support and defend the integrity of the Social Security system, the foundation of the economic life of millions of Americans. That system will be strong and reliable and protected under a Reagan administration."[64] Cutting Social Security was one of the least popular options in regaining fiscal certainty. Internal White House polling found that a balanced budget was a priority and was popular, but "reducing Social Security" was the "least acceptable proposal presented" and the "plan fails to get a majority in any [demographic] category."[65]

The proposal endorsed by the Reagan administration (specifically by budget hawk and Office of Management and Budget director David Stockman) was a proposal that would cut the benefits of recipients of Social Security if they retired before the age of 65. Specifically, the program would reduce "the benefit levels of those who retire after 1981 at the age of 62, restricting disability benefits and deferring a cost-of-living increase by three months next year [1982] and reducing the base used to determine future retirement benefits. Those who retire at 62 would receive 55 percent of the benefit they would have got at 65, rather than 80 percent, as they would under current law."[66] Although not a "cut" in the truest sense, the Reagan Social Security proposal took away benefits retirees were counting on (especially those who had planned to retire before learning about the program).[67]

At the heart of its inability to lead public opinion was the White House's failure to do enough to sell its proposals to the public after the plan was formulated. Indeed, the conditional theory from chapter 2 suggested that it is difficult to lead if presidents cannot or do not convey their message to the public. From January until May, when Congress unanimously voted his proposal down, the president only addressed the public once on the issue of Social Security and not at all on his proposals to reform Social Security. At a prime-time address primarily devoted to his economic policy, the president only inattentively remarked, "Now, I know that exaggerated and inaccurate stories about these cuts have disturbed many people, particularly those dependent on grant and benefit programs for their basic needs. Some of you have heard from constituents, I know, afraid that social security checks, for example, were going to be taken away from them. Well, I regret the fear that these unfounded stories have caused, and I welcome this opportunity to set things straight."[68]

He concluded that "the full retirement benefits of the more than 31 million social security recipients will be continued, along with an annual cost-of-living increase."[69] This would be a promise broken since the proposal from the White House would technically penalize early retirees by cutting the full benefits for some citizens. The president may not have wanted to publicize support for a policy that was not anticipated to be well received by the public, a tactic consistent with findings suggesting that presidents will not make a public appeal when their policy is not in accord with the public or when their position is unpopular relative to Congress.[70] Still, Senator Charles Grassley (Republican from Iowa) urged, "President Reagan should get out on television and explain it [the plan] to the public."[71]

But the White House, hoping to keep the policy change under the radar, did not speak publicly about this proposal until it was too late. In fact, part of the reason the proposal did not gain any traction in leading public (or congressional) opinion was the absence of the president as champion of the proposal. The public proposal was left to White House aides James Baker and Dick Darmin (deputy secretary of the U.S. Treasury) and was "without a White House label."[72] Even the announcement of the proposal was relegated to cabinet-level status, where the announcement was announced "the next day by [Secretary Dick] Schweiker at Health and Human Services rather than the White House" and the "Social Security plan would henceforth be known as 'Dick Schweiker's plan.'"[73]

Without a public push to lead the public (or Congress) and on a particularly sensitive issue like Social Security, not surprisingly the president's proposals found little favor and continued to lose favor after the president introduced them. Figure 6.2 lists two different sets of polls taken over the life span of the Reagan administration's proposals: (1) approval of the president's Social Security plans broadly and (2) approval of the specific plans to reduce benefits for early retirees. The trends are both consistent: fewer percentages of the public supported the president's plan as time went on. For instance, the percentage of the public approving of all the president's proposals to reform Social Security declined from 33% to 26% from May (just before the Congress took up the matter) to July. Those responding "don't know" were unchanged at 18%. Similarly, the percentage of the public approving of the president's plan to reduce benefits for early retirees declined from 43% in May to 40% in June and 27% in September. Tellingly, a late May (a week after the proposal was made public) memorandum from Dick Wirthlin to Edwin Meese, James Baker, and Michael Deaver suggested, "Thus, in less than a week we surfaced what must be designated as the most unpopular position taken to date."[74] The percentage of the public responding "don't know" also dramatically jumped from 5% to 27%, suggesting extreme uncertainty about the plan.

This failed leadership on the Social Security plan revealed cracks in the armor of the "Teflon president." Pollster Dick Wirthlin noted that "unfortunately this particular issue reinforced some latent fears we know the electorate has carried about the president and more specifically about his economic program. Sixty-three percent now agree or agree strongly with the statement, 'Regardless of what the President says, we can't cut 49 billion dollars from the Federal Budget without hurting the old or the sick who depend on Government checks.' In April that number was 54%—an increase of 9%. This shift clearly triggered by the discussion about Social Security undoubtedly cast a shadow (hopefully a transient one) over the spending reduction elements of the President's programs."[75] Wirthin urged that "it will take the President—using his communications skills—to convince Americans that the changes yet to be proposed in the social security are in their best interest in the long run—not an easy task under the best of circumstances."[76] The White House did not, however, use the bully pulpit here as they had successfully in passing tax and budget reforms earlier in the year (see chapter 5).

Had the administration engaged in more forethought on the packaging or the communication of the issue, they still would have found that the issue was not popular and that the public was uncertain about the reform of the cornerstone program of the New Deal. In poll results examined after the issue had died in Congress, pollster Dick Wirthlin found opposition to "raising the Social Security payroll tax," "raising the age for full retirement benefits to 68," and "reducing the benefits for early retirement from 80% to 50% of full bonus." However, he found "mild acceptance" of "reducing the cost of living increases to a rate a few points lower than it is now" and "using other government funds including general income taxes to maintain the current fund."[77] Although not determinative, these findings suggest avenues for reform that the administration could have convinced the public to accept.

The White House also sought to determine where they stood with their core constituencies on the important issue of Social Security, especially after they found that their approach to the issue found no favor

President Reagan's Social Security Proposals

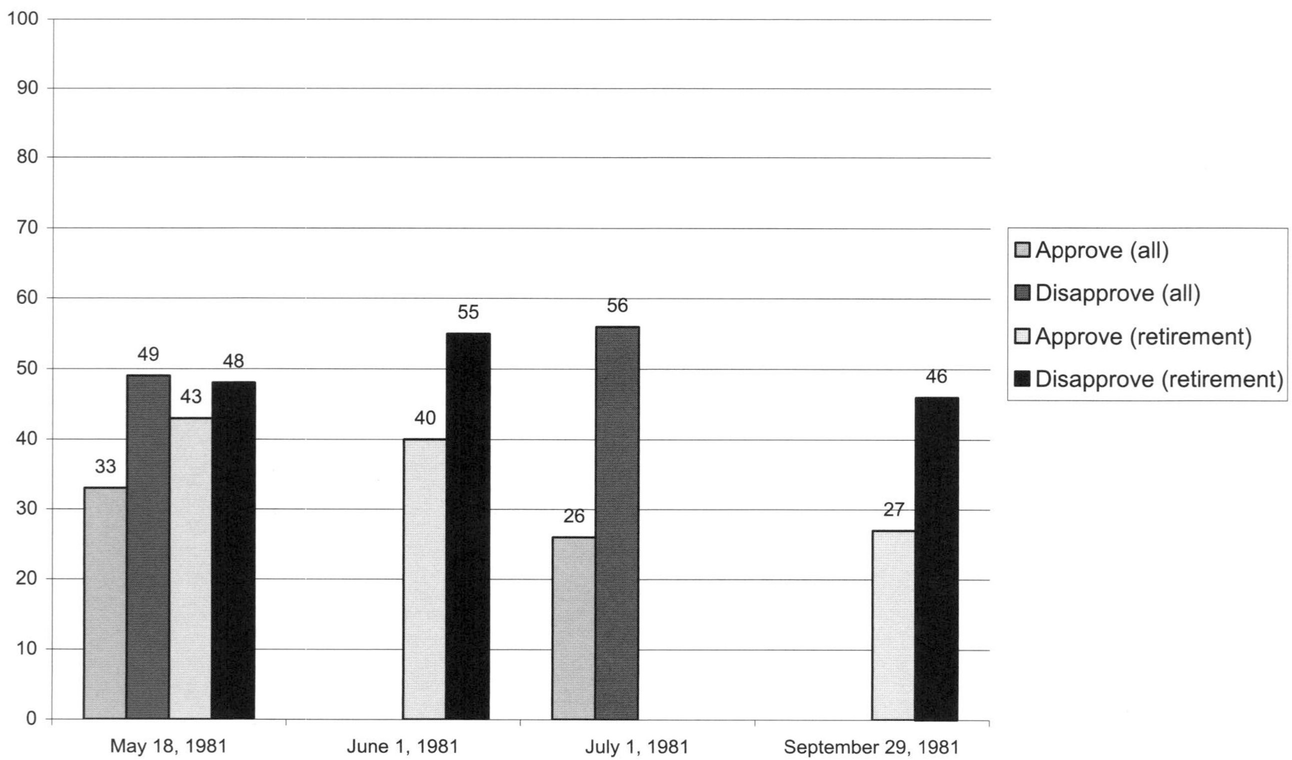

with the mass public. Poll results from July of 1981 (two months after the Congress voted their proposals down) revealed that "as to be expected, those already receiving Social Security benefits are less inclined to think that the system needs major changes: indeed, a check in the hand appears to be worth at least 15 percentage points, as retirees and those over 65 years of age disagree dramatically with the overall population on the need for Social Security reform." Wirthlin continued that "those in the working population who are currently contributing to a rapidly diminishing social security fund, are the ones who feel the most strongly about the need for reform" where 72% of those in the 25 to 44 age groups agreed for the need for "major reforms." In terms of party, Wirthlin reported that "support for reform exists across all levels of party affiliation, yet Democrats are more likely to ignore the need for reform than Republicans and Independents; to wit, 66% of the Republicans, 63% of the Independents and 60% of the Democrats agree with the statements calling for changes."[78] Thus, the president had not lost his core public, even if by pursuing this legislation he jeopardized the White House's ability to garner mass public support or a bipartisan solution.

Fig. 6.2. (opposite). President Reagan's Social Security proposals. Unfortunately, the polls are not the exact wording from each time period (in fact, no same worded polls on the issue were found). However, the polls are worded similarly enough and the potential responses phrased similarly. The May 14 poll was a Washington Post/*ABC News Polls that asked, "Generally speaking, do you approve or disapprove of the Reagan administration's plans to change the Social Security program?" The July 1981 poll was conducted by Cambridge Reports and asked, "Recently, the Reagan Administration asked Congress to reduce various Social Security benefits in order to improve the financial situation of the Social Security system. Based on what you've heard, do you favor or oppose President Reagan's proposals for Social Security?" The poll conducted May 18, 1981, by NBC News/Associated Press asked, "Another of the proposals (by the Reagan administration to save the Social Security system money) is to cut further the benefits people can receive from Social Security if they retire early, between ages 62 and 65. Do you favor or oppose this proposal, or don't you know enough to have an opinion?" The poll conducted July 1, 1981, by CBS News/*New York Times *asked, "Ronald Reagan has proposed that the Social Security benefits for people who retire early, that is, at age 62 instead of 65, be sharply reduced. Do you approve or disapprove of doing this?" The poll conducted September 29, 1981, by NBC News/Associated Press asked, "President Reagan has proposed cutting the benefits people receive from Social Security if they retire early, between ages 62 and 65. Do you favor or oppose this proposal?"*

Ultimately, the administration's halfhearted attempts to lead public opinion ended in the proposal not being passed by Congress. In fact, the Senate (controlled by the Republicans at the time) "went on record 96 to 0 against any proposal that would precipitously and unfairly penalize early retirees" or reduce benefits more than necessary "to achieve a financially sound system and the well-being of all retired Americans." Almost at the same time, House Democrats unanimously adopted a statement characterizing the administration's proposals as an "unconscionable breach of faith, especially with early retirees."[79] The Social Security program failure was "the major domestic policy misstep of the Reagan administration" and "an extraordinary political misjudgment" by the administration.[80] These critical views complicated the prior ability of the White House to get the public behind these policies and certainly limited the White House's ability to get its legislation passed.

Although several factors would have played positively for the president in leading public opinion, according to the findings from chapter 4, the White House either misplayed its hand or was disadvantaged by political circumstances that mitigated the positive effect of these factors. For later presidents, it was found that a "honeymoon" was a negative condition for leadership success. The Reagan administration's honeymoon period quickly began to wane after early budget skirmishes (described in the previous chapter) and demonstrated to the Democrats in Congress that they could assert themselves politically.[81] The president's mandate was short-lived and "for the first time since taking office, President Reagan and his main advisers have suffered a painful lesson in the political limits of the President's popularity and his mandate. A White House that boasted it was too proud to compromise was forced to initiate peace talks with Democratic Congressmen on the issue of cutting taxes, and, as Mr. Reagan flew to California last week, his aides were grudgingly admitting that their abrupt call for tightened Social Security benefits was, indeed, a mistake that marred an otherwise successful record in legislative politics."[82]

Congressional opposition resulting from divided government also significantly hurt the president. Poll analysis from the *Washington Post*/ABC News noted, "Until now, many Democrats on Capitol Hill have said that they opposed much of Reagan's economic recovery program but were voting with the president because he clearly commanded overwhelming public support. With leaders in Congress already expressing opposition to the proposed changes in the Social Security program, public resistance to it could well prod Congress into a confrontation on an issue in which it, not the president, enjoys public backing."[83] Congress quickly unanimously voted down the program that was "jeered by the Democrats, who were amazed that Reagan had given them such an easy opportunity."[84] A bipartisan solution was the only way forward, and the White House would not engage in another discussion about Social Security until such common ground was reached.[85] The day after the defeat in Congress of his proposals, the president sent a letter to congressional leaders stating, "I have today asked Secretary Schweiker to meet with you and other leaders of the Congress as soon as possible to launch a bipartisan effort to save Social Security. I have also asked him to make the full resources of his department available for this undertaking. And of course, you can count on my active support of this effort."[86]

Even if the White House had followed the edicts confirmed in this book and used the bully pulpit more effectually, a more sustained effort was needed to carry out the leadership of public opinion. The conditional theory of public opinion leadership presumes an active president willing to regularly take his message to the public. In this case, the White House also did not plan the advance of the issue well, in part because the president caught the staff off guard by making a quick decision and putting the policy in play sooner than expected.[87] Contemporary observers echoed this advice at the time: "'The only time you announce something suddenly,' said a leading Republican pollster after the recent events, 'is when it's a popular move.'" Another White House staff member similarly lamented, "I don't think we took enough soundings."[88] This is the difference between the administration's success in passing their budget and tax proposals earlier in 1981 (see chapter 5) and their failure to get the public on their side on Social Security reforms.

Conclusion

As discovered in chapter 3, and as several recent scholars of presidential leadership of public opinion have asserted, presidents do not typically have much luck leading public opinion. The circumstances that might engender leadership, including an effective medium of communication, a strong economy, an attentive and persuadable public, and muted competing political voices, typically do not neatly line up in presidents' favor. Until this point, however, pinpointing the precise conditions that may limit presidential leadership has been difficult. The previous chapter, read in tandem with this chapter, establishes a criterion that presidents must typically meet in order to garner opinion movement. This is not to imply that all of these factors must be present or absent for leadership to be present or absent. Rather, these individual conditions provide guidelines for understanding leadership success and failure in a broader and more systematic way.

As found in the aggregate results in chapter 4 and in the case studies from chapter 5, in leading public opinion, communication is a necessity. The presidents studied in this chapter were not ineffective communicators. However, the conclusions here suggest that leading the public is as much about the communications tactics and timing used as the content of the prose. On this measure, all three presidents failed to effectively employ their message through the bully pulpit. It was perhaps not always a matter of choice. For President Kennedy, using the persuasive power of the White House would have antagonized an already reluctant and hostile Congress. For President Ford, it was difficult to determine on which economic issue (unemployment or inflation) the White House should have focused. For President Reagan, "going public" meant advertising an issue on which he was not on the popular side.

These case studies also provide a lesson in the difficulty in keeping one's campaign promises, or especially, not breaking one's campaign promises. For President Kennedy, offering a policy to cover the elderly with health insurance was a popular political choice but securing funding from a recalcitrant Congress was another difficulty altogether. Promise of additional spending in tough economic times was a promise tailor-made to be broken. Similarly, President Ford promised to "Whip Inflation Now" from his first days in office (the president had no benefit of a campaign to make promises). However, tackling such an enormous problem, especially when multiple interconnected economic troubles plagued the nation, proved to be a challenge too great for any administration and a promise that the Ford White House could not keep. On the other hand, President Reagan promised in the 1980 campaign not to cut Social Security, but the easy option of saving billions of dollars from the bountiful reservoirs of the program proved to be a "cut" too tempting to pass up. To follow through on one's campaign promises is critical for reelection, and ensuring these promises are kept (or not broken) is a function of leadership ability.

The nature and involvement of public opinion also matters in leading public opinion. The public was uninformed or uncertain in each of the issues identified above, suggesting that the president was unable to convince them of the correctness of the White House's policy or that the president's voice was crowded out by competing agents. These conditions clouded the public's certainty about these policy initiatives. Getting the public to accept the nature of the problem (as in the case of President Ford) or the value of the solutions (as in the case of Presidents Kennedy and Reagan) is paramount in leading public opinion. Even though some of the reforms were popular on paper, the failure of the president to communicate his message to the public caused the public to be ambivalent about the proposals. The role of the public in accepting presidential proposals, understanding them, and being convinced to endorse them is key in presidential leadership.

CHAPTER 7

Successful Leadership in Foreign Policy

One of the ironies of presidential leadership of public opinion is that although presidents are presumed to fail at leading on domestic policy issues, they are widely thought to be successful at leading public opinion on foreign policy issues. Theoretically and empirically, this should be true because of the presumed advantages of the White House in formulating international and military policy, advantages that result from information asymmetries and deference to the president on foreign policy issues.[1] Foreign policy issues often emphasize the inherent symbolism and drama of the presidency, which can be used as an effective marketing tool for presidential persuasion. This, combined with the president's unique role in the constitutional system, should foster unique leadership accomplishments in foreign policy because of the president's significant persuasive advantage in these circumstances.

Chapters 5 and 6 linked the aggregate findings to particular moments in presidential history to underscore the leadership conditions that fostered presidential leadership on domestic policy. Similarly, in this chapter I illustrate three instances of successful opinion leadership on foreign policy, again using archival data that correspond to the theoretical ideas from chapter 2 and the empirical findings from chapter 4. First, to illuminate these conditional patterns of success, I look at President Johnson's leadership efforts in 1965 to convince the public of the correctness of the administration's policies on the Vietnam War. Second, I examine President Carter's gradual leadership of the public on the Panama Canal treaties and their eventual ratification through the Senate. Third, I explore perhaps the clearest case, that of President George H. W. Bush's leadership of public opinion during the Gulf War.

Evolution of Johnson's Vietnam Policy

During his tenure in the White House, Lyndon Johnson received the full scope of public support and public ire on the Vietnam War. When the conflict began, his support in the public and Congress, especially in the wake of the passage of the Gulf of Tonkin Resolution, could scarcely have been higher. By the end of his term (hastened in part by the growing stalemate in Vietnam) the public and Congress were significantly split concerning the course of the war, and frustration was mounting. This case study focuses on the Johnson administration's efforts to hold together support for his Vietnam policy at the critical middle juncture when the Johnson administration escalated the conflict (in mid to late 1965), risking public backlash.[2] During this time, support for the war had not fallen off as it would in the middle of 1966—at this point in 1965, the public still generally supported the administration's policy objectives in Vietnam. The Johnson administration's effort did not occur by manifest. Indeed, it spent considerable time and energy leading public opinion and keeping the support for the war high, behavior that is consistent with the conditional theory of successful leadership.[3]

Despite the high popularity of the president in early 1965 (just above 70%), and despite sizeable majorities in both houses of Congress following the 1964 elections, the White House was still concerned with the durability of public opinion. For the Johnson administration, the ongoing conflict in Vietnam represented an elongated struggle to win public opinion on foreign policy in spite of mounting casualties and the potential of a damaging international stalemate. Hayes Redmon (special assistant to the president) sent a memorandum to press secretary Bill Moyers that framed the administration's approach to public opinion: "Polls do not make policy. Yet, I think it is essential that we do all we can to insure public support for our policies. Polls can tell us what people will and will not support."[4] As a result, the administration argued for a "partial mobilization" (rather than a "total mobilization") of the home front over an extended duration of time until the war could be concluded so that neither the "hawks" nor "doves" would be riled.[5] This was about to change as the administration's policy grew more aggressive.

A sustained conflict situation like Vietnam provides a consistent opportunity, born out of necessity, for presidents to lead public opinion on foreign policy. In a memorandum titled "Leadership on Vietnam,"

Horace Busby argued that the "continuing public silence" from the White House on Vietnam was a growing concern. He continued:

> The pro-negotiation element in Congress has admittedly had a harmful effect on our position in Saigon. But the harmful effect at home may be just as great—or even greater. The Senators are bound to be making the majority of the American people anxious and nervous over our future in Southeast Asia. The people, as you said so often during the Korean War, are probably ahead of Congress—and certainly equal in their understanding to the Executive. If the people could hear you speak to the small groups at the White House, I am certain the confidence and support they would extend to you would be overwhelming—and would be effectively felt in Congress itself. The consequences of the public not hearing you speak in this manner and spirit disturbs me.[6]

Busby went on to argue that the president should appeal directly to the nation: "I have come to believe that you have little to lose and a very great deal to gain by appearing before the nation to address a Joint Session of the Congress—and I do recommend serious consideration of this."[7] Using the president and his role as national leader was key and would cement "the country's vivid image of you as a national leader to trust" if the conflict escalates or ends.[8] Busby's point was that the public needed to be convinced that the Johnson administration was actively pursuing peace even when the war was actually escalating. The president's aides argued that this needed to be done on the national stage. The medium here was the correct choice, since, as found in chapter 4, leading foreign policy through televised strategies is an effective strategy.

The president decided in early 1965 that "abandoning Vietnam seemed unthinkable," but at the same time, "public and congressional support for a full-scale conflict seemed unlikely to outlast substantial human and material costs." As a result, Johnson "chose measured increases in U.S. military action and continuing efforts to negotiate a settlement."[9] Indeed, the president was careful to walk a fine line, as he was advised to do in the memorandum from aides that outlined the limits of the public's willingness to accept escalation. For instance, in April of 1965 the president gave a speech at Johns Hopkins University that was designed to reaffirm the administration's strategy of fighting until negotiations had begun. The president argued that the spread of Communism must be stopped but that "our objective is the independence of South Viet-Nam, and its freedom from attack. We want nothing for ourselves—only that the people of South Viet-Nam be allowed to guide their own country in their own way. We will do everything necessary to reach that objective. And we will do only what is absolutely necessary." The "escalation with restraint" theme is found prominently in this speech. The president concluded, "Until that bright and necessary day of peace we will try to keep conflict from spreading. We have no desire to see thousands die in battle—Asians or Americans. We have no desire to devastate that which the people of North Viet-Nam have built with toil and sacrifice. We will use our power with restraint and with all the wisdom that we can command. But we will use it."[10]

The White House needed another dramatic event to solidify its policies in the public mind. In particular, in early 1965 it was in need of such an event because several of the president's military advisers indicated to him that he needed to respond to attacks from the North Vietnamese or risk losing the public's confidence.[11] The event came on February 7, 1965, in the form of a Viet Cong attack at an air base in Pleiku that killed eight U.S. military advisers and wounded 126 others.[12] It ignited a significant retaliation by the Johnson administration that changed the course of the Vietnam conflict. Specifically, in response, the White House decided on systematic bombing of North Vietnam (first dubbed "Flaming Dart," then "Rolling Thunder").[13] "Rolling Thunder" was only supposed to last eight weeks but ended up being the dominant offensive tactic of the Johnson White House in the Vietnam War.

In following the attacks in Vietnam, the White House was strong at leading public opinion. Vice President Humphrey argued that the president "needed to assure public backing" and that "there has to be a cogent, convincing case if we are to enjoy sustained public support."[14] Several specific communications efforts in the early spring of 1965 initiated a favorable response from the public. Two major speeches were conducted (nationally televised on April 7 and May 2), few press conferences were held, and the president was consistently talking about Vietnam in public. These strategies paid off for the Johnson White House, as supported by the conclusions from chapter 4 which found that presidents who talked about the issue on television, not in a press conference, and over consecutive days in public assisted their own leadership efforts.

During this progressive escalation throughout 1965, the Johnson administration believed themselves to be on solid ground. The media (even newspapers who had initially expressed reservations about the conflict) and a generally anti-Communist Congress resoundingly supported the president's decision.[15] In addition, after the initiation of bombing in early February 1965, the White House was able to lead the public. A confidential memorandum to the president stated that the "trend is more towards getting war to N. Viet Nam than towards negotiation but dominant view still is hold the line. There has been a notable rallying behind the President on Viet Nam. Support for air raids and clear, overwhelming mandate to send as many U.S. troops there as necessary to withstand the Viet Cong attacks during Monsoon season."[16] Other polling reports indicated that the percentage of the public approving the president's handling of the situation rose from 41% (before the bombing) to 60%, and the percentage favoring the course of "continu[ing] to hold the line as we are doing now" rose from 40% in January 1965 to 46% in February 1965.[17] Rallies are not always positive (they are actually negative when examining all cases grouped together), but particular circumstances could make a rally positive, especially if it was in response to a direct attack on U.S. service personnel.

The evidence clearly shows that the public followed the president's lead on the administration's new course of action in Vietnam. In a February memorandum sent to the president from long-time aide Horace Busby (just after the beginning of Rolling Thunder), Busby notes, "The public confidence in you rests heavily on the man-in-the-street's instinct that while you want peace as he does, you also will not allow the Communists to push the U.S. around, as the man-in-the-street believes he would not."[18] The increasing escalation of the conflict was a risk for the Johnson administration in that it jeopardized their ability to secure a peaceful settlement to the conflict and risked alienating the public who believed them to be escalating the conflict with no real end. However, the president himself recognized that "Americans placed their faith in the president in difficult moments, and opinion surveys bore him out. Almost 70 percent of the nation gave him a 'positive' rating, along with the same proportion supporting a bombing strategy as the 'only way' to 'save' Vietnam."[19] The White House argued that the bombing of North Vietnam in retaliation for the attacks was "appropriate and fitting . . . which is how they described the raid after the Tonkin Gulf 'incident' six months earlier."[20]

Other findings confirm this rise in support resulting from the president's leadership efforts during the middle of 1965. Table 7.1 demonstrates

TABLE 7.1
Moving Opinion on Vietnam, 1965

	Hold line	Negotiate and withdraw	Carry war to North Vietnam
Late September	59%	11%	30%
August	49	25	26
July	45	30	25
May	47	31	22
March	49	38	13

Note: Table reproduced from Lyndon Johnson Library, White House Central Files, PR 16 7/15/65–11/2/65, "Redmon to Moyers," October 28, 1965, Box 346. The question was "All in all, what do you think we should do about Vietnam now? We can follow one of three courses: carry the ground war into North Vietnam, at the risk of bringing Red China into the fighting; try to negotiate and withdraw our support and troops from South Vietnam; or continue to hold the line there to prevent the Communists from taking over South Vietnam. Which do you favor?"

the gradual rise in the percentage of the public favoring the "hold the line" course while the percentage favoring "negotiate and withdraw" declined. The percentage favoring "carrying the war to the north" also steadily rose during this time. And the support for escalating the conflict garnered support from nontraditionally Democratic groups. For instance, "the most dramatic shift in public support for holding the line in Vietnam has taken place among normally Republican voters who cast their ballots in 1964 for Mr. Johnson" while those in favor of carrying the war to North Vietnam were "people who voted for Barry Goldwater" in 1964. In geographical terms, "the belief that we should carry the war to the North is strongest in the South and West where 37% now favor that course. This is an increase since August from 24% in the South and 33% in the West."[21]

The president's popularity was also helpful in his leading public opinion during this time. As we saw in chapter 4, popularity conjures up several additional kinds of leadership opportunities favorable to the president. Having just been reelected during the previous year by a massive popular and Electoral College landslide, and enjoying the support of almost 70% of the public in February 1965, the president was riding high. And, although opposition to the escalation of Vietnam was beginning (especially after the decision to initiate Rolling Thunder), "State Department aides discounted serious public opinion difficulties over Vietnam, because they imagined that the president's huge approval ratings in general would carry the nation along whatever course he chose."[22] In addition, the issue was foremost on the public's mind, which by itself has a small negative effect on leadership. But because the president was highly popular, the issue's heightened salience triggered a successful moment to lead public opinion. Both the president's popularity and the high salience of the issue together contributed to relatively easy leadership of public opinion.

But the White House's ability to lead public opinion was not permanent. In Table 7.1, there is a slight dip in the percentage of the public who supported the "hold the line" position in July of 1965. Because the president chose to announce a new troop increase in a press conference (which was found in chapter 4 to be ineffective at inducing leadership) rather than a televised address to Congress (which was found to be effective at leading on foreign policy), the president's policy choice was aggressively questioned. Johnson erroneously thought that "we can get our people to support us without having to be provocative," but ironically, drawing out the conflict grew potential opposition.[23] The president had hoped to make the announcement during the day (when the television audience was smaller) and thereby "muffle" the decision.[24] However, the format of a press conference subjects the president's message to challenges by exposing those elements of a policy that the public most fears (in this case, a prolonged war with significant military escalation). For instance, questions at the president's press conference addressed several unpopular outcomes to the conflict such as the intervention of China (as when a reporter asked, "Is the United States prepared with additional plans should North Viet-Nam escalate its military effort, and how do you anticipate that the Chinese Communists will react to what you have announced today?"), the duration of the conflict (as when another reporter asked, "And do you think the American people ought to think of that possibility [of a five- to seven-year war]?"), and the proper role of Congress (as when a reporter asked, "What are the borders of your power to conduct a war? At what point might you have to ask Congress for a declaration?"). These questions limited the White House's ability to communicate its message clearly and changed the nature of the reporting of the story.[25]

After a turbulent year of escalation in Vietnam in 1965, the administration sought to take stock of where they were politically with the

Vietnam conflict. The Johnson administration sought to identify which groups still supported their policies in Vietnam. A report from December of 1965 (summarized by White House aide Jack Valenti) found that "two out of three people feel the U.S. was right in staying in Vietnam even when Americans became involved in a land war. Only one American in five thinks we should have pulled out before American troops were involved in combat." He continued that "those who agree with our policy of remaining in Vietnam include a disproportionate number" of men, young people (age thirty or under), the better educated, people who are more knowledgeable about Vietnam. And of those who agreed that Vietnam is essential to the United States' commitment to stopping Communism, "those more knowledgeable about Vietnam and our involvement, young people and college educated people" were more likely to support the administration.[26]

While the president's policies were still popular in April of 1965, the support for the president's handling of the situation began to erode. In results from a Harris-conducted poll done privately for the Johnson administration, Harris noted that the president's handling of the situation in Vietnam was still high (57%) but that "right after the retaliatory bombing started, it went up to 60.40—a month ago it was down to 55.45—this represents something of a leveling out on the positive side."[27] Beginning with the initial bombing of North Vietnam in February 1965 and the buildup of troops in July of 1965 (called "Phase I"), a "permissive majority" of the public supported President Johnson, but a lasting split in public opinion (concerning the course of the war) would begin in late 1965.[28] The Johnson administration knew that this favorable opinion would not last long. They suspected that "these 'opinions' [favoring the policies in Vietnam] reflected a temporary surge of patriotism in response to an international crisis."[29] The more the public learned about the situation (from April to July of 1965), the more uncertain the public became about the course of action chosen by the Johnson administration.[30]

The results were not all bad for the Johnson White House, however. Data collected toward the end of 1965 indicated that the public still supported the president's military policies, especially on specific strategies of escalation. In November of 1965, the president still had the ability to lead the public on escalating the conflict. In particular, on specific courses of action, such as "We should bomb Hanoi" (20% favoring in October and 22% in November) and "We should blockade North Vietnam" (38% favoring in October and 40% in November), the president still maintained positive momentum in public support.[31] This support suggested to the president's staff that the public would continue to support these policies. Hayes Redmon wrote to Bill Moyers that "the most significant figure" was that "we should keep fighting until we achieve negotiations" and that "people are determined to support the president in his quest for negotiations to save South Vietnam."[32]

Similarly, Bill Moyers concluded a month later (in December of 1965) in a memorandum to the president, "Yet, if the public supports our military increases to date, they are even more overwhelmingly in favor of attempts at negotiated settlement."[33] Additionally, in a memorandum to President Johnson, Moyers wrote, "All this indicates that the public has supported our policies—including increased military efforts—to date. This is primarily because they want us to be in a position to negotiate from strength. They want—and even anticipate—a negotiated, compromise peace. They have supported escalation because they hope it will bring peace more quickly."[34]

Moyers also suggested "to maintain public support we need a series of moves—preferable [*sic*] dramatic—to assure them [the public] that we are active in the pursuit of peace."[35] Moyers concluded the memorandum by noting, "The great danger for the future lies in frustration of this goal [peace]."[36] Charting that balance would consume the remainder of the president's time in office. The lesson was that the president needed to keep constant pressure on the issue, a prospect that the White House was unwilling to do because of fears of angering either the hawks or the doves, contributing to the erosion of the president's support and his decision not to run for reelection in 1968.

Carter and the Panama Canal Treaties

Although not a political priority for the Carter administration upon arrival in the White House, the negotiation and finalization of the Panama Canal treaties, which returned the control of the Panama Canal to Panama, would be seen as one of the president's major foreign policy accomplishments.[37] The president saw this issue as the key to future relations with Panama and "diffused a sensitive controversy of long standing."[38] The return of the canal, although initially not favored by Governor Carter in the 1976 campaign, became part of the legacy of the administration's return to human rights principles in foreign policy.[39] These treaty negotiations are also instructive as case studies in presidential leadership because of the Herculean task the White House faced in moving public opinion on foreign policy, and their eventual victory demonstrates the correctness of several of the predicted conditions of success. The White House approached leading public opinion in a cavalier way at first, but after acknowledging the importance (and necessity) of moving public opinion, it impressively utilized the power of the bully pulpit to lead public opinion. According to Jones, the Carter White House "demonstrated the capacity to change public opinion and build a coalition for an unpopular issue and policy."[40]

The treaty negotiations began in February of 1977 with the president sending representatives to Panama. The public was almost instantly against the idea. Memoranda from the secretary of state's office noted "the general public perception on Panama is that we are giving away the Canal—giving up what is 'rightfully ours.'"[41] In May of 1977, public polls indicated that 78% of the public favored "the United States continuing its ownership and control of the Panama Canal" and 8% favored "turning ownership and control of the Panama Canal over to the Republic of Panama."[42] Five months later, after the treaties had been in principle agreed to by both parties, only 31% of the public approved of the treaty that called "for the U.S. to turn over ownership of the canal to Panama at the end of this century" even with the caveat that "the U.S. will maintain control over the land and installations necessary to operate and defend the canal."[43] It was clear, then, that the Carter administration had its work cut out for it.

Early attempts at opinion leadership, after the initiation of negotiations, were very limited. The White House was largely quiet on the matter, and those times when they did address the public on the matter, it was in the wrong format for successful leadership. As we saw in chapter 4, press conferences negatively affect public leadership efforts. The president faintly noted in a press conference on February 23 (his first public statement since sending negotiators to Panama), "We have begun again, within the last week, our discussions on the Panama Canal treaty. We have two extremely good negotiators, and I hope that we will have success there. There is no way that I can say at this point what degree of progress we have made. It's just beginning."[44] In fact, even when an agreement was achieved, a strategy memorandum from the Department of State suggested the president announce the "in principle" agreement (a major step forward) in a "special press conference (or perhaps part of a regularly scheduled press conference, depending on timing) at the

White House to make a personal statement of the Treaty agreement."[45] Additional followup media work would be done by Ambassadors Linowitz and Bunker on the morning television and radio news programs. In addition, there were scarcely two consecutive days when the president discussed the issue in public, that is, only once (from September 6 to 8) during 1977. These public relations efforts were not sufficient to lead public opinion, even on issues of foreign policy where President Carter presumably had an advantage.

Perhaps not surprisingly, given the lackluster effort to lead public opinion on the treaty, the public was reticent to embrace it. However, despite the outpouring of public opposition, much of the internal polling used by the Carter administration suggested that the opposition was soft and that opinion could be changed in advance of congressional approval. For instance, in June of 1977 a State Department aide noted,

> The most recent polls we have seen reflect evidence that the prevailing opposition to a new Panama Canal Treaty is *susceptible to change.* Comparisons between two Roper polls (June 1976 and January 1977) show that in the later poll there was an increase in public preferences for the status quo *in the absence* of countervailing arguments. Roper's more recent poll also indicates the relative persuasiveness of arguments for and against a new Treaty. In January, among those people *shown* sets of arguments opposing and favoring revision of the Treaty, 47% opposed revision and 33% supported a change; of those *not* shown arguments, 53% opposed revision and 24% supported it.

The memorandum concluded, "These results all indicate the need to get responsible information to the public in a timely fashion. Given the possibility of a conceptual agreement soon, we must move quickly with education of the public."[46] Patrick Caddell (the White House pollster) summed this up in December of 1977: "All of this suggest [*sic*] that opinion is extremely fluid. The public does not have hard and fast ideas on the Canal Treaties; they do not have information. Giving them information (and particularly giving them the idea that the Canal can still be defended) increases the support for those treaties. Most people always argue that those who oppose them do so from ignorance; in this case it just happens to be true. Giving the people knowledge about the treaties has to be a high priority item."[47] With the right kind of persuasion, the public would follow the president's lead.

It was shortly after this point that the White House began to focus more on leading opinion on the canal by taking advantage of the bully pulpit, a key to leading opinion in the conditional theory of opinion leadership. President Carter's efforts to persuade the public on the treaty were not working, through what chief of staff Hamilton Jordan called a "misunderstanding" caused by "distorted rhetoric and demagoguery."[48] However, through a concerted effort that included top administration foreign policy experts briefing opinion leaders, as well as the president briefing key editors, and top advisers briefing heads of national women's organizations, Senate staffers, and senior citizens organizations, Jordan reported to the president that "administration efforts to build public support for the Panama Canal Treaties are staring to bear fruit."[49] A concerted, consistent approach to presidential leadership on foreign policy would pay off for the White House. A memorandum from the State Department to Jordan argued that "even though much still remains to be done, all the signs are very promising and there is good reason to believe that with a sustained effort, public opinion will be sufficiently prepared by early '78 to enable the Senate to cast the two-thirds vote required for approval of treaties."[50]

The White House was confident about its ability to lead public opinion on the treaty, perhaps reflecting the supposition that the bully pulpit afforded the White House strong ability to lead on foreign policy.[51] The White House began to acknowledge the importance of shaping (and in this case, changing) public opinion on the prospect of a Panama Canal treaty. For instance, an internal opinion poll memorandum at the State Department indicated that the findings from individual polls differed substantially enough to suggest that opinion is moveable and that, quoting Senator Robert Byrd, "you're not going to get two-thirds of the Senate to ratify that treaty until there's a substantial change in the polls."[52] To accomplish this task, Jordan argued in September of 1977 for a "fireside chat" to "demonstrate continued commitment and Presidential interest" and defining the case for the ratification "by anticipating the objections of the opponents and dealing with them first."[53] A memorandum to national security adviser Zbigniew Brzezinski confirmed this thinking by asserting that "the job of explaining the Canal issue to the American public is not getting any easier."[54] The White House was beginning to recognize the value of public opinion in gaining support for the treaties.[55]

In October of 1977 Patrick Caddell did an initial survey of public attitudes and again found the public to be persuadable on key issues. He argued in the summary of findings that "the primary reason for opposing the treaty is the feeling that it is seen as a 'give away' of American property" and "other responses by treaty antagonists had to do with the security issue: the fear of a Communist takeover and the need to protect the U.S."[56] But, given that a majority of the public did not feel informed enough to make a good decision about the treaty, Caddell argued that "the issue does not seem to be all that important to the average American voter, given his admitted lack of knowledge and the ease with which opinions seem to be changed" and that "it is possible to change the views of a fair number of voters who oppose the Canal treaty."[57] Again turning to core constituencies for leadership opportunities, Caddell noted that "strongest political support for the treaty come from Democrats, the liberally inclined, those favorable to Carter and those who think Carter is doing a good job" and that "professionals, college graduates, those in high-income categories, and thirty-five years old and under are more inclined to favor the treaty" whereas the "strongest opposition comes among Republicans, conservatives and Carter detractors" and "older Americans, the poor, and less-educated segments of the population."[58]

Hamilton Jordan's suggestion to "go public" in a major way was followed as the White House got savvy about how to press the policy in the public. The president went public on television several times over the course of the ratification debate in the Senate. Jordan noted, "We have more weapons in our arsenal. If we do a 'Fireside Chat' now but feel that we need another dose in late October or January, we can do a Town Hall meeting on the treaty and/or you [the president] can make highly publicized trips to target states."[59] It was found in chapter 4 that talking continuously about an issue in the public (especially for two consecutive days) assisted presidents in leading public opinion. The White House thus had an important strategy change on this dimension in 1978. For instance, although I found only one instance where the president spoke in consecutive days about the treaty during 1977, the president did so several times beginning in 1978, and he generally spoke more frequently about the importance of the treaty. These included several "town hall" meetings where citizens could ask questions of the president on the issue.

Echoing these themes and following his aides' advice on public communication, the president addressed the issue on a nationally televised stage at several critical moments before the Senate debate over ratification. First, in his State of the Union message to Congress on January 19, 1978, the president said:

> Finally, the world is watching to see how we act on one of our most important and controversial items of business—approval of the Panama Canal treaties. The treaties now before the Senate are the result of the work of four administrations—two Democratic, two Republican. They guarantee that the canal will be open always for unrestricted use by the ships of the world. Our ships have the right to go to the head of the line for priority of passage in times of emergency or need. We retain the permanent right to defend the canal with our own military forces, if necessary, to guarantee its openness and its neutrality. The treaties are to the clear advantage of ourselves, the Panamanians, and the other users of the canal. Ratifying the Panama Canal treaties will demonstrate our good faith to the world, discourage the spread of hostile ideologies in this hemisphere, and directly contribute to the economic well-being and the security of the United States.[60]

Not surprisingly, the language employed by the president in the State of the Union address matched the concerns Caddell declared that the public had about the transfer of the canal to the Panamanian government, especially the United States' ability to use and defend the canal. Indeed, Caddell's advice to Jordan was that "if treaty supporters can convey the idea that this right to defend the canal is, indeed, part of the treaty we already have, they will be able to win public support for the treaties."[61] In accord with chapter 4, where we found that this strategy was positive for presidential leadership on foreign policy issues, the president and White House were tactically intelligent in going public in this manner.

President Carter also more specifically outlined the treaties in another televised address to the nation two weeks later, again emphasizing the points that Caddell found to be popular: "Throughout the negotiations, we were determined that our national security interests would be protected; that the canal would always be open and neutral and available to ships of all nations; that in time of need or emergency our warships would have the right to go to the head of the line for priority passage through the canal; and that our military forces would have the permanent right to defend the canal if it should ever be in danger. The new treaties meet all of these requirements."[62]

The president directly addressed the two "big" questions that the public had about the ratification of the treaty. He asked, "Will our Nation have the right to protect and defend the canal against any armed attack or threat to the security of the canal or of ships going through it? The answer is yes, and is contained in both treaties and also in the statement of understanding between the leaders of our two nations." He later asked, "Another question is: Why should we give away the Panama Canal Zone? As many people say, 'We bought it, we paid for it, it's ours.' I must repeat a very important point: We do not own the Panama Canal Zone. We have never had sovereignty over it. We have only had the right to use it."[63]

Evidence from late 1977 indicated that the public was beginning to respond favorably to the president's speeches. A memorandum from the State Department to Hamilton Jordan argued that, although the public did not support the treaty in mid-1977, "no one is scoffing anymore and the administration's efforts to build public support are starting to bear fruit."[64] Specifically, poll numbers from October to November 1977 showed a "shift of 14 percentage points in the differential between pro and con" and once the public knew "simple details of the treaties" (such as the United States ability to defend the canal from invaders), both Gallup and Harris polls revealed significant jumps toward favoring the treaty.[65] Specifically, Harris polls in September 1977 and January 1978 (the only two moments when identical questions were asked) found that the percentage of the public that favored the treaty rose from 26% to 29%.[66] The percentage of the public responding "don't know" also declined, demonstrating that the White House was effectively educating the public on the issue. Indeed, in December 1977 pollster Caddell found in a follow up to his survey of October 1977 that "some increase support for the Panama Canal treaties over the last few months" registered in several polls. There was also a concurrent decline in the percentage of the public responding "don't know" from 55% to 47%. He continued, "Looking at where the changes come, we see that there have been fairly uniform gains in support among Democrats, Republicans, and Independents."[67]

Burton Kaufman also notes that "thanks largely to the White House's lobbying efforts . . . opinion about the treaties began to turn around."[68] The first treaty was passed (the one that returned the waterway to Panama) on March 1. On April 18, 1978, the second of the treaties (the ability of the U.S. to defend the canal if necessary) was passed. Although I did not find identically worded poll questions, polls from early and mid-1978 suggest movement of the public with the president's persuasive efforts.[69] For instance, in February, 43% of the public approved of the treaties (with the specification that the United States could defend the canal if needed).[70] By the end of February 1978, just before the full vote in the Senate, 54% of the public supported the treaty with the "defense" idea mentioned.[71] In late March, just before the vote on the second treaty, 72% of the public would agree with the treaty if it would "allow the use of U.S. military force to defend the Panama Canal in an emergency and to allow U.S. warships priority in going through the canal in an emergency."[72] The president's "handling" of the issue also improved during the discussion of the treaties, improving from 26% "positive" on March 6 to 33% "positive" on April 28.[73]

Perhaps as important as the means of communication used were the means of communications *not* used. The administration (by late 1977) had recognized that public opinion needed to be changed and the White House set out to do so. They wisely avoided attempting to communicate much through the media. The White House focused attention on the public and on Congress, choosing a direct route to focus the their persuasion rather than filtering their message through the media. For instance, the president, beginning in January 1978, held several question-and-answer town hall meetings in Mississippi, New Mexico, Maine, and New Hampshire to directly communicate with the public. In addition, the president himself spoke with every member of the Senate at least twice to gain support from the treaties, engaging in "intense pressure" on the body.[74] Communicating through the media was an important strategy, of course, but the president himself was directly involved in briefings to key party and political officials at the state and national level.[75]

Bush and the Initiation of the Gulf War

Seldom does one witness a president with such highs and lows as President George H. W. Bush. From record highs in approval ratings (at the time of the Gulf War) to his failed reelection bid just two years later, President Bush's time in office was a roller-coaster ride. In discussing presidential leadership of foreign policy, however, the focus here is on the president's leadership during the run-up to the Gulf War, the event that brought him skyrocketing popularity. Ironically, the invasion of Kuwait by Iraqi forces on August 2, 1990, was initially met with only passing interest from the Bush administration; however, Saddam Hussein's increasingly bullish rhetoric about his weapons capability alarmed the

White House.[76] The president, relatively popular throughout the first half of his term, by 1990 had several important issues on his agenda, including the economy and the Soviet Union. Reelection, only two years away, was also on the president's mind. Zaller argues that politicians seeking reelection (and George Bush on the Gulf War in particular) who are under the threat of electoral retribution "take great care to lead public opinion only toward goals that the public will, in retrospect if not always in prospect, applaud."[77] The president and his team would have to navigate around particular concerns in the public regarding the scope of the intervention of military forces, and would ultimately prove very successful in leading public opinion on this issue.

As with so many other cases of leadership, the White House turned to internal polling (especially focus groups) to help persuade the public before the initiation of the conflict. These focus groups helped determine the boundaries of public opinion, and the Bush White House was interested in circulating the results of the focus group to key principles such as defense secretary Cheney, General Colin Powell (chairman of the Joint Chiefs of Staff), and General Brent Scowcroft (national security adviser), "as well as whoever might be writing the president's remarks regarding the Gulf."[78] Focus groups are designed to elicit specific ideas or phrases identified by a focus group participant, and these views are assembled by demographic category.[79] Eleven focus groups were conducted in December of 1990 (after the Iraqi invasion and after President Bush moved troops to Saudi Arabia) in four cities (New York, San Francisco, Dallas, and Kansas City) with eight to ten people in a group.[80] The focus group findings largely outlined the persuasive language the Bush administration used to communicate with the public over the course of the conflict.[81]

The Vietnam War left the American public skeptical toward foreign intervention unless using force was considered necessary to protect self-defined interests.[82] In particular, the public is shown to be more permissive toward restraining aggressive militaries abroad rather than engaging in long-term internal political change.[83] Thus, the first critical step for the Bush administration was to ensure that the public approved of the potential actions to be taken in response to Saddam Hussein's invasion of Kuwait, and specifically, that Desert Shield was not like Vietnam (which the president routinely attempted to do).[84] In short, administration officials had their work ahead of them if they were to convince the public to use force in the Middle East. Roger Ailes (one of the president's political strategists) noted to the president in a memorandum that the president's pollsters "believe the President must have public support for a war and they believe that support does not currently exist [in December of 1990]."[85] The findings showed that the "people seem to be quite informed about the reasons for our interest and involvement," but "in many cases, *they have not embraced the cause.*"[86]

For this reason, attempting to sell the public on the necessity of intervention in the Gulf was critical—at the time of the focus groups (in December of 1990) the percentage of Americans who felt the country was escalating to war "too quickly" rose to almost 50%.[87] The White House understood this dynamic and made sure to involve the public in its decision making, a connection that worked.[88] This reticence to engage internationally was linked to the "Vietnam syndrome" where the public was reticent to use force abroad. The focus group report notes that the "most dramatic and pervasive theme" was the "necessity of avoiding 'another Vietnam.'"[89] The decision to not invade Baghdad at the conclusion of the war may have been a result of not wanting to get bogged down in a quagmire like in Vietnam or in an internal regime change unpopular with the public.[90]

Ultimately, those in the focus groups indicated "most all do believe that the U.S. could conceivably win an all-out, short term, military battle" assuming we "use all our resources." Several respondents indicated that "no one wants to drag this out for too long," noting that the military should "make it quick," "get it over with," and "the faster the better."[91] The administration was clearly concerned with the "time as a weapon" problem the report describes and publicly sought to assuage the public's concerns. Many of these trepidations related to the possible duration of the conflict. For instance, many respondents in the focus groups indicated that they viewed the Iraqi military as "just as difficult, or even more difficult to fight as the North Vietnamese were in the not-so-distant past." Another set of respondents indicated they were hesitant because the Vietnam War was "a war we had to watch—*night after night.*"[92]

In convincing the public to support the plan, Ailes argued that, in the pre-invasion focus group, "people responded positively when reminded: Saddam started it, of all the steps taken by the President to resolve this peacefully, we are showing restraint and the U.S. is not the aggressor." He concluded by offering that "the people don't necessarily need more information, but a bit more persuasion."[93] Even with public opinion focused primarily on domestic issues at the time, "Bush and his spokesman adroitly brought it [public opinion] along, step-by-step, to support not only military intervention to defend Saudi Arabia but, when all else failed, the launching of the most massive assault since World War II to drive Iraqi forces from Kuwait."[94] The White House echoed these themes in its public briefings on the matter, and the president, as the chief spokesperson, was adept at pronouncing these popular themes when speaking in public.

Although normally reluctant to utilize the bully pulpit, the president made a concerted push to shape public perceptions in the case of the Gulf War.[95] In a press conference (carried by all the major networks) three days after the Ailes memorandum, the president reflected the themes from the focus group:

> As a democracy we've debated this issue openly and in good faith. And as President I have held extensive consultation with the Congress. We've now closed ranks behind a clear signal of our determination and our resolve to implement the United Nations resolutions. Those who may have mistaken our democratic process as a sign of weakness now see the strength of democracy. And this sends the clearest message to Iraq that it cannot scorn the January 15th deadline.
>
> Throughout our history we've been resolute in our support of justice, freedom, and human dignity. The current situation in the Persian Gulf demands no less of us and of the international community. We did not plan for war, nor do we seek war. But if conflict is thrust upon us we are ready and we are determined. We've worked long and hard, as have others including the Arab League, the United Nations, the European Community, to achieve a peaceful solution. Unfortunately, Iraq has thus far turned a deaf ear to the voices of peace and reason.
>
> Let there be no mistake: Peace is everyone's goal. Peace is in everyone's prayers. But it is for Iraq to decide.[96]

Several themes already found to be popular from the focus groups were referenced in the president's statement: caution, restraint, and cooperation.

However, because this was a give and take with the press, the president's message was not unchallenged. Several reporters probed the president on whether or not he had already made up his mind for war regardless of the stated deadlines. Another reporter confronted the president by asking, "Mr. President, there's only three days left until the deadline, which isn't enough time for Saddam Hussein to pull out his troops. In fact, you, yourself, wouldn't let Jim Baker go to Baghdad on this date because there wouldn't be enough time. Do you see the possibility of anything happening in these last few days that could avert war or any chance that he will pull his troops out?" This line of questioning resonated with the public's dissent. A commensurate dip in the approval of the president's policy during the winter of 1990 may have resulted specifically from congressional and media scrutiny of his decisions and decision making and from lack of certainty among the public over the proper course of action.[97]

The communications plans were given serious forethought by the administration. In a communications plan that governed the administration's public discourse on Operation Desert Shield in November of 1990, David Demarest (assistant to the president for communications) outlined for the president several communications activities "over the next three weeks to strengthen public support for Operation Desert Shield." One suggestion indicated the presidents should engage in a "live, 10-minute address to the nation which would be a personal reflection of the Gulf situation, and would talk about the troops, and their dedication and sense of purpose." Another tactic suggested exploiting the "barnstorming" technique, a "White House on the road" concept, which would involve "senior administration officials working Desert Shield speeches into existing beyond-the-beltway travel plans. Possible venues would include local American Legion and VFW halls, civic and business organizations, and conferences and conventions."[98]

Television, as the cornerstone in presidential leadership efforts on foreign policy, was effective in communicating the White House's message to the public. On January 12, the president addressed the nation. He began by indicating, "Just 2 hours ago, allied air forces began an attack on military targets in Iraq and Kuwait. These attacks continue as I speak. Ground forces are not engaged." Then he followed up by blaming Saddam Hussein for initiating this sequence of events.[99] Again reflecting the themes of the focus groups, the president argued, "The United States, together with the United Nations, exhausted every means at our disposal to bring this crisis to a peaceful end. However, Saddam clearly felt that by stalling and threatening and defying the United Nations, he could weaken the forces arrayed against him." Further, in addressing the duration of the conflict, he noted, "Prior to ordering our forces into battle,

Attitudes Toward Military Action in the Persian Gulf

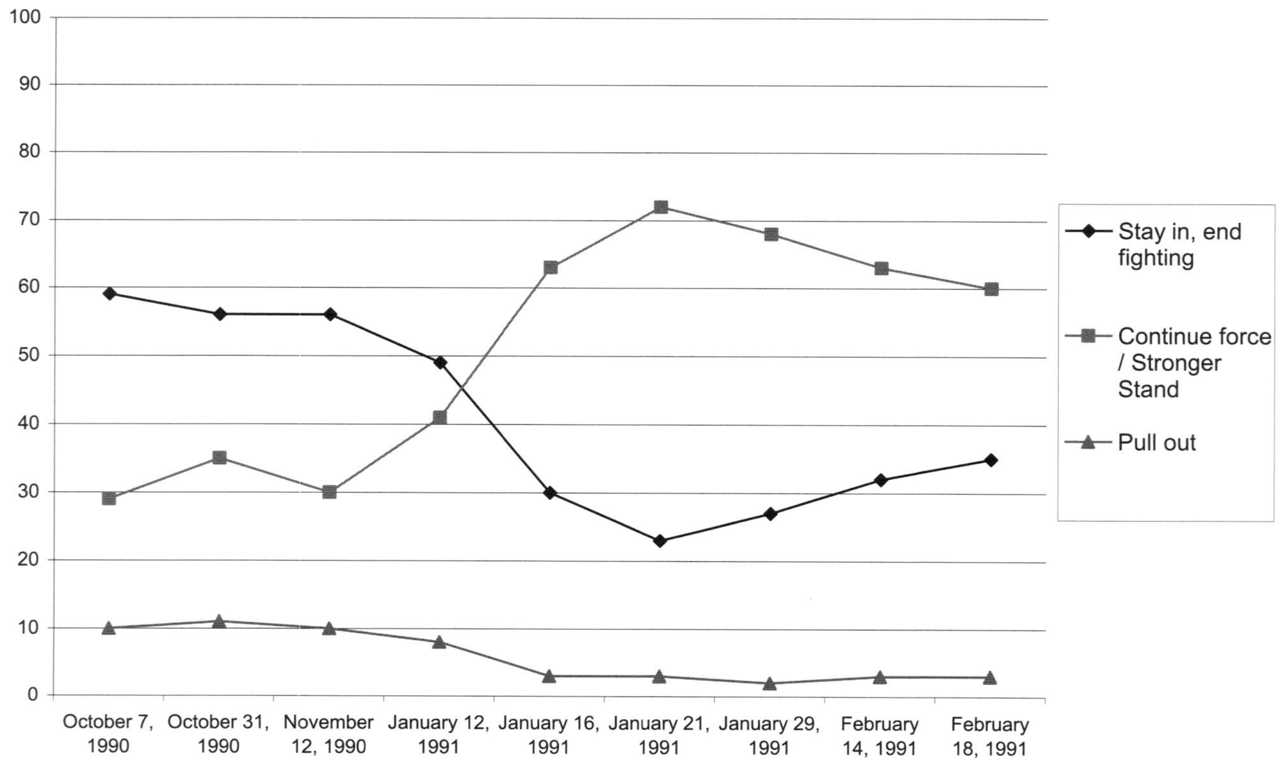

I instructed our military commanders to take every necessary step to prevail as quickly as possible, and with the greatest degree of protection possible for American and allied service men and women. I've told the American people before that this will not be another Vietnam, and I repeat this here tonight." At the end of the hostilities, the president again addressed the nation on television (via a joint session of Congress) on January 29 and March 6.

The cumulative leadership efforts paid off for the president. The White House's internal data suggested that their leadership efforts worked from the start. Figure 7.1 identifies opinion trends over the substantial duration of the conflict. Increasing percentages of the public gradually supported the president's commitment of U.S. military personnel into harm's way. Indeed, in the days following the president's address to the nation on the initiation of military hostilities (January 12), a significant swing in public opinion was registered in those agreeing that the United States should take a stronger stand against Iraq. John Mueller finds a significant approval spike for several groups during this time, including those disagreeing the United States made a mistake in entering the conflict, those approving of Bush's handling of the war, those approving of the job he was doing as president, those trusting him to make the right decisions in the war, and those considering the American actions in the Mideast to be "morally justified."[100]

The president was able to hold a firm majority of the public in his corner and lead them to more strongly support his position. In internal polling results, the president saw an increase in the percentage of the public who favored going to war or using force if Iraq did not withdraw by January 15 (42%) from December of 1990 (35%) and in the percentage who indicated that the United States should still go to war if ten thousand lives would be lost in January (50%) from December of 1990 (43%).[101] Further, those groups agreeing more strongly about the "use of force in the Middle East should Iraq not vacate Kuwait by January 15" included

Fig. 7.1. (opposite). Attitudes toward military action in the Persian Gulf. Data are reproduced from the George H. W. Bush Library, White House Chief of Staff Files, Polling 1991 (2 of 3), "Teeter to the President," February 15, 1991, CF 00473. Although the poll dates encompassed several days of polling, only the closing date of the poll was included (unless the polling was completed in a single day, such as for the polls of January 16 and February 18, 1991). Responses for "don't know" and/or "refused" were not included in the original table.

several groups President Bush was courting for reelection in 1992. For instance, "Reagan Voters" increased support from 64% in December to 69% in January, "New Bush Voters" (those voters who voted for Bush but not Reagan) increased support from 53% to 59% and "Conservative GOP" affiliates increased support from 63% to 69%.[102]

Similarly, Table 7.2 also identifies a trend analysis of internal White House polling on the subject of whether the White House made the "right decision" in sending troops and using military force. The data again reveal that the president's initial efforts to persuade the public in his January 16 televised appeal worked. The percentage supporting the decisions to send troops increased from 67% to 77% during the first days of the conflict. There was also a concurrent rise in those who agreed that a military solution was a good option, rising from 64% agreeing to 73% agreeing. The generally positive media coverage of the swiftness of victory and the expediency with which the White House resolved the situation likely contributed to this increase in favorable opinion.[103] Also, not surprisingly, the percentage of the public who responded "don't know" to the question declined from 7% to 5%, reflecting saturated media coverage of the probable conflict and presidential attention to the issue.

Prior to the start of hostilities, the president requested that Congress pass a resolution endorsing his ability to use force and also immediately began lobbying both the public and Congress for it with a "full-scale lobbying campaign."[104] These efforts paid off on January 12 when Congress approved a resolution (the Persian Gulf War Resolution) to provide the president with the capacity to engage militarily with Saddam Hussein's forces in the Middle East. Still, the vote in the Senate was 52 to 47 and the vote in the House was 250 to 183, reflecting the dissent felt by opponents in Congress. Although there was doubt about the proper course of action, the president's ability to craft a convincing argument was persuading Congress to go along with the White House's plans, although that would change if the United States were to encounter any significant casualties.[105] Although both the public and Congress were initially reluctant to follow the president's lead, the persuasion from the White House and its carefully crafted arguments kept each of the constituencies appeased.[106] And, while significant opposition voices to the president's can limit his persuasive opportunities, President Bush here, along with a less than critical media, was able to persuade Congress through the public.[107] Mueller noted about President Bush that "a trusted, determined president is in a compelling position."[108]

TABLE 7.2
Approval of President Bush's Policies in the Middle East

	January 16	January 17–21	January 28–29	February 11
Sending troops				
Did the right thing	67%	77%	77%	76%
Should have stayed out of the situation	26	18	18	14
Don't know	7	4	5	8
Refused/No answer	0	0	0	2
Using military force				
We are doing the right thing	64%	73%	72%	*
Should have waited longer	30	24	23	*
Don't know	5	3	4	*
Refused/No answer	1	0	1	*

Note: Table reproduced from George H. W. Bush Library, White House Chief of Staff Files, Polling (2 of 3) 1991, "Steeper to Rogers," February 20, 1991, CF 00473. The "Using Military Force" question was not asked during the February 11, 1991, period. The "Sending Troops" question was "Do you think we did the right thing sending troops to Saudi Arabia or should we have stayed out of the situation?" The "Using Military Force" question was "Do you think we are doing the right thing in using military force against Iraq, or do you think we should have waited longer for the economic sanctions and diplomatic pressure to work?"

The president and the White House met virtually all the criteria that were set out in chapter 4 as being necessary to lead public opinion. First, presidential popularity has a modest effect on presidential leadership in foreign policy, and even before the hostilities started, President Bush was popular according to Gallup polls.[109] Given that the issue was the most salient issue for the months leading up to and after the initiation of hostilities, the White House had a popular leader and an important issue that buttressed its leadership efforts. Second, presidential deployment of troops is also key to leadership success on foreign policy. Because the invasion of Iraq took place in August of 1990, President Bush sustained a leadership moment for the remainder of 1990 that led into the beginning of hostilities in early 1991. Third, according to the data from chapter 4, a "major address" strategy (utilizing the television to speak to the American people) was an effective tool in foreign policy. The president took to the airwaves several times during the course of the Persian Gulf conflict in a strategic communications approach that was a textbook example of leadership success.

Yet, beyond the mass public, the White House communications strategies were also directed toward the president's core constituency groups in "selling" the Gulf War. Indeed, Zaller finds support greater among core Republican constituencies (especially with exposure to the media) than for other groups.[110] In the "Communications Plan" for Operation Desert Shield, David Demarest wrote to chief of staff John Sununu that "target groups" including "potential surrogates (groups and individuals) who already support the president should be given immediate priority. With proper briefing materials and talking points, veterans groups, key business leaders, Members of Congress, foreign policy experts, friendly columnists, administration officials and party leaders can give the president's message resonance almost immediately."[111] Polling results after the conflict began indicate that men were more likely than women to favor bombing of military targets where civilians might be located.[112] More generally, the public evaluated the president in terms of foreign policy, a policy choice that advantaged Republicans.[113]

However, like other moments of presidential leadership, the effect of the president's leadership efforts lasted only temporarily. Figure 7.1 identifies a gradual decline (after an initial surge described above) from a height of 72% supporting "continuing the force and taking a stronger stand" in mid-January to 60% supporting. Other findings from mid-January are that the percentage of the public who favored the policy to "continue using military force until Iraq surrenders completely" declined to 75% in January 21 from a height of 81% on January 19. Similarly, the percentage of the public indicating that "we are doing the right thing" in Iraq declined to 66% on January 21 from a height of 76% on January 17.[114] Mueller also notes that between the beginning of the air war (January 16) and early February that "there was some erosion of war support during the course even of the Gulf War with its low casualties."[115]

Part of the problem of the decline in approval of the president and his policies, according to the president's pollsters, was that the public quickly forgot about the success in the Gulf War. Indeed, once Iraq slipped from the national agenda and the concerns over the budget and taxes took over, "the President had slipped to his lowest rating during his first term."[116] Total media coverage began to decline and domestic criticism began to rise.[117] In addition, by early 1992 (a year after the hostilities ended), the president was losing key support of his core constituency. Fred Steeper (one of the president's pollsters) noted "with upper-income, non-union men, he has dropped 28% in approval (49% approve and 50% disapprove). With Southern men, he has dropped 26% (46% approve and 52% disapprove). The two groups of men are now just moderately more positive than voters, in general, when they should be significantly more positive."[118]

Conclusion

These case studies demonstrate that presidents do find considerable success in leading public opinion on foreign policy, and these vignettes have helped to advance our understanding of the ways in which certain political conditions positively affect presidential leadership of foreign policy. Of course, there are particular conditions that significantly help to ensure leadership is effective for presidents. In terms of communications strategies, utilizing a "major address" or talking about the issue for consecutive days are potent communications tools in leading public opinion on foreign policy. The blanketing of the president's message, given the assumptions about the White House's natural advantage in setting the agenda and selling its foreign policy messages to the public, is most practical via the television. In each of the three cases described in this chapter, the presidents utilized the bully pulpit in this way, talking directly to the public from the Oval Office, and each time it was effective in leading public opinion. In addition, and similar to all other moments of presidential leadership, discussing the issue in public on multiple consecutive days is an effective way to keep the issue on the agenda and hammer the administration's message home with repeated appeals.

Similar to the findings from chapter 5 on domestic policy, presidents are able to actively facilitate the enactment of their preferred policy agenda by Congress. Presidents Carter and Bush were able to secure agreements needed from Congress or were provided broad authority for action by Congress in part because they were able to motivate public opinion to their side and create an environment where Congress was more inclined to grant the president's policy wishes. This ability was especially telling in the case of the Panama Canal treaties because Congress was initially against the treaties. For Presidents Johnson and Bush, while there was dissent about escalation or intervention, the White House teams managed to maneuver around it with their rhetoric. A president with the public on his side in a foreign policy matter, especially one involving armed conflict, makes it difficult for Congress to challenge the White House. This reality is another reason why presidents are effective leaders in foreign policy and why communications tactics are more pronounced during these time periods.

These findings also speak to the importance of framing in leading public opinion on foreign policy. In each case, the president was able to muster support for an action, even if the cost could be financial or in the form of casualties, but he did so acknowledging the important role of the public and the limitations the public forced on the president. Polling data allowed the White Houses to pinpoint public concern and educate the public on issues on which they may be less informed. But, public opinion also placed constraints on presidential framing of foreign policy, an outcome that is especially telling since presidents are thought to possess uniform persuasive powers on foreign policy issues. Presidents do care about public opinion on foreign policy, and importantly, this opinion tends to rein in the ability of the White House to shape foreign policy outcomes with its rhetoric alone. These results suggest that the public is not easily manipulated by presidential rhetoric, a reality that speaks to the powerful role of public opinion in presidents' ability to lead public opinion. The president as public educator therefore is an important component to leadership of public opinion.

CHAPTER 8

Unsuccessful Leadership in Foreign Policy

It is clear from the few presidents studied in the previous chapter that presidents find success at leading public opinion on foreign policy issues—indeed, provided enough space, I could expand this discussion to several more moments of leadership where the president has persuasively functioned as commander-in-chief. That presidents find particular moments of success in leading public opinion on foreign policy is important but not necessarily surprising since it is largely expected that presidents have an advantage on these issues. But perhaps more surprising are those moments of presidential leadership on foreign policy that fail, even with some favorable conditions present. This chapter is an investigation into three of those moments where presidents fail to lead public opinion on foreign policy. This set of explanations can help to refine our understanding of the advantages or disadvantages of executive public persuasion in international diplomacy and military issues.

Similar to the discussion of domestic policy failure in chapter 6, the value in this investigation is to describe how, absent positive political conditions or including negative conditions outlined in chapter 4, presidents are not as successful in leading public opinion on foreign policy. Again, three cases are identified. The first case study ascertains why President Nixon was unable to lead public opinion on his military and diplomatic choices during the Vietnam War in early 1972. The second case study looks at President Reagan's inability to lead the public to accept his policies on aid to the Contras in Nicaragua (and the administration's surprising unwillingness to abandon the position when they proved unable to lead the public). Third, the chapter ends by examining President Clinton's lack of success in leading the public on the issue of military intervention in Somalia. This again presents a case where one might expect a foreign policy issue would assist the White House in leading opinion but where there was no leadership success. Although these cases have been examined before, the value added here is that we can more clearly understand why presidents failed to lead public opinion when we apply the aggregate findings from chapter 4.

Nixon (Temporarily) Escalates Vietnam

By the time "Johnson's War" became "Nixon's War," President Nixon inherited a conflict about which the American public was growing more dissatisfied. Karnow hypothesizes that President Nixon "was largely responsible for his own doom. The domestic opposition to the conflict that grew during his first term in office exacerbated his sense of beleaguered isolation, prompting him to sanction the accumulation of offenses that became Watergate."[1] The president's early military strategy was to "Vietnamize" the conflict, whereby U.S. forces would gradually withdraw and the South Vietnamese government would eventually take over the fighting, even though he perceived that this might lead to a collapse of South Vietnam.[2] For instance, in January of 1972, the president announced (to the surprise of the public) that the administration had been in secret negotiations to end the war—a move toward ending the conflict that a majority of the public supported.[3]

This resolve (and policy) would be tested in the spring of 1972 when the North Vietnamese attacked multiple points in South Vietnam with their largest force since the Tet Offensive in 1968. The offensive began on March 30 when "an estimated 15,000 North Vietnamese troops with armored vehicles, artillery, and mobile antiaircraft guns attacked across the DMZ from the north and northwest" an attack that caught the U.S. military forces by surprise.[4] The attack "struck in three successive waves" over South Vietnam's northern provinces, the central highlands, and in the area north of Saigon.[5] The timing of this offensive was not unexpected since both President Nixon and secretary of state Henry Kissinger "foresaw a massive Communist drive unfolding in 1972, timed to influence American voters during the presidential election campaign."[6] The president and his advisers had to walk the fine line of limiting military involvement (consistent with the plan involving removal of troops) but also responding to these attacks.

On April 26, 1972, the president addressed the nation on the United States' planned retaliation for the North Vietnamese attack. The president framed the problem in Vietnam by claiming, "Now, Hanoi's answer to this offer [of peace talks] was a refusal even to discuss our proposals and, at the same time, a huge escalation of their military activities on the battlefield. Last October, the same month when we made this peace offer to Hanoi, our intelligence reports began to indicate that the enemy was building up for a major attack. And yet we deliberately refrained from responding militarily. Instead we patiently continued with the Paris talks, because we wanted to give the enemy every chance to reach a negotiated settlement at the bargaining table rather than to seek a military victory on the battlefield—a victory they cannot be allowed to win."[7] The president drew on past examples to demonstrate that, while the United States was committed to peace and did not wish any land in Vietnam, the North Vietnamese had repeatedly vacated the peace table.

The president reiterated that he would take a number of steps to bring the conflict to a close: "First, I have decided that Vietnamization has proved itself sufficiently that we can continue our program of withdrawing American forces without detriment to our overall goal of ensuring South Vietnam's survival as an independent country. Consequently, I am announcing tonight that over the next months 20,000 more Americans will be brought home from Vietnam. This decision has the full approval of President Thieu and of General Abrams. It will bring our troop ceiling down to 49,000 by July 1—a reduction of half a million men since this administration came into office."

Second, he desired to resume the peace discussions in Paris with an eye toward a "firm expectation that productive talks leading to rapid progress will follow through all available channels." Third, the bombing of military installations in North Vietnam would be resumed until the aggression from the North Vietnamese had ended. The president reminded the public that before the invasion by the North Vietnamese, 90% of the troops had been withdrawn and the sorties flown over the North had been cut in half. But with the recent escalation, the president claimed (as in the past), "I would act to meet that attack."[8] The day after the North Vietnamese attacks, the president ordered "protective reaction missions" to hit targets in North Vietnam (which began on April 15) and "dusted off" blueprints for mining Haiphong harbor (which began on May 8).[9]

Strangely, President Nixon did not immediately go on television to convey his policy to the public—he waited almost a month to discuss the issue. In fact, the president did not mention Vietnam in public speeches from the date of the offensive (March 30) until his prime-time speech on April 26. The decision to give the televised address was debated (the alternative was a press conference) and delayed because of the president's doubts about the proper course of action.[10] The White House may have also delayed its reaction to the March events because of Nixon's impending visit to the Soviet Union and an uncertainty about how to press Soviet premier Leonid Brezhnev for a response to the North Vietnamese incursion.[11] The delay in addressing the nation may have truncated the probable effect of more consistent leadership.

The president's policies were initially popular with a majority of the public; however, this popularity did not aid him in moving opinion after his April 26 speech. Tom Benham (one of the president's pollsters) in the post-speech poll results argued that "while the public splits in their approval of President Nixon's handling of the Vietnam situation overall, they strongly back him in the various specifics of his position as questioned in the survey."[12] However, the president's speech did little to *enhance* the public's favorable reaction to his handling of the "Vietnam situation." As a result, polls indicated that approval of the president's handling of Vietnam had fallen from 53% in early March to 48% in mid-April to 47% in the days following the speech.[13] Melvin Small claimed that the administration's "hands were tied" because the public was growing impatient (and often downright belligerent) about seeing the end of the war.[14] Nixon himself noted that he did "not want to do anything in the April announcement that will in any way reduce the chances for some success on the negotiating front."[15]

Although the president's policies were initially looked on favorably by the public, this approval did not last long. The president acknowledged that the "rally" did not indicate long-term support and that "his support would slip" soon.[16] This phenomenon comports with the negative effect of rally moments that we saw in chapter 4. Indeed, the president's speech garnered the lowest "very favorable" or "somewhat favorable" reaction of any of the president's other major Vietnam speeches (especially compared to the president's January 1972 speech in which he announced popular troop withdrawals and covert peace negotiations). For instance, Benham's polls indicated that the president's earlier "Report on Vietnam" speech in April 1971 was received favorably by 63% of the public and his "Vietnam Announcement" in January 1972 was received favorably by 73% of the public. In contrast, the April 1972 speech, "Vietnam Invasion Announcement," was received favorably by only 61% of the public, lower than any of the other speeches on any topic.[17] Likewise, from the January 1972 speech to the April 1972 speech, the percentage of respondents answering "don't know" rose from 3% to 7%, implying that the public

TABLE 8.1

Who Is to Blame for Little Progress in Peace?

	U.S. more to blame	North Vietnam more to blame	Both sides to blame	No opinion
Polling date				
July 28–August 4, 1969	6	40	43	11
March 28–April 21, 1970	5	38	47	10
April 27–April 29, 1971	4	35	50	11

Note: Table reproduced from Richard Nixon Library, National Archives II, H. R. Haldeman Files, Distribution of Vietnam Invasion Poll—April 27–29, 1972, "Vietnam Invasion Poll," April 30, 1972, Box 350, p. 8. The question was "In your opinion, which side is more to blame for the fact there has been little progress in the Paris negotiations and the war is still continuing? Is the U.S. more to blame, the North Vietnamese more to blame, or do both sides share the blame?"

was less informed or less certain about the president's message, a sign of increasing apathy about the president's policy to end the long conflict.

In addition, although the president emphasized establishing peace in his April 1972 speech and the role the United States would play in that effort, a growing majority of the public felt that "both sides share the blame" for little progress in ending the war. Table 8.1 reveals that after the president's speech smaller percentages of the public thought that either the United States or North Vietnam (individually) were to blame, but more of the public thought that the blame was shared equally (43% in August 1969, 47% in April 1971, and 50% in April 1972). Benham concluded, "The public's reaction to the Paris negotiating sessions are a measure of frustration and an [*sic*] evidence of the public's unhappiness with ambiguity."[18] The ambiguity of the plan clearly hurt the president's efforts to lead public opinion, as shown by the lack of movement of "don't know" in Table 8.1. Peace and an end to the conflict were the pathway to greater public approval and public trust. The public would not follow the president's lead on anything short of that effort.

The president's pledge that "I have flatly rejected the proposal that we stop the bombing of North Vietnam as a condition for returning to the negotiating table" was also examined by pollsters. Initially, this proved popular, with 66% of the public agreeing with the president's position.[19] However as the months went by, fewer and fewer in the public agreed that this was the best course of action. Gallup polls taken before and after that time suggests that the public was not moved by the president's arguments to escalate the bombing. In April, Gallup polls reported that 45% of the public favored "stepped up bombing of North Vietnam" while only 41% of the public favored that strategy in September 1972 when "Operation Linebacker" was still in full force.[20] The percentage of respondents answering "don't know" also increased from 11% to 15% between the two polls. Substantiating these findings of nonleadership, it is also important to note that again during this time, on May 8, 1972, the president appealed to the public by going on television to announce additional conditions for a peace agreement and a more aggressive bombing of North Vietnam to deny them "the weapons and supplies it needs to continue the aggression."[21] This appeal had no effect because the public clearly did not believe the plan would work. Other than this address on May 8, there were few other moments when the president publicly discussed his Vietnam policy.

Several of the conditions found to detract from leadership were present in the political environment in 1972. In particular, it was found that during an election year a president is less likely to lead public opinion. This phenomenon was clearly affecting the Nixon administration because the media and the public were taking their frustrations out on the president for not ending the war as he had promised in 1968. The "crunch period" of the elections also fostered greater desire for the Nixon White House to return to the negotiating table.[22] Government officials in Hanoi were counting on this pressure and banked that the president would not expand military operations before the 1972 elections.[23] Indeed, the initial phase-out of troops was prolonged over "the course of the year in order to help Nixon politically in the upcoming presidential election."[24] The president's rivals would also limit his hand—President Nixon was concerned about increased bombing during the Democratic National Convention and its likely political effect on the voters.[25] Pressure from the president's electoral opponents created a difficult environment in which to lead public opinion because of opposing messages.

This case study also demonstrates the limitations of a rally effect and helps to put the negative finding from chapter 4 in context. Although the attack by North Vietnam on South Vietnam would fall under a classic rally moment for definitional purposes, the public did not respond to it. Several events may have limited a rally. First, as described above, the president did not immediately take advantage of the rally by going public. Second, the public was conditioned to a longstanding conflict replete with attacks and counterattacks, so another escalation by the North Vietnamese did not cause much of a stir (especially considering the president did little except maintain troop withdrawal plans and increase the bombing). Third, without the immediate success at the peace table that the administration had hoped to find with this increased bombing, the escalation would be branded a failure and, according to secretary of state Kissinger, "the demands for 'political' alternatives would mount."[26] Short of a peaceful end to the conflict, the public would not consider the president's actions a success.

Also, President Nixon's popularity was not above average during this time (53% approved of his job as president in March 23, 1972).[27] But even worse for the White House, the president's popularity in the days after the speech was slipping, especially among swing voter groups. Bruce Kehrli (White House staff secretary) and Gordon Strachan (White House aide to the chief of staff) wrote to H. R. Haldeman in early May 1972 that "the President's 2 percentage point drop in popularity is reflected in the statistically significant decreases among union families and independents." In particular, the independents' perception of the situation in Vietnam may have hurt their overall impressions of the president. They noted that "the increased fighting in Vietnam may account for the drop in approval," a particularly bad problem to have before an election. Indeed, Bob Teeter, another of the president's pollsters, argued that "over the years ticket-splitters have provided the winning margin in most of the priority states, and they are vital to us this year."[28] However, considering President Nixon's "southern strategy," the news was positive because the president received a 5% increase in approval in the South.[29]

Ironically, President Nixon's chosen form of communication was the most valuable in leading public opinion.[30] Speaking to the nation from the Oval Office should have produced significant gains for the president. Yet the circumstances illustrate how, consistent with the constraint theory on the importance of message delivery, gains can be significantly limited. Tom Benham found that the television audience was *lower* for this speech than most other speeches, in part because the advance publicity generated a great deal of attention. He also found that "awareness" of the speech was only 60%, lower than that for any other major speech given on Vietnam by the president since early 1971.[31] He argued that the administration should "build interest and suspense rather than have the main content leaked in advance."[32] This case offers an important caveat to findings about the success of the "major address" strategy in leading opinion on foreign policy. As George Edwards notes, without attention from the audience to a presidential message, the president's leadership ability is significantly restricted.[33]

The value of a televised announcement is not only the impact of the speech on the viewing public (which Benham found to be small) but also on the media for the days following the speech. Arguing the White House's point several days in a row is a sound way to lead public opinion. Yet the president had been absolutely silent on the public stage (on the issue of Vietnam but also in general) since April 21, 1972, five days before the televised address. In fact, the previous mention of the president's policy stance on Vietnam was on April 13, 1972, nine days before the president's speech, and it came in the form of a letter sent to delegates to a White House Conference on Youth![34] After the speech, he was also quiet on the issue of Vietnam until a press conference on April 30 in Texas.[35] Without a constant message from the White House, it is not surprising that the president was unable to lead public opinion in this case.

However, despite the difficulties in managing an increasingly unpopular war, President Nixon was able to lead opinion in small, temporary amounts, generally by framing his unpopular Vietnam policies in terms of sensitive issues the public would never deny, such as linking staying in Vietnam to protecting the lives of the prisoners of war or preventing a Communist takeover. Figure 8.1 identifies a trend in opinion in these two questions beginning in mid-1971. The president's speech on April 26, 1972, explaining the administration's response to a full-scale invasion of South Vietnam by the North (by bombing military targets in North Vietnam), temporarily increased the percentage of the public willing to stay in Vietnam given the unwanted consequences of putting POWs in danger or permitting a complete Communist takeover of South Vietnam. In his April 26 speech, the president indicated, "As far as we are concerned, the first order of business will be to get the enemy to halt his invasion of

Fig. 8.1. (following page). Tradeoffs to withdrawal from Vietnam. Data were taken from the Richard Nixon Library, National Archives II, H.R. Haldeman Files, Distribution of Vietnam Invasion Poll, April 27–29, 1972, "Vietnam Invasion Poll," n.d. The "POW" question reads "Would you favor withdrawal of all U.S. troops by the end of 1972 even if it threatened the lives or safety of U.S. POWs held by North Vietnam?" The "takeover" question reads "Would you favor withdrawal of all U.S. troops by the end of 1972 even if it meant a Communist takeover of South Vietnam."

Tradeoffs to Withdrawal from Vietnam

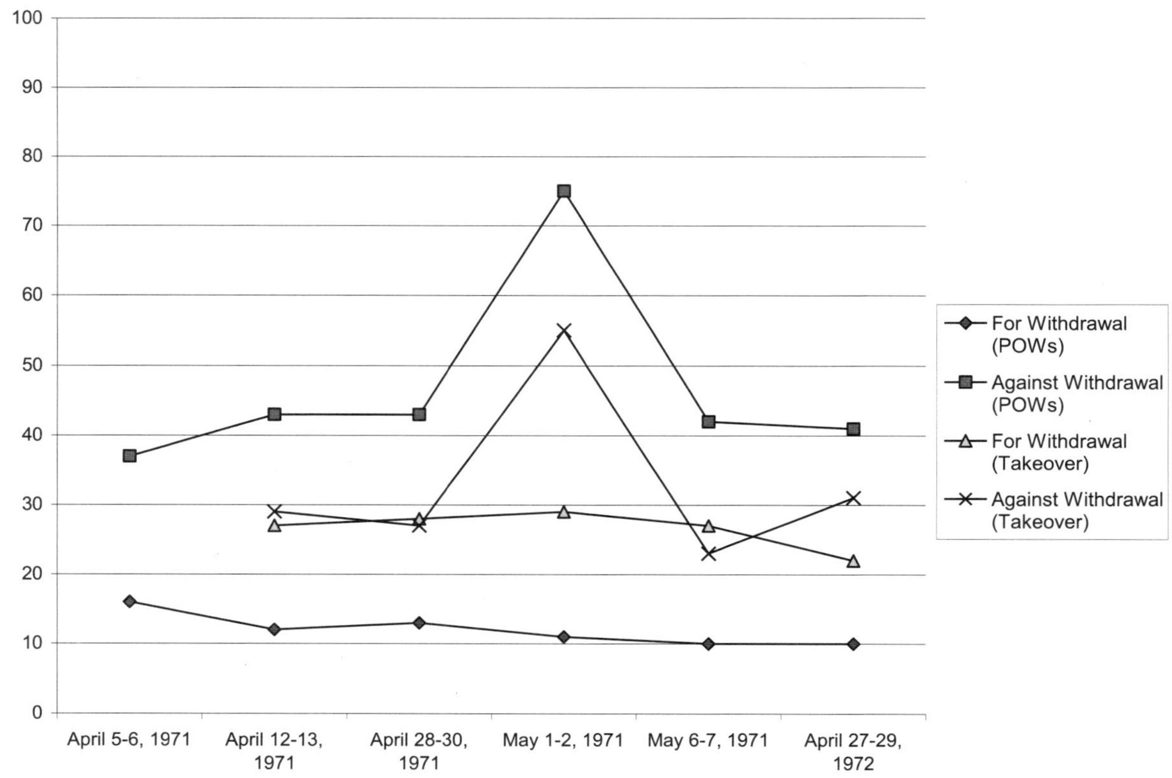

South Vietnam and to return the American prisoners of war," largely following the public's lead on this issue.[36] However, just as quickly as it rose, support for staying in Vietnam fell again, and support for withdrawal climbed as high as it had been before the president's speech. Again, this experience demonstrates how framing matters to leadership of foreign policy, as discussed in the previous chapter.

Reagan Presses for Contra Funding

With reelection secured in 1984 in a resounding victory over Walter Mondale, President Reagan sought to make political headway with his policy to aid rebels in Nicaragua who sought to overthrow their government. The president tapped into public frustration with revolutions in Latin America by espousing a tough stance against Communist revolution.[37] Although the public was generally concerned about the scope of Communist influence, extending a policy of intervention to Central America was still not at the top of the public agenda. This case study examines the White House's attempt to arouse public concerns over the spread of Communism in Nicaragua and the White House's unsuccessful efforts to move public preferences to support its policies.

The administration generally found little public support for its policies in Central America during Reagan's first term in office. A Wirthlin Poll from June of 1983 found that public concern was highest on the troubles in Central America when the arguments reflected a potential detrimental effect on the U.S. economy of between two and ten million "feet people" (refugees) from Central America arriving on American soil.[38] But the public was *not* more likely to support the president's position when presented with several other scenarios, including "concentration-type camps" in Nicaragua, increasing economic aid to El Salvador, "rightist killings" in El Salvador, or a lack of popular domestic support of the El Salvador government.[39] Especially troubling to the White House was the fact that "even among his base Republican support group Reagan does not receive a majority approval" on his handling of the situation in Central America.[40]

This decline in popular support can be traced to the public's unwillingness to engage in any conflict, no matter how uncomplicated the military task may appear. The Reagan administration's quick resolution to prior events in Lebanon and Grenada had done little to quell the public's concerns about a marauding U.S. military engaged in foreign conflicts.

Eugene Wittkopf explained that the public's desire to help its southern neighbors prevent a Communist takeover was strong in the 1940s, 1950s, and 1960s, but when confronted with real-life scenarios in the 1980s, the public opposed sending military aid.[41] The lack of significant levels of public support limited the administration's policy in Nicaragua and El Salvador to that of giving covert military aid and offering forceful rhetoric but no troops.[42] Wittkopf and James McCormick conclude that the Central American affair was "a story of failure in that the president of the United States fought a long political battle against a determined domestic opposition and came up short."[43]

Acknowledging low public support for policies of intervention in early 1985, the White House engaged in a major campaign to build public support and win congressional sanction. Their ultimate goal was to get Congress to approve a $14 million military aid package to the Contras.[44] To focus the public and Congress on the issue, "White House officials have decided to devote their attention to a major political offensive on behalf of the Contras next month, after Congress votes on the MX missile, possibly including a nationally televised speech by the president."[45] The White House believed "that it would lead public opinion with policy sculpted around the anticommunist beliefs that Reagan held so dearly."[46] The White House had been successful at such endeavors in the past, since it was able to promote higher levels of policy support with public speeches designed to increase support for intervention in Lebanon and Grenada.[47] The president's partisans were convinced this would work—an aide on the Senate Foreign Relations Committee commented that "the President has thrown the moral issue into sharp relief" and "the more he talks and the more people know, the more momentum he'll create on the issue."[48]

Through several speeches, President Reagan attempted to persuade the public that the issue of intervention in Central America was important. The spring of 1985 was "consumed by a public relations battle mounted across the country."[49] Robert Pastor reported that the president outlined his position in nearly every medium available to him, including the 1985 State of the Union address, a press conference on February 21, and in his radio address of March 30.[50] For instance, in his 1985 State of the Union message, he argued:

> We must stand by all our democratic allies. And we must not break faith with those who are risking their lives—on every continent, from Afghanistan to Nicaragua—to defy Soviet-supported

> aggression and secure rights which have been ours from birth. The Sandinista dictatorship of Nicaragua, with full Cuban-Soviet bloc support, not only persecutes its people, the church, and denies a free press, but arms and provides bases for Communist terrorists attacking neighboring states. Support for freedom fighters is self-defense and totally consistent with the OAS [Organization of American States] and U.N. Charters. It is essential that the Congress continue all facets of our assistance to Central America. I want to work with you to support the democratic forces whose struggle is tied to our own security.[51]

President Reagan's rhetoric was inflammatory and had the familiar ring of language used to describe the conflict with the Soviet Union. Gutman notes that Reagan, through his speeches, "laid down a concept (rollback by proxy), rhetoric ('freedom fighters'), and a shrill tone."[52] The president also frequently invoked the establishment of democratic principles (similar to the American founding) in the Nicaraguan case.[53] He emphasized his prerogative as commander-in-chief by claiming that "there are some situations in which only the president can and does know all the facts; he should be permitted to lead the nation and make decisions based upon what he knows and the trust placed in him by the voters."[54] He frequently appealed to the public for support, referring in several speeches to "the rebels as 'our brothers' and urging public support of the rebel cause."[55] The president was attempting to frame the issue in his favor.

In pressing harder for a military victory to overthrow the Sandinistas, President Reagan indicated in a particularly notable press conference on February 21, "Now if the present government would turn around and say, all right, if they'd say: 'Uncle.' 'All right, come on back into the revolutionary government, and let's straighten this out and institute the goals.'"[56] The president's remarks were immediately chastised by the Democrats in Congress. House Speaker Thomas P. (Tip) O'Neill Jr. (Democrat from Massachusetts)

> attacked President Reagan for saying the United States will continue to back rebels in Nicaragua unless the leftist Sandinista government there cries "uncle," and predicted that Congress will reject attempts to restore funding for the rebels. "The United States has played 'uncle' in Latin America for far too long," O'Neill said. "It is time to play brother. . . . The way to peace in Central

> America is through nonaggression and through . . . regional negotiations. . . . I don't believe he [Reagan] has the votes in either the House or the Senate for either overt or covert aid to the rebels."[57]

The president also utilized the media (through press conferences) five times between January and June of 1985 (three of these were rare prime-time conferences) to attempt to lead public opinion. As is common in such interactions, the press aggressively challenged the president on several points that coincidentally corresponded to the public's concerns on the administration's policies. For instance, referencing the president's earlier "Uncle" statement and following up on several other similar questions, CBS News correspondent Bill Plante asked,

> Mr. President, I wonder if we might return to Nicaragua. In answer to Sam's [Donaldson] question, when he pressed you, you said that you—or you seemed to be saying that you wouldn't advocate the overthrow of the government, not if the present government would turn around and say, "Uncle." Well, aren't you really saying that you want the present government out, and secondly, sir, should the United States be trying to influence a government of another nation in this hemisphere?[58]

Tough questions, like the one asked by Bill Plante, illustrate the significant limitations of using the media to lead public opinion. As we discovered in chapter 4, using the media (especially modern presidents doing so through press conferences) is a strategy that actually limits presidential ability to lead public opinion.

Ultimately, the public was not biting, and Reagan's advisers began to take note. Dick Wirthlin mailed a personal letter to President Reagan asking him to publicly refrain from supporting the Contra rebels. He argued, "In response to the question as to whether or not it is necessary for us to provide aid to those fighting the regime in Nicaragua, only 28% favor it and 70% of all Americans now oppose. . . . I, thus, strongly recommend, Mr. President, that you *not* take your case concerning aid to the Contras to the public in some dramatic and/or symbolic fashion. Rather, I believe that you should use press conferences and other lower profile activities to reaffirm your constituent support of the rebels."[59] However, according to the findings from this book, such tactics as press conferences were the wrong strategy. "Going public" on television was found to significantly help presidents lead public opinion whereas barnstorming and press conferences produce slow or negative results.[60]

For all the efforts the president and the White House put in to moving public opinion, "public support remained low."[61] Even considering the president's landslide victory in 1984, "the nation's overwhelming support for Reagan did not translate directly into support for the contra war in Nicaragua. Polls still showed the American people opposed the covert war, insofar as they knew about it."[62] Specifically, in poll results from April 1985, Dick Wirthlin's polls indicated, "U.S. policy in central America continues to divide the nation. An unchanged 50% still disapprove of his handling of the situation in Central America." Indeed, the president's rhetoric may have hurt his efforts because his "own sharp language polarized the mood in Congress, and some members said his credibility had been hurt."[63] The public was inattentive to many of the president's efforts, as most did not know what the administration's policies were or what the nature of the conflict was.[64] Again, with the public paying little attention and the president's inability to educate them (which would increase their information on the matter or make them more certain about the correct course) the White House's leadership efforts were destined to fail.

Finding little support in the public or in Congress, the president switched tactics. In April of 1986, the White House suggested that the $14 million allocation to the Contras would be used for humanitarian purposes only for two months; after two months, if the rebels' ceasefire with the Nicaraguan (Sandinista) government did not produce a peaceful arrangement, the money would revert to military uses.[65] Even with the change, Dick Wirthlin found that "strong opposition registers over providing even 'humanitarian' aid to the rebels in Nicaragua. Last month, the American public was asked if they felt it was 'absolutely necessary that we provide 14 million dollars in military aid to those fighting the regime in Nicaragua.' At the same time, 70% disagreed with that statement. This month, the word 'humanitarian' was substituted for 'military' and the rest of the statement was left unchanged. The change made no difference."[66]

Similarly, public polls taken around the time of the president's public push for the $14 million aid package indicated his efforts found little success in the public. For example, in consecutive Harris polls (in June and August of 1985), the percentage favoring the Reagan administration's policies over Congress's went from 34% to 28%.[67] Further, in polls asking directly "Do you favor or oppose . . . sending $14 million in military aid to the rebels in Nicaragua?" by Harris and Associates, 28% favored the proposal in March of 1985 while only 23% favored it in May of 1985.[68] Ironically, Reagan's "handling" of the situation did improve, but the public did not approve of the policy itself. The failure to gain public acceptance of the policy and the inability of the administration to secure passage in Congress left the president "fighting to obscure errors which have temporarily undermined his image."[69] Other public pollsters commented, "The President's standing definitely is on the wane. Polls during the past two weeks show a downturn . . . with Democrats and independents accounting for most of the decline."[70] Ultimately, public opinion played a "limiting though not defining" role in removing aid to the Contras.[71] Indeed, a president's ability to frame an issue is limited by the role of public opinion, a phenomenon that clearly limited President Reagan's ability to lead public opinion.[72]

Interestingly, again, when confronted with political difficulty (especially on its core agenda), the White House relied on and attempted to lead its core allies. Wirthlin urged organizational allies such as the Republican National Committee and the Heritage Foundation to "contact their constituents who are firmly committed to our Central American objectives and urge them to call and write their Congressmen and Senators."[73] In attempting to sell the plan to the American people, "a conservative group, 'Citizens for America,' working in consultation with [Oliver] North, organized a public relations campaign to take the President's case right to the people, to hop right over the national media."[74] The campaign cost "about $300,000 and included visits by 22 Central American business officials to cities across the United States and then to the offices of selected congressmen."[75] These efforts may have restricted a more dramatic falloff in public support and eventually helped to pass a "limited" humanitarian assistance bill through Congress.[76]

Additionally limiting the president's ability to lead was that the public was not well informed about the United States' role in Central America. A better-informed public, as consistently found throughout this book, would have assisted the president's efforts to lead the public. A polling memorandum from Dick Wirthlin in April of 1985 argued, "A majority of the adult population (58%) have not even heard or read anything recently about the President's proposal to use aid to the Contras for humanitarian purposes."[77] Indeed, President Reagan himself claimed in a radio address in August that the public was "confused about what we're supporting in Central America."[78] Wirthlin's personal note to Reagan in April argued that although the president was effective in educating the public in the past, on the Nicaragua issue the educational approach is "not appropriate in boosting support for the Nicaraguan aid request. While the public is misinformed about many of the consequences of such aid, it is not misinformed about the Nicaraguan government. Seven out of ten know it is a communist totalitarian regime engaged in a variety of activities that threatens its neighbors militarily." Wirthlin concludes, "By raising the political stakes and the public salience of this particular issue, you would not only put into jeopardy the favorable job approval you now enjoy, but, more importantly, you will generate more public and congressional opposition than support."[79]

Other political conditions also limited the president's ability to lead public opinion to endorse increased aid to the Contras. First, negative voices from Congress significantly hurt the president. Through his public push the president was "trying to turn the heat up" on Congress (through the public), but this strategy failed.[80] In fact, the proposal's reception was downright chilly as "the Administration's wilder claims about the Sandinista Government and the need to support the 'freedom fighters' in Nicaragua appear to have failed miserably to win legislative support."[81] Even the president's copartisans and supporters in Congress were abandoning him. According to the *Washington Post,* Senator Richard Lugar (Republican from Indiana), the chair of the Senate Foreign Relations Committee, said that the president's program was no longer "viable." "Lugar's assessment is the latest of a series of signals to the Reagan administration from Republican and Democratic lawmakers that an expected request for new aid faces difficult if not insurmountable obstacles in the 99th Congress."[82] Second, as we saw in Wirthlin's warning against "raising the political stakes," as well as in the aggregate findings in chapter 2, the higher the salience of the issue, the less likely presidents are able to lead if they are not popular. These realities partially explain President Reagan's lack of success.

Clinton Withdraws from Somalia

President Clinton came into office with little foreign policy experience. The primary thrust of the 1992 campaign was a focus on domestic matters that the Clinton campaign team argued had been ignored under the globe-trotting President Bush.[83] As Craig Allen Smith described it, "The sign in the Clinton headquarters read, 'It's the economy, stupid,' and pundits used it to dramatize the campaign's focus on economic frustrations as their vehicle for unseating George Bush."[84] In his inaugural address as the first president elected since the end of the Cold War, Clinton claimed that the "new world" was "more free but less stable" than before and used his rhetoric during his presidency to craft an explanation for what the United States' role would be in the post–Cold War world.[85] The president had a rude awakening on international matters as his administration would deal with several foreign policy flare-ups during his term, including Cuban refugees, the civil and ethnic conflicts in Bosnia and Haiti, and nuclear inspectors being denied entrance to North Korea.[86] The administration's response to a crisis in Somalia, however, would be the first test of the president's public leadership abilities and his new foreign policy.

The initial commitment of U.S. military forces in Somalia originated in 1992 in the Bush administration, and thus was a policy inherited by the Clinton administration. Civil strife and growing famine conditions in Somalia convinced President Bush that "U.S. forces were needed," and in December of 1992 "a force of 1,300 U.S. Marines landed in Mogadishu, and within weeks more than 25,000 U.S. soldiers were on the ground in Somalia" under Operation Restore Hope.[87] President Clinton "pledged to stay the course in Somalia, and he proved as good as his word," even adding reinforcement troops.[88] William Berman argued that Clinton, by continuing to commit troops "already dispatched to this poor East African country to help in the distribution of food supplies sent to cope with widespread famine, he quickly found himself at war with rival gangs contesting for control in the country's capital."[89] On October 3, 1993, in an attempt to capture clan leader Mohamed Farah Aideed and his top lieutenants in Mogadishu, the operation ran into trouble—by the end of the mission, two Black Hawk helicopters were shot down and eighteen American soldiers had been killed and one captured.[90] The images of a dead American solider being dragged through the dusty streets of Mogadishu the next day lingered in the public's mind and prompted the president to act.

On the afternoon of October 7, 1993, the president addressed the nation on the mission in Somalia. The stakes were high, especially since the president needed the support of Congress on his other policies in Bosnia and Haiti in the near future.[91] Moreover, failure on this issue would make the administration's handling of foreign policy seem incompetent. The president argued that more troops and military resources were necessary to stabilize the situation and protect the troops already in the field. He argued, "This past week's events make it clear that even as we prepare to withdraw from Somalia, we need more strength there. We need more armor, more air power, to ensure that our people are safe and that we can do our job. Today I have ordered 1,700 additional Army troops and 104 additional armored vehicles to Somalia to protect our troops and to complete our mission. I've also ordered an aircraft carrier and two amphibious groups with 3,600 combat Marines to be stationed offshore. These forces will be under American command."[92] However, he noted, a withdrawal of all troops would take place no later than March 13, 1994.

Unfortunately for the president, in addressing his Somalia policy, he only chose to utilize the powerful platform of the bully pulpit this *one time*. As we saw in chapter 4, when the issue is foreign policy, the public responds to the president more when the speech is presented on television. Although presidents likely reach some point of diminishing returns on their utilization of televised "formal" speeches (in the form of lessened patience or dwindling viewership among the public or the unwillingness of television networks to carry the speech), President Clinton would have been wise to approach the public through additional televised speeches on this policy issue. Another potential mistake was the decision that the speech would be delivered in the afternoon, rather than in prime time, because of a debate about "elevating" an unpopular issue to a "high profile" problem for the White House.[93] If persuasion was the goal, delivering the address in the middle of the day was not the best option.

The president's single televised appeal to the nation, in the afternoon, was not his only mistake in leading opinion on Somalia. The president may have utilized the media too much in his attempts to communicate his message to the public. As we discovered in chapter 4, press conferences do not positively influence presidential leadership of public opinion. In the week following his address to the nation, the president met with the press (either formally or informally, but always on the record) a total of seven times. Managing a political message through the press is not an easy task under any circumstances, but the confluence of forces that occurred during the Clinton presidency (such as the rise of interest in the candidates' personal lives and the ubiquity of cable television and the Internet, with which "no other prior presidential administration had been forced to contend") limited the president's ability to rely on the media to report his message unfiltered.[94]

On a potentially positive note, the president did talk about the issue for multiple consecutive days (which was found to be a positive harbinger of success in leading opinion within three months). However, of the eleven public statements he made in the week following his afternoon address, only three of those were in settings where the press was *not* granted access to ask questions. Further, although the president gave speeches in Washington, D.C., Connecticut, and North Carolina in the days following his televised address, his mentions of the Somalia policy were usually lost in a litany of other issues. For example, in his speech in New Haven, Connecticut, the president remarked: "You know, I was thinking just sitting here about the incredible events that our country has seen unfold in the last three-and-a-half weeks at home and abroad: the developments in the Middle East and in Russia; the efforts we are making here to deal with health care; and the signing of the national service bill, which was one of the things that drove me into the campaign for president; the efforts we're making to pass the trade agreement with Mexico and Canada; the continuing troubles of Somalia."[95] Here the president referenced the troubles in Somalia only as part of his larger foreign policy rather than as a specific policy in need of additional public support. Furthermore, in his address to the fall meeting of the Democratic National Committee, President Clinton "made only a passing reference to the American military deployment in Somalia, saying it was most important that the public focus on matters at home."[96] Such barnstorming efforts may have paid off quickly if the president was highly popular, but since the president was only modestly popular during that time, this effort was less effective.

The results of the president's lackluster leadership of public opinion were that, consistent with the aggregate findings in this book, public opinion did not move in the direction of favoring the president's policy (and in some instances moved away from the president's position). Table 8.2 reports the results of two poll questions taken before and after the president's afternoon speech on October 7 that query the role of U.S. troops in the region. The survey's first question was about whether the public thought that sending more troops (as the president proposed in his speech) would "insure safe withdrawal" of U.S. forces or whether more troops would "more deeply involve" the country in the conflict in Somalia. On this question, there was absolutely no change in opinion from before the president's speech to after the speech. Similarly, the second question asked whether sending additional troops to make sure that food and supplies got through to the people of Somalia was "worth the cost" of human life. Before the president's speech, 45% of the public agreed that it was worth the cost, but after the president's speech, only 42% of the public agreed it was worth the cost. The percentage of the public responding

TABLE 8.2
United States Troops and Somalia

	October 6–7	October 13
Sending more troops . . .		
"Will insure safe withdrawal"	24%	24%
"Get U.S. more deeply involved"	67	67
Don't know	9	9
Sending troops to make sure food got through to the people . . .		
"Worth the cost of American life"	45%	42%
"Not worth the cost"	45	44
Don't know	10	14

Note: For the first poll questions, the CBS News poll asked, "Do you think that sending more troops to Somalia now will insure that all U.S. (United States) troops can be safely withdrawn within a few months, or do you think that sending more troops now will just get the U.S. more deeply involved in Somalia?" For the second poll question, the CBS News poll asked, "Given the loss of American life, the financial costs, and other risks involved, do you think sending U.S. (United States) troops to Somalia to make sure food got through to the people of Somalia was worth the cost, or not?"

"don't know" also increased during this time, suggesting an uncertain commitment to the president's program. It seems clear that the public questioned the role of the military in Somalia.

Another way to look at this question is to examine the public's view of the president's "handling" of the situation in Somalia. Figure 8.2 charts this poll question from the days after the October 3 downing of the American Black Hawk helicopter until October 19. A few trends are important to point out. First, the public consistently disapproved of the

Fig. 8.2. (following page). President Clinton's handling of Somalia. The poll question asked (by different survey organizations) was "Do you approve or disapprove of the way (President) Bill Clinton is handling the situation in Somalia?" The October 5 survey by CBS News registered 14% "no opinion." The October 6 survey by CBS News registered 21% "don't know." The October 7 survey by CBS News registered 18% "no opinion." The October 10 survey by the Washington Post *registered 6% "no opinion." The October 13 survey by ABC News registered 4% "no opinion." The October 19 survey by CBS News registered 13% "no opinion."*

President Clinton's Handling of Somalia

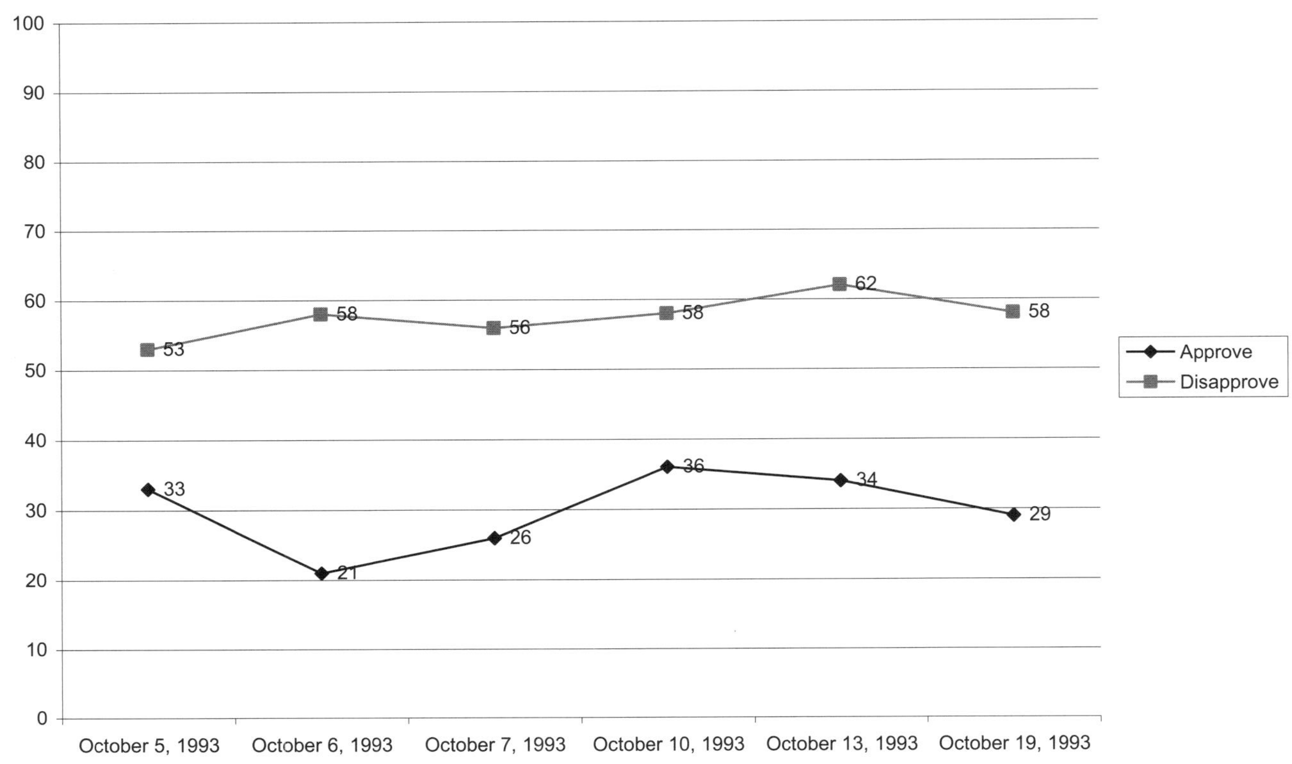

president's handling of the conflict in Somalia, a clear implication that the public does not support his policy in the region. Second, the register of disapproval does not vary much over this period, even after the president's afternoon address to the nation on October 7 (in fact, the percentage of disapproval actually rises slightly in the days following his address). Third, the public's approval of Clinton's handling of the situation fluctuates more than the public's disapproval. There is a modest increase in "handling" approval after his speech on October 7 (from 26% on October 7 to 36% on October 10), but this effect is ephemeral since his approval rating returned to below 30% in the days following his address. And, since his disapproval also increased, this suggests little or no net movement of public opinion to his position.

Ultimately, public opinion pressured the White House to more rapidly withdraw troops from Somalia. After the fiasco on October 3, "Clinton was under enormous domestic pressure to remove those troops from the scene, which he later did."[97] William Hyland also argued that "the temper of public opinion had never been enthusiastic about keeping troops in Somalia after the famine was overcome; pulling out was what the public wanted."[98] No amount of leadership or presidential persuasion was able to significantly alter the outcome in this circumstance. Illustrating this lack of leadership, polls taken before and after the president's October 7 address to the nation asked the public whether the troops should stay in Somalia until the situation is peaceful or withdraw troops "as quickly as possible." On October 6, 32% of the public agreed that troops should stay until the situation was peaceful, and on October 19 (after the president's speech), 33% agreed.[99] This modest movement of public support was certainly not sufficient to justify maintaining present troop levels. The administration feared "mission creep" where the need for more troops would create the need for more troops.[100] The public feared this also; in early October 1993, 56% of the public feared that Somalia could become like Vietnam, and that number rose to 62% in late October.[101]

There were several factors that have been found to benefit a president in leading public opinion on foreign policy but were not present for the White House during this period. Presidential approval was found to be a positive characteristic helping presidents lead public opinion by enhancing other conditions. President Clinton's approval rating at this time, however, was not above average and had largely been stuck in the midforties since the summer of 1993.[102] Strangely for a foreign policy situation involving foreign attacks on military personnel, the president's approval rating actually declined from 50% on October 8 (immediately after his address to the nation) to 47% on October 13 to 48% on October 28 and November 2.[103] Had he enjoyed above-average popularity, certain factors would have benefited him (such as a presidential barnstorm or a higher salience issue), but, without above-average popularity, the effect of his approval ratings on public leadership was modest.

These findings again help to explain why a rally moment is contingent upon several factors, many of which are not automatic and are not in the president's control. In the days following the images of American servicemen being paraded in the streets of Mogadishu, "the nation's emotional reaction was immediate, and it registered strongly on Capitol Hill."[104] Similarly, in his address to the nation on Somalia on October 7, the president directly addressed the tragic events on October 3. He opined, "This past weekend we all reacted with anger and horror as an armed Somali gang desecrated the bodies of our American soldiers and displayed a captured American pilot, all of them soldiers who were taking part in an international effort to end the starvation of the Somali people themselves. These tragic events raise hard questions about our effort in Somalia."[105] With the hopes of rallying the public, he also drew on support for the U.S. military:

> When our troops in Somalia came under fire this last weekend, we witnessed a dramatic example of the heroic ethic of our American military. When the first Black Hawk helicopter was downed this weekend, the other American troops didn't retreat although they could have. Some 90 of them formed a perimeter around the helicopter, and they held that ground under intensely heavy fire. They stayed with their comrades. That's the kind of soldiers they are. That's the kind of people we are.[106]

Yet as we have seen, the public did not increase their support for the mission, felt no greater stake in the mission, and did not increase approval of the president at all. In fact, his approval rating declined.

Why did the public not rally around the White House's policy? Several explanations are plausible. First, the president delayed making his policy announcement for four days (the incident in Mogadishu occurred on October 3 and his speech was on October 7). The emotional effect of the powerful images of chaos in the streets of Somalia may have mitigated by then. Second, the rally may actually have backfired and precipitated the public's isolationist response to interventions that may inflict military casualties. The "emotions aroused by a new picture [of the bodies of U.S. servicemen being dragged through the streets] and the deaths it represents are putting pressure on the Administration to end the mission that began with such acclaim less than a year ago."[107] Substantiating this interpretation of the public's response, scholars have found that rally effects diminish when presidents use force and that support for conflict declines when cumulative actions escalate a conflict without solving it.[108] The public's frustration over the situation created a reaction against continued intervention and limited their desire for a forceful response. Third, public support for the policy had already dropped to its lowest point in September of 1993 (when the military shifted its objective from delivering food to a "peace-enforcement goal of targeting Somali warlord Mohamed Farah Aideed") and it was simply not going to go higher.[109]

Also damaging for the White House was that the Clinton team had just been elected eleven months before the Somalia crisis. The young Clinton administration was still immersed in an unhappy (by virtue of being unpopular) honeymoon with the media and Congress, a finding that the analysis in chapter 4 reveals to be a negative prospect for leadership. Contemporary observers noted, "President Clinton is a little over a week away from the purely imaginary marker that has measured presidential debuts ever since Franklin Roosevelt—the first 100 days. In Mr. Clinton's debut, he has impressed many with his energy and engagement, . . . [but] his honeymoon is over already, one of the shortest on record."[110] The White House was also still dealing with significant economic problems and trying to gain a foothold on its policy agenda (especially on health care), generally to little success. Indeed, the early years of the Clinton administration were replete with messages from multiple and competing groups. Lynda Kaid, John Tedesco, and Julia Spiker find "this new use of political advertising, to compete for public support on issues normally decided by the interplay of executive and legislative forces, has added an entirely new element to the policy environment."[111] Each competing group limited the president's ability to clearly and effectively disseminate his message to the public on his Somalia policy.

As a complement to the White House's short honeymoon, the chaotic nature of the issue agenda in 1993 contributed to a difficulty in focusing the president's persuasive power on the public. Of course, there are always several issues on the president's plate at once. But when the White House is focusing on too many issues, or when its focus on one issue negates its focus on another, the possibility of message entanglement from the White House is created. Edwards argued that the Somalia situation came in the middle of several other issues that the president was attempting to sell to the public. He notes that "there were important distractions" from the president's main focus at the time of the Somalia troubles: health-care legislation.[112] The president had to devote attention to Somalia, "so the president returned from his health care trip to California and focused on events abroad."[113]

Conclusion

Although conventional wisdom holds that presidents can lead on foreign policy, it is clear that not all foreign policy situations are alike. The fact that a president has the opportunity to engage the public on a foreign policy issue is not necessarily by itself an unlimited formula for success. Presidents still must follow the same set of rules and patterns that make political leadership work in other contexts, whether these moments involve the use of U.S. troops in a region (Somalia) or the defense of a particular ideology (funding of the Nicaraguan rebels or escalating conflict in Vietnam). The fact that these case studies find presidents unable to lead public opinion in several foreign policy moments refines the work of previous scholars who argue that presidents can uniformly move public opinion on foreign policy and provides a more nuanced view of the conditions of leadership on foreign policy. As argued in the previous chapter, a president with public opinion on his side is a tough opponent for Congress, but when the president can't move public opinion, presidential powers on foreign policy are less formidable.

These case studies can also tease out the nature of a rally effect and what value it retains for the White House. President Nixon had a built-in rally when an antagonistic military attack on U.S. military personnel sparked his retaliatory bombing, but his actions were too slow to capitalize on the emotion and enthusiasm in the public. President Reagan attempted to create his own rally moment with fierce and dramatic rhetoric—a prospect that, without accompanying events to shock the public, was unsuccessful at raising public interest or knowledge. In fact, attempts to frame the issue to his favor backfired. President Clinton also had a natural rally moment (similar to President Nixon's) but without a defined objective to link to his policy and without follow-up rhetorical support, the Somalia policy rally was emaciated and therefore ineffective at leading public opinion. Similarly, in each case the media was unsupportive or critical of the mission or the president's actions. Each case helps to put the "non-rally" finding from chapter 4 into context.

Ironically, each president whom we studied in these cases used the "major address" strategy, a good tactical move according to the aggregate findings. However, particular circumstances limited the reach of these speeches. For instance, in the case of Richard Nixon, his pollsters found that the audience for his speech was lower than that for any other recent Vietnam speech, limiting the effectiveness of the televised appeal. President Clinton addressed the public in the afternoon (instead of in prime time) as a way to suppress the potentially unpopular elements of the policy. President Reagan used several means of communications but the impact of the Contra aid discussion was either limited by other issues on the agenda (such as the funding negotiations for the MX missile or the debate over increasing farm subsidies) or the cacophony of dissent coming from the halls of Congress. Perhaps the president did not go public enough on television. Several of the president's aides (led by Patrick Buchanan) urged the president to use the television more (especially just before the House rejected the $14 million Contra funding in April) to public opinion because the issue required sustained persuasion, but Buchanan's proposal was rejected by presidential aides Michael Deaver and Ed Rollins.[114]

Politics and diplomacy also limit what the president can do by way of persuasive communications. For instance, both Presidents Nixon and Clinton (and advisers to President Reagan) were unwilling to speak publicly with any great frequency on the issues that confronted them for fear of jeopardizing international diplomacy, a future balance of policy objections in Congress or alienating the public with an unpopular policy. If the White House is unwilling to attempt to sell its policies to the public, it is not startling to discover that leadership of public opinion does not result. These failures of leadership are less about policy falling "on deaf ears" (as Edwards notes) and more about the White House's desire to whisper. The communication component is therefore a necessary condition for political leadership and one which a president bent on leading (foreign or domestic policy) must employ.[115]

As we have seen in these three cases, poor or inopportune timing in relation to elections or presidential first years in office can hurt leadership efforts because these factors take the focus off presidents or add unwanted focus onto presidents. Political moments close to elections negatively affect opportunities for presidential leadership of public opinion. For instance, President Nixon's unsuccessful attempts to lead public opinion occurred only months before the 1972 election. The president's actions hurt his chances to convince the public that peace in Vietnam was close and highlighted his broken promise of 1968 to end the conflict. Presidential honeymoons, especially for later-serving presidents, also negatively impact presidential efforts to lead public opinion. President Reagan's reelection in 1984 was a clear indication of his political wherewithal, but the choice of an unpopular policy and perceptions of him as a "lame duck" president limited his effectiveness in leading public opinion to support increasing aid to the Contras. The nascent Clinton administration had not even finished their honeymoon before they were confronted with a critical situation abroad, and the president's lack of experience communicating to the public on foreign policy became apparent.

CHAPTER 9

Implications for Leadership and the Public Presidency

As observers and scholars of presidential history, we are obsessed with ranking the presidents who are thought to be the "best leaders." Early attempts (such as Arthur M. Schlesinger's survey of historians in 1948) and more recent attempts (such as James Taranto and Leonard Leo's *Presidential Leadership: Rating the Best and Worst in the White House*) address the puzzle of presidential leadership from multiple perspectives but without a consensus on the criteria used for evaluation.[1] Routinely, Presidents (Franklin) Roosevelt, Kennedy, and Reagan come out on top while, typically, Presidents Nixon, Ford, and Carter hover around the bottom. These rankings are traditionally based on reputation, perceived presidential "skill," success in the policy arena, and ability to handle the various crises facing each president. Rankings like these supply magnificent evidence for a spirited debate about the effectiveness of presidents, comprising the interaction of political forces with presidential political acumen and qualities that make strong leaders.

Methodologically, these rankings also provoke a reasonable debate about how presidential leadership is measured (especially in reference to presidential "greatness"). However, it is difficult to assess presidential leadership from select cases because information may be stressed that is thought to be important for evaluation (when it potentially is not) or information may be missing that is important for appraisal. Scholars also tend to assume that presidential moments of successful leadership are self-induced and transcend the peculiar moments of economic, international, or political circumstances.[2] Too much faith is put in these moments as "revealers" of presidential greatness when presidents simply happened to be serving at a fortuitous moment in time for enhancing leadership.[3] The moments, issues, or events that scholars select as vehicles to examine presidential leadership success or failure come with methodological trade-offs—a kind of empirical "zero sum" game where only selected moments of presidential history, White House policy, or presidential actions are examined and from which presidential leadership is generalized. Such studies also presume that one can understand *when* presidents *should* have led, often without verification of that elusive fact.

In this concluding chapter, I review the evidence presented in this book to assess what this study has contributed to the literature on the public presidency and the role of presidents as leaders of public opinion. Of course, this analysis presumes that presidents desire to lead mass public opinion to further their policy goals when other rhetorical goals may take priority in certain instances, including leading individual groups, directly influencing Congress with their rhetoric, neutralizing critics of the administration's policies, or exploiting other opportunities presented by a broad confluence of political forces.[4] The analysis from this book does not preclude these explanations but rather takes as its central goal to offer empirical evidence for when presidents are likely to temporarily lead public opinion and which tactics are most effective. Understanding these political, social, and economic contexts more clearly, we can begin to paint a clearer picture of the constraints presidents face when leading public opinion as well as the opportunities for leadership not previously found in the literature.

The literature on the subject of presidential leadership has produced several contradictory theories along with concurrent empirical variation. Some scholars claim presidential leadership can be achieved by effective presidents; some claim it is an illusion. Other scholars claim leadership of opinion is central to and present in presidential political success; others dispute this claim. In this book I seek to use the data to resolve these differences and add to an understanding of how and under what conditions presidents lead public opinion. The findings here support and complement several theories in the literature. However, these findings also challenge several existing findings or recast assumptions pertaining to presidential behavior regarding public opinion. Although this book will not be the final word on the subject (given the myriad of ways in which scholars might define leadership of public opinion), it has gotten us closer to a more refined understanding of the moments where presidents succeed at leading public opinion.

Refining Our Understanding of Presidential Leadership

Absent the power to *command*, the president's power to *compel* may be the most significant tool in the White House's arsenal of persuasive techniques. Leadership of public opinion is a time-honored tradition for the White House, dating back to the early days of the presidency and maturing in the age of polls, and this type of policy leadership has been the impetus for the growth of power in the modern presidency. The trouble is that assumptions abound pertaining to the effectiveness of this approach to policy advocacy. Presidents, the public, and pundits alike assume that opinion leadership is an unquestionably good strategy. However, despite much enthusiasm for opinion leadership, the findings from this book show that presidents are not able to lead public opinion with great consistency. Most presidents rarely break the 50% barrier in leading public opinion (leading half the time) and are less effective at leading opinion in significant (greater than 5%) amounts. This is a modest-to-mediocre record of public persuasion, especially considering the emphasis the political system puts on this strategy.

This is not to suggest, of course, that presidents do not find moments of success. We can identify several conditional moments of leadership success, which are reflected in the themes from this book. When there is movement of opinion from before the president speaks to after he speaks, the opinion tends to move modestly in the direction of the president's policies (typically in small increments of between 1% and 5%). Leadership of opinion in larger percentages is more rare but does occasionally occur, especially by certain presidents or on certain issues. It is clear that a sustained effort to lead public opinion from the White House is therefore necessary if the president hopes to consistently move public opinion to his favor. This reality is supported by evidence from the aggregate findings (as the "two days before" findings reveal) and in the case studies of successful leadership. Michael Genovese confirms this thinking in his advice to incoming presidents on presidential persuasion: "Your power will always be fragile and variable; and it must be won anew every day."[5]

The need for a sustained effort from the president in order to consistently lead public opinion is the core theoretical connection to the arguments in this book. In chapter 2 I argued that the president would be more likely to lead public opinion when fewer countervailing agents or elements obscured his direct communication with the public. Presidents should succeed at leading public opinion when they make consistent, solid, and unwavering attempts to do so. The more the president can avoid the political echo chamber associated with partisan battles or communications, the better the chance he has to lead public opinion. In particular, the ability to lead public opinion is *provisional* (hence this book's title) because certain factors enhance leadership success and certain factors detract from it. These findings complement the work by scholars who are interested in explaining how presidents interact with a political environment that is set up so that, given the right strategic resources, they can succeed, but without these resources they will fail. The implication is that the president's political environment and his strategic use of the White House's communications strategies is more telling of his ability to lead public opinion than are his rhetorical skills or institutional setting.

Indeed, the communications strategies that most directly connect to the public find the most success in leading public opinion. For instance, a "barnstorm" strategy works best when a president is popular or when he has enough time to allow the strategy to mature (three months). A "major address" strategy works best for all presidents grouped together, especially on matters of foreign policy, but is less effective for later presidents. And, importantly, a strategy of talking about the issue for two consecutive days (at least) helps to lead the public. Generally, the case studies also reveal that these tactics were effective when used in combination with each other and when they enabled the White House to avoid relying on the media to disseminate the president's message. For instance, unveiling a policy through a televised address then stumping for it across the nation was often found to be effective. Or, beginning a speaking tour of the nation and parlaying that momentum into a televised speech is also often effective. Utilizing multiple avenues on the same issue is important to keeping the public and the media focused on that message. As this communications focus wanes, so do the prospects for leadership.

Of course, in discovering the situations where presidential leadership succeeds, we can also by extension more closely examine why presidents *fail* to lead public opinion, the most frequently presumed outcome of presidential actions. So, why do presidents not find success in leading public opinion? The conditional leadership theory suggested that when there are more countervailing influences present in the political system, this leads to less leadership success for presidents because the president's voice is crowded out. As evidence, we can observe that later-serving presidents, afflicted with a new political reality replete with a more aggressive media and greater partisanship, are more disadvantaged than earlier presidents who did not have to deal with these challenges to as great an extent. This new political reality severely limits modern presidential leadership.

Similarly, other issues (countervailing elements) may crowd out the president's agenda and complicate his ability to focus the media and public on an issue. An administration may miscalculate the ability of the political system (especially Congress) to deal with multiple issues simultaneously, as in the case of the Kennedy administration and their pursuit of several policies at once in Congress in addition to Medicare. This phenomenon may reflect a lack of planning but also may reflect economic or electoral needs to rush passage of several pieces of legislation. The opposition (or support) from interest groups also plays a role, one that is important to evaluating the limits to presidential leadership, especially in modern presidential policymaking. More issues on the agenda mean more voices to compete with the president's message. As a result, especially in foreign policy cases, the president has less success when the issue has high salience, since more political activity is generated by more visible issues.

The "size" of the president's agenda (or the number of issues concomitantly pursued) clearly has an effect on his ability to lead public opinion, especially related to his ability to sustain public attention to that agenda. A White House's agenda is inherently limited, and, according to Paul Light, "the President's domestic agenda also reflects the allocation of resources, which often are fixed and limited. As the President moves through the term, each agenda choice commits some White House resources—time, energy, information, expertise, political capital."[6] The restrictions that emerge in the modern presidency limit the resources presidents can devote to too many subjects—focusing on one single issue (at a time) is critical. This slow, "spoon feeding" approach is important because it allows for a timely digestion by the public and the media (and eventually Congress) rather than a rapid-fire, adversarial approach that may sour stomachs. The reality of limited resources directly connects to the conditional theory of presidential leadership that requires presidents to focus on single issues with intense focus.

Indeed, there are several examples of how presidents fail to lead public opinion when too many issues are pursued at once or when a White House's laserlike focus on an issue enabled successful leadership. For instance, President Kennedy's rush to pursue several major pieces of legislation in 1961 and 1962 crowded the political agenda and complicated his ability to put the force of the White House's popularity behind his Medicare legislation. President Ford's inability to secure passage of his anti-inflation proposals was not aided by his own reluctance about the proposals (in that the proposal was eventually withdrawn), the White

House's loose commitment to solving the inflation problem over the unemployment problem, and the rush of the plan to the media. On the other hand, President Reagan focused exclusively on tax and budget proposals in his first months in office and secured congressional passage of both pieces of legislation. Likewise, President Clinton's intense focus on the issue of the budget late in his first term allowed him to focus public attention early, commit the information resources of the White House, and effectively organize his troops for battle against an averse Congress.

Many scholars see a direct trade-off between bargaining with Congress and appealing to the public. The more presidents "go public" the less likely they are able to compromise with Congress, having thrown down a gauntlet by requiring Congress to respond. Yet anecdotal evidence suggests that, depending on the political situation, the two are not mutually exclusive. For instance, although President Reagan was unable to convince the public or Congress to accept his proposals for military aid to the Contras, the White House was ultimately able to get Congress to agree to $27 million in "nonlethal" humanitarian aid (albeit through a long negotiation and not in the original format the president desired).[7] President Clinton was able to pursue an aggressive public stance on balancing the federal budget, encapsulating his ideas and concurrently bargaining with Congress to enact his preferred policy. In that sense, the two strategies reinforced each other, illustrating how Kernell's "going public" has practical promise.[8]

If the president can temporarily move opinion through specific tactics, he may find traction in Congress at key moments in the legislative process. Several of the presidents in these case studies used the power of the bully pulpit to alter or diffuse congressional opposition or create Congressional acquiescence. Taking their message to the public in this fashion may provide presidents with the necessary bargaining leverage needed to pressure additional members of Congress to support their positions. In short, "going public" can work, but it does not necessarily work all the time or because presidents utilize the bully pulpit. Presidents must choose selected times and tactics in a combination that favors their success.

The media also clearly play a limiting role in the president's political leadership, which is ironic given the tremendous resources the White House brings to the public relations battle.[9] The White House's relationship with the media is altogether symbiotic, tense, playful, and strategic.[10] Since the media is a vessel for the president's message, the president must find ways to bring his message to the public with as little filtering as possible. Not unpredictably, then, press conferences are particularly difficult moments to attempt to lead public opinion because the media is the sieve through which the White House's message is funneled. On this point, one measure that was explored too briefly but which needs more attention is media coverage of the policy itself. If the media frames an issue in a way that limits the president's appeal to the public or if the media has primed the public to believe other issues are more important, the effect on leadership would be tangible. Thus, absent a particular kind of coverage, leadership may be made easier, or with the benefit of a certain type of coverage, leadership could be made easier.

Reflecting these trends in the media, two specific temporal moments also consistently damage presidential leadership of public opinion: during election years or during a president's honeymoon year in office. Theoretically, both moments provide an opportunity for presidents to more clearly communicate with the public. This is true in the case of elections since the media and public are focused on them, and in the case of the president's first year in office, the media are less critical of presidential decisions and the public is more patient with presidential actions. Yet presidents find no quarter in these moments and as a practical matter can do very little to work around these time periods since they cannot avoid talking during their first or fourth years in office. Indeed, the negative coverage trends have been exacerbated in recent years. As a result, presidents must seek to lead opinion more strategically during these critical moments rather than assume that they will have carte blanche to invigorate their agenda on the national stage. Bargaining with Congress privately during these times would also be a safer, calculated tactic.

The Fate of the Public Presidency

Recent scholarship has argued that leadership is categorically impossible for presidents as they try to communicate their message to the public. Both Edwards and Jeffrey Cohen suggest that the limitations of partisanship, media attention, and public attention hamper the president's ability to present his unvarnished message to the American people.[11] Susan Herbst argues that because of these boundaries presidential speech is "hurtling towards its demise."[12] I take a different viewpoint here. I argue that these limiting conditions are clearly present, but in instances where presidents have a clearer window of communication, they have an easier time leading public opinion. The findings from this book nuance categorical claims about presidential inability to lead public opinion. Within the framework identified by these authors, the argument and findings in this book suggest that, when such negative conditions are not present, presidents are more able to communicate their message and lead opinion. Indeed, the findings here concerning audience attention (changes in the percentage of the public responding "don't know") and the importance of the issue both comport with earlier findings reflecting the difficulty presidents find leading public opinion. Presidents may lead at the margins but they still lead.

In fact, presidents are not always hapless victims of political circumstances where an unfavorable environment perpetually disadvantages their ability to lead public opinion. Several time periods, conditions, and tactics are used by presidents to their advantage, especially when it is more likely that the president's message is able to get through with direct, televised communication, through consistently utilizing the bully pulpit, or when more effectively "teaching" the public. These findings imply that presidents have some control over their own political fortune and that presidents can strategically lead public opinion, even though this success is conditioned on the degree of public information, the prominence of the issue, the time period, and the tactic used. These findings concur with Edwards's edicts from *The Strategic President* in that presidents are admonished to use their skills to recognize the opportunities for leadership. The present book has helped to put the president's ability to lead public opinion in context—a critical step to evaluating the impact of presidential rhetoric on the public, Congress, and the larger political system.

In assessing presidential leadership, Edwards argues that "presidents cannot reshape the contours of the political landscape to pave the way for change by establishing an agenda and persuading the public, Congress, and others to support their policies."[13] But this is too broad an indictment of the president's inability to foster a political environment to be more receptive to his policies. The case studies here have demonstrated, complemented by the aggregate findings, that presidents are able to control the agenda, frame issues, and get their policies passed by taking their case to the public. The ability of Presidents Nixon and Reagan to persuade a reluctant Congress or mute congressional opposition to their economic policies illustrates how presidents can lead public opinion to their advantage. President Clinton's battle with Republicans in Congress in 1995 and 1996 also illustrates how the bully pulpit can pressure

Congress to respond to the president's policies. In foreign policy cases, Presidents Carter and Bush were able to secure support from Congress despite initial dissent as a result of their ability to gather popular support behind their initiatives. These findings do not imply that the president's strategy always works, as we saw in chapters 6 and 8 that such leadership efforts do fail, but when the conditions are right for the president and the pathways of communication are clearer, the president has the ability to cultivate a favorable environment.

Where does this leave our understanding of the public presidency? One primary critique of the "new" public role of the president (through the rhetorical presidency) is that presidents have surpassed their constitutionally proscribed roles and run the risk of political demagoguery as they persist in communicating directly to the public.[14] Although manipulation and secrecy are clearly components of the ways in which presidents shape public opinion,[15] the findings here reveal that presidents are generally incapable of moving public preferences on public policy except under specific conditions. And, importantly, these conditions are often temporary (major addresses or a barnstorm), ephemeral (popularity or salient issues), or issue based (foreign policy) so that a president will have only a momentary opportunity to take advantage of the political circumstances. Similarly, when opinion moves, it moves in small amounts and temporarily. These findings mitigate (or minimize) the instances in which presidents might engage in incendiary rhetoric to manipulate the public.

Fears of a rhetorically demagogic presidency often reflect the delicate balance of powers between the executive and legislative branches. Is the new rhetorical presidency a recipe for political gridlock in Congress? Several scholars are concerned that the use of the bully pulpit may backfire and anger the executive's coequal counterpart.[16] Kernell contends, "Going public violates [congressional] bargaining in several ways. First, it rarely includes the kinds of exchanges necessary, in pluralist theory, for the American political system to function properly. At times, going public will be merely superfluous—fluff compared with the substance of traditional political exchange. Practiced in a dedicated way, however, it may displace bargaining."[17] This is a real concern because presidents are constantly "going public" and the almost ubiquitous presence of divided government necessitates political bargaining (although several scholars have pointed out that the "going public" strategy has yet to prove effective as originally theorized).[18] The polarization in the public and Congress may spell political disaster for a president who is unwilling to compromise.

Coalitional politics are also affected by presidential leadership attempts. There is a danger that a president, sensing or experiencing a lack of success in leading mass public opinion, may resort to more concentrated or localized appeals, ignoring mass public opinion altogether.[19] Narrow communications outlets (like cable television, specialized publications, local media, and the Internet) make ignoring public opinion more possible than ever before. Evidence from the case studies suggests that presidents' core constituencies within the public are important resources to them in difficult times, implying that, as political circumstances worsen and presidents find themselves embattled, they are more likely to retreat to their base.[20] To the extent that there is a trade-off between what is good for the entire nation and what is good for the president's core public, retreating to the base is a worrisome trend.

Yet this danger is mitigated because presidents who stray too far from the core concerns of the public (the mass public or their core constituents) find themselves in precarious political circumstances and without core *or* mass support. Presidents need minimum levels of public support to maintain confidence in their policies, whether it is congressional support, electoral support, or bureaucratic support. Without a policy at least tacitly endorsed by the public, the president's ability to retain control of the agenda, implement public policy, and lead public opinion is lessened. This balance of forces (political, social, and economic) prevents presidents from employing their power as dictators, even if their rhetoric occasionally slips into demagoguery. The republic has withstood presidents of all shades beginning from the nascent days of presidential governance, some aggressive with power, some meek with power, and public opinion has played a role in each phase of this development.[21] To ignore public opinion for too long is to ignore the foundation of government—a chance presidents rarely take.

The role of the public themselves in the process of presidential leadership is also critical and cannot be overlooked. Their role is particularly acute as evaluators of the president's use of rhetoric as a way to usurp political power. Public opinion forms the limits of what presidents can do, as we found throughout this book. Presidents are most effective at leading when the public is more certain or informed about a policy, not when they are less informed. Presidents are persuasive "teachers" of the public; the public attains higher levels of information on the subjects the president talks about. If knowledge and certainty lead to good judgments, this phenomenon suggests that presidents cannot move opinion where the public is unwilling to go. There are moments of real concern during "rally" moments and "honeymoon" years when presidents theoretically lead an information-impoverished public, but the findings in this book suggest that the president's ability to lead in these instances is not absolute nor is it frequent. The case studies involving presidents' attempts to frame foreign policy further demonstrate the ephemeral nature of presidential leadership. Knowledgeable public opinion is critical to the role of democracy, and in this book I suggest that the public, the media, and other institutional actors must be vigilant when the president frames foreign policy to ensure that the public is not being taken for a ride. Even so, the public is skeptical enough to not simply buy every presidential argument.

Presidential framing of issues (highlighting certain words or phrases) provides the president the opportunity to lead public opinion, but the limits of the public's understanding or support are strongly considered by the White House.[22] In several instances in the case studies, presidents were able to frame issues in particular ways that enhanced support for less popular policies (see Nixon on Vietnam in chapter 8), but they did so acknowledging the important role of the public and the limitations the public forced on them (see Bush on the Gulf War in chapter 7). This reality minimizes presidents' manipulation of the public through their leadership; although presidents developed an infrastructure to change public preferences, the limitations forced on them by these preferences also encourages responsiveness to them.[23] Presidents are concerned about violating public opinion, and importantly, this opinion tends to rein in the ability of the White House to shape policy outcomes with their rhetoric alone. This is especially true since, consistent with the theory presented here, presidents will also be challenged in their messages by competing actors—this competition in framing issues has been shown to lessen support for initial positions.[24] The public is not easily manipulated by presidential rhetoric, a finding that powerfully impacts presidents' ability to lead public opinion.

Similarly, the higher the salience of the issue being discussed by the president, the less likely presidents are to lead public opinion. In none of the statistical models did the higher visibility of salient issues provide presidents with a more potent platform to lead public opinion. In fact, as consistently shown in the aggregate findings, the higher the salience of the issue the less likely presidents were to lead public opinion. The implication of these findings is that presidential communications, even at the hub of government, do not always provide the White House with a clear pathway to the ears of the public—other groups (countervailing agents) are very likely to join the cacophony of voices advocating their preferred policy. In such circumstances the president's message can get obscured or challenged, making his ability to lead more difficult and likewise limits his ability to railroad the political system with his position, at least from a rhetorical standpoint.

Provisional but Powerful

Ultimately, the whims of popular passions that caused the authors of the *Federalist Papers* to express such dismay seem to have given way to recognition of the importance and influence of public opinion on presidential decision making—a strong connection, but a refereed one. Modern presidents of all levels of popularity, personality, interpersonal skill, education, and occupation adhere to the changing philosophy of presidential politics in which presidents, as guardians of the nation's interests, look to the public for input and guidance on policy but also attempt to shape the public's views. President Woodrow Wilson's revolutionary assertion that "there is but one national voice in the country, and that is the voice of the President" creates a paradigm of modern presidential necessity to communicate with and lead the public.[25] Even if "provisional" by political situation, temporal circumstance, or presidential tactic, this persuasive power is still relevant and still shapes the president's centripetal role in the political system.

Epilogue

Presidents 43 and 44

The data (and most of the case studies) in this book end with the Clinton presidency. As described throughout this book, several detrimental modern political factors negatively affected the leadership efforts of later-serving presidents (Presidents Carter to Clinton). These factors all relate to the story presented in Chapter 2—as presidents face more constraints on their leadership (in the form of countervailing elements or agents), their ability to communicate with the public (and therefore lead the public) declines. Yet it seems clear that the political environment for opinion leadership has gotten worse, not better. Presidents Bush (43) and Obama (44) served during times when the difficulties presidents face in leading public opinion have been dramatically exacerbated since the Clinton administration. For instance, more recently, the media is even more ubiquitous, the sources of media are more prolific, political partisanship has intensified as the "center" of American politics has disappeared, and technology has emerged that individualizes consumption of political information.

In this epilogue my purpose is to look briefly at the two presidencies since Bill Clinton's second term in order to identify specific trends in their leadership tactics and the success or failure of these efforts. This is not a comprehensive study of these presidencies, their leadership tactics, or their relationship with the American people. Indeed, these are more appropriately left to a longer treatise on the subject. Furthermore, such a feat would be difficult considering the Obama administration only recently arrived in office as of this writing. Here I reexamine the trends discovered in the previous nine chapters and compare and contrast them with selected trends identified as key legislation or issues important to the Bush and Obama administrations. Generally confirming the findings from this book, the political environment serves as a critical backdrop to the ability of these presidents to lead public opinion, and, perhaps as importantly, their success is predicated on timing, issues, intensity, and degree of public information. But in each instance, the president has some control over these conditions and can therefore use the bully pulpit provisionally.

President Bush (43)

George W. Bush's ascendancy to office wasn't as smooth as that of past presidents. The president's narrow election victory demonstrated a highly divided electorate and a congested political environment. Reflecting this tension, a prolonged legal battle and concurrent political struggle following election night nibbled away at the president's momentum in the early days of his administration.[1] Partly as a result, the transition of the president selling himself as a candidate to selling his policies while in office was clearly blurred as the Bush administration made the strategic choice to "govern by campaigning."[2] The Bush White House cleverly used its campaign networks to communicate its messages to their supporters.[3] This tactic enabled the new administration to have a continuous message in front of the American public, even if the number of supporters it won was often limited to those who agreed with the president. And, despite these political limitations, President Bush demonstrated that a president is not always crippled by "thin electoral margins, bare majorities in Congress, or by modest or even low levels of popular approval."[4]

Tax Cuts. Proposing a significant round of cuts to federal income taxes was a centerpiece of President Bush's political campaign and one of the first proposals on which he used the bully pulpit to persuade the public. The government was in the black with record budget surpluses and the president was pushing a $1.35 trillion tax cut.[5] This promise was a major part of the president's campaign in 2000 and a big part of the president's philosophy of government that was built around allowing taxpayers to keep more of the money they made.[6] The plan called for lowering the marginal income tax rates for all taxpayers, including a reduction of the percentage of income paid in each tax bracket, reducing the "marriage penalty," giving a child tax credit, and eliminating the estate tax. As a central part of his agenda, the president took to the stump vigorously to persuade the American public that these tax cuts were good for them and for the economy.

Some argue that, despite these efforts, the president failed to lead public opinion. For instance, Edwards reports that public opinion on the president's tax policy did not move much from early February 2001 to the end of April 2001, with 56% supporting it in February and the same number supporting it in April.[7] Yet two details are overlooked in Edwards's analysis of President Bush's "going public" tactics. First, the president did probably effect a change (albeit small) in public opinion. He delivered an address to a joint session of Congress on February 21 where he argued, "I hope you will join me in standing firmly on the side of the people. You see, the growing surplus exists because taxes are too high and Government is charging more than it needs."[8] As we discovered in chapter 4, a public address of this nature has a positive effect on a president's ability to lead public opinion. Similarly effective in leading public opinion is a barnstorm trip around the nation. In the three days following his address to Congress, President Bush visited Pennsylvania, Nebraska, Iowa, Georgia, and Arkansas. As a result, before the president's speech (February 19–21) the tax cut program received 53% approval, while after the president's speech and barnstorm trip, approval of the program rose modestly to 56% (March 5–7).[9] And, importantly, scholars have suggested that this approach of building support was effective in passing these tax cuts.[10]

Second, buttressing the argument from chapter 2 about the nature of the president's message transmission, those individuals exposed to the president's speech were more likely to be persuaded. A Gallup/CNN/*USA Today* poll of adult watchers of the president's February 27 address showed that 68% of watchers approved before the president's speech while 79% approved after watching the speech. The percentage of respondents responding "don't know" declined from 8% to 2%.[11] Again, this direct and unvarnished message to the public had success in moving public opinion, although such success is clearly contingent on people watching the address. Still, these findings suggest that the president's message was persuasive, even if temporarily, and the public was learning about the proposals and becoming more sure they would work. Therefore, the central successful conditions governing public opinion leadership explained throughout this book hold. Congress's approval for the policy was secured and the White House had its first major policy victory.

Iraq. Not surprisingly, the president's efforts to persuade the American public that the administration's plans to initiate conflict with Iraq were successful. Leaving aside the veracity of their claims regarding the presence of weapons of mass destruction, the context of the "war on terror," or the gradual degeneration of public support as the conflict drug on, the administration's public relations efforts in 2003 leading up to the initiation of hostilities conformed to the prototype of how presidents lead public opinion on foreign policy. Figure 10.1 charts the percentage of the public approving or disapproving of the commitment of military action to remove Saddam Hussein from power. The percentage approving held steady in the mid-sixties range for much of February to early March, partly because the administration was not educating the public enough on their positions.[12] Then, following a Saturday radio address and two prime-time addresses in mid-March, the percentage rose from 76% to 80%. In late March through mid-April, the percentage declined again but hovered in the high 70% range.

A number of factors identified in the previous chapters played favorably for the administration in terms of leading public opinion on President Bush's Iraq policy. First, he made two prime-time speeches (March 17 and 19) to the American public. Again, tactics such as direct communication with the public are successful in communicating the White House's message. Second, the president talked about the issue virtually every day from late January to the beginning of the conflict in late March 2003. The administration's continuous pressure on an issue that they had made their central focus gave the president a wider platform from which explain his positions. Third, the White House committed troops to the conflict, an activity that was found to boost leadership capability in foreign policy cases. Fourth, the activities were *not* in an election year or in his honeymoon period, both factors that have been found to limit presidential ability to lead public opinion.

Contrasting with this interpretation, Edwards argues that the percentage favoring sending ground troops to remove Saddam Hussein from power only rose modestly during the first three months of 2003.[13] First, this is true of the question asking about "ground troops" (Gallup) but not of the more generic "military action" question, a distinction Edwards recognizes.[14] Second, the question posed by Gallup about "ground troops" (used by Edwards) is only asked through March 15; the president gave national addresses to the public on March 17 and 19 (as well as initiated hostilities on those days), which clearly caused the public to activate their

*Fig. 10.1. (following page). Support for military action in Iraq. The question was "Do you approve or disapprove of the United States taking military action against Iraq to try to remove Saddam Hussein from power?" All polls were conducted by CBS News/*New York Times. *The top line is the percentage approving while the bottom line is the percentage registering "don't know."*

Support for Military Action in Iraq

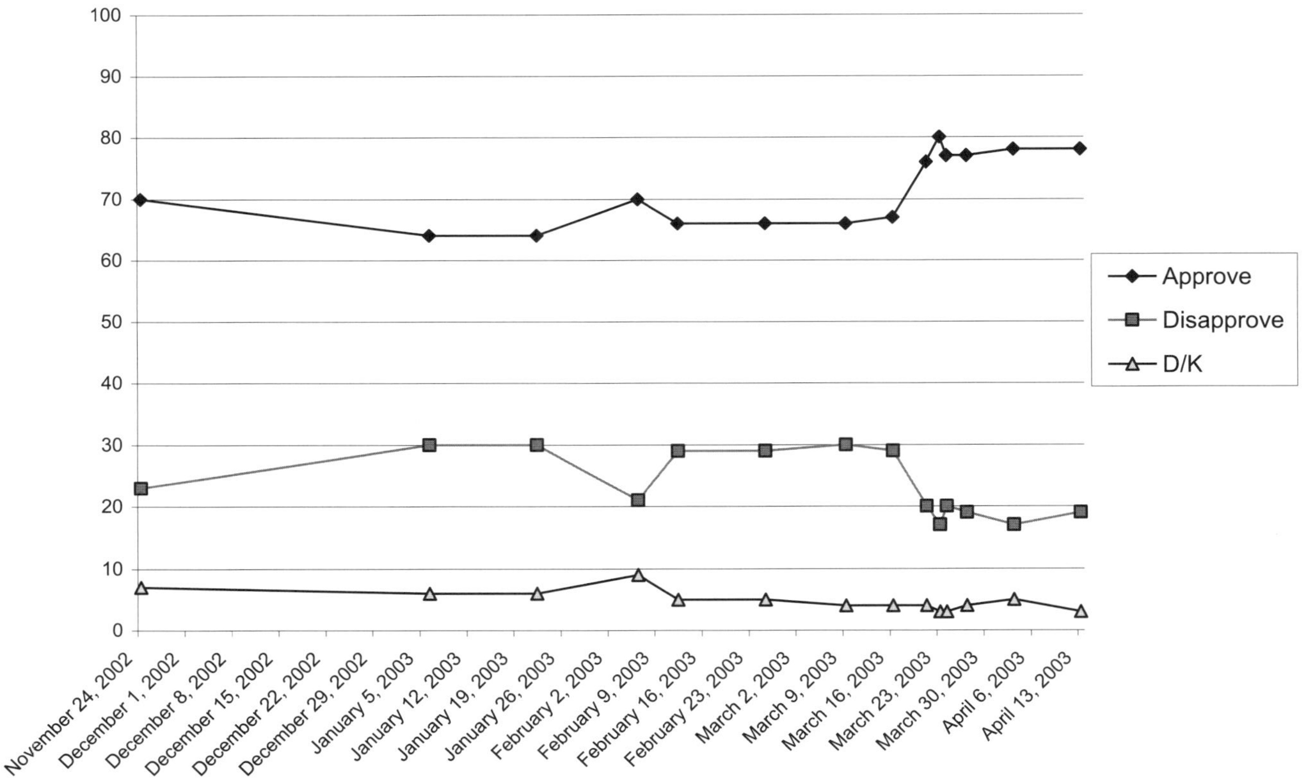

support for him and decrease the percentage of the public responding "don't know," both factors shown to be effective elements of presidential leadership. The differences in timing and wording of polls helps to explain why Edwards's findings are different from those presented here. Ultimately, Congress approved a resolution for the use of force, again showing that a president with public opinion on his side in foreign policy is a powerful force. This is especially true when the media are unwilling to report few deviations from the official government line.[15]

Immigration Reform. In his second term, the Bush administration pushed for two policy issues that were major campaign promises: reforming the immigration policies and reforming Social Security by offering private accounts (described below). On immigration reform, the president's proposals were often at odds with his party since the administration supported a temporary worker program, allowing illegal immigrants to return to their home country and apply for temporary work permits in the United States.[16] In addition, provisions for increased border enforcement (and even a wall along the southern U.S. border) proved to be sticking points. The conservative members of the president's party had concluded that an "enforcement-only" approach to the immigration issue would be a more appealing election issue for their base in the 2006 midterm elections.[17]

Still, despite a significant partisan divide and a highly salient issue, the president did manage to (modestly) convince the public that he was "handling" the immigration issue better (although not nearly a majority). For instance, table 10.1 tracks a longitudinal trend from April to June of 2006 when the president was pressing his case with the American public. The Senate passed a reform plan containing many features desired by the administration in late May and the president was attempting to use the bully pulpit to pressure the House to pass the bill as well.[18] The percentage of the public who approved of the president's handling of the issue rose from 26% at the end of April to 38% after the president's prime-time speech on immigration on May 15 (in the early June poll). However, halting this effect, the president did not himself aggressively press the issue, as he only spoke one time on the issue for consecutive days for the rest of the summer. The majority of the administration's public relations efforts emanated from the White House Press Office where press secretary Tony Snow handled a bulk of the questions posed by reporters. Perhaps not surprisingly, the percentage of the public approving of the president's

TABLE 10.1
President Bush's Handling of Immigration (2006)

	April 28–30	May 11–15	May 16–17	June 9–11	June 14–15
Approve	26	34	36	38	33
Disapprove	64	56	50	55	50
Don't know	9	10	13	7	18

Note: The question was "Do you approve or disapprove of the way George W. Bush is handling . . . immigration?" All polls are Gallup Organization polls from 2006.

handling of the issue fell again from 38% to 33% in early to mid-June, and the overall percentage never reached majority status. Still, even this small movement did not overcome an overall lack of support for the policy in public or in Congress.

Social Security Reform. On the president's efforts to reform Social Security (described in the preface), several scholars have documented the administration's and the President's failures to move public opinion on this issue.[19] The all-out information and persuasion campaign was one of the largest of the Bush administration, and the president (and the press and communications staff) believed that he could convince the public by taking his case directly to them.[20] But, all told, the president not only failed to move the public after a considerable amount of traveling and talking but also did not get any legislation out of any committee in Congress. Again, political partisanship limited the administration's ability to lead public opinion because the nation was so polarized by the issue. Not surprisingly, this echo effect precluded Congress from coming to any agreement and the president's spending of his political capital was wasted.

Considering the findings from this book, President Bush was limited by two specific tactical factors. First, the president never took the national stage to attempt to convince the public to support his policies. This tactic was found to be one of the most potent in assigning presidential leadership, and, save for a few minutes during his State of the Union in 2005, the president stuck to his strategy of mobilizing local subgroups of the public. Second, related to the previous point, and demonstrated earlier this book, the president's much heralded "sixty cities in sixty days" barnstorm didn't achieve leadership success because later presidents are generally less likely to find success with such a tactic (unless they enjoy above-average popularity, which President Bush did not). The findings from the previous chapters did suggest that concerted efforts to lead public opinion would pay off, but the limitations faced here by the Bush administration clearly outweighed any presidential effort.

In addition to these communications factors, several other effects described in the preceding chapters limited the president's ability to lead public opinion. The greater salience of the issue clearly complicated the administration's hope to present their proposals unvarnished to the American people—the press coverage of the administration was more negative than that of past administrations, and the Democratic Party and major interest groups (like the American Association of Retired Persons) vociferously and vocally opposed the president's plan.[21] Related to the partisanship argument, the public's hardened preferences (stable numbers of individuals responding "don't know") restricted the president's ability to convince an open-minded public that his proposals were viable and necessary. This also provides additional evidence that partisanship can limit presidential leadership. The evidence from the previous chapters also suggests that a higher-salience issue and a honeymoon year both have negative effects on presidential leadership. The implication is that the second honeymoon appears to be more challenging for presidents than their first.

Trends. What has been learned from President Bush's successes and failures to lead public opinion? First, as the findings for later presidents demonstrate, the rising tone of partisanship creates difficulties in presidential leadership.[22] Although presidents may be able to lead public opinion in small amounts, divides within a party or polarization of the public create obstacles to moving mass public opinion very far. This reality was discovered most clearly in President Bush's efforts to lead the public on immigration reform (where he moved public opinion modestly but not enough to reach a majority) and Social Security reform (where public opinion did not move much at all). This phenomenon is linked to the arguments in chapter 2 and findings from chapter 4 that higher-salience issues or times when the president was likely to find opposition (honeymoons, election years) limited a president's ability to lead public opinion. But, where he could build consensus, the president's ability to rally the public around his policy objectives did work in securing support from Congress (in the cases of tax cuts and Iraq).

Second, presidents are more inclined now to avoid leading mass public opinion and instead target smaller, specific groups with which to communicate directly. Specifically, presidents may want to communicate with groups to whom his influence and persuasion is likely to be most acceptable. These groups are likely to include core political constituencies by race, gender, political party, interest group, and otherwise. This concept of "narrowcasting" is at the core of "going public." Presidents seek to speak to certain segments of the public in order to have these groups put pressure on individual members of Congress. In this scenario, attempting to persuade the mass public is more work than is needed; presidents may be interested in motivating *particular groups* of the public to engage their elected representatives which in turn fortifies the president's bargaining position in Congress. Not surprisingly, presidents therefore look for opportunities to find their public subgroups in states where the elected officials are reluctant to support presidential initiatives on Capitol Hill.[23]

This phenomenon was found in several of the case studies, where presidents attempted to curry favor with their base, in spite of or concurrent with leadership of mass opinion. President Bush did more than any president to date to court his base. Indeed, according to James E. Campbell, considering the importance of the Republican Party's conservative base in the 2000 and 2004 elections and the closeness of the contests, the Bush White House was "eminently reasonable" for governing with these constituencies in mind.[24] President Bush has used this philosophy to "go local" to take the administration's message to local public groups (and media) rather than to the national media.[25] An examination of the partisan divide and the president's Social Security reform proposals reveals a similar pattern. In responses to a poll question on whether or not the president's barnstorm trip made them more or less likely to approve of the president's proposals (reported in table 10.2), only self-identified Republicans and conservative respondents approved of the proposals more after hearing the president's message (69% and 59%, respectively). Not surprisingly, Democrats and liberals were less likely to indicate that they liked the proposals more (7% and 2%, respectively). So, although mass public opinion did not move, the White House was able to stimulate their base.

Despite the occasional missed opportunity or lack of interest on the part of the public, President's Bush's ability to lead public opinion comports broadly with the factors found to enhance or detract from presidential leadership. First, on the positive side, major televised addresses are profitable for leading public opinion. Second, stumping for the issue for

TABLE 10.2
Persuaded by President Bush's Social Security Proposals?

	Republican	Democrat	Independent
Liked it more	69%	7%	21%
Liked it less	13%	54%	30%
Didn't change	40%	22%	33%

	Liberal	Moderate	Conservative
Liked it more	2%	37%	59%
Liked it less	32%	46%	19%
Didn't change	14%	45%	38%

Note: Source was CBS/*New York Times* poll, June 10–15, 2005. The question was "Would you say that the more you've heard about the Bush Administration's proposals on Social Security the more you've liked them, or the more you've heard about the Bush Administration's proposals on Social Security the less you've liked them, or haven't you changed your mind about them?"

several days often yielded positive results (when the president was more popular). Third, on foreign policy, the president's information advantage and position as national leader provide a platform for more consistent leadership of public opinion. On the other hand, the negative conditions also prevail. For instance, the greater the contentiousness of the issue, the less likely presidents are to lead. Higher-salience issues and presidential honeymoon years (even second honeymoons) are also similarly difficult times to facilitate presidential leadership. The effects of presidential leadership are also temporary, so regardless of how effective particular tactics are at leading public opinion, levels of public support often decline to their initial positions. But, although these effects may be small or temporary, the potential is still there for the president's persuasive efforts to have a positive effect on the president's legislative success.[26]

President Obama (44)

President Barack Obama's historic election in 2008 underscored a dramatic shift in American politics. With a significant margin of victory in the popular and Electoral College votes and sizeable Democratic majorities in both houses of Congress, the Obama presidency ushered in a new era of government and vowed to break from recent past partisan acrimony and take the country in a new direction. The president's victory was sealed by increases in demographic groups voting for him across most categories (compared to John Kerry in 2004) and victories in states that had not been won by a Democratic candidate since President Bush was elected in 2000 (including Florida, Nevada, Ohio, and Indiana). However, despite a clear victory and mandate for political change, the road ahead for the nascent administration would not be as smooth as his monumental election. President Obama inherited several challenging global and economic issues, including two wars and a growing domestic and international financial panic.

First on the president's agenda, and the only major issue on the table at the time of this writing, was a push for a multibillion dollar economic stimulus package designed to jumpstart the sluggish U.S. economy. Among other items, the stimulus package included targeted tax cuts (rebates, an education tax credit, and homebuyers' tax credits), additional spending on public roads, bridges, schools, funding to modernize healthcare records, and investment in alternative energy—a total spending package of almost $800 billion.[27] Even with the president's calls for bipartisanship, selling the plan to Republicans would be a challenge. The president began his push with five short television interviews ("sit downs" with the network news anchors). Although the president stressed the importance of his plan and answered critics who argued the spending priorities were misplaced or not needed, his message was detoured a bit by the surprise withdrawal of Tom Daschle as the nominee-designate for the Department of Health and Human Services due to Daschle's nonpayment of taxes.[28]

The cornerstone of the administration's push for passage of key legislation was President Obama's first prime-time press conference, a rare event for recent presidents.[29] Although the president chose to take his message to the public through a press conference, two elements to that press conference helped to minimize the otherwise negative effect of press conferences on public leadership. First, Obama held his press conference on the same day as a barnstorm trip to Elkhart, Indiana, a city that had been hard hit by the economic slump. The president began the press conference with a narrative about the hurting city and linked the policies from his economic stimulus proposal to ways in which the citizens of Elkhart (and others) would be helped by investment in education, infrastructure, and social benefits. Moreover, the next day following the press conference, the president departed for several states, including Florida, Virginia, and Illinois, to continue to stump for the plan, and he continued to talk about the need for the spending proposed by the legislation.[30] The barnstorm tactic by itself is a positive enhancer of the president's ability to lead public opinion, especially if the president is popular (which President Obama was with 66% of the public approving of his handling of his job as president).[31] Such a barnstorm effort by a president is shown to work effectively for all presidents grouped together, but is less effective for later-serving presidents. Yet the political circumstances surrounding the new president seem to have changed this leadership capability in President Obama's favor.

Second, the president took only fourteen questions in the hour-long press conference, spending a majority of his time answering questions with lengthy speeches, each of which allowed him to stay on message and control the floor. By controlling the content more carefully, the president was able to use the press conference to his advantage. In addition, the questions were not all focused on the contentious stimulus package: several reporters asked the president about foreign affairs (Iran and Afghanistan), Department of Defense policies regarding the photographing of killed soldiers' returning flag-draped coffins, and one asked about New York Yankees baseball player Alex Rodriguez's admission about steroid usage. These temporary diversions from President Obama's main message didn't help him but also didn't hurt him as much as negative or probing questions on his core agenda might have.

Working against the president, according to the findings from this book, were the higher salience of the issue (along with concurrent criticism from putative opponents), later-serving presidents' short (or nonexistent) honeymoon, the fact that the president didn't use the medium of a nationally televised address, which the White House could control to sell his proposals, and the fact that the president attempted to use a press conference as a vehicle to lead public opinion. Yet, working in the president's favor was his popularity and the salience of issue (a potent combination when taken together), as well as the fact that the public was "persuadable," in that they were less informed or certain about the impact of the stimulus package (in part due to its complexity), and that the president pressed the issue in public for several consecutive days.[32]

The president's full-court press worked. A majority of the public approved of the stimulus plan in late January and early February (52%), and after his press conference (February 9) and barnstorm during the following two days, the percentage of the public who approved of the plan rose to 59%.[33] This 7% movement toward the president's position occurred even with the presence of stiff opposition from the Republican Party. Further, the percentage of the public who responded "don't know" to the question fell from 11% in late January to 8% in mid-February, suggesting that the public became more informed about the issue because of the amount of coverage of the issue and the president's public relations efforts. The legislation passed both houses of Congress, although the bill only attracted a handful of Republican votes in the Senate and no Republican votes in the House. Still, the opposition was muted enough to provide smooth passage of the legislation through Congress.

Trends. Although the president (as of this writing) has only engaged in one significant campaign to court public opinion, the results from this enterprise both confirm and amend the findings from this book. First, challenging the nonleadership findings during the "honeymoons" of later presidents, President Obama successfully navigated his first leadership challenge at a time when the findings from chapter 4 suggested he should not succeed. Perhaps the nature of the president's victory prompted a resurgence of the presidential honeymoon, replete with less opposition and less critical media coverage. Similar to this trend, the president's press conference of February 9, 2009, did little to stifle the momentum of the White House's public relations efforts, again suggesting that the nature of press coverage is important to presidents and that President Obama may have been the recipient of enough positive coverage (or beneficiary of the absence of negative coverage) to mitigate the otherwise deleterious effects of presidential press conferences. The president did not use a major address strategy that other presidents used with positive effects, although there is no doubt that such a tactic will eventually be employed by the administration.

Other trends discovered in the early Obama administration do comport with the findings from the previous chapters. First, the combination of a highly salient issue and a very popular president provided a boost to the president, especially given the depth of the crisis and the risk aversion of Congress to do nothing to forestall the crisis. Second, presidential "barnstorm" and "two days before" strategies have a positive effect on presidential leadership, again confirming that presidents who actively and continually press their message with the public are more likely to achieve public persuasion. Similarly, the higher the degree of public learning or an increase in public certainty about an issue, the greater the president's ability to lead public opinion. On a complicated, interconnected, and vastly large issue like the stimulus package proposed by the Obama administration, the potential for public confusion was significant. Yet the White House, in using the bully pulpit to explain its position to the public (as well as to counteract opposing voices) was able to educate the public and convince them to be more certain about the need for the plan.

The Obama White House also has the potential to engage in "narrowcasting" in a similar manner to the Bush White House. The Obama presidential campaign made skilled use of personal technology (including instant messages, text messages, and online networking sites) to communicate their political messages to their base. This use of technology was especially valuable when introducing new policies or in combating criticism from opponents. Should these trends continue, the Obama administration, when attempting to sell their policies to the American public, will have an easier time reaching their base if they can keep the same communications network connected while in office. The effectiveness of "going public" during President Obama's term rests on the Obama administration's ability to transfer their network from campaigning to governing and to translate the aggressiveness of the Obama supporters to communicating the president's message to members of Congress.

APPENDIX A

Case Selection, Matching Statements, and Opinion Polling

This appendix spells out the specific methodological choices I made in selecting policy statements, matching public opinion polls to these statements, and defining presidential leadership. Some of this material is discussed in chapter 3 but is repeated and extended here.

Random Selection of Cases. A random selection of cases is the cornerstone of the project design. As noted in chapter 3, I used the pages of the *Public Papers of the President* from Dwight Eisenhower to Bill Clinton (1953–2001) as the universe for presidential statements. This necessitated using the hard copy of the *Papers,* since the sample element was the page itself (although, as of this writing, an online, page-specific searchable version is available for the years 1992 to 2004). The *Public Papers* data are a standard and traditional source of presidential statements, and a favorite among political scientists seeking to catalogue presidential rhetoric.[1] The *Papers* are reliable because each president since Harry Truman has systematically recorded every public statement (no matter how trivial).[2] The data are also easily available and comparable over time. Beginning with President Carter, the *Public Papers* also included information printed in the *Weekly Compilation of Presidential Documents.*[3] In order to systematize the statements collected, the information from the *Weekly Compilation* documents had to be excluded since these documents only appear after 1977 in the *Public Papers.* In any event, based upon the search parameters described below, the *Weekly Compilation* tended to be excluded anyway since these documents were generally procedural rather than policy-related.

I decided upon a 4% random sample since it would yield a manageable number of statements to match with opinion polling. It also provides a data set that has a randomly selected dependent variable, allowing us to make causal and generalizable inferences with the statistical models employed. Such a random selection picks up many different kinds of presidential speeches, ceremonial statements, radio addresses, speeches to local volunteer organizations, and many more. The value of this selection process is that we are able to select a cross-sectional sample of different kinds of presidential speeches and incorporate several different genres of speech into a single measure. Among other advantages, a cross-sectional sample provides a more global measure of presidential speeches and prevents singling out only "important" speeches such as televised speeches or annual addresses. Additional details on selection bias are presented below and in appendix C.

Once a page was randomly selected, the *first statement* on that page that qualified under the coding rubric (see below) was utilized as the statement for the case in question. This seemed to be the most systematic, consistent, and relatively simple manner in which to select a case on the page. The *Public Papers* are organized chronologically, but I could identify no logical possibility of bias in selecting the first such statement on a page. Although the placement of page breaks in the president's speech is not technically or purely random, it is various and unpredictable enough to not present any consistent selection bias. If the end of a sentence was continued from a previous page, the first full sentence on the sampled page was the starting point for searching for assertions. If the final sentence on the page was the only policy statement (and it was selected for coding), the end of the sentence on the subsequent page was fully coded.[4]

The primary trouble with this method of selection is that the text size per page is larger (that is, fewer words) for the *Public Papers* of Presidents Eisenhower and Ford than for other presidents. To remedy this disparity, a 3% sample was used for the statements of Presidents Eisenhower and Ford and a 4% sample was used for the statements of all the other presidents. Because the unit of analysis is the policy statement on the page, counting the same percentage of pages for dense and less dense numbers of statements per page runs the risk of undercounting the total number of statements per president. Under this rule of "undersample" of less dense pages, there is an equal probability of selecting a page eligible for determining whether it contains a valid statement. Since each denser page provides more words among which one might find a statement, these pages must be weighted upward so there is greater chance of providing an

TABLE A.1
Total Pages and Random Selection of Pages

President	Total pages in papers	Percentage of pages	Total sample pages
Eisenhower	5,784	3%	221
Kennedy	2,637	4	102
Johnson	6,873	4	257
Nixon	6,995	4	232
Ford	5,784	3	171
Carter	9,878	4	416
Reagan	13,023	4	507
Bush	7,521	4	284
Clinton	17,968	4	667

Note: Data compiled by the author. As noted, because of density of word differences, smaller percentages of the *Public Papers* of Eisenhower and Ford were taken.

equal "codable" assertion to a given number of words that the president utters. Table A.1 below identifies the total pages and total sample pages searched for each president in the sample.

"Selection" Error. As with any random sample, there is some error surrounding the selection of the cases. A complete count of the total statements for each page (subsequent to the selection of the statement that was coded as the dependent variable) was kept to identify the precise sample error. We are interested in the error associated with selecting a particular statement on a particular page. Table A.2 reports the total statement for each president, the average assertions per page, and the average standard error per president. In order to tabulate the standard error, I used the following equation: (se = $(\sqrt{((pq)/(\sqrt{N}))}$, where p is the proportion of pages selected, q is the proportion of pages not selected (calculated by taking the total number of sampled pages from table A.1 and dividing it by the number of ultimate cases coded in the dataset that contained viable matched opinion data), and N is the total number of assertions per president. This equation yields the probability of selecting a particular page and a particular statement within that page. The standard

TABLE A.2
Policy Statements and Standard Errors

President	Total statements	Average statements per page selected	Proportion of pages selected	Standard error
Eisenhower	821	5.78	64%	.089
Kennedy	675	8.04	82	.075
Johnson	1,201	7.70	61	.082
Nixon	1,508	9.61	68	.074
Ford	859	6.66	75	.079
Carter	1,601	5.93	65	.075
Reagan	2,009	6.11	65	.071
Bush	1,390	6.38	77	.068
Clinton	3,392	6.91	74	.057
Total	10,054	5.08		

Note: Data compiled by the author. In order to tabulate the standard error, the following equation was used (se = $(\sqrt{((pq)/(\sqrt{N}))}$, where p is the proportion of pages selected and q is the proportion of pages not selected (calculated by taking the total number of sampled pages and dividing it by the number of ultimate cases coded in the dataset which contained viable matched opinion data) and N is the total number of assertions per president.

errors, as reported table A.2, are reasonably near each other, making the probability across presidents similar to each other.

The design I present above does not account for whether or not there is a presidential speech on a topic. The unit of analysis is the *presidential speech*. But, similar to exposure effects in advertising, the question here is not whether or not there would be an effect *if* the president *didn't* speak.[5] Here we ask, When presidents *do* speak (as they do on most every issue of the day) does that speech have an effect on public opinion? In short, the assumption is that presidents are continually talking about most issues (even ones that may disadvantage them in their attempt to "spin" the issue their way). It is the *effect* of these speeches that is of interest here. This approach, which focuses on effects, is a useful approach because it allows for a more certain assertion that the president was trying to lead public opinion (since he spoke on the issue) than does an alternative design. See appendix C for an additional discussion of the methodological ramifications of these issues.

"Valid" Statements. As noted, on each page several statements ultimately would qualify as a "valid statement;" for instance, the first-appearing statement on the page was coded. The most basic desire in the statement coding was to capture an opinion on a particular policy matter. An item was considered valid if (1) it came from the president (not subordinates, other actors, or attributions to other actors), (2) it was directly or tacitly endorsed by the president (both "I stand by my decision to send troops to Haiti" and "I applaud the efforts of the Republicans in Congress in passing a raise in the minimum wage" would count), (3) it was about U.S. government–based action, (4) the issue occurred within the confines of the president's term in office (e.g., discussions of the Civil Rights Act of 1964 were not coded during the Clinton administration), and (5) it advocated a *specific policy issue* (even if particular action on the issue was vague).[6] Thus, the policy issue had to be specific (e.g., "We need to reduce the deficit" or "I support a raise in the minimum wage") rather than vague (e.g., "We need to work for peace in the world" or "We need to help the neediest people with our programs") and/or make clear the president's advocacy of a particular policy approach. However, if the intended effect or assisted group was vague but was attached to a policy, the president was coded as supporting the policy (e.g., "We need to pass my health-care bill to protect our kids"). The line is drawn here in order to capture the most specific issue possible.

Of course, because presidents talk about a wide range of topics generally, and often within the same speech, special rules had to be developed for when an individual statement would count as valid. At the sentence level, if a sentence referred to several advantages or several reasons for presidential support in a statement, the first such claim listed was coded as the dependent variable and the additional advantages within the sentence were counted as individual statements for purposes of calculating standard errors (on the assumption that the president would desire to individually enumerate them).[7] For instance, if the president said, "Our tax bill will reduce the deficit, give tax cuts to the middle class, and remove the capital gains restrictions," the tax bill "reducing the deficit" was the coded statement and the remaining two were counted in the list of total statements. Similarly, at the paragraph level, if the president listed ten separate advantages (or features) of the same bill, the first sentence was coded and the remaining nine were counted in the list of total assertions. If the president mentioned a policy in a sentence without explicitly mentioning that he opposed it (such as a particular tax-cut legislation, Medicare reform, etc.), it was assumed he was in favor of the policy (and it was coded this way for poll-matching purposes).

This process also required excluding several types of statements that violated the general principle. Statements that were not coded include those that were too vague, as well as procedural and ceremonial statements, political speculation, economic predictions, conditional statements ("might" or "maybe" or "considering"),[8] or personnel decisions. Other statements specifically excluded were the announcement of the creation of or findings of a task force or commission, raw economic data, specific military victories or actors, information on earnings, appointments, nominations, general "thank you" or "welcome" letters (to members of Congress or foreign dignitaries), treaty "transfers" to the Senate, veto statements or signing statements (unless spoken in a speech), quarterly reports (economic or foreign policy), mandatory reports to Congress on budget matters, the president's schedule or potential schedule, or the announcement of a "ceremonial week" (such as "Nurse Appreciation Week"). Since these were not statements and espoused no particular policy, they were excluded from the analysis.

Special considerations needed to be developed for particular kinds of statements that presented coding complications. Statements dealing with relations between the United States and other countries were generally straightforward enough to be coded based upon the coding rules. Specifically, if the president visited another country or another country's rulers visited with the president, the president would often make statements to the effect that the "relationship with country X is strong and valuable." Also, presidents are statutorily obligated to inform Congress of emerging or continuing "emergencies" (generally involving enemies, such as Iran or Iraq), and these "emergency declarations" were considered procedural and were not coded. Trade negotiations were also occasionally spoken of by the president, in which case, the issue was coded as "trade" and the specific proposal in question was also coded. For instance, if the president indicated the administration's stance was that tariffs on Japanese goods needed to be raised, the general issue is trade and the specific issue is the president supporting increased tariffs on Japan.

Discussion of economic conditions and the effect of economic policy also complicated the coding of economic policy statements. The reason is that when presidents speak of an economic policy, especially a successful one, they generally combine the endorsement of the policy with an evaluation of how it affected (or will affect) the nation's economy.[9] Generally, the stated policy, proposal, or stance the president took on a particular issue was isolated from the president's interpretation of the effects. So, taking credit for reducing unemployment or lowering interest rates was coded, and if the president indicated his economic plan caused these economic results, the president's support of his economic plan was coded. If the president took credit in a speech for "lowering the deficit" or "lowering inflation" but it was not linked to any discernable policy proposal or support for a particular plan, it was coded (and matched to a more general "handling" question).

Limitations. The issue of timing and cataloging of speeches opens several questions. Opinion may have fluctuated after the first coded poll (in the time between the first poll and the president's statement). Presidents may also have attempted to shape the opinion environment before attempting to lead public opinion on the matter. For instance, Hill and Hinton-Anderson argue that reciprocal opinion between elites and the mass public shape liberal policies at the state level.[10] But the search method balances this out since we explore a random set of speeches (rather than single speeches) across a president's term, so any "pre-statement priming" is reasonably likely to be distributed evenly across the observations.

Matching Polls to Statements

The Roper Center has a comprehensive archive dating back to 1930 and is the most complete record of all public opinion polling available to researchers. The online searchable component makes it relatively easy to select the most appropriate poll to match with a statement. To obtain a wide range of both dates and polling organizations, I used the online polling archive at the Roper Center for Public Opinion Research at the University of Connecticut to search for public polling data that could be matched up with the randomly selected presidential policy statements. The Roper Center houses all major polls released publicly, including Gallup, Harris, Roper, ABC, CBS, CNN, NBC, *Los Angeles Times, New York Times, USA Today,* and the *Wall Street Journal,* as well as many university-sponsored or independent polls from NORC, NES, and GSS.

In addition, frequently several "special topics" polls (longer polls on particular issues or events) and other polls conducted by private contractors were included.

Great care was taken to search all of the germane polling data to ensure that the policy expressed in the president's statement matched the policy in the poll. This process was usually uneventful because the issues in the statements were specific enough that poll questions tended to be clear about whether or not the public favored the policy, favored spending more money on an issue, or favored a particular country. But if no poll was found to match the policy, or there was ambiguity about the connection between poll and statement, no data were coded for that entry. Of course, I had to make certain interpretations or evaluations had to be made in cases where the poll data and statement did not *perfectly* match. Several of these conditions are described below, along with examples of "easy" and "hard" matches.

Matching Examples. To demonstrate the process of matching, I have selected an "easy" case and a more challenging case to provide perspective on the data. First, the easy case—on December 5, 1994, President Clinton indicated he endorsed "opening up NATO membership to eastern bloc countries" (page 2145). On October 25, 1994, a Gallup poll queried the public: "Some people believe that NATO (North Atlantic Treaty Organization) should be expanded to include Poland, Hungary and the Czech Republic, thereby committing the United States to defend them against attack in the same way as we are committed to defending Western Europe. Do you think NATO should or should not be expanded to include those three countries?" to which 46% of the public responded affirmatively. This result presented a straightforward statement of support for a doctrinal policy choice.

For the more difficult case—on July 26, 1994, President Clinton indicated he was "proud of the role the United States played in fostering peace in the Middle East" (page 1315). On September 10, 1993, a CNN/*USA Today* poll queried the public: "Israel and the P.L.O. (Palestine Liberation Organization) have reached a new (peace) agreement in the Middle East. It would give the Palestinians control over some land in the occupied territories. In return, the P.L.O. has agreed to end terrorism and recognize Israel's right to exist. Do you generally favor or oppose this agreement?" to which 80% responded affirmatively. This question presents a slightly more tenuous matching connection because, although the

Clinton administration helped to initiate the proceedings, they did not explicitly draft the agreement. This poll was coded as a match because it seemed clear that the president was asking for (and receiving) credit for this accomplishment.

The Polls that Counted. Poll responses were grouped together to reflect a dichotomous, majoritarian viewpoint. For instance, poll answers that were divided into "very favorable" and "favorable" were collapsed into one category, similar to answers that an issue required "great urgency" and "some urgency" or policies that were "strongly approved" or "somewhat approved." When matching statements about the "closeness" or "importance" of a country to the United States, and the poll in question had a feeling thermometer or some other larger range of options, the response categories were split directly in half to preserve the dichotomy of the coded categories. Occasionally a question asked about respondents' knowledge about a subject and their approval of the subject (for instance, "Have you heard about President Carter's plan to combat inflation and do you strongly approve, somewhat approve, somewhat disapprove, strongly disapprove or don't you know?"). If this was the case, only the percentages of individuals claiming they had heard or had knowledge of the policy (depending on how it was worded) were coded. Those respondents responding "Don't know" or "No opinion" were left out of the primary pro/con code.

I sought poll data that reflected the exact language of the policy statement, which necessitated excluding poll results when the questions were loaded or biased (e.g., linking policies like inflation and taxes together).[11] Of course, if a particular contingency was specified in the president's statement (e.g., "We need to save Social Security before we cut taxes"), I sought polling questions that reflected that contingency. A challenge to this process was matching the language used by the president and the language used by the pollsters. The politicization of legislation or policy choices along with clever phrasings by the White House made this issue difficult on certain issues.[12] In general, I searched several analogous words in the Roper archive to ensure that the poll language that was ultimately recorded best reflected the language used by the president. For instance, presidential references to "smarter" government or "rethinking government" were treated the same as "efficiency" of government in poll questions. Presidential references to "clean water" or "clean air" were treated as tantamount to poll language referencing "natural resources" or "environment." Similarly, descriptions of "tax relief" (or even more specific references to "death taxes" or "marriage penalties") were treated as "tax cut" since pollsters generally favor this language.

As with isolating a particular policy statement, particular cases necessitated creating a unique rule to deal with a matching case. Periodically, presidents would use language in their speeches that reflected the desire to end (or diminish) something, such as inflation, unemployment, or violence. If this was the case, poll questions that asked "if the government is doing enough to solve" the particular problem were permitted to be coded as a positive (pro) response. Also, poll questions referring to the number one "economic problem" (from a list of such problems) was considered usable if the president spoke in a general way about the economy. Such polls were limited to instances where presidents used this language.

Searching for Salience Counted. The category of issue "salience" was based upon the pollsters' question "What is the most important problem facing the country today?" This poll question came in several forms, generally every few months, but I coded only questions that were (1) open ended to the respondent and (2) requested only one (rather than two or three) "top issues." These criteria preserved the spontaneous and singular "problem" nature of the public's single greatest concern. In general, policy statements on an issue were matched in a general way to polls posing questions on the salience of the issue.[13] It was usually a straightforward connection but occasionally required searching for a broader category of poll salience. For instance, policy statements regarding conflicts between Israel and other nations or Soviet involvement in Central America were captured in general categories such as "Mideast peace" or "Latin America" rather than by specific topic. The most specific category was used where possible.

APPENDIX B

Case Study Selection and Archival Data Collection Methods

In this appendix I outline the process of selecting and constructing case studies (including advantages and disadvantages) and describes the document search procedure at the presidential archives.

Case Studies as Political Analysis

A comprehensive search of presidential archives is an informative way to analyze presidential history. As noted in chapter 5, it is difficult, but not impossible, to treat archival data analysis of this sort in a truly systematic manner. In that sense, as is the situation with most works based on case studies, scholars are unable to definitively *prove* their assertions. However, given the range of cases and the interpretation of theories of behavior and leadership, it can be claimed with some certainty that the assertions here are plausibly correct. Ultimately, though, I attempted to be careful when discussing casual connections and in proposing absolute conclusions. In this section, I explore the advantages and disadvantages of addressing theoretical questions with archival material so I can be clear about the contributions and limitations of the analysis. In addition, I discuss the case selection method.

A case study is defined as "an intensive study of a single unit (a relatively bounded phenomenon) where the scholar's aim is to elucidate features of a larger class of phenomena."[1] Therefore, the case studies employed in this book are fixed in time to a particular moment (typically a month or shorter) in which to analyze presidential behavior and public reaction. This limit provides a sufficient amount of time to understand the event and reaction to it in varying political situations. My goal in using these case studies is to illuminate and explain with greater depth the aggregate empirical findings from the statistical models presented.

In this way I attempt to avoid problems of ambiguity in case study research, about which Gerring notes, "Writers should be clear about which propositions are intended to describe the unit under study and which are intended to apply to a broader set of units."[2]

The primary evidence used in the case studies are documents collected from presidential archives (more on this below) containing information on public opinion or public opinion polling. Polling data or polling memoranda presented in this project conform to a basic standard or qualification that I applied when selecting a valid document. Heith, in her comprehensive study of the polling memoranda sent by and to White House staffers during the Nixon administration through Bush administrations, defines the material she selected as including formal and informal memoranda, handwritten notes, pollster reports, and other various written documents.[3] The documents selected for this book generally conformed to these criteria. The document search included poll and focus group results from a variety of sources, including memoranda detailing the utilization of public opinion in any form and handwritten notes documenting the flow of material to and from individuals in the White House.

Reliance on historical data for purposes of testing theories has several advantages and disadvantages. One major advantage of presidential archival research is that empirical investigation can be conducted inside the "black box" of presidential policy making. Further, as Page notes, untangling the connection between policy and opinion may be best conducted by just such a method since it provides a relatively clear and valid explanation of the players' thoughts and arguments.[4] Others have successfully employed these techniques to mid-twentieth-century presidents.[5] Armed with the fertile information from the actual time of decision making, researchers can find out what the president and his staff knew and when they knew it. We can therefore identify important timing sequences to investigate how public opinion had an effect on decision making, a key consideration for testing the hypotheses and getting a fresh look at the theoretical quandary of connecting policy and opinion.

A prominent disadvantage in using archival research is the problem of possible selection bias. For all presidential administrations, many small but significant events, such as personal thoughts or phone calls, were not recorded.[6] Important and relevant documents could have been lost or discarded either by the principal author or by staffers when sorting materials.[7] Some of the materials uniquely relevant to an analysis of presidential involvement with public opinion is also not yet open to the public. This might be especially true for the Bush White House since many of the materials have not yet been opened by archivists.[8] Similarly, even if the material has been reviewed, certain holds can be placed on the material based upon a "P-5" classification (confidential advice from staff member to the president) by an archivist or the material may be restricted by a "deed of gift." The approach I use in this book, however, remedies this selection problem by relying on a wide range of available documents (both primary and secondary) to explain the positions and evaluate the arguments.

Although I am confident in our search strategy, the sheer volume of presidential documents precludes a full accounting of *all* the White House poll results or memoranda in which polling was discussed among the senior staff. Indeed, one can never be fully certain that a complete set of polling documents can be found. Also, one set of polling data may be interpreted in one way by an individual adviser, while another interpretation from another staff member may be missing, excluded, misfiled, or simply destroyed. Relying on a single document for an evaluation of "what the White House was thinking" can therefore often be misleading. For this reason, I have selected a multiple case study approach to the analysis—one that allows us to gain perspective on the depth and scope of the discussion inside the White House. In addition, I use supplementary primary and secondary sources to corroborate the archival findings.

The cases selected for this book span a broad range of types of issues (economic, budget, foreign policy), interventions and negotiations (wars and arms control talks), varieties of conflict duration (both short and drawn out), and several episodes involving different presidents across time (mid- to late-twentieth-century presidents), and across electoral circumstances (first- and second-term presidents), thus allowing for a great deal of variation in the cases to examine our expectations. Although narrowly presented and stylized, the cases selected and observations discussed reflect a breadth and depth necessary for successful description and exposition of analytical claims.[9] Although these case studies were not randomly selected, they do conform to a standard cross-sectional design, allowing us to determine if the two variables studied (presidential rhetoric and movement of public opinion) are associated.[10] Evidentiary proof in this context lies in the preponderance of documentation all pointing in the same direction.[11] The longitudinal nature of the data also allows for appropriate time-ordered causal claims.

Searching for Archival Documents

The quality of archival research is only as good as the archivists and the findings aids (or the time-intensive search process an individual researcher will spend). A comprehensive search of a presidential archive would entail sifting through several hundred million documents. For comparative purposes, the Johnson Library contains 35 million documents, the Nixon Materials Project contains 45 million documents (only 7 million of which are open to the public), the Ford Library contains 21 million documents and the Bush Library contains 38 million documents. Many of the documents in question are lost to history because of inadequate finding aids. It is therefore necessary to rely rather heavily on the archival finding aids, although thinking "outside the box" and pursuing alternative research strategies is often productive and necessary to find appropriate and germane data.

No researcher could ever hope to uncover all available references to polling data in his or her lifetime (even of one president). The sheer volume of memoranda, letters, reports, and recommendations prohibits such an expansive exploration. However, it is generally simple to locate most of the actual polling data used, since such documents have historically been catalogued in their own files as a stand-alone topic. What follows is a description of the most time-efficient and targeted search for public opinion data and public opinion polling memoranda. Although it did not likely turn up every instance of public opinion, chances are that these search procedures captured most all of the important data.

The document search for this book included poll results from a variety of sources, including memoranda detailing the utilization of public opinion polling in any form and handwritten notes documenting the flow of material to and from individuals in the White House concerning polling (described above). Oral history interviews conducted with members of the White House staff and other individuals connected the president were surveyed for references to public opinion and public opinion polling. Papers of key individuals that served as administrative secretaries, press department officials, policy advisors, or department secretaries (especially in the area of foreign affairs) were systematically selected for review with the assumption that these individuals would be the most likely to use public opinion polling data and would have access to these data. If one staff member had access to polling data, that person's files were checked more carefully with the assumption that more would be found. General papers of the president were also surveyed for evidence of public opinion polling, including the White House Central Files, the White House Official Files, the President's Personal Files, the President's Secretary's Files, the American Institute of Public Opinion Files, and the White House Telegraph Office Files. If time permitted, specific issues that were known to be the subject of opinion polling (such as President Ford's "Whip Inflation Now" campaign or the Gulf War under President Bush) were searched in the White House Subject File.

Organization of the Archives. Presidential archives are each arranged in similar ways; however, the archives of Franklin Roosevelt, Harry Truman, and Dwight Eisenhower have systems of internal organization (remaining from the old White House filing system) that are different from archives that were established after John Kennedy's presidency. The White House filing system before Kennedy was staffed by permanent civil servants (some of whose tenure began under the administration of William McKinley). This filing system possessed no true centralized or numerical system (and relied on an antiquated and anachronistic U.S. Army filing system) which makes research more erratic.

The White House Central Files in the Roosevelt, Truman, and Eisenhower administrations are divided into the Official File, the General File, the Confidential File, and the President's Personal File (or often the President's Secretary's File). The White House Official Files contain a substantial quantity of factual materials on major issue of public policy, including executive orders, records of press conferences, and bills and resolutions signed. They generally consist of copies of letters sent in acknowledgment of other letters or reports sent to president or additional hard copies of White House administrative materials, usually from important or influential citizens. The General Files contain letters from individual citizens, interest group organizations, and occasionally members of Congress on matters of interest. These documents are usually simple acknowledgments from the White House staff and give no internal insight on presidential thinking. The White House Confidential Files consist of correspondence, memoranda, telegrams, and reports (often once security-classified material) that originate or are sent to senior White House staff or the president. The President's Personal File contains a president's social correspondence, congratulatory letters, and other memos to and from the White House staff. In some archives, these papers are called the President's Secretary's Files and include private documents initiated, received, or kept by the president's personal secretary. It is in these files where one can get a window into the day-to-day operations of the White House staff and often an intimate view of the president's viewpoints on a range of issues.

The White House Central Files in the presidential archives including and subsequent to John Kennedy are divided into two types of files: General and Executive Files. General Files were handled by lower-level White House staff members and include memoranda, letters, or reports from individual citizens or "less important" interest groups. Executive Files are similar memoranda, letters, or reports except that these forms were from higher profile (or "important") groups such as members of Congress, former presidents, influential citizens, or members of the media, and these letters were written by or to senior White House Staff. It is therefore more appropriate to view the Executive Files with greater concern and with more intensity because it is where most of the evidence of important policy decision making is found, in particular, those files where polling might be used to formulate policy. Locating particular important documents in these archives is easier because every document is cross-referenced back to the Central Files holdings. For instance, if a polling memoranda is known to be in the files of the Attorney General, that poll is cross-listed to the White House Central Files folder on public opinion polling (but only if the poll is known to be located in that file). In contrast, in the pre-Kennedy filing system, documents were not centrally classified by subject and could not be cross-referenced.

Beyond the official federal records of a president's administration, which I have just described, all presidential archives contain the personal papers of many cabinet members, staff members, friends of the president, influential advisors, or family members. These documents (usually indicated by "files" or "papers" instead of "records") are typically donated to the presidential archive after the president's term in office. These papers are also a valuable source of information on issues or events that may contain a different or value-added perspective. Often, however, these documents are simply duplicates of documents contained in the official records (several copies of each official documents are made) and are typically not cross-referenced to the original document.

Of course, certain archives have particular sets of papers or files unique to the administration or endemic to specific individuals within the auspices of the president in question. These documents are also often a valuable source of information, as they are specific to an individual, event, or organization. For instance, President Eisenhower's personal secretary, Ann Whitman, created several chronological files containing items the president saw that week or documents he requested. Also, papers of the political parties (and often key individuals) involved during the term of the president's service are often a wealth of quality data, since much of the early polling data originated from these sources. These diverse sets of inimitable papers or files were searched sporadically, when available.

APPENDIX C

Data and Models

In this appendix I discuss the methodological choices that I made in employing statistical models to evaluate the data, as described in chapters 3 and 4. The data collection process and the matching of opinion polls to presidential statements are relevant here but are more thoroughly described in appendix A. Here I also present several alternative models (with similar variables but different specifications) that demonstrate the robustness of the results in the text.

Regression Model

A linear regression model makes a causal claim that the change in *y* (dependent variable) is caused by a change in *x* (independent variable). Thus, the β coefficient is the change in *y* associated with a one unit change in *x* when the other independent variables are held constant. The ordinary least squares (OLS) present a coefficient based upon the minimum sum of squared differences between the data point and the predicted line. This is expressed as:

$$Y = \beta_1 * x_1 + \beta_2 * x_2 + \ldots + \beta_n * x_n + c$$

where each β is an independent variable (1 to *n*) and *c* is the constant term (including the error term). The dependent variable (Y) is continuous here (the percentage movement of public opinion from before to after the president's speech). The "goodness of fit" measure (adjusted R^2) is the amount of variance in the dependent variable explained jointly by the independent variables, adjusted for the number of variables. A score of 1 indicates a "perfect" explanation. The adjusted R^2 in the models in chapter 4 generally explain about a third of the variance (some lower and some higher), a reasonable amount.

In interpreting the OLS regression model, it is important to understand that the coefficients (effects of the independent variable on the dependent variable) are relative to the baseline. In this case, because the unit of observation is a presidential speech rather than an issue (upon which a presidential speech may or may not have been made), the baseline figure is a presidential speech. But, more than that, the baseline is a presidential speech in which the characteristics of the independent variables are not present. So, the baseline is a presidential speech delivered during unified government, not during a honeymoon or a presidential election year, not for two consecutive days, not during a "barnstorm" tour, not from the Oval Office, and so on. Essentially, the controls are the different kinds of speeches, different characteristics of the president, and the different elements present in the political environment. I further discuss the ramifications for the sampling issue in appendix A.

Sampling Problems?

There are three potentially problematic sampling issues with this method (as outlined in chapter 3 and in appendix A). Each is discussed below, along with explanations and alternative models (where appropriate).

Availability of Polls. Pollsters do not poll on every issue. They are more likely to poll when the information is needed for news coverage. And, since the polling industry developed over the time period from the 1950s to 2000 (the range of our presidential statement sample), there may be more polling data available for later-serving presidents. Although we randomly select and directly observe the president's speeches and the public opinion polling associated with each statement, we do not observe the public opinion polls for all presidential statements (or all issues). Specifically, I only observe public opinion polls for those statements that are randomly sampled, not the universe of public opinion on that issue. That is, there is a degree of "self selection" in that pollsters only poll on particular issues (rather than all or a random sample of issues), making sample selection bias a possible problem.

One solution to this problem is a Heckman model to statistically control for selection bias. Since there is a nonrandom assignment to the treatment variable (and thus a censored sample), a Heckman model may be appropriate.[1] In practice, we are attempting to measure unobserved data (presence of a poll). The Heckman model uses a selection equation which is essentially a separate model that isolates the first stage of the equation. The Heckman model requires the presence of a unique variable instrument that affects the chance for observation of the dependent variable.[2] Specifically, in these alternative models, the variables in the selection equation affect the chance whether or not public opinion exists on the issue (and hence may necessitate a poll). In effect, pollsters who typically poll to provide topical and up-to-date public opinion for newspaper coverage (or on behalf of newspapers) do so when there is an election, or in more recent times, when there is more need to conduct polls. Therefore, the unique instrumental variables are if the poll was conducted (1) in a congressional election year, (2) in a presidential election year, and (3) later in the sampling period (for later-serving presidents).

The Heckman model in table C.1 uses the full data, not truncated by the one- or three-month window, because the number of cases was too small. The Heckman model reveals that there may be a small selection effect when it comes to the sample of polling issues. The inverse Mills' ratio is significant at $p > .10$, suggesting a possible selection effect. But the Heckman model results are also very similar to the models from the text and to the logistic regression models (also using a dichotomous dependent variable) listed below. The signs of most of the variables are identical (State of the Union promise, second term, approval, issue salience, decrease in "don't know," and all of the communications tactics). In addition, the statistical significance in each model is also very similar to the main findings from the models in the text (State of the Union promise, issue salience, decrease in "don't know," and all of the communications tactics).

However, this model is not used in the main text for several reasons. First, it would be impossible to know on which issues a pollster *would have* polled in different circumstances. Conducting a Heckman model requires the presence of a unique variable instrument that affects the chance for observation of the dependent variable,[3] and this information is difficult to manifest. The selection equation used in table C.1 is very sensitive to the variables included and can be easily altered. Second, without a good instrument for the first stage of the selection (and a nonsignificant inverse Mills' ratio), the results would be the same as a logistic regression model (which are similar; see below). The significance is close to not meeting conventional levels of significance (and other minor changes to the selection equation reduced the significance). Third, several other techniques were used to account for any potential selection

TABLE C.1
Heckman Selection Model: Poll Selection

Variable	Successful leadership	Selection model
Political conditions		
Divided	.045	
	(.086)	
State or the Union promise	.157*	
	(.085)	
Honeymoon	–.054	—
	(.151)	
Second term	–.189*	—
	(.102)	
Presidential approval	.013***	—
	(.004)	
Election coming	.017	
	(.046)	
Rally	.211***	
	(.082)	
Public attention issue		
Issue salience	–.006*	—
	(.003)	
Decrease in "don't know"	.011***	—
	(.004)	
Communications tactics		
Two days before	.160*	
	(.091)	
"Barnstorm"	.287***	—
	(.102)	
Major address	.243**	—
	(.116)	
Press conference	–.186***	—
	(.077)	

TABLE C.1
Continued

Variable	Successful leadership	Selection model
Going international	.362	—
	(.231)	
Control variables		
Popular before statement	–.004*	—
	(.002)	
Second equation		
Congressional election year		–.091
		(.106)
Presidential election year		–.222*
		(.112)
Later-serving president		.214*
		(.099)
Constant	1.26	–1.35
	(.856)	(.171)
N	1,084	
ρ	–1.00	
σ	.984	
λ (Mills' ratio)	–.984	
	(.536)*	
Probability > F	.000	

Note: Data compiled by the author and conducted with Heckman selection equation (calculated using the SPost for Stata from Long and Freese [2006]). The selection equation is to the right of the full model. Dependent variable: dichotomous variable indicating movement of public opinion from before presidential statement to after (post-statement poll minus pre-statement poll). Dependent variable for the selection equation is whether or not there was a poll taken on the issue. Standard errors in parentheses. Dashes denote variables removed because the data overlapped. Statistical significance: ***$p < .01$; **$p < .05$. *$p < .10$.

bias in the models in chapter 4. One solution was a random selection of the speeches, which tended to produce a diverse sample of issues. Some of these issues are likely to have polling (salient issues) while others were less likely (nonsalient issues). If the sample was random, there is a more even chance that there will be a poll on the issue in question. Another solution was to truncate the data by time period, so that it could be determined whether or not all presidents grouped together looked different than later-serving presidents.

Selection of Speeches. A second possible sampling issue is the selection of presidential speeches. The design does not capture moments where presidents do not speak on an issue—it only captures moments where the president has spoken. Therefore, there is no variation on presidential speech except by type of speech. So, we cannot know whether or not public opinion would have changed *without* a presidential speech. This also relates to the endogeneity problem (described further in the following section). But, as noted above in the discussion of the interpretation of the OLS model and in the sampling description in appendix A, this endogeneity problem is seen as strength of the design. The research question addressed in this book is, When the president speaks on an issue, which conditions enhance his ability to lead public opinion? In that sense, a design that samples from all speeches (rather than all issues) is more appropriate since the assumption is that presidents speak on most issues, and the desired knowledge is based upon some exposure to presidential speech. The interpretation in the text reflects this assumption. This sampling approach is also useful because it allows for a more certain assertion that the president was trying to lead public opinion (since he spoke on the issue).

An alternative way to collect these data would have been to take a sample of issues, then search for presidential speeches on the issue. But this method is problematic for several reasons. First, the selection of the universe of issues the president might discuss would be very difficult, especially since there is a large range of issues from highly salient to not salient. Compiling a list of such issues would also be difficult since it would be a challenge to find agreement among several sources. Second, creating such a list could bias the selection of issues to known issues, which are often more salient, by missing smaller issues presidents might discuss (for instance, minor foreign policy issues explored in chapter 4). Third, presidents talk about most issues of the day, complicating the researcher's ability to control for whether or not the president spoke meaningfully on the issue. Fourth, the present design allows for a greater degree of certainty that the president was trying to lead public opinion on the issue—after all, the president chose to include it in a public speech. Finally, although I decided conceptually that this was the wrong way to approach the issue, I did run several Heckman models with a specific issue as the dependent variable in the selection equation (including Social Security, taxes, the budget, and foreign policy) with only the salience of the issue as the predictors of the selection equation—in none of the results were there enough cases to complete the analysis.

"Attempts" to Lead. In a third possible selection effect, it may be the case that the president's ability to lead public opinion is different when he *attempts to lead* on that issue versus when he does not attempt to lead on that issue. In a short discussion in the introduction to the theory in chapter 2, I suggested that one measure employed in the models in chapter 4 was a good proxy for the president's "attempt" to lead public opinion: whether or not he brought up the issue on each of the two days prior to the speech captured in the sample. Therefore, there could be a selection effect where the president's choice to lead affects his ability to lead. Put another way, it could be the case that presidents only attempt to lead on certain issues where they are more certain they will succeed. Again, a model to control for this possible selection effect can be tested to determine whether or not the selection effect exists.

In the model in table C.2, the dependent variable for the selection equation was the dichotomous measure of whether or not the president spoke on the issue for two consecutive days. The variables selected for the selection equation were the presence of divided government and the degree of polarization of Congress (comporting with Kernell's argument that presidents are more likely to "go public" during these times) and whether or not the issue was brought up in the State of the Union address (defined in the text in chapter 2).[4] In these instances, presidents should be more likely to "go public" during these times. The results reveal a modest selection effect since the inverse Mills' ratio (lambda) is statistically significant. Still, these results are substantially similar to the results in the tables in the text. For instance, the sign and significance of the mutual findings are nearly identical, including "major address," change in "don't know," issue salience, honeymoon, and second term. These results again demonstrate the robustness of the findings across model specifications.

TABLE C.2
Heckman Selection Model: "Attempts" to Lead

Variable	Successful leadership	Selection model
Political conditions		
Divided	–.034	
	(.205)	
Honeymoon	–.411*	—
	(.242)	
Presidential election	–.458**	—
	(.156)	
Second term	–.461***	—
	(.152)	
Presidential approval	.016	—
	(.010)	
Public attention issue		
Issue salience	–.019***	—
	(.005)	
Decrease in "don't know"	.009*	—
	(.005)	
Communications tactics		
"Barnstorm"	.024	—
	(.168)	
Major address	.674*	—
	(.347)	
Press conference	–.039	—
	(.151)	
Going international	.108	—
	(.225)	
Control variables		
Popular before statement	–.001	—
	(.003)	

TABLE C.2
Continued

Variable	Successful leadership	Selection model
Selection model		
Polarized government		–.398
		(.705)
Divided government		–.082
		(.162)
State of the Union promise		.606
		(.169)
Constant	1.67	–2.13
	(.899)	(.424)
N	1,640	
ρ	–.935	
σ	.698	
λ (Mills' ratio)	–.653*	
	(.364)	
Probability > F	.001	

Note: Data compiled by the author and conducted with Heckman selection equation (calculated using the SPost for Stata from Long and Freese [2006]). The selection equation is to the right of the full model. Dependent variable: dichotomous variable indicating movement of public opinion from before presidential statement to after (post-statement poll minus pre-statement poll). Dependent variable for the selection equation was whether or not the president spoke on the issue for two consecutive days. Standard errors in parentheses. Dashes denote variables removed because the data overlapped. Statistical significance: $^{***}p < .01$; $^{**}p < .05$; $^{*}p < .10$.

Endogeneity

It could be the case that presidents take positions on only popular issues, on issues where they are more certain they can lead, or on issues where they are losing support. That is, they may only talk about issues when they are sure they can lead public opinion. I have taken several steps to control for these or test for these potential problems. First, several control variables are included to control for endogeneity issues and presidents taking positions on only popular issues. These control variables are included to ensure our model correctly specifies the political environment, or to "furnish a 'rival hypothesis'" to make the explanations more plausible.[5] First, I control for early and late presidents (divided as Eisenhower to Ford and Carter to Clinton). I also divided the sample of presidents by early and late presidents in several models in chapter 4 to capture any changes in modern political communications tactics changing during the 1970s or the emergence of an aggressive media.[6]

Second, to control for the overall popularity of the issue, I also use a measure of the popularity of the president's statement (or issue) before the president spoke ("popular before statement"). This measure controls for presidents taking positions based on the popularity of issues, in case presidents more frequently make speeches on popular or unpopular issues.[7] This measure controls for the popularity of the polled policy before the president spoke so we can hold constant the popularity of the issue with regard to whether or not the president led on that issue. This poll-gauged measure of the popularity of a proposal is described in the measurement section in chapter 3 (and coded as a continuous variable). So, if 90% of the public approve of a policy before the president speaks and 91% approve afterward, the 90% figure is included in the model to control for the public's prior approval of a policy.

Third, because I only have measures of issues on which presidents took positions, not ones for those they did not, the sample is inherently incomplete and susceptible to endogeneity problems because of no control variable.[8] Models that were run (but not shown here) in which dummy variables were included for certain "mandatory" issues (the budget and Social Security) on which the president is "expected" to take a position (in effect, modeling a control variable) demonstrate no substantive change in the models presented.

Fourth, considering that the president can choose on which issues to speak, I also include controls for those issues that are in the president's core agenda (in the form of the mentions of policy that are concurrent with the president's State of the Union message) or for those issues about which the White House cared greatly to persuade the public by continually referencing the policy for consecutive days ("two days before"). In order to provide another control for the possible endogenous effects of presidents talking about all issues without regard to importance, I use a measure of policy statement mentions from the State of the Union speech

("State of the Union promise") to match to the president's statement. That is, if the president mentioned the policy issue in question during his most recent State of the Union message, it is a variable coded "1" (and "0" otherwise). Because of the importance and weight of the annual speech, I assume that if the president mentions the issue in his State of the Union message and then again during that year, then the president is attempting to "go public" with the issue and lead public opinion.[9] This assumption also effectively models a "control variable" that distinguishes between *all issues* and *issues the president cares about.*

Fifth, the random selection of the unit of analysis (presidential statement) helps correct for any potential endogenous effects of biased presidential speech selection. Because the design captures speeches from several time periods and political circumstances within and between administrations, the chance is equal of getting a speech in a particular time period when the president may be speaking because he believes it will advantage his ability to lead. This design is therefore better able to measure presidential leadership because it relies on all presidential speeches rather than only high-profile speeches (such as State of the Union speeches or Oval Office speeches).

Supplements to Models from the Text

Table C.3 includes additional area-specific variables from table 4.6 in chapter 4. Few of these coefficients are significant.

Alternative Models

Ordinary Least Squares. In an alternative OLS model (not shown), I regressed the percentage approving of the president's policy choice before he made it (t_1) on the percentage approving of the statement after he made it (t_2). This model corresponds with Page, Shapiro, and Dempsey who conduct a similar analysis.[10] In it, the percentage approving of the president's policy before the president made the statement ("popular before statement") was statistically significant, implying that presidents are able to affect public opinion with their rhetoric. The coefficients for "prepoll" percentage were positive and significant at the $p > .001$ level, suggesting leadership effects. In addition, like Page, Shapiro, and Dempsey, I find substantial agreement between this model and a model employing change in approval from t_1 to t_2 as the dependent variable (as in table 4.1

TABLE C.3

Regression Model for Opinion Movement Within One Month (from Table 4.6)

	All foreign policy issues		Minor foreign policy issues	
Variable	Eisenhower to Clinton	Carter to Clinton	Eisenhower to Clinton	Carter to Clinton
Specific issues				
Latin America	−4.76	−4.40	10.4	8.11
	(9.12)	(8.84)	(6.96)	(7.12)
Asia	2.94	7.59	4.19	3.53
	(5.01)	(8.65)	(4.81)	(5.40)
Russia	.940	5.41	3.94	5.95**
	(3.58)	(3.84)	(2.62)	(2.83)
Mideast	−5.02	−1.62	−7.76	−3.98
	(4.38)	(4.60)	(9.29)	(9.15)

Note: Dependent variable: continuous variable indicating movement of public opinion from before presidential statement to after (post-statement poll minus pre-statement poll). Standard errors in parentheses. Statistical significance: $^{**}p < .05$.

in the text). Comparing the models, the coefficients are identical in sign and statistical significance but lose some of the substance of the coefficient. Because the coefficients and standard errors were identical on all those variables except the pre-statement poll measure, I have chosen not to reproduce them here.

Logistic Regression Models. Because the leadership variable could be limited to a dichotomous variable (either public opinion moves in favor of the president's position or it does not), the models below are run as alternative models to those from chapter 4 with a dichotomous dependent variable. The data from these alternative models are run with a logistic regression model. In the models below, a "0" signals that the post-poll measure was greater than the pre-poll measure (opinion did not move toward the president's position, including "no change") while a "1" signals that the post-poll measure was greater than the pre-poll measure (opinion moved toward the president's position). Thus, the models presented in the text can be run in an alternate format to test for the robustness of the findings. In the models below, the coefficients by themselves are not interpretable—in a more formal treatment of these findings, the coefficients would be converted to predicted probabilities. But the important part here is to understand the sign and significance of the coefficients, and to determine the degree of congruence between these results and the OLS results displayed in chapter 4, rather than directly comparing the impacts.

Table C.4 mimics the same variable specification from table 4.1 in chapter 4. Only the models for all presidents are shown because the models truncating the data to later-serving presidents failed to converge (there were too few cases). Happily, the findings here and in the OLS models in the text are significantly similar. At the one-month column in table C.4, compared to table 4.1 in the text, the decrease in "don't know," two days before, major address, and press conference variables are all the same sign and similar level of significance. The differences are that, in table C.4, the "rally" variable is positive and significant (where it was negative in table 4.1) and the presidential election variable is not significant (where it was significant in table 4.1). In the second column of table C.4, the results for presidents at the three-month window are nearly identical, with, again, the decrease in "don't know," two days before, major address, and press conference variables are all the same sign and similar level of significance matching table 4.1. On balance, the results are substantively similar.

Table C.5 mirrors table 4.2 from the text (except that the second model with the interaction between a popular president and a popular issue failed to converge). For the first model (interaction of popular president and high salience), the sign and significance of all of the variables is the same in both models with the single exception of the interaction variable between popular president and high salience issue. In the second column of table C.5 (mirroring the third column of table 4.2, the interaction between popular issue and high-salience issues), the results are also very similar. Again, the results between the models are substantively similar and provide added certainty about the robustness of the findings.

Finally, table C.6 mirrors table 4.5 in the text. The first column reports all presidents grouped together. Most conditions here are the same as in table 4.5 from the text: presidential election, honeymoon year, decrease in "don't know," deployment of troops, two days before, and major address. Only one variable (issue salience) is significantly different—the sign is positive in the logistic regression model but negative in the OLS model (table 4.5). The second and third columns in table C.6 are

TABLE C.4
Opinion Movement for All Presidents at One and Three Months

Variable	One month Eisenhower to Clinton	Three months Eisenhower to Clinton
Political conditions		
Divided government	–2.64	–1.42
	(2.08)	(.928)
Honeymoon	1.29	2.33
	(2.55)	(1.65)
Second term	6.74	2.24
	(5.61)	(1.35)
Presidential approval	–.185*	–.068
	(.107)	(.048)
“Rally”	13.5**	3.18
	(7.02)	(1.14)
Presidential election	4.15	.749
	(3.39)	(1.13)
Carter–Clinton	–7.59	–2.91
	(4.23)	(1.30)
Public information		
Issue salience	–.159	–.098
	(.119)	(.044)
Decrease in “don’t know”	1.98**	.450***
	(.941)	(.142)
Communications tactics		
Two days before	7.69**	2.46***
	(3.87)	(1.00)
“Barnstorm”	1.82	.274
	(2.19)	(1.15)
Major address	11.4**	3.08
	(5.87)	(1.15)
Press conference	–4.25*	–1.04
	(2.40)	(.828)

TABLE C.4
Continued

Variable	One month Eisenhower to Clinton	Three months Eisenhower to Clinton
Control variables		
Popular before statement	.024	−.019
	(.059)	(.024)
State of the Union promise	5.78	1.26
	(3.83)	(1.00)
Constant	−1.35	5.01
	(8.72)	(4.47)
N	82	100
Probability > F	.000	.000
Pseudo-R^2	.747	.514
Proportional reduction of error	76.4%	69.5%

Note: Dependent variable: dichotomous dependent variable signifying a change of greater than 5% in opinion movement. One- and three-month columns capture the outer time boundary of survey dates for those data. Standard errors in parentheses. Statistical significance: ***$p < .01$; **$p < .05$; *$p < .10$.

truncated to only minor issues. These variables are also significantly similar to their counterparts in table 4.5 in both sign and significance: issue salience, election year, decrease in "don't know," popular before the statement, press conferences, State of the Union promises, and the constant (for only later presidents in column 3). Two variables are of the same sign but are significant in table C.6: two days before and presidential elections. Otherwise, the findings are in substantial agreement.

TABLE C.5
Opinion Movement at One Month (Alternate Specifications)

	Model specification	
Variable	1	3
Political conditions		
Divided government	–.027	–.498
	(.872)	(.977)
Honeymoon	–3.65*	–3.29
	(2.10)	(1.92)
Second term	.050	.134
	(1.02)	(1.07)
Presidential approval	.003	–.029
	(.070)	(.070)
"Rally"	–.082	.267
	(.874)	(.903)
Presidential election	–2.21*	–2.41
	(1.02)	(1.09)
Carter–Clinton	1.82	2.05
	(1.16)	(1.23)
Above-average salience	.241	—
	(1.29)	
Popular issue	—	–3.11
		(1.86)
Popular president	.296	.778
	(1.42)	(1.60)
Public information		
Issue salience	.008	.035
	(.056)	(.040)
Decrease in "don't know"	.176**	.210**
	(.078)	(.086)
Communications tactics		
Two days before	3.13**	3.44
	(1.50)	(1.40)

TABLE C.5
Continued

	Model specification	
Variable	1	3
"Barnstorm"	1.63	1.88
	(1.01)	(1.06)
Major address	1.68*	1.62
	(1.01)	(1.08)
Press conference	−1.81	−2.00
	(.816)	(.797)
Interacted variables		
Popular president × High salience	1.37	—
	(1.60)	
Popular president × Popular issue	—	1.40
		(1.55)
Popular issue × High salience	—	—
Control variables		
State of the Union promise	.783	.531
	(.862)	(.896)
Popular before statement	−.026	.030
	(.023)	(.042)
Constant	−2.92	−3.41
	(4.21)	(4.26)
N	78	81
Probability > F	.001	.000
Pseudo-R^2	.381	.416
Proportional reduction of error	63.8%	69.4%

Note: Dependent variable: continuous variable indicating movement of public opinion from before presidential statement to after (post-statement poll minus pre-statement poll). Standard errors in parentheses. Dashes denote variables removed because the data overlapped. Statistical significance: $^{**}p < .05$; $^{*}p < .10$.

TABLE C.6

Opinion Movement on Major and Minor Foreign Policy Issues Within One Month

	All foreign policy issues	Minor foreign policy issues	
Variable	Eisenhower to Clinton	Eisenhower to Clinton	Carter to Clinton
Political conditions			
Divided government	.078	.205	.229
	(.891)	(.566)	(.697)
Honeymoon	−7.48***	.132	.452
	(2.82)	(.655)	(.747)
Presidential election	−3.18**	−.954*	−1.15*
	(1.43)	(.537)	(.627)
Second term	.882	−.436	−.318
	(1.18)	(.574)	(.627)
Presidential approval	.139**	−.025	−1.15
	(.069)	(.022)	(.627)
Carter–Clinton	2.93**	−.191	—
	(1.45)	(.664)	
Public attention issues			
Issue salience	.103**	−.044**	−.051**
	(.052)	(.020)	(.023)
Decrease in "don't know"	.396***	.142***	.155***
	(.139)	(.050)	(.056)
Foreign policy variables			
Deployment of troops	10.0***	—	—
	(3.69)		
Airstrikes	2.20	—	—
	(1.70)		
Congressional authorization	10.5	—	—
	(81.0)		

TABLE C.6
Continued

	All foreign policy issues	Minor foreign policy issues	
Variable	Eisenhower to Clinton	Eisenhower to Clinton	Carter to Clinton
Communications tactics			
Two days before	6.10***	.699	1.06**
	(2.18)	(.510)	(.561)
"Barnstorm"	1.68	.774	.746
	(1.32)	(.526)	(.569)
Major address	1.88*	.856	1.66
	(1.14)	(1.11)	(1.30)
Press conference	−3.09***	−.559	−.865*
	(1.15)	(.497)	(.574)
Control variables			
State of the Union	.611	1.27**	1.37*
	(.891)	(.675)	(.762)
Popular before statement	−.048	−.046***	−.046***
	(.032)	(.014)	(.015)
Constant	−12.2**	3.20	3.39*
	(5.75)	(2.06)	(1.91)
N	81	143	125
Probability > F	.001	.000	.000
Pseudo-R^2	.516	.237	.277
Proportional reduction of error	77.7%	32.2%	38.4%

Note: Dependent variable: continuous variable indicating movement of public opinion from before presidential statement to after (post-statement poll minus pre-statement poll). Standard errors in parentheses. Blank spaces denote variables removed because the data overlapped. Statistical significance: $***p < .01$; $**p < .05$; $*p < .10$.

Notes

Preface

1. Levine and Levine, *People and the President.*

2. Casey, *Cautious Crusade.*

3. The Roosevelt-Wallace ticket received 55% of the popular vote and 449 Electoral College votes to the Willkie-McNary ticket's 45% of the popular vote and 82 Electoral College votes.

4. Franklin D. Roosevelt Library, President's Secretary's Files, Public Opinion Polls, 1942–1944, "From Hadley Cantril, October 8, 1941," Box 157. Interviewing between July 11 and July 19, 1941.

5. Franklin D. Roosevelt Library, President's Secretary's Files, Public Opinion Polls, 1942–1944, "Cantril to Rosenberg," July 3, 1941, Box 157.

6. Franklin D. Roosevelt Library, President's Secretary's Files, Public Opinion Polls, 1942–1944, "Cantril to Rosenberg," September 20, 1941, Box 157.

7. Franklin D. Roosevelt Library, President's Secretary's Files, Public Opinion Polls, 1942–1944, "Trial tabulations on the Far Eastern situation," December 5, 1941, Box 157.

8. Emphasis in original. Ronald Reagan Presidential Library, Files of David Chew, State of the Union '86 (1), "Chew to Regan," January 13, 1986, OA 14170.

9. Ibid.

10. Ibid.

11. Ronald Reagan, "Address before a Joint Session of Congress on the State of the Union," February 4, 1986, in Public Papers of the President of the United States, Ronald Reagan, vol. 2: 1986 (Washington, D.C.: Office of the Federal Register).

12. Ronald Reagan Presidential Library, PR 15, 366001–37700, "Analysis of the February 4, 1986, State of the Union," Box 11. The document was seen by the president on February 3, 1986.

13. The December 12, 1985, question from the ABC News–*Washington Post* survey asks, "Well, the Gramm-Rudman law requires automatic cuts in spending for many social and military programs each year that Congress doesn't reduce the budget deficit on its own. Do you approve or disapprove of the Gramm-Rudman budget balancing law, or is that something you don't have an opinion on?" The February 20, 1986, question from the *Los Angeles Times* asks, "As you know, Gramm-Rudman sets a series of declining deficit ceilings so that, by 1991, the deficit will be entirely wiped out. If the budget, for any year, fails to make the required reductions, Gramm-Rudman calls for automatic across-the-board spending cuts divided equally between military and nonmilitary programs. In principle, are you in favor of the Gramm-Rudman Bill, or are you opposed to it?"

14. Sandlow, "Bush Claims Mandate."

15. Edwards, "Changing Their Minds?"

16. Morin and VandeHei, "Social Security Plan's Support Dwindling."
17. Sanger, "Bush's Road Tour Rolls On."
18. Ibid., 20.
19. Fine and Waterman, "New Model of Presidential Leadership."

Chapter 1

1. Edwards, *On Deaf Ears;* J. M. Hogan et al., "Report of the National Task Force on the Presidency and Public Opinion."
2. Page, Shapiro, and Dempsey, "What Moves Public Opinion?"
3. Page and Shapiro, "Presidents as Opinion Leaders"; Page and Shapiro, *Rational Public.*
4. Canes-Wrone, *Who Leads Whom?;* Kernell, *Going Public;* Cohen, *Presidential Responsiveness and Public Policy-making;* Canes-Wrone and Shotts, "Conditional Nature of Presidential Responsiveness"; Stimson, MacKuen, and Erikson, "Dynamic Representation"; Jacobs and Shapiro, *Politicians Don't Pander;* Eshbaugh-Soha, *President's Speeches.*
5. Edwards, *On Deaf Ears.*
6. See Medhurst, "Eisenhower's Rhetorical Leadership"; Finbow, "Presidential Leadership or Structural Constraints?"; Sloan, *Reagan Effect;* and others.
7. Canes-Wrone, *Who Leads Whom?;* Cohen, *Presidential Responsiveness and Public Policy-making.*
8. See Edwards, *On Deaf Ears.*
9. Waterman, Wright, and St. Clair, *Image-Is-Everything Presidency.*
10. Jacobs and Burns, "Second Face of the Public Presidency."
11. Rosen, "Test of Presidential Leadership of Public Opinion."
12. Hart, *Sound of Leadership,* 14.
13. Kingdon, *Agendas, Alternatives, and Public Policies;* Cohen, "Presidential Rhetoric and the Public Agenda"; Cohen, *Presidential Responsiveness and Public Policy-making;* Hill, "Policy Agendas of the President and the Mass Public"; Edwards and Wood, "Who Influences Whom?"; Eshbaugh-Soha and Peake, "Presidents and the Economic Agenda."
14. Brace and Hinckley, *Follow the Leader;* Brace and Hinckley, "Presidential Activities from Truman through Reagan"; McGraw, Best, and Timpone, "What They Say or What They Do?"; Druckman and Holmes, "Does Presidential Rhetoric Matter?"; Canes-Wrone, "Public Presidency, Personal Approval Ratings, and Policy Making."
15. Kernell, *Going Public.*
16. Finbow, "Presidential Leadership or Structural Constraints?"
17. Jacobs and Shapiro, "Rise of Presidential Polling."
18. Edwards, *On Deaf Ears:* Edwards, *Strategic President.*
19. Edwards, *On Deaf Ears,* 28.
20. Edwards, *On Deaf Ears,* 48.
21. See also Cohen, "Presidential Leadership in an Age of New Media"; Cohen, *Presidency in the Era of Twenty-four-Hour News.*
22. See, for instance, Kellerman, *Political Presidency;* Lammers and Genovese, *Presi-*

dency and Domestic Policy; Gergen, *Eyewitness to Power;* and Greenstein, *Presidential Difference,* just to name a few selected compendiums of these findings.

23. Wenger and Gerber, "John F. Kennedy and the Limited Test Ban Treaty."

24. Sloan, *Reagan Effect.*

25. Jacobs and Shapiro, "Rise of Presidential Polling."

26. Bailey, Sigelman, and Wilcox, "Presidential Persuasion on Social Issues."

27. Koch, "Political Rhetoric and Political Persuasion."

28. Sloan, "Meeting the Leadership Challenges of the Modern Presidency"; Wenger and Gerber, "John F. Kennedy and the Limited Test Ban Treaty"; Medhurst, "Eisenhower's Rhetorical Leadership."

29. Wood, *Politics of Economic Leadership.*

30. Cohen and Hamman, "Polls: Can Presidential Rhetoric Affect the Public's Economic Perceptions?"

31. See Canes-Wrone, *Who Leads Whom?*

32. Sigelman, "Disarming the Opposition."

33. Rosenblatt, "Aggressive Foreign Policy Marketing."

34. Kernell, *Going Public.*

35. Edwards, *On Deaf Ears,* xi.

36. Edwards, *Strategic President,* 190.

37. J. M. Hogan et al., "Report of the National Task Force on the Presidency and Public Opinion," 306.

38. Ibid., 310.

39. Qualitative studies are Eisinger, *Evolution of Presidential Polling;* Heith, "One for All." Quantitative studies are Page and Shapiro, "Presidents as Opinion Leaders"; Page, Shapiro, and Dempsey, "What Moves Public Opinion?"; Cohen, *Presidential Responsiveness and Public Policy-making.*

40. See Edwards, *On Deaf Ears:* Eshbaugh-Soha, *President's Speeches;* Cohen, *Presidency in the Era of Twenty-four-Hour News.*

41. Key, *Public Opinion and American Democracy.*

Chapter 2

1. Hamilton, Madison, and Jay, *Federalist Papers,* 459.

2. See Sheehan, "Madison v. Hamilton."

3. Tulis, *Rhetorical Presidency.*

4. Kernell, *Going Public.*

5. Woodrow Wilson, *Leaders of Men,* 42.

6. Ibid., 45.

7. Woodrow Wilson, *Congressional Government,* 202.

8. J. M. Hogan, *Woodrow Wilson's Western Tour;* Kernell, *Going Public;* Mellow, *State of Disunion.*

9. Lowi, *Personal President.*

10. Pious, *American Presidency.*

11. Kellerman, *Political Presidency.*

12. DiIulio, "Hyper-Rhetorical Presidency."

13. Cornwell, *Presidential Leadership of Public Opinion,* 6.
14. Burns, *Presidential Government.*
15. Burns, *Running Alone,* 6.
16. Rockman, "When It Comes to Presidential Leadership," 327.
17. Kernell, *Going Public.*
18. Ibid., x.
19. Ibid., 2.
20. Laracey, *Presidents and the People.*
21. Canes-Wrone, "President's Legislative Influence from Public Appeals"; Canes-Wrone, *Who Leads Whom?*
22. See Heith, *Polling to Govern.*
23. Jacobs and Shapiro, "Rise of Presidential Polling."
24. Eisinger, *Evolution of Presidential Polling;* Rottinghaus, "Reassessing Public Opinion Polling in the Truman Administration."
25. Heith, *Polling to Govern.*
26. Edwards, *Strategic President.*
27. Kernell, *Going Public,* 192.
28. Hart, *Sound of Leadership,* 2.
29. Barrett, "Going Public as a Legislative Weapon."
30. Maltese, *Spin Control,* 2.
31. See Jacobs and Shapiro, *Politicians Don't Pander.*
32. Chong and Druckman, "Framing Public Opinion in Competitive Democracies."
33. Barrett, "Press Coverage of Legislative Appeals by the President."
34. Geer, *From Tea Leaves to Opinion Polls.*
35. For instance, if the president discussed increasing the minimum wage on a particular day, I searched the president's statements made during the two days prior to that particular day to ascertain whether he made a similar statement about the minimum wage.
36. Baum and Groeling, "What Gets Covered?"
37. See Edwards, *On Deaf Ears;* Cohen, *Presidency in the Era of Twenty-four-Hour News.*
38. Barrett, "Gone Public"; Barrett, "Going Public as a Legislative Weapon."
39. Edwards, *On Deaf Ears,* 128; see also Peake and Eshbaugh-Soha, "Agenda-Setting Impact of Major Presidential TV Addresses."
40. Edwards, *Strategic President.*
41. Cohen, "Presidential Leadership in an Age of New Media."
42. Not every conditional expectation directly speaks to presidential *leadership* as defined in chapters 1 and 2, since few studies measure "leadership" in the same way. However, taken as a whole, this broad literature links presidential decision making across several political dimensions.
43. For purposes of analysis, presidents coded as "early" were those from President Eisenhower to President Ford and those coded as "late" were those from President Carter to President Clinton. This distinction makes sense substantively because President Carter was the first to provide office space in the West Wing full-time to a public opinion pollster. Also, breaking up the data into these two time periods cuts the data roughly in half. Eisinger, *Evolution of Presidential Polling.*

44. Kessel, *Presidents, the Presidency, and the Political Environment.*

45. Geer, *From Tea Leaves to Opinion Polls;* Geer and Goorha, "Declining Uncertainty."

46. Jacobs, *Health of Nations.*

47. Maltese, *Spin Control;* Eisinger, *Evolution of Presidential Polling.*

48. Light, *President's Agenda,* 92.

49. See Tulis, *Rhetorical Presidency;* Laracey, *Presidents and the People.*

50. Jacobs and Shapiro, *Politicians Don't Pander.*

51. Ibid., xv. Emphasis in original.

52. Hargrove, *President as Leader.*

53. Neustadt, *Presidential Power and the Modern Presidents,* 84.

54. Ibid., 89.

55. See Alvarez and Brehm, *Hard Choices, Easy Answers.*

56. A simple example of this is a "rally" event where the there is a "follower" effect. Specifically, the public (1) becomes more informed about a subject and (2) is persuaded by the president's message on that subject.

57. Geer, *From Tea Leaves to Opinion Polls,* 44–45.

58. Althaus, *Collective Preferences in Democratic Politics.*

59. Converse, "Information Flow and the Stability of Partisan Attitudes," 583.

60. Zaller, *Nature and Origins of Mass Opinion.*

61. Zaller, *Nature and Origins of Mass Opinion;* see also Zaller and Feldman, "Simple Theory of the Survey Response."

62. The post-poll percentage of the public responding "don't know" is subtracted from the pre-poll percentage of the public responding "don't know." Therefore, positive numbers indicate the percentage of respondents responding "don't know" decreases. Responses of "don't know" can indicate either lack of knowledge or lack of certainty over the opinion that the respondent has. For purposes of analysis in this chapter, we assume both effects are at work. Sanchez and Morchio, "Probing 'Don't Know' Answers"; Coombs and Coombs, "'Don't Know': Item Ambiguity or Respondent Uncertainty?"

63. Light, *President's Agenda.*

64. Canes-Wrone and Shotts, "Conditional Nature of Presidential Responsiveness," 701.

65. Druckman and Holmes, "Does Presidential Rhetoric Matter?"

66. Cohen, "Presidential Rhetoric and the Public Agenda."

67. Hill, "Policy Agendas of the President and the Mass Public."

68. The exact wording of the Gallup Organization's question used in the analysis is "What do you think is the most important problem facing this country today?" When appropriate, and to capture a poll as close to the date of the statement as possible, other answers to similar questions were recorded, as long as the questions (1) allowed for open-ended response available to the respondent and (2) requested only one (rather than two or three) "top issues." This preserves the spontaneous and singular "problem" nature of the issue in question.

69. Schattschneider, *Semisovereign People.*

70. Russett, *Controlling the Sword;* Jordan and Page, "Shaping Foreign Policy Opinion."

71. The exact wording of the Gallup Organization's question is "What do you think

is the most important problem facing this country today?" The variable recorded is the percentage of the public responding that a particular issue was the most important.

72. Stimson, MacKuen, and Erikson, "Dynamic Representation."

73. Canes-Wrone, Herron, and Shotts, "Leadership and Pandering"; Rottinghaus, "Rethinking Presidential Responsiveness."

74. Jacobs and Shapiro, *Politicians Don't Pander,* 3.

75. Canes-Wrone and Shotts, "Conditional Nature of Presidential Responsiveness."

76. Light, *President's Agenda,* 64.

77. See Skewes, *Message Control.*

78. Cox Han, Governing from Center Stage; Tenpas, *Presidents as Candidates.*

79. Doherty, "Elections: The Politics of Permanent Campaign."

80. Presidential popularity is measured by Gallup's question on presidential job approval. The question was "Do you approve or disapprove of the way [the incumbent] is handling his job as president?" Data were taken from Ragsdale, *Vital Statistics on the Presidency.*

81. Neustadt, *Presidential Power and the Modern Presidents.*

82. Buchanan, *Citizen's Presidency;* see also Todd M. Schaefer, "Persuading the Persuaders."

83. Page, Shapiro, and Dempsey, "What Moves Public Opinion?"; Zaller, *Nature and Origins of Mass Opinion.*

84. Brody, *Assessing the President.*

85. Wildavsky, "Two Presidencies."

86. However, other scholars have revised these initial findings, suggesting the advantage only exists for Republican presidents and that the effect was mitigated after the end of the Vietnam War. But these works look at policy passage, not opinion leadership, where presidential credibility on the issue is more important. Bond and Fleisher, "Limits of Presidential Popularity"; Sigelman, "Rallying to the President's Support."

87. See Edwards, "Public Presidency," 43; Hess, *Presidential Decisions for War.*

88. Bostdorff, *Presidency and the Rhetoric of Foreign Crisis.*

89. Brody, *Assessing the President,* 77.

90. Mueller, *War, Presidents, and Public Opinion.*

91. Hetherington and Nelson, "Anatomy of a Rally Effect."

92. Cohen and Hamman, "Polls: Can Presidential Rhetoric Affect the Public's Economic Perceptions?"

93. Cohen, *Presidential Responsiveness and Public Policy-making.*

94. Rosenblatt, "Aggressive Foreign Policy Marketing."

95. Kernell, *Going Public;* see Neustadt, *Presidential Power and the Modern Presidents.*

96. See Crockett, *Opposition Presidency.*

97. Hart, *Sound of Leadership,* 83; Canes-Wrone, "President's Legislative Influence from Public Appeals."

98. Peterson, *Legislating Together.*

99. Bond and Fleisher, "Limits of Presidential Popularity."

100. Tulis, *Rhetorical Presidency;* Kernell, *Going Public.* Although there are literally dozens of strategies by which the president might communicate with the public, we isolate these four communications tactics because they help to advance our understanding

of presidential leadership, they are each prominently discussed in the literature, they are attainable easily from the *Public Papers of the President,* and they are clearly comparable over time.

101. Tenpas, *Presidents as Candidates;* Edwards, "Changing Their Minds?"

102. Kernell, *Going Public.*

103. Concurrent with Lammers and Kernell, I coded "travel" as days away from Washington, D.C., engaged in public political activity and a speech longer than 200 words. These excluded short speeches to reporters and vacation travel. Lammers, "Presidential Attention-Focusing Activities"; Kernell, *Going Public.*

104. See Brace and Hinckley, *Follow the Leader.*

105. Gleiber and Shull, "Presidential Influence in the Policymaking Process," 456.

106. Kernell, *Going Public,* 121.

107. J. M. Hogan, *Woodrow Wilson's Western Tour,* 19.

108. Charnock, McCann, and Tenpas, "Goin' Mobile"; Doherty, "Elections."

109. Kernell, *Going Public,*121.

110. Holbrook, "Did the Whistle-Stop Campaign Matter?"; Barrett, "Gone Public."

111. Cohen and Powell, "Building Public Support from the Grassroots Up."

112. Ostrom and Simon, "Man in the Teflon Suit?"

113. See Eshbaugh-Soha and Peake, "Going Local"; Barrett and Peake, "When the President Comes to Town."

114. Again, commensurate with Lammers and Kernell, televised speeches were coded as those delivered or broadcast from Washington, D.C., and "focused on more than a narrow potential audience" (Lammers, "Presidential Attention-Focusing Activities"; Kernell, *Going Public,* 136). These events did not include radio addresses.

115. Cox Han, Governing from Center Stage.

116. Cornwell, *Presidential Leadership of Public Opinion,* 32; Simon and Ostrom, "Impact of Televised Speeches and Foreign Travel," 61.

117. Jamieson, *Eloquence in an Electronic Age.*

118. Cohen, "Presidential Rhetoric and the Public Agenda"; Druckman and Holmes, "Does Presidential Rhetoric Matter?"

119. Brace and Hinckley, "Presidential Activities from Truman through Reagan."

120. Cox Han, Governing from Center Stage, 169.

121. Cohen, "Presidential Rhetoric and the Public Agenda"; Cohen, *Presidential Responsiveness and Public Policy-making.*

122. Ostrom and Simon, "Man in the Teflon Suit?"

123. Ostrom and Simon, "Man in the Teflon Suit?" 74; see also Shaw, "Study of Presidential Campaign Event Effects," 410.

124. Edwards, *On Deaf Ears.*

125. Wattenberg, "Changing Presidential Media Environment."

126. Neustadt, *Presidential Power and the Modern Presidents,* 84.

127. Aberbach and Rockman, "Hard Times for Presidential Leadership?"

128. Cohen, *The Presidency in the Era of Twenty-four-Hour News.*

129. Welch, "Presidential Success in Communicating with the Public."

130. Edwards, *On Deaf Ears,* 130.

131. Wattenberg, "Changing Presidential Media Environment."

132. West, "Television and Presidential Popularity in America."

133. Baum and Kernell, "Has Cable Ended the Golden Age of Presidential Television?"; Young and Perkins, "Presidential Rhetoric, the Public Agenda, and the End of Presidential Television's 'Golden Age.'"

134. Ragsdale, *Vital Statistics on the Presidency.*

135. Welch, "Presidential Success in Communicating with the Public."

136. Welch, "Was Reagan Really a Great Communicator?"

137. Barabas, "Presidential Policy Initiatives."

138. Baum and Kernell, "Has Cable Ended the Golden Age of Presidential Television?"

139. Welch, "Was Reagan Really a Great Communicator?"

140. Lammers, "Presidential Press Conference Schedules."

141. Barrett, "Going Public as a Legislative Weapon."

142. Kumar, "Presidential Press Conferences." We define these events as those occasions when the White House press corps was allowed direct access to the president and permitted to pose questions to him. Such occasions involved longer give-and-take sessions with members of the press as well as shorter question volleys back and forth in between other official events. Commensurate with Kumar's definition, these events were found in the *Public Papers of the President,* a consistent and standard source for defining them. If press officials who were able to ask any questions attended the event, the event was coded as a "press conference." These include the president's brief, spontaneous interactions with the press while traveling to or from an event or a scheduled formal press conference, and also joint press conferences where the president was asked questions by the press with another person (often a visiting dignitary). In keeping with the rubric for policy issue coding, only the president's statements were coded. These events are often in prime time (and on television); however, this was not a condition to be coded affirmatively in this category and for purposes of analysis. Where appropriate, televised press conferences have been separated from nontelevised press conferences to test the impact of television on media-based communication strategies. Kumar, "Source Material: 'Does This Constitute a Press Conference?'"

143. Grossman and Kumar, *Portraying the President.*

144. Clayman and Heritage, "Questioning Presidents"; Clayman et al., "Historical Trends in Questioning Presidents."

145. Kumar, "Presidential Press Conferences," 174.

146. Kernell, *Going Public.*

147. Mayer and Rozell, "A Presidency Transformed," 3, 210.

148. Kumar, "Presidential Press Conferences."

149. Lammers, "Presidential Press Conference Schedules."

150. Eshbaugh-Soha, "Presidential Press Conferences Over Time."

151. Kernell, *Going Public,* 119.

152. Simon and Ostrom, "Impact of Televised Speeches and Foreign Travel."

153. Brace and Hinckley, *Follow the Leader,* 52; Simon and Ostrom, "Impact of Televised Speeches and Foreign Travel," 69.

154. Kernell, *Going Public,* 122.

155. Brace and Hinckley, *Follow the Leader,* 54.

156. Hart, *Sound of Leadership,* 24.

157. Brace and Hinckley, *Follow the Leader,* 57.
158. Kernell, *Going Public;* see also Brace and Hinckley, *Follow the Leader.*
159. Brace and Hinckley, "Presidential Activities from Truman through Reagan," 392.
160. Woodrow Wilson, *Congressional Government,* 76.

Chapter 3

1. Rockman, "When it Comes to Presidential Leadership, Accentuate the Positive."

2. This process also required excluding several types of statements that violated this definition. Generally, statements that were not coded include those that were too vague, procedural statements, ceremonial statements, political speculation, economic predictions, observations on the general state of the economy, conditional statements ("might" or "maybe" or "considering"), or personnel decisions.

3. An examination of the data offers face validity in that presidents tend to discuss the significant policies that, historically, one would expect them to discuss (e.g., Eisenhower on the farm program, Kennedy on the missile gap, Johnson and Nixon on Vietnam, Ford and Carter on energy policy, Reagan on the Strategic Defense Initiative and taxes, Bush on the Gulf War, and Clinton on balancing the budget).

4. Page and Shapiro argue that a one-year lag in opinion and policy congruence is a reasonable time interval and base their results on this thinking (see Page and Shapiro, "Effects of Public Opinion on Policy," 177).

5. This method, although limited to one point of observation before and after the president's statement, addresses the specific question of whether or not presidents move opinion with particular speeches. Because public opinion is relatively stable (see Page and Shapiro, *Rational Public*), we can be confident that we are not observing opinion that will change greatly. Given this stability, our ability to control for external validity (or "control history") and for the same pre- and post-instrument, this quasi-experimental approach has merit (Campbell and Stanley, *Experimental and Quasi-Experimental Designs for Research,* 39, 42). Similarly, longer time periods may inject exogenous uncertainty into the equation, limiting the ability to claim that, causally, certain political factors (which may change in the intervening time period) influence the opinion movement.

6. There are instances where questions were prefaced differently or with respect to the timing of an event or speech. For instance, a question might preface, "As you may know," or alternatively, "Turning our attention to . . ." In addition, a preface to the question might reference the same point, legislation, or event but would alter the temporality. For instance, a question might have a preface "Legislation being considered by Congress" before the legislation passes and "Legislation recently passed by Congress" after the legislation passed. Ultimately, the questions are worded similarly enough to not make a significant change in the question wording.

7. The question (on both dates) was "Do you favor or oppose the nationwide ban on assault weapons?" Both polls were conducted by CBS News/*New York Times.*

8. The key here is that we are measuring polled opinion *before* and after the president speaks, and only for polls that employ the same question and answer choices. This matching can be difficult because pollsters often poll *after* a president speaks on an issue or do not use the same questions before and after our cataloging of the president's

statement on a particular date. This accounts for the relatively low number of yielded cases from the original sample of 1,976. Indeed, Page and Shapiro, and Page, Shapiro, and Dempsey, conduct a similar analysis of before-and-after quasi-experimental testing over a comparable time period and also produce a comparable small number of cases (actually fewer). However, this design adds to the uniqueness of this relationship because we have a valid measure of how popular the issue was before the president discussed it publicly. This method also allows us a continuous measure to match statement to opinion, since public opinion is measured as a continuous variable (the percentage of the public supporting the policy assertion). Page and Shapiro, "Presidents as Opinion Leaders"; Page, Shapiro, and Dempsey, "What Moves Public Opinion?"

9. Edwards, *On Deaf Ears.*

10. See, for instance, Reagan, *Reagan Diaries.*

11. Cohen, *Presidential Responsiveness and Public Policy-making;* Shaw, "Study of Presidential Campaign Event Effects."

12. See Page and Shapiro, *Rational Public.*

13. Repeated polls for longer time periods can make causal arguments more difficult because we do not have concurrent measures of presidential statements beyond the first moment of presidential speech recorded here. A repeated time-series design would require collection of all presidential statements within that (often lengthy) period. As a result, we focus on short-term leadership as a starting point for this inquiry. In any event, the trends in policy favorability or unfavorability will average out over repeated trials, making our approach reasonable.

14. Hart, *Sound of Leadership;* Page and Shapiro, *Rational Public,* 343–50.

15. Genovese, "Celebrity in Chief," 20.

16. Hargrove, *President as Leader;* Edwards, *On Deaf Ears,* 156.

17. Edwards, *Public Presidency;* Hart, *Sound of Leadership;* Eshbaugh-Soha, "Political Agendas."

18. Kumar, "Office of the Press Secretary"; Zarefsky, "Presidential Rhetoric and the Power of Definition."

19. Jacobs and Shapiro, *Politicians Don't Pander,* 320.

20. Light, *President's Agenda,* 160, 238.

21. Skewes, *Message Control.*

22. Genovese, "Celebrity in Chief."

23. See for instance Stout and Zeleny, "Bush Is Firm as Criticism over Iraq Mounts."

24. Farnsworth and Lichter, *Mediated Presidency.*

25. Quantitative approach: Page and Shapiro, "Presidents as Opinion Leaders"; Page, Shapiro, and Dempsey, "What Moves Public Opinion?" Qualitative approach: Edwards, *Public Presidency;* Kernell, *Going Public;* Edwards, *On Deaf Ears:* Wood, *Politics of Economic Leadership.*

26. Sigelman and Rosenblatt, "Mythological Considerations in the Analysis of Presidential Persuasion"; see also Cunion, "Second-term Presidents?"

27. Sigelman, "Rallying to the President's Support."

28. For instance, see discussion of the Clinton administration's belief that they could lead public opinion on health-care policy (Jacobs and Shapiro, *Politicians Don't Pander,* 116).

29. This figure of 49% is derived from the total number of statements of which there are valid opinions both before and after the president's statement (665) out of the total cases where there was positive movement from time 1 to time 2 (305). So, no change is excluded from the denominator. This measure excludes the cases for which there was only matched opinion either before or after the statement. Of the total cases, 34% (665 out of the 1,976 total) contained usable data.

30. Edwards, *On Deaf Ears;* Cohen, "Presidential Leadership in an Age of New Media."

31. Geer, *From Tea Leaves to Opinion Polls.*

32. The issues addressed in each of the windows of time are not the same, making a direct comparison not appropriate for the data. These data do, however, provide a sense of the exponential emergence of the president's message on the policy in question across various time periods and the effect at various times. The same speech is not necessarily affecting opinion, but rather is affecting the echo of that speech (see text for explanation).

33. Cohen, *Presidential Responsiveness and Public Policy-making;* Cohen and Hamman, "Polls: Can Presidential Rhetoric Affect the Public's Economic Perceptions?"

34. We cannot say for certain that each president was trying to lead public opinion with these statements, but my reading of the literature suggests that presidents are seeking to gain influence with each speech made, so we presume that presidents are trying to lead public opinion on these matters. See Hart, *Sound of Leadership.*

35. The total numbers within the category are presented at the base of the bar. The number on top of the bar is the percentage. For the nonpooled data, the chi square (5.37) is not statistically significant at $p > .05$, but the gamma statistic (-.004) is statistically significant at $p > .05$ and Kendall's tau-b (-.002) is statistically significant at $p > .05$. For the significant data (greater than 5% opinion movement), the chi square (14.6), gamma statistic (-.05), and Kendall's tau-b (-.031) are statistically significant at $p > .05$.

36. Genovese, *Memo to a New President,* 125.

37. Murray and Howard, "Variation in White House Polling Operations."

38. Underscoring the minimal differences between the "early" and "late" presidents, the chi square (.984) is not statistically significant at $p > .05$. But the Kendall's tau-b (-.03) is statistically significant at $p > .05$.

39. The chi square (3.60), gamma statistic (-.193), and Kendall's tau-b (-.03) are statistically significant at $p > .05$.

40. See, *The Presidency in the Era of Twenty-four-Hour News.*

41. Furthermore, there appears to be no significant party effect, as both Republicans (46%, $n = 159$) and Democrats (48%, $n = 146$) are successful at leading opinion in approximately equal amounts. The chi square (.227) is not statistically significant at $p >.05$ for the party variable when cross-tabulated with the leadership dichotomous variable.

42. Cunion, "Second-Term Presidents: Free Birds or Lame Ducks?"

43. Hetherington, "Political Relevance of Trust."

44. Maltese, *Spin Control.*

45. Wood, *Politics of Economic Leadership.*

46. Drew, *Showdown.*

47. The total n for first-term successful leadership cases is 221 (out of 487 total).

The total n for second-term successful leadership cases is 84 (out of 178 total). The chi square (.172) is not statistically significant at standard levels of significance, but the Kendall's tau-b (.01) is statistically significant at $p > .05$.

48. For second term presidents, the total n is 178. The chi square (.345) and the Cramer's V (-.022) are not significant at $p > .05$, but the Kendall's tau-b (-.02) is statistically significant at $p > .05$.

49. Of course, aggregating terms may mask subtle differences for individual presidents. Figure 3.1 does reveal that President Eisenhower was more successful at leading in his second term, while Presidents Nixon, Reagan, and Clinton were not. President Eisenhower governed with a strong economy, low inflation, strong employment, and solid economic growth. These political circumstances may have helped him to more successfully lead public opinion. Presidents Nixon, Reagan, and Clinton dealt with major, protracted institutional scandals in their second terms that may have damaged their credibility generally and negatively affected their ability to lead public opinion. These political contingencies are explored with more detail, including controlling for the effects of popularity and economic decline, in subsequent chapters.

50. Neustadt, *Presidential Power and the Modern Presidents,* 40.

51. Kernell, *Going Public.*

52. Jamieson, *Eloquence in an Electronic Age.*

53. Klein, *The Natural.*

54. Edwards, "Does the Messenger Matter?"

55. Sorensen, *Kennedy,* 310.

56. Giglio, *Presidency of John F. Kennedy,* 258–59.

57. Cannon, *President Reagan,* 751; Welch, "Presidential Success in Communicating with the Public."

58. L. Berman, *Looking Back on the Reagan Presidency.*

59. Sloan, "Meeting the Leadership Challenges of the Modern Presidency."

60. Schneider, "Political Legacy of the Reagan Years," 63.

61. Dowd, "Leaders as Followers."

62. Jacobs and Shapiro, *Politicians Don't Pander,* 95.

63. Frisby, "Clinton Seeks Strategic Edge with Opinion Polls"; Murray and Howard, "Variation in White House Polling Operations."

64. Neustadt, "Weakening White House"; Edwards, *On Deaf Ears.*

65. Edwards, *Strategic President.*

Chapter 4

1. Edwards, *On Deaf Ears,* 15.

2. Page, Shapiro, and Dempsey, "What Moves Public Opinion?"; Neustadt, "What Moves Public Opinion?"; Edwards, *On Deaf Ears;* Cohen, *Presidency in the Era of Twenty-four-Hour News.*

3. Aberbach and Rockman, "Hard Times for Presidential Leadership?"; Edwards, *On Deaf Ears.*

4. Roper, "Contemporary Presidency."

5. In separate models run but not displayed here, a variable capturing the number

of days between the president's statement and the post-poll date was included. Not surprisingly, the variable was negative and generally significant, although the effect was small across these alternative specifications. Yet in terms of the robustness of the results, the main effects between the models with this variable and without it are substantially similar (where the coefficients for communications tactics, public knowledge, and temporal circumstances such as rally effect and elections are nearly identical through each specification). The main differences are that the "two days before" variable loses significance and the "going international" tactic is often significant.

6. With relatively few cases and relatively many independent variables, there is a danger that the model is "overfitted." To test against this, I ran a number of checks. First, I reran the models with only the key variables (communications tactics, voter knowledge, and issue salience) to see if these variables were still significant without including other variables. The results between this test and table 4.1 were significantly similar. Second, I altered the dependent variable to only include negative opinion change to see if the variable signs reversed themselves, as would be expected. The signs did reverse themselves, which demonstrates that the effects are robust.

7. Baum and Kernell, "Has Cable Ended the Golden Age of Presidential Television?"; Edwards, *On Deaf Ears;* Young and Perkins, "Presidential Rhetoric, the Public Agenda, and the End of Presidential Television's 'Golden Age'"; Clayman et al., "Historical Trends in Questioning Presidents." We also split the data in this manner to mirror the beginning of "modern" polling practices in the White House with the introduction of an in-house pollster (instead of external consultants) during the Carter administration. We do so with the assumption that later presidents are better equipped with the knowledge of popular policies, as asserted in Conditional Expectation 1 (chapter 2). An alternative model with a slightly different specification, where "late" presidents were classified as Reagan to Clinton, yielded substantially similar results across the models.

8. Similar to Meernik and Ault, "Public Opinion and Support for U.S. President's Foreign Policies." The change in "don't know" is measured as the percentage of respondents answering "don't know" to the recorded survey question before the president spoke minus the percentage responding "don't know" after the president spoke. Negative integers here correspond to a decline in the percentage of "don't know," or to an increase in the information the public reports having about a policy issue.

9. In an alternative OLS model (discussed in appendix C), I regressed the percentage approving of the president's policy choice before he made it (t_1) on the percentage approving of the statement after he made it (t_2). Like Page, Shapiro, and Dempsey, who conduct a similar analysis, I found substantial agreement between this model and a model employing change in approval from t_1 to t_2 as the dependent variable (as in table 4.1). See Page, Shapiro, and Dempsey, "What Moves Public Opinion?"

10. Correlations were run between all of the dependent and independent variables. In the few instances where there were correlations, these correlations did not generally exceed .25. The largest relationship was a .41 correlation between the dependent variable and the change in "don't know." This is on the large side but not troublesome enough to remove it from the model. And, for substantive reasons such as the need to understand the shifts in the public's knowledge, the change variable was needed for the explanation. None of the principle communications strategies (barnstorm, press confer-

ence, going international, or major address) were highly correlated with themselves when they were interacted with "don't know"—the largest was the "major address" at .45. None of the other correlations were above .20. However, the interacted variables were correlated to varying degrees with change in "don't know," as follows: major address (.32), barnstorm (.41), and press conference (.46). But, again, for substantive reasons, these were included in the model in table 4.1 to demonstrate the interacted effect. This inclusion is also common with such models using interacted variables.

11. These alternatives include different models to capture dichotomous effects of the dependent variable and selection bias models to capture any selection effect by several issues.

12. Edwards, *Strategic President,* 104.

13. Alternative specifications including pre-poll and/or post-poll "don't know" percentages in the model as straight independent variables yielded substantially similar results.

14. Carter, *Keeping Faith.*

15. Jimmy Carter Library, WHCF, Subject File (PR 75), PR 15 1/20/77–8/31/77, "Hutcheson to the President," June 10, 1977, PR 75.

16. Ibid.

17. A July 1977 Cambridge Survey Research poll asks, "On the whole, how would you rate the job Congress has been doing as it works on President Carter's energy program: excellent, good, only fair or poor?" Harris Polls on October 13 and November 7, 1977, asked, "How would you rate him on . . . his overall energy program—excellent, pretty good, only fair or poor?" (for the October poll, 57% responded negatively and 10% responded "don't know"; for the November poll, 55% responded negatively and 8% responded "don't know.")

18. An alternative model was run with all press conferences (not limited to those on television) and the effect was substantively the same.

19. See Kumar, "Source Material: 'Does This Constitute a Press Conference?'"; Kumar, *Managing the President's Message.*

20. Kumar, "Presidential Press Conferences"; Mayer and Rozell, "A Presidency Transformed."

21. See Welch, "Presidential Success in Communicating with the Public"; Welch, "Was Reagan Really a Great Communicator?"; Young and Perkins, "Presidential Rhetoric, the Public Agenda, and the End of Presidential Television's 'Golden Age.'"

22. Hart, *Sound of Leadership.*

23. Welch, "Was Reagan Really a Great Communicator?"; Farnsworth and Lichter, *Mediated Presidency.*

24. Interactions with the "two days before" strategy did not improve the statistical significance of the measure. Removing the interaction with change in "don't know" also does nothing to change the sign or significance.

25. Schaefer, "Bill and Hilary's Excellent African Adventure."

26. Brace and Hinckley, *Follow the Leader,* 56.

27. Ibid., 57.

28. In an alternative specification that excludes international summits in which the United States was involved (included in Mueller's original definition) from the "rally"

variable, the coefficient was still negative and of similar size but did not reach statistical significance. However, given that Mueller's definition of "rally" included these summits, I chose to keep the rally definition as close to the original as possible.

29. See Edwards and Swenson, "Who Rallies?"; Callaghan and Virtanen, "Revised Models of the Rally Phenomenon"; Norrander and Wilcox, "Rallying around the Flag and Partisan Change."

30. Lian and Oneal, "Presidents, the Use of Military Force, and Public Opinion."

31. Oneal and Bryan, "Rally 'round the Flag Effect"; Lian and Oneal, "Presidents, the Use of Military Force, and Public Opinion."

32. Baum and Groeling, "What Gets Covered?"

33. Hetherington and Nelson, "Anatomy of a Rally Effect."

34. Canes-Wrone, "Public Presidency, Personal Approval Ratings, and Policy Making."

35. Page and Shapiro, "Presidents as Opinion Leaders"; Page, Shapiro, and Dempsey, "What Moves Public Opinion?"

36. The coefficient is very high here, especially for later presidents, suggesting they may be artificially inflated. But in an alternative model where the two variables that were highly correlated to the honeymoon variable were dropped (approval at .23 and "major address" interacted with "don't know" at .14), the results were substantially the same, suggesting that the findings are accurate.

37. Brody, "Is the Honeymoon Over?"

38. Kumar, *Managing the President's Message.*

39. Grossman and Kumar, *Portraying the President;* Clayman et al., "Historical Trends in Questioning Presidents."

40. Edwards, *On Deaf Ears;* Cohen, *Presidency in the Era of Twenty-four-Hour News.*

41. The Vanderbilt Television News Archive database was accessed from http://tvnews.vanderbilt.edu/.

42. These variables are all dummy variables and each has been constructed from other dummy variables. Above-average popularity in the sample was popularity above 54%. Above-average salience for an issue was greater than 10.82%. Above-average issue popularity for an issue was greater than 55%.

43. In alternative models, run without the Gallup-measured approval variable, the results were substantively the same.

44. Neustadt, *Presidential Power and the Modern Presidents.*

45. Miroff, *Pragmatic Illusions.*

46. R. Sobel, *Public Opinion in U.S. Foreign Policy.*

47. Wildavsky, "Two Presidencies"; Edwards, *Public Presidency;* Lian and Oneal, "Presidents, the Use of Military Force, and Public Opinion"; Powlick and Katz, "Defining the American Public Opinion/Foreign Policy Nexus"; Canes-Wrone, *Who Leads Whom?*

48. Specific issues coded as "minor" included statements pertaining to foreign aid, trade, arms control, relationships between countries, and recognition of nations. "Major" issues, on the other hand, included dealing with national security threats, relations between the superpowers, international associations (NATO or the United Nations), or emerging or ongoing conflicts.

49. See R. Sobel, *Impact of Public Opinion on U.S. Foreign Policy.*

50. Canes-Wrone, *Who Leads Whom?*

51. Peake, "Presidential Agenda Setting in Foreign Policy," 69; but cf. Wood and Peake, "Dynamics of Foreign Policy Agenda Setting."

52. We also control in table 4.6 for three exogenous variables that might correspond to opinion movement: the president's order to send troops, air strikes initiated by the president and the congressional authorization of the use of force. Several studies include the duration of foreign conflict as a variable, and these events have consistently positive effects on presidential ability to move approval ratings, although the effect is sometimes small (Parker, "Toward an Understanding of 'Rally' Effects"; Oneal and Bryan, "Rally 'round the Flag Effect"; Lian and Oneal, "Presidents, the Use of Military Force, and Public Opinion"). Others have also found significant "rallies" associated with the use of force by sending troops, in particular with the United States as revisionist or originator of a dispute (Baker and Oneal, "Patriotism or Opinion Leadership?"). Mueller, in *War, Presidents, and Public Opinion,* finds that citizens are especially likely to support a president's decision to engage militarily. The data on declarations of war and appropriation of troops was taken from "CRS Report for Congress: Declarations of War and Authorizations of the Use of Military Force, Congressional Research Service" (Elsea and Grimmett, *Declarations of War and Authorizations for the Use of Military Force*). The data on supplementary budget requests were collected from a search on Lexis-Nexus of newspaper accounts of these requests.

53. Sigelman, "Disarming the Opposition"; Rosenblatt, "Aggressive Foreign Policy Marketing"; Schubert, Stewart, and Curran, "Defining Presidential Moment"; Foyle, "Evolution of Presidential Polling"; Western, "War over Iraq."

54. Interactions between presidential popularity and any of the communications tactics ("Oval Office speech," "two days before," and "going international") did not prove to be statistically significant when included in the same model, implying that (1) our findings on the communications tactics are robust and (2) very little can be done by presidents to alter the circumstances under which presidents successfully communicate to the public.

55. Ronald Reagan Presidential Library, Craig Fuller Files, President Reagan's Record of Communications, 1981–1983 (1 of 4 to 4 of 4), OA 10974.

56. Rosenblatt, "Aggressive Foreign Policy Marketing."

57. In a model run but not shown, interactions with the "change in don't know" variable and each communication tactic reveals similar results. The coefficient for the interaction of "change in don't know" with "Oval Office speech" is half as large (but still statistically significant), while interactions with "two days before" and "going international" are not statistically significant.

58. Whereas there were 281 instances where minor issues were discussed during elections, these issues were only discussed 99 times during election years.

59. Stoll, "Guns of November"; Fordham, "Politics of Threat Perception of the Use of Force."

60. The correlations between rally effects and the individual foreign policy events are small and not significant. The Pearson *r* coefficients for correlations between our defined "rally" moments were as follows: troops (-.007), airstrikes (.043), and congressional authorization (.026). Similarly, the correlations between these events and an Oval

Office speech are also low: troops (.005), airstrikes (-.026), and Congressional authorization (.016). The occurrences where a presidential speech was an Oval Office speech (99 total) and was connected to an event were also low: troops (6), airstrikes (3), and congressional authorization (2).

61. The variables for use of force were removed from the analysis of minor issues in table 4.6 because, by definition, these events are major events.

62. James and Rioux, "International Crises and Linkage Politics"; Sigelman et al., "As Time Goes By."

63. Ronald Reagan Presidential Library, David Gergen, Press Plans/Communications Plan (2) November '81–July '82, "Gergen to Baker, Meese, Deaver and Clark," OA 10530.

64. See Cohen, "Presidential Leadership in an Age of New Media;" Cohen, *Presidency in the Era of Twenty-four-Hour News.*

65. Eshbaugh-Soha and Peake, "Going Local"; Barrett and Peake, "When the President Comes to Town"; Kumar, "Presidential Press Conferences."

66. See Marra, Ostrom, and Simon, "Foreign Policy and Presidential Popularity," 616.

67. Neustadt, *Presidential Power and the Modern Presidents,* 90.

Chapter 5

1. Page, "Democratic Responsiveness?"

2. Foyle, *Counting the Public In;* Western, *Selling Intervention and War.*

3. Yin, *Case Study Research.*

4. Small, *Presidency of Richard Nixon,* 30.

5. Ibid., 203.

6. Richard Nixon Materials Project, National Archives II, H. R. Haldeman Files, Polls Image Study (1), "Benham to Haldeman," June 9, 1971, Box 343.

7. Richard Nixon Materials Project, National Archives II, H. R. Haldeman Files, Polls Image Study (1), "Derge to the President," July 4, 1971, Box 343.

8. Weber, In Pursuit of Price Stability, 9.

9. Richard Nixon Materials Project, National Archives II, H. R. Haldeman Files, Polls Image Study (1), "Benham to Haldeman," June 9, 1971, Box 343.

10. Richard Nixon Materials Project, John Whitaker Files, Polls (3 of 4), "Whitaker to Erlichman," June 14, 1971, Box 92. Emphasis in original.

11. Small, *Presidency of Richard Nixon,* 209.

12. In a poll from May of 1971, with the Vietnam War excluded from the list, 44% of the public counted "Inflation/High cost of living" as the "most important problem facing people here in the United States." The second most important problem was "Pollution/Ecology" at 25% followed by "Unemployment" at 24%. Richard Nixon Materials Project, National Archives II, H. R. Haldeman Files, Polls—Chron, September–October 1971, "Strachan to Haldeman," September 22, 1971, Box 335.

13. Weber, In Pursuit of Price Stability, 130.

14. Genovese, *Nixon Presidency,* 67.

15. Weber, In Pursuit of Price Stability, 124.

16. Richard Nixon Materials Project, National Archives II, H. R. Haldeman Files, Polls Image Study (1), "Benham to Haldeman," June 9, 1971, Box 343, p. 2.

17. Richard Nixon Materials Project, National Archives II, Polls (1 of 4) (1969–1972), "Chapin to Haldeman," August 19, 1971, Box 22.

18. Reeves, *President Nixon,* 357.

19. Richard Nixon, "Address to the Nation Outlining a New Economic Policy: The Challenge of Peace," August 15, 1971, American Presidency Project, www.presidency.ucsb.edu./ws/?pid=3115. See Reeves, *President Nixon,* 359.

20. Richard Nixon, "Remarks to the 89th Annual International Meeting of the Knights of Columbus in New York City," August 17, 1971, American Presidency Project, www.presidency.ucsb.edu./ws/?pid=3119.

21. Richard Nixon, "Address to the Congress on Stabilization of the Economy," September 9, 1971, American Presidency Project, www.presidency.ucsb.edu./ws/?pid=3140.

22. Haldeman, *Haldeman Diaries,* 351.

23. Small, *Presidency of Richard Nixon,* 210.

24. Emphasis in original. Richard Nixon Materials Project, National Archives II, Patrick Buchanan Files, Haldeman 1971 (2 of 2), "Haldeman to Buchanan," August 26, 1971, Box 3.

25. Richard Nixon Materials Project, National Archives II, Charles Colson Files, Polls, "Rumsfeld to Colson," June 30, 1972, Box 100.

26. Ibid., 15.

27. Nixon, *Memoirs of Richard Nixon,* 520.

28. Richard Nixon Materials Project, National Archives II, H. R. Haldeman Files, Polls—Chron, January–February 1972, "Haldeman to Strachan," January 31, 1972, Box 335.

29. Small, *Presidency of Richard Nixon,* 207.

30. Reeves, *President Nixon,* 377.

31. Richard Nixon, *Memoirs of Richard Nixon,* 521.

32. Richard Nixon Materials Project, National Archives II, Charles Colson Files, Harris and Associates (accordion folder), "Peterson to the President," August 19, 1972.

33. Ibid.

34. Greene, *Limits of Power,* 76.

35. Richard Nixon Materials Project, National Archives II, Charles Colson Files, Harris and Associates (accordion folder), "Peterson to the President," October 24, 1972.

36. Ibid.

37. Greene, *Limits of Power,* 77.

38. Ibid., 76.

39. Richard Nixon Materials Project, National Archives II, Charles Colson Files, Polls, "Rumsfeld to Colson," June 30, 1972, Box 100.

40. Ibid., 18.

41. Dallek, *Ronald Reagan.*

42. Wicker, "Reagan's Real Test."

43. Foley, "Presidential Leadership and the Presidency."

44. From January to October of 1981, the president's popularity was in the mid- to high fifties. This increase partly followed the attempted assassination of the president in March of 1981. See Ragsdale, *Vital Statistics on the Presidency.*

45. Dallek, *Ronald Reagan.*

46. Emphasis in original. Ronald Reagan Presidential Library, Richard Beal Files, Strategic Plans: Phase III, July 8, 1981 Version (1), "Beal to Meese," July 2, 1981, OA 465. Phase III represented the period from October 1, 1981, to January 15, 1982, the period in which the president's proposals began to lose public favor.

47. J. Hogan, "Federal Budget in the Reagan Era," 222.

48. Reagan, *An American Life,* 234.

49. Weatherford and McDonnell, "Ideology and Economic Policy," 140.

50. Sloan, *Reagan Effect,* 125.

51. Niskanen, *Reaganomics,* 75.

52. Reagan, *An American Life,* 286.

53. Weatherford and McDonnell, "Ideology and Economic Policy," 141.

54. Ronald Reagan, "Remarks in Atlanta, Georgia, at the Annual Convention of the National Conference of State Legislatures," July 30, 1981, American Presidency Project, www.presidency.ucsb.edu./ws/?pid=44131.

55. Ronald Reagan Presidential Library, Richard Beal Files, CFOA 465, Social Security, "Wirthlin to Richards," July 30, 1981, Box 4 of 6.

56. Niskanen, *Reaganomics.*

57. Schneider, "Political Legacy of the Reagan Years," 54.

58. Erickson, *Reagan Speaks,* 46.

59. Ronald Reagan, "Address at Commencement Exercises at the University of Notre Dame," May 17, 1981, American Presidency Project, www.presidency.ucsb.edu./ws/?pid=43625.

60. Ronald Reagan Presidential Library, Richard Beal Files, CFOA 465, Social Security, "Wirthlin to Richards," July 30, 1981. Box 4 of 6. The question was "Suppose most of President Reagan's economic proposals are passed by Congress. From what you've heard and read, do you feel that, on the whole, these proposals will help or hurt the economy?"

61. In September of 1981, Wirthlin noted that "timing is the key." He was challenging poll reports from the *Washington Post* that indicated a lack of support for the Reagan plan. Wirthlin argued that the support now was higher than it had been and his data discovered that it would take at least a year to yield success. Ronald Reagan Presidential Library, Edwin Meese Files, Wirthlin 1981 (1), "Wirthlin to President Reagan, et al.," September 23, 1981, OA 6518.

62. Ronald Reagan Presidential Library, Edwin Meese Files, Wirthlin 1981 (7), "Wirthlin to Richards," August 21, 1981, OA 6518.

63. Sloan, *Reagan Effect,* 156.

64. J. Hogan, "Federal Budget in the Reagan Era," 218.

65. These numbers were taken from a poll done by Opinion Research Corporation (and shared with the Reagan White House) for the Chamber of Commerce of the United States. Ronald Reagan Presidential Library, Richard Beal Files, Polls, "Public Attitudes toward the Reagan Economic Program," April 1981, OA 7239, Box 5 of 6.

66. Peterson and Rom, "Lower Taxes, More Spending, and Budget Deficits," 214.

67. Reagan, *An American Life,* 285.

68. Weatherford and McDonnell, "Ideology and Economic Policy," 141.

69. Ronald Reagan Presidential Library, Edwin Meese Files, Wirthlin 1981 (6), "Wirthlin to Richards," October 19, 1981, OA 6518.

70. Ibid., 2.

71. Ronald Reagan Presidential Library, Edwin Meese Files, Wirthlin 1981 (6), "Wirthlin to Meese, Baker and Deaver," October 14, 1981, OA 6518.

72. Broder, "Rising Opposition to Reagan . . ."

73. Edsall, "Reagan Legacy."

74. Edwards, "Presidential Rhetoric?"

75. Stephanopoulos, *All Too Human.*

76. Drew, *Showdown,* 319.

77. Morris, *Behind the Oval Office,* 485.

78. Ibid., 489.

79. Bill Clinton, "The President's Radio Address," November 11, 1995, American Presidency Project, www.presidency.ucsb.edu./ws/?pid=50757.

80. Jones, *Clinton and Congress.*

81. Drew, *Showdown,* 218.

82. Jacobs and Shapiro, *Politicians Don't Pander,* 278.

83. Jones, *Clinton and Congress,* 145.

84. Bill Clinton, "The President's News Conference," January 9, 1996, American Presidency Project, www.presidency.ucsb.edu./ws/?pid=52570.

85. Morris, *Behind the Oval Office,* 491. Morris's poll question was "Last week the Republican majority in Congress passed bills they say will balance the budget in 7 years. The bill contains $270 bill in cuts in Medicare spending, $70 bill cuts in education spending, major cuts in environmental programs, and tax changes which would raise taxes on some working families, but lower then on others." Sixty-three percent opposed the plan while 33% supported it.

86. The *Washington Post*/ABC News poll asked on November 13 and 19, "On another subject, the Republicans in Congress have proposed a budget that they say will balance the federal budget in seven years and cut taxes for most Americans. (Bill) Clinton says this budget makes too many cuts in domestic programs and gives tax breaks to the wealthy. Who do you think is right, Clinton or the Republicans in Congress?" (the preface "on another subject" was removed in the November 19 poll). In the November 13 poll, 32% responded "Republicans," 2% responded "both," 2% responded "neither," and 7% responded "no opinion." In the poll of November 19, 29% responded "Republicans," 3% responded "both," 6% responded "neither," and 3% responded "no opinion."

87. The Hart and Teeter Research Company poll asked, "As you may know, Republicans in Congress are in the process of passing a federal budget that they say will balance the budget in seven years and reduce taxes for most families. President (Bill) Clinton says he will veto the budget because he believes it cuts too much from certain domestic programs and gives tax breaks mostly to the wealthy. In your view, should the President sign or veto this budget?" Thirty-two percent responded "sign the budget" and 7% responded "not sure."

88. Jacobs and Shapiro, *Politicians Don't Pander,* 289.

89. Morris, *Behind the Oval Office,* 492.

90. Drew, *Showdown,* 331; Stephanopoulos, *All Too Human,* 405.

91. Drew, *Showdown,* 335.

92. Jacobs and Shapiro, *Politicians Don't Pander,* 275.

93. Jones, *Clinton and Congress,* 156.

94. Morris, *Behind the Oval Office,* 492.

95. Clinton, *My Life,* 694.

96. Bill Clinton, "Address before a Joint Session of the Congress on the State of the Union," January 23, 1996, American Presidency Project, www.presidency.ucsb.edu./ws/?pid=53091.

97. Drew, *Showdown,* 358.

98. W. Berman, *From the Center to the Edge,* 56.

99. Arnold, "Clinton and the Institutionalized Presidency."

100. Morris, *Behind the Oval Office,* 187.

101. Stephanopoulos, *All Too Human,* 404.

102. Clinton, *My Life,* 682.

103. W. Berman, *From the Center to the Edge,* 51.

104. Clinton, *My Life,* 684.

105. Bill Clinton, "Address before a Joint Session of the Congress on the State of the Union," January 23, 1995, American Presidency Project, www.presidency.ucsb.edu./ws/?pid=53091.

106. Wood, *Politics of Economic Leadership.*

Chapter 6

1. Sorensen, *Kennedy,* 342.

2. Schlesinger, *A Thousand Days,* 644.

3. Giglio, *Presidency of John F. Kennedy,* 102.

4. Reeves, *President Kennedy,* 327.

5. John Kennedy, "Special Message to the Congress on Health and Hospital Care," February 9, 1961, American Presidency Project, www.presidency.ucsb.edu./ws/?pid=8222.

6. Sorensen, *Kennedy,* 343.

7. The Gallup Poll question of October 24, 1961, asked, "Do you think that the government in Washington is spending too much tax money for welfare programs to help the people in the United States or do you think it isn't spending enough?"

8. John Kennedy Library, President's Office Files, Staff Memos (Louis Harris), "Public Reaction to President Kennedy During the First 60 Days of his Administration." Box 64a, p. 6. The polls were conducted in Seattle, Washington, and in the state of Kentucky (not a nationwide poll).

9. Ragsdale, *Vital Statistics on the Presidency.*

10. Dallek, *An Unfinished Life,* 586.

11. Speech queries for "Medicare," "elderly" and "aged" were all searched, since the legislation was referred to in several ways.

12. Sorensen, *Kennedy,* 343.

13. An Opinion Research Corporation poll conducted on August 31, 1962, asked, "As you may know, Medicare was one of Kennedy's proposals rejected by Congress. . . . How much have you read or heard about president Kennedy's Medicare plan for the aged—a great deal, a fair amount, or very little?" Twenty-two percent responded "a great deal" and 39% responded "a fair amount."

14. John Kennedy, "Annual Message to the Congress on the State of the Union," January 30, 1961, American Presidency Project, www.presidency.ucsb.edu./ws/?pid=8045.

15. Giglio, *Presidency of John F. Kennedy,* 103.

16. John Kennedy, "Address at a New York Rally in Support of the President's Program of Medical Care for the Aged," May 20, 1962, American Presidency Project, www.presidency.ucsb.edu./ws/?pid=8669.

17. Sorensen, *Kennedy,* 343.

18. Ibid.

19. John Kennedy Library, President's Office Files, Louis Harris 1/60–9/63, "Harris to the President," July 26, 1962, Box 20.

20. Ibid., 3.

21. Dallek, *An Unfinished Life,* 496.

22. John Kennedy Library, President's Office Files, Louis Harris 1/60–9/63, "Harris to the President," July 26, 1962, Box 20.

23. Schlesinger, *A Thousand Days,* 721.

24. John Kennedy, "The President's News Conference," March 8, 1961, American Presidency Project, www.presidency.ucsb.edu./ws/?pid=8524.

25. Giglio, *Presidency of John F. Kennedy,* 102.

26. Reeves, *President Kennedy,* 327.

27. John Kennedy Library, President's Office Files, Staff Memos (Louis Harris), "Public Reaction to President Kennedy During the First 60 Days of his Administration," Box 64a, p. 7.

28. Jacobs and Shapiro, *Politicians Don't Pander.*

29. Sorensen, *Kennedy,* 342.

30. Giglio, *Presidency of John F. Kennedy,*102. Because the administration perceived it would have problems getting the legislation passed in the House, it actually offered the program in the Senate as an amendment to the Public Welfare bill already passed in the House.

31. Giglio, *Presidency of John F. Kennedy.*

32. John Kennedy Library, President's Office Files, Louis Harris 1/60–9/63, "Harris to the President," n.d., Box 30. Although this memorandum is not dated, the context of the argument suggests that it was early 1963.

33. Porter, *Presidential Decision Making,* 101.

34. L. Sobel, *Ford and the Economy,* 1.

35. Gerald Ford, "Address to a Joint Session of the Congress on the Economy," October 8, 1974, American Presidency Project, www.presidency.ucsb.edu./ws/?pid=4434.

36. Greene, *Limits of Power,* 72.

37. L. Sobel, *Ford and the Economy,* 38.

38. L. Sobel, *Ford and the Economy,* 33.

39. Ford, *A Time to Heal.*

40. Gerald Ford Presidential Library, Robert Hartmann Files, President Ford's Anti-Inflation Program, "President Ford's Anti-Inflation Program: The Public Reaction," October 1974, Box 33, p. 19.

41. Ibid., 53.

42. Porter, *Presidential Decision Making.*

43. Gerald Ford Presidential Library, Robert Hartmann Files, President Ford's Anti-Inflation Program, "President Ford's Anti-Inflation Program: The Public Reaction," October 1974, Box 33, p. 22.

44. Ibid., 47.

45. Greene, *Presidency of Gerald Ford,* 75.

46. The question from Harris and Associates was "(Let me ask you about some specific things President Ford has done. On . . . Keeping inflation under control . . . would you rate him excellent, pretty good, only fair, or poor?" In December 1974, 75% disapproved and 7% were "not sure." In February 1975, 81% disapproved and 5% were "not sure." In March 1975, 83% disapproved and 4% were "not sure."

47. Unfortunately, polls with identical question wording could not be found. The December 6, 1974, poll question from the Roper Organization asked, "President Ford in an address to Congress in early October (1974) made ten proposals for dealing with inflation. Here is a list of those proposals. Would you go down that list and for each one tell me whether you are in favor of or opposed to it, or are you uncertain about it?) . . . A one-year, 5% surcharge on income taxes for families with $15,000 or more taxable income." The December 23, 1974, poll from Harris and Associates asked, "President Ford has put forth a program both for curbing inflation and for getting the country out of the recession. Let me read you some key parts of what President Ford has proposed. For each, tell me if you favor or oppose it. Put a 5% surcharge on taxes paid on incomes over $15,000 for families and $7,500 for individuals."

48. Gerald Ford Presidential Library, Robert Hartmann Files, A Study of National Issues: March 1975, "National Impact Study #2, March 1975," Box 32, p. 27.

49. Ibid., 42.

50. Ibid., 34.

51. Ibid., 37.

52. Gerald Ford Presidential Library, Foster Chanock Files, Polls—General (2), "Slight to Jones," August 22, 1975, Box 2.

53. Gerald Ford Presidential Library, Robert Hartmann Files, DMI—The Public's Perceptions of Economic Issues, "The Public Perceptions of Economic Issues," February 1975, Box 30, p. 30.

54. Ibid., 28.

55. *U.S. News and World Report,* January 6, 1975.

56. Gerald Ford Presidential Library, Foster Chanock Files, Robert Teeter, "Spencer and Teeter to Cheney," November 12, 1975, Box 4.

57. Ibid.

58. Crain, "How Gerald Ford's WIN Effort Became a Loser."

59. Gerald Ford Presidential Library, Foster Chanock Files, Robert Teeter, "Spencer and Teeter to Cheney," November 12, 1975, Box 4.

60. Greene, *Presidency of Gerald Ford,* 72.

61. Gerald Ford Presidential Library, Robert Hartmann Files, President Ford's Anti-Inflation Program, "President Ford's Anti-Inflation Program: The Public Reaction," October 1974, Box 33, p. 31.

62. Edel, *Reagan Presidency,* 63.

63. Cannon, *President Reagan.*

64. Kneeland, "Reagan Vows to Support Social Security Program."

65. Ronald Reagan Library, Edwin Meese Files, Wirthlin (5) 1981, "Wirthlin to Richards," September 29, 1981, OA 6518. Other revenue sources that were tested included reducing foreign aid (84% approve), cutting federal jobs (68% approve), reducing welfare payments (68% approve), and consolidating departments of Education and Energy (40% approve).

66. Tolchin, "Byrd Assails Cuts in Social Security."

67. Cannon, *President Reagan.*

68. Ronald Reagan, "Address before a Joint Session of the Congress on the Program for Economic Recovery," February 18, 1981, American Presidency Project, www.presidency.ucsb.edu./ws/?pid=43425.

69. Ibid.

70. Canes-Wrone, *Who Leads Whom?*

71. Cattani, "Public Outcry: 'Don't Touch Our Social Security.'"

72. Cannon, *President Reagan,* 213.

73. Ibid.

74. Ronald Reagan Library, Edwin Meese Files, Wirthlin (10) 1981, "Wirthlin to Meese, et al.," May 28, 1981, OA 6518.

75. Ibid.

76. Ibid., 2.

77. Ronald Reagan Library, Richard Beal Files, Social Security, "Wirthlin to Richards," July 29, 1981, Box 4, p. 3.

78. Ibid.

79. Dewar, "Senate Unanimously Rebuffs President on Social Security."

80. Niskanen, *Reaganomics,* 38

81. Cattani, "Reagan Honeymoon Wanes as Congress Stirs on Key Issues."

82. Raines, "White House Learning the Limits to President's Mandate."

83. Sussman, "By 3 to 2, Americans Disapprove of Reagan Plan for Social Security."

84. Cannon, *President Reagan,* 213.

85. Ibid.

86. Ronald Reagan, "Letter to Congressional Leaders on the Social Security System," May 21, 1981, American Presidency Project, www.presidency.ucsb.edu./ws/?pid=43849.

87. Cannon, *President Reagan.*

88. Raines, "White House Learning the Limits to President's Mandate," *New York Times,* May 25, 1981, 9.

Chapter 7

1. Page and Shapiro, "Presidents as Opinion Leaders"; Canes-Wrone, *Who Leads Whom?*

2. See Herring "War in Vietnam," 28.

3. See L. Berman, *Lyndon Johnson's War.*

4. Lyndon Johnson Library, White House Central Files, PR 16 12/15/65–1/21/66, "Moyers to President," December 27, 1965, Box 346.

5. Gardner, *Pay Any Price,* 253; Rottinghaus, Brandon, "Following the Mail Hawks."

6. Lyndon Johnson Library, Aides Files (Busby), Memos to President—February '65, "Busby to President," February 27, 1965.

7. Ibid.

8. Ibid.

9. Dallek, *Flawed Giant,* 245.

10. Lyndon Johnson, "Address at Johns Hopkins University: 'Peace without Conquest.'" April 7, 1965, American Presidency Project, www.presidency.ucsb.edu./ws/?pid=26877.

11. Karnow, *Vietnam: A History,* 428.

12. Gardner, *Pay Any Price,* 168.

13. Burke and Greenstein, *How Presidents Test Reality.*

14. Dallek, *Flawed Giant,* 252.

15. L. Berman, *Planning a Tragedy.*

16. Lyndon Johnson Presidential Library, White House Central Files, PR 16 Public Opinion Polls (April—June 1965), "On Continuing US Air Raids," August 9, 1965, Box 80.

17. Lyndon Johnson Presidential Library, White House Central Files, PR 16 Public Opinion Polls (April—June 1965), "Moyers to the President," February 16, 1965, Box 80.

18. Lyndon Johnson Presidential Library, Aides Files (Busby), Memos to the President—Feb. '65, "Busby to President," February 27, 1965, Box 52.

19. Karnow, *Vietnam: A History,* 430.

20. Ibid.

21. Lyndon Johnson Library, White House Central Files, PR 16 7/15/65–11/2/65, "Redmon to Moyers," October 28, 1965, Box 346.

22. Gardner, *Pay Any Price,* 170.

23. Dallek, *Flawed Giant,* 277.

24. Karnow, *Vietnam: A History,* 441.

25. Lyndon Johnson, "The President's News Conference," July 28, 1965, American Presidency Project, www.presidency.ucsb.edu./ws/?pid=27116.

26. Lyndon Johnson Presidential Library, White House Central Files, PR 16 11/27/65–12/14/65, "Valenti to the President," December 13, 1965, Box 346.

27. Lyndon Johnson Presidential Library, White House Central Files, PR 16 10/29/64–5/19/65, "Moyers to the President," February 16, 1965, Box 346. The note from Moyers to the President reads, "Attached are the results of the polls I mentioned to you last night. Lou Harris asks that we not let anyone know he did it for us." The text describing the polling data reads, "Dictated by Lou Harris, N.Y. City—4/6/65."

28. R. Sobel, *Impact of Public Opinion on U.S. Foreign Policy,* 33.

29. Dallek, *Flawed Giant,* 254.

30. Barrett, *Uncertain Warriors,* 47.

31. Lyndon Johnson Library, Aides Files (Moyers), BDM Memos, September 1965–March 1966, "Redmon to Moyers," November 27, 1965, Box 11.

32. Ibid.

33. Lyndon Johnson Library, White House Central Files, PR 16 12/15/65–1/21/66, "Moyers to President," December 27, 1965, Box 346.

34. Ibid.

35. Ibid.

36. Ibid.

37. Kaufman, *Presidency of James Earl Carter Jr.*, 117.

38. Moore, "The Carter Presidency and Foreign Policy," 69; Hargrove, *Jimmy Carter as President.*

39. Haas, *Jimmy Carter and the Politics of Frustration*, 100.

40. Jones, *Trusteeship Presidency*, 158.

41. Jimmy Carter Library, Chief of Staff Files, Panama Canal 8/77 (1), "Schuker to Aragon," June 17, 1977, Box 36.

42. The poll question from Opinion Research Corporation asked, "Do you favor the United States continuing its ownership and control of the Panama Canal, or do you favor turning ownership and control of the Panama Canal over to the Republic of Panama?" Fourteen percent responded, "Don't know."

43. The poll question from the Gallup Organization asked, "The proposed new treaty between the U.S. and Panama calls for the U.S. to turn over ownership of the canal to Panama at the end of this century. However, the U.S. will maintain control over the land and installations necessary to operate and defend the canal. Do you approve or disapprove of this proposed new treaty?" Fifty-three percent disapproved and 16% responded "no opinion."

44. Jimmy Carter, "The President's News Conference," February 23, 1977, American Presidency Project, www.presidency.ucsb.edu./ws/?pid=6887.

45. Jimmy Carter Library, Chief of Staff Files, Panama Canal 8/77 (1), "Schuker to Aragon," June 17, 1977, Box 36.

46. Ibid., 2. Emphasis in original.

47. Jimmy Carter Library, Chief of Staff Files, Panama Canal Treaties, 1977 (3), "Caddell to Jordan," December 20, 1977, Box 50.

48. Jimmy Carter Library, Chief of Staff Files, Panama Canal Treaty—10, 11, 12 (3), "Aragon to Jordan," November 30, 1977, Box 36.

49. Jimmy Carter Library, Chief of Staff Files, Canal Treaty, 1977, "Jordan and Moore to the President," December 13, 1977, Box 50.

50. "Aragon to Jordan," November 30, 1977.

51. See Canes-Wrone, *Who Leads Whom?*

52. Jimmy Carter Library, Chief of Staff Files, Panama Canal 8/77 (2), "Blair to Read et al.," August 22, 1977, Box 36.

53. Jimmy Carter Library, Chief of Staff Files, Panama Canal 9/77, "Jordan to Carter," September 19, 1977, Box 36.

54. Jimmy Carter Library, White House Central Files Subject Files, PR 15 1/20/77–8/31/77, "Pastor to Brzezinski," May 16, 1977, Box PR 75.

55. J. M. Hogan, "Public Opinion and American Foreign Policy."

56. Jimmy Carter Library, Chief of Staff Files, Panama Canal Treaty—10, 11, 12 (1), "An Analysis of Public Attitudes toward the Panama Canal Treaties," October 1977, Box 36.

57. Ibid.

58. Ibid., 12, 13.

59. "Jordan to Carter," September 19, 1977. Although it extends beyond our analy-

sis here, other types of public communication from the White House were employed, such as the State Department's speakers bureau, State and Defense Department officials making speeches, materials mailed from the White House Press Office to over 4,000 columnists, and the use of surrogates such as President Ford, Henry Kissinger, George Meany, William Buckley, Averell Harriman, and John Wayne. See "Aragon to Jordan," November 30, 1977.

60. Jimmy Carter, "State of the Union Address Delivered before a Joint Session of the Congress," January 19, 1978, American Presidency Project, www.presidency.ucsb.edu./ws/?pid=30856.

61. Jimmy Carter Library, Chief of Staff Files, Panama Canal Treaties, 1977 (3), "Caddell to Jordan," December 20, 1977, Box 50.

62. Jimmy Carter, "Panama Canal Treaties Address to the Nation," February 1, 1978, American Presidency Project, www.presidency.ucsb.edu./ws/?pid=29995.

63. Ibid.

64. "Aragon to Jordan," November 30, 1977.

65. Ibid.

66. The Harris poll asked "As you know, the Senate now has to debate the treaties that President Carter signed granting control of the Panama Canal to the Republic of Panama in the year 2000. Do you approve or disapprove of those treaties." The polls ended on September 26, 1977 (51% disapproved and 23% were "not sure") and January 12, 1978 (51% disapproved and 20% were "not sure").

67. "Caddell to Jordan," December 20, 1977.

68. Kaufman, *Presidency of James Earl Carter Jr.*

69. In locating polls to evaluate public opinion, we tried to find polls that matched most closely the actual impact of the treaties. Patrick Caddell also notes in his followup survey that the final poll results depend a great deal on the wording of the questions "and the amount of information they convey about the treaties." "Caddell to Jordan," December 20, 1977.

70. The February 13 Gallup poll question was "Actually, the treaties would give Panama full control over the Panama Canal and the Canal Zone by the year 2000, but the United States would retain the right to defend the canal against a third nation. Do you favor or oppose these treaties between the U.S. and Panama?" Thirty-eight percent disapproved and 19% stated "no opinion."

71. The February 22 NBC News poll question was "The new treaty between the United States and Panama calls for the United States to turn over ownership of the canal to Panama at the end of this century. However, this treaty still has to be approved by the Senate. Would you favor or oppose approval of the Panama Canal treaty if amendments were added specifically giving the United States the right to intervene if the canal is threatened by attack and the right to send our warships to the head of the line in case of emergency?" Forty percent disapproved and 6% were "not sure."

72. The March 21 Harris poll asked, "The second (Panama Canal) treaty has been changed to allow the use of U.S. military force to defend the Panama Canal in an emergency and to allow U.S. warships priority in going through the canal in an emergency. In general, do you tend to approve or disapprove of these changes in the Panama Canal treaty?" Nineteen percent disapproved and 9% stated "not sure."

73. The Harris Polls from February 18 and April 20 asked, "Now let me ask you about some specific things President Carter has done. How would you rate him on . . . his handling of the Panama Canal Treaties—excellent, pretty good, only fair or poor?" In the February poll, 59% were "negative" and 15% were "not sure" while in the April poll, 56% were "negative" and 11% were "not sure."

74. Shoup, *Carter Presidency and Beyond,* 183.

75. Haas, *Jimmy Carter and the Politics of Frustration,* 101.

76. J. E. Smith, *George Bush's War.*

77. Zaller, "Strategic Politicians, Public Opinion, and the Gulf Crisis," 250.

78. George H. W. Bush Library, White House Chief of Staff Files, Polling 1991 (1 of 3), "Ailes to Sununu and the President," February 9, 1991, CF 00473 (2 of 4).

79. Heith, "One for All."

80. The "respondent types" included were "Mainstreamers" (ages 25–60), "Succeeders" (25–60), "Reformers" (25–60), "College Students" (18–24), and "Young Non-College" (18–24). A footnote indicates that African Americans were underrepresented by this study.

81. Rottinghaus, "Foreign Policy and the Limits of Crafted Talk."

82. Wittkopf, *Faces of Internationalism,* 4.

83. Jentleson "Pretty Prudent Public"; Jentleson and Britton "Still Pretty Prudent."

84. See R. Sobel, *Impact of Public Opinion on U.S. Foreign Policy,* 147.

85. "Ailes to Sununu and the President," February 9, 1991.

86. George H. W. Bush Library, White House Chief of Staff Files, Polling 1991 (1 of 3), "The Persian Gulf: Viewpoint of the American People," December 1990, CF 00473 (3 of 4), Box 44. Emphasis in original.

87. R. Sobel, *Impact of Public Opinion on U.S. Foreign Policy,* 162.

88. Woodward, *Commanders,* 337; Mueller, *Policy and Opinion in the Gulf War,* 116.

89. "The Persian Gulf: Viewpoint of the American People," December 1990, p. 11.

90. R. Sobel, *Impact of Public Opinion on U.S. Foreign Policy,* 156; see Jentleson, "Pretty Prudent Public."

91. "The Persian Gulf: Viewpoint of the American People," December 1990, p. 17.

92. Ibid., 9.

93. George H. W. Bush Library, White House Chief of Staff Files, Polling 1991 (1 of 3), "Ailes to the President," January 9, 1991, CF 00473 (2 of 4).

94. J. E. Smith, *George Bush's War,* 161.

95. See Cox Han, "Rose Garden Strategy Revisited."

96. George H. W. Bush, "The President's News Conference," January 12, 1991, American Presidency Project, www.presidency.ucsb.edu./ws/?pid=19213.

97. Woodward, *Commanders,* 325; Greene, *Presidency of George Bush,* 124.

98. George H. W. Bush Library, White House Chief of Staff Files, Persian Gulf Working Group, "Demarest to the President," November 14, 1990, CF 00472, Box 12. President Bush handwrote a message on the memorandum asking, "How much of this has been done? What more can be done? Let's discuss next week."

99. George H. W. Bush, "Address to the Nation Announcing Allied Military Action in the Persian Gulf," January 16, 1991, American Presidency Project, www.presidency.ucsb.edu./ws/?pid=19222.

100. Mueller, *Policy and Opinion in the Gulf War,* 70.

101. George H. W. Bush Library, White House Chief of Staff Files, Polling 1991 (1 of 3), RNC U.S. National Survey, January 4–12, 1991, January 23, 1991, CF 00473.

102. RNC U.S. National Survey, January 4–12, 1991, January 23, 1991, p. 11. Polls in December were taken over the period of December 7–12, 1990, and polls in January were taken over the period January 4–12, 1991. There were no indications from this or other documents pertaining to how "Reagan" voters or "New Bush" voters were determined.

103. Mueller, *Policy and Opinion in the Gulf War,* 75; see also Iyengar and Simon, "News Coverage of the Gulf Crisis and Public Opinion."

104. Woodward, *Commanders,* 358.

105. Ibid., 289.

106. Ibid., 323.

107. Entman and Page, "News before the Storm."

108. Mueller, *Policy and Opinion in the Gulf War,* 60.

109. His popularity hovered between the mid-sixties and mid-seventies between August of 1989 and August of 1990 (when Iraq invaded Kuwait).

110. Zaller, "Strategic Politicians, Public Opinion, and the Gulf Crisis."

111. Emphasis in original. George H. W. Bush Library, White House Chief of Staff Files, Persian Gulf Working Group, "Demarest to Sununu," November 28, 1990, CF 00472, Box 12.

112. George H. W. Bush Library, White House Chief of Staff Files, Polling 1991 (2 of 3), "Steeper to Teeter," February 15, 1991, CF 00473.

113. Iyengar and Simon, "News Coverage of the Gulf Crisis and Public Opinion."

114. RNC U.S. National Survey, January 4–12, 1991, January 16, 1991. The first poll question was "Here are some positions people are taking on the war. For each one, please tell me if you favor or oppose it." The second poll was "Do you think we are doing the right thing in using military force against Iraq, or do you think we should have waited longer for the economic sanctions and diplomatic pressure to work?"

115. Mueller, *Policy and Opinion in the Gulf War,* 77.

116. George H. W. Bush Library, White House Chief of Staff Files, Polling 1991 (1 of 3), "Steeper on 'The Tax Issue,'" January 9, 1991, CF 00473 (1 of 4).

117. Brody, "Crisis, War, and Public Opinion," 220.

118. George H. W. Bush Library, White House Press Office, Marlin Fitzwater Files, Political File (1) OA 6548, "Steeper to Teeter," March 2, 1992, Box 22.

Chapter 8

1. Karnow, *Vietnam: A History,* 592.

2. Palmer, *The Twenty-five-Year War.*

3. See L. Berman, *No Peace, No Honor.*

4. Kimball, *Vietnam War Files,* 302.

5. Karnow, *Vietnam: A History,* 655.

6. Karnow, *Vietnam: A History,* 644.

7. Richard Nixon, "Address to the Nation on Vietnam," April 26, 1972, American Presidency Project, www.presidency.ucsb.edu./ws/?pid=3384.

8. Ibid.

9. Karnow, *Vietnam: A History*, 658.

10. Kimball, *Nixon's Vietnam War*, 304.

11. Karnow, *Vietnam: A History*, 659.

12. Richard Nixon Library, National Archives II, H. R. Haldeman Files, Vietnam Invasion Poll—April 27–29, 1972, "From Tom Behman," April 30, 1972, Box 350.

13. Richard Nixon Library, National Archives II, H. R. Haldeman Files, Distribution of Vietnam Invasion Poll—April 27–29, 1972, "Vietnam Invasion Poll," April 30, 1972, Box 350.

14. Small, *Presidency of Richard Nixon*, 66.

15. Quoted in Kimball, *Vietnam War Files*, 204.

16. Karnow, *Vietnam: A History*, 661.

17. "Vietnam Invasion Poll," April 30, 1972, p. 4.

18. "From Tom Behman," April 30, 1972.

19. "Vietnam Invasion Poll," April 30, 1972, p. 6.

20. The Gallup poll asked, "Do you favor or oppose the stepped up bombing of North Vietnam?" Results came out on April 24, 1972, and September 25, 1972.

21. Clodfelter, *Limits of Air Power*, 157.

22. Palmer, *The Twenty-five-Year War*, 122.

23. Karnow, *Vietnam: A History*, 654.

24. Ibid., 204.

25. Kimball, *Nixon's Vietnam War*, 311.

26. Clodfelter, *Limits of Air Power*, 158.

27. The president's popularity hit 62% in May 1972 and 59% on June 16, 1972. See Ragsdale, *Vital Statistics on the Presidency*.

28. Richard Nixon Library, National Archives II, H. R. Haldeman Files, Wave II Ala.–NJ, "Teeter to MacGregor," July 15, 1972, Box 367.

29. Richard Nixon Library, National Archives II, H. R. Haldeman Files, Vietnam Invasion Poll—April 27–29, 1972, "Kehrli and Strachan to Haldeman," May 2, 1972, Box 350.

30. The administration was debating holding a press conference wherein the president would make the same announcement (Kimball, *Nixon's Vietnam War*, 304).

31. "Vietnam Invasion Poll," April 30, 1972, p. 4.

32. Richard Nixon Library, National Archives II, H. R. Haldeman Files, Distribution of Vietnam Invasion Poll, April 27–29, 1972, "Memorandum from Tom Benham," n.d.

33. Edwards, "Changing Their Minds?"

34. Richard Nixon, "Letter to Delegates of the 1971 White House Conference on Youth Transmitting a Report of Executive Branch Review of Conference Recommendations," April 13, 1972, American Presidency Project, www.presidency.ucsb.edu./ws/?pid=3373.

35. Richard Nixon, "Remarks and a Question-and-Answer Session with Guests following a Dinner at Secretary Connally's Ranch in Floresville, Texas," April 30, 1972, American Presidency Project, www.presidency.ucsb.edu./ws/?pid=3390.

36. Nixon, "Address to the Nation on Vietnam," April 26, 1972.

37. Pastor, "Reagan Administration and Latin America."

38. Ronald Reagan Presidential Library, WHCF, Subject File, PR 15, 153001–167000, “Wirthin to Meese, Baker and Deaver,” July 13, 1983, Box 3.

39. Ibid.

40. Ibid.

41. Wittkopf, *Faces of Internationalism.*

42. R. Sobel, *Impact of Public Opinion on U.S. Foreign Policy.*

43. Wittkopf and McCormick, “Domestic Politics of Contra Aid,” 73.

44. Wicker, “A Bone in His Throat.”

45. Hoffman, “Reagan to Push ‘Contra’ Funds.”

46. R. Sobel, *Impact of Public Opinion on U.S. Foreign,* 111.

47. Rosenblatt, “Aggressive Foreign Policy Marketing.”

48. Moffett, “Reagan Raises Level of Rhetoric.”

49. Kagan, *Twilight Struggle,* 368.

50. Pastor, “Reagan Administration and Latin America,” 374–75.

51. Ronald Reagan, “Address before a Joint Session of the Congress on the State of the Union,” February 6, 1985, American Presidency Project, www.presidency.ucsb.edu./ws/?pid=38069.

52. Gutman, *Banana Diplomacy,* 271.

53. R. Sobel, *Impact of Public Opinion on U.S. Foreign,* 117.

54. Reagan, *An American Life,* 484.

55. Moffett, “Reagan Raises Level of Rhetoric.”

56. Ronald Reagan, “The President’s News Conference,” February 21, 1985, American Presidency Project, www.presidency.ucsb.edu./ws/?pid=38249.

57. Goshko and Shapiro, “Speaker O’Neill Assails President.”

58. Reagan, “President’s News Conference,” February 21, 1985.

59. Ronald Reagan Presidential Library, WHCF, Subject File, PR 15, 307001–318000, “Wirthin to President,” April 10, 1985, Box 5. Emphasis in original.

60. Several of the president’s speechwriters (including Patrick Buchanan) argued for a televised address to the nation, but Oliver North argued against it. In 1986, when requesting an additional $100 million in aid ($70 million of it military aid), the president was able to move public opinion after an appeal on television (see Kagan, *Twilight Struggle,* 427).

61. R. Sobel, *Impact of Public Opinion on U.S. Foreign Policy,* 117.

62. Kagan, *Twilight Struggle,* 345.

63. H. Smith, “Rebuff for the President.”

64. R. Sobel, “Public Opinion about United States Intervention”; R. Sobel, *Impact of Public Opinion on U.S. Foreign Policy.*

65. Hoffman, “President Keeps Pushing ‘Contra’ Aid.”

66. Ronald Reagan Presidential Library, WHCF, Subject File, PR 15, 307001–318000, “DMI Executive Summary,” April 1985, Box 5.

67. The Harris Poll question was “Recently, President Reagan has had some serious disagreements with Congress. Now who do you think was more right—Reagan or Congress—in their differences over . . . sending military aid to the Contra rebels in Nicaragua, which is favored by Reagan and opposed by Congress?” In June, 59% favored Congress (1% favored both) and in August, 64% favored Congress (1% favored both).

68. In March 1985, 66% opposed the aid proposal and 6% were unsure. In May 1985, 73% opposed the aid proposal and 4% were not sure.

69. Brummer, "Why the President Still Holds All the Cards."

70. Saikowski, "Reagan Moves to Recapture Political Momentum."

71. R. Sobel, *Impact of Public Opinion on U.S. Foreign Policy,*100.

72. Rottinghaus, "Foreign Policy and the Limits of Crafted Talk."

73. Ronald Reagan Presidential Library, WHCF, Subject File, PR 15, 307001–318000, "Wirthin to President," April 10, 1985, Box 5.

74. Ibid.

75. Kagan, *Twilight Struggle,* 369.

76. Pastor, "Reagan Administration and Latin America."

77. Ronald Reagan Presidential Library, WHCF, Subject File, PR 15, 307001–318000, "DMI Executive Summary," April 1985, Box 5.

78. Quoted in R. Sobel, *Impact of Public Opinion on U.S. Foreign Policy,* 114.

79. "Wirthin to President," April 10, 1985.

80. Cannon and Goshko, "Fight Over Further Aid to 'Contras' Intensifies."

81. Brummer, "Why the President Still Holds All the Cards."

82. Dewar, "Lugar Says Congress Is Likely to Deny Further 'Contra' Aid."

83. Berman and Goldman, "Clinton's Foreign Policy at Midterm."

84. C. A. Smith, "Rough Stretches and Honest Disagreements," 226.

85. Drew, *On the Edge,* 18; Edwards and Valenzano, "Bill Clinton's 'New Partnership' Anecdote."

86. Jones, "Campaigning to Govern."

87. Western, *Selling Intervention and War,* 133.

88. Woods, "Clinton, Fulbright, and the Legacy of the Cold War," 102.

89. W. Berman, *From the Center to the Edge,* 36.

90. Drew, *On the Edge,* 316.

91. Ibid., 326.

92. Bill Clinton, "Address to the Nation on Somalia," October 7, 1993, American Presidency Project, www.presidency.ucsb.edu./ws/?pid=47180.

93. Drew, *On the Edge,* 329.

94. Bode, "Clinton and the Press," 23.

95. Bill Clinton, "Remarks at Yale University in New Haven, Connecticut," October 9, 1993, American Presidency Project, www.presidency.ucsb.edu./ws/?pid=47190. His remarks were more pronounced in a speech at the University of North Carolina on October 12, 1993, in part because he included an additional sentence expressing his "sympathy and gratitude" to those soldiers from Fort Bragg in North Carolina who died in Somalia.

96. Berke, "Clinton Sounds a Rallying Cry," 10.

97. W. Berman, *From the Center to the Edge,* 36.

98. Hyland, *Clinton's World,* 59.

99. The October 6 and 19 CBS News poll asked, "What should the United States do now? Do you think the United States should keep its troops in Somalia until the situation in Somalia is peaceful, or should the United States withdraw its troops as quickly as possible?" In the October 6 survey, 59% responded "withdraw" and 9% responded

"don't know." In the October 19 survey, 60% responded "withdraw" and 7% responded "don't know."

100. Henriksen, *Clinton's Foreign Policy,* 10.

101. The October 6 and October 26 polls from NBC News asked, "Do you feel the situation in Somalia could turn into another Vietnam for the United States or don't you feel that is a real danger?" The percentage of the public registering a "not sure" was 7% and 4%, respectively.

102. See Ragsdale, *Vital Statistics on the Presidency.*

103. Ibid.

104. Drew, *On the Edge,* 318.

105. Clinton, "Address to the Nation on Somalia," October 7, 1993.

106. Ibid.

107. Goodman, "Effect of Images on Government Policy."

108. James and Rioux, "International Crises and Linkage Politics"; Sigelman et al., "As Time Goes By."

109. Klarevas, "Polls-Trends," 526.

110. Ingwerson, "Clinton's First 100 Days."

111. Kaid, Tedesco, and Spiker, "Media Conflicts over Clinton Policies," 103.

112. Edwards, "Presidential Rhetoric?"

113. Ibid., 247.

114. Cannon, "Buchanan Urges Speech on Nicaragua."

115. Edwards, "Changing Their Minds?"

Chapter 9

1. Taranto and Leo, *Presidential Leadership.*

2. Beschloss, *Presidential Courage.*

3. Fine and Waterman, "New Model of Presidential Leadership."

4. Cohen, "Presidential Going Public"; Eshbaugh-Soha, *President's Speeches;* Edwards, "Changing Their Minds?"; Edwards, *On Deaf Ears,* 25.

5. Genovese, *Memo to a New President,* 7.

6. Light, *President's Agenda,* 2.

7. Pastor, *Condemned to Repetition,* 375.

8. Kernell, *Going Public.*

9. Cohen, *Presidency in the Era of Twenty-four-Hour News.*

10. See Kumar, *Managing the President's Message;* Cohen, *Presidency in the Era of Twenty-four-Hour News.*

11. Edwards, *On Deaf Ears;* Cohen, *Presidency in the Era of Twenty-four-Hour News.*

12. Herbst, "Rhetorical Presidency and the Contemporary Media Environment."

13. Edwards, *Strategic President,* 188.

14. See Tulis, *Rhetorical Presidency.* See also Ceaser, "Demagoguery, Statesmanship, and the American Presidency."

15. See Jacobs and Shapiro, *Politicians Don't Pander;* Parry-Giles, *Rhetorical Presidency, Propaganda, and the Cold War.*

16. Lee, "Dividers, Not Uniters."

17. Kernell, *Going Public,* 3.
18. Eshbaugh-Soha, *President's Speeches.*
19. Cohen, *Presidency in the Era of Twenty-four-Hour News.*
20. See, for instance, Dreazen, "Bush 9/11 Tour Aims to Bolster Republicans."
21. Laracey, *Presidents and the People.*
22. Rottinghaus, "Foreign Policy and the Limits of Crafted Talk."
23. Jacobs, *Health of Nations.*
24. Chong and Druckman, "Framing Public Opinion in Competitive Democracies."
25. Woodrow Wilson, *Constitutional Government in the United States.*

Epilogue

1. C. Campbell, "Managing the Presidency or the President?"
2. Edwards, *Governing by Campaigning.*
3. Edwards, "Changing Their Minds?" 10.
4. Rockman, "Legacy of the George W. Bush Presidency," x.
5. Jacobson, *A Divider, Not a Uniter;* Schier, *Panorama of a Presidency.*
6. Fleischer, *Taking Heat,* 62.
7. Edwards, *Governing by Campaigning;* see also Edwards, "Riding High in the Polls," 33.
8. George W. Bush, "Address before a Joint Session of the Congress on Administration Goals," February 27, 2001, American Presidency Project, http://www.presidency.ucsb.edu/ws/?pid=29643.
9. Edwards, *Strategic President,* 91.
10. Jacobs, "Promotional Presidency and New Institutional Toryism."
11. The poll question was "Do you favor or oppose the federal income tax cuts President (George W.) Bush has proposed?" The pre-poll percentages were obtained February 25–26 and the post-poll percentages were obtained after the speech. In the pre-poll, the percentage opposing was 24%, and in the post-poll, the percentage opposing was 19%.
12. Neal, "Bush Looks to Rally the Public."
13. Edwards, *Governing by Campaigning.*
14. Ibid., 96.
15. Bennett, Lawrence, and Livingston, *When the Press Fails,* 13.
16. Jones, "U.S. Congress and Chief Executive George W. Bush."
17. Jacobson, *A Divider, Not a Uniter,* 264.
18. Schier, *Panorama of a Presidency.*
19. Edwards, *Governing by Campaigning;* Jacobs, "Promotional Presidency and New Institutional Toryism."
20. Schier, *Panorama of a Presidency.*
21. Ibid., 112.
22. Jacobson, *A Divider, Not a Uniter,* 4.
23. Edwards, *On Deaf Ears;* Cohen, *Presidency in the Era of Twenty-four-hour News.*
24. J. E. Campbell, "Presidential Politics in a Polarized Nation."
25. Eshbaugh-Soha and Peake, "Going Local"; Eshbaugh-Soha, "Local Newspaper Coverage of the Presidency."

26. Blinder, "Going Public, Going to Baghdad."

27. Branigin and Shear, "Senate Passes Economic Stimulus Bill."

28. Kornblut and Shear, "Obama Says He Erred in Nominations."

29. Kumar, *Managing the President's Message.*

30. President Obama also gave an exclusive interview with ABC's *Nightline* that aired the evening of his visit to Fort Myers, Fla.

31. In a three-day rolling Gallup poll conducted February 6–8, 2009, the question was "Do you approve or disapprove of the way Barack Obama is handling his job as president?" Twenty-one percent disapproved.

32. Zeleny, "Already Back on the Trail."

33. The poll was a *USA Today*/Gallup poll taken January 27, February 4, and February 10, 2009. The poll question was "As you may know, Congress is considering a new economic stimulus package of at least 800 billion dollars. Do you favor or oppose Congress passing this legislation?"

Appendix A

1. Hart, *Sound of Leadership;* Cohen, "Presidential Rhetoric and the Public Agenda"; Cohen, *Presidential Responsiveness and Public Policy-making;* Edwards and Wood, "Who Influences Whom?"

2. President Roosevelt was the first to publish the collected public statements of his presidency, but the selection procedures are not uniform and do not match those of the government-printed versions, including the public statements of President Hoover and Presidents Truman to George W. Bush.

3. These documents contain presidential proclamations, messages, executive orders, communications to Congress and federal agencies, retirements, resignations, nominations sent to the Senate, or other acts approved by the president.

4. If it was the case that a bill or policy is mentioned on a page without reference to the exact nature of the bill, an effort was made to seek out the content of the bill by searching through the previous pages.

5. Petty and Cacioppo, *Communication and Persuasion.*

6. Advocacy of a policy came in several different forms, including taking credit for the effects of legislation or a program, signing a bill, promoting a treaty or agreement, requesting action from Congress, identifying "problem" issues, vetoing or directing executive agencies to take action.

7. If two adjectives were used to describe a policy or bill or program, the policy was only coded once. For instance, "This health care bill is the right thing to do and is smart" would only count once.

8. Rhetorical questions, popular with President Clinton, were excluded for this reason.

9. Wood, *Politics of Economic Leadership.*

10. Hill and Hinton-Anderson, "Pathways of Representation."

11. Modest exceptions here are cases where presidents stood for reelection after their first term. If polling questions referenced the election in a general way, the poll could be included, assuming it met the standard criteria. Such poll questions were not used if the question mentioned the president's opponent or his opponent's policies.

12. Jacobs and Shapiro, *Politicians Don't Pander.*

13. When counting the position of the issue (the order in an ascending list), "miscellaneous" issues, "don't know," or other general categories ("health-care issues") were excluded. These tended to be rather small percentages.

Appendix B

1. Gerring, "What Is a Case Study and What Is It Good For?" 341.
2. Ibid., 345.
3. Heith, *Polling to Govern,* 10–11.
4. Benjamin I. Page, "Democratic Responsiveness?"
5. Foyle, *Counting the Public In;* Western, *Selling Intervention and War.*
6. Howell and Pervenier, *From Reliable Sources.*
7. Hill, *Archival Strategies and Techniques.*
8. For instance, at the Bush Library, some files in White House Office of Records Management (WHORM) subject file were processed systematically from 1993 to 1998. These are official government files rather than papers donated to the library. Overall, most of the files are not open. Many documents relating to the elections of 1988 and 1992 are closed due to "personal privacy" issues.
9. King, Keohane, and Verba, *Designing Social Inquiry.*
10. Schutt, *Investigating the Social World.*
11. Yin, *Case Study Research.*

Appendix C

1. Heckman, "Sample Selection Bias as a Specification Error"; Achen, *Statistical Analysis of Quasi-Experiments.*
2. Sartori, "An Estimator for Some Binary-Outcome Selection Models without Exclusion Restrictions."
3. Ibid.
4. The data on political polarization was taken from Poole and Rosenthal's DW-NOMINATE scores, available at http://voteview.com/dwnl.htm. The means of the parties for each Congress was subtracted and the absolute value taken to provide a relative measure of distance between the parties. For further reference see McCarty, Poole, and Rosenthall, *Polarized America.*
5. Campbell and Ross, "Connecticut Crackdown on Speeding."
6. Baum and Kernell, "Has Cable Ended the Golden Age of Presidential Television?"; Edwards, *On Deaf Ears;* Young and Perkins. "Presidential Rhetoric, the Public Agenda, and the End of Presidential Television's 'Golden Age'"; Clayman et al. "Historical Trends in Questioning Presidents."
7. Canes-Wrone, *Who Leads Whom?*
8. Campbell and Ross, "Connecticut Crackdown on Speeding."
9. Cohen, *Presidential Responsiveness and Public Policy-making.*
10. Page, Shapiro, and Dempsey, "What Moves Public Opinion?"

Bibliography

Achen, Christopher H. *The Statistical Analysis of Quasi-Experiments.* Berkeley: University of California Press, 1986.

Althaus, Scott L. *Collective Preferences in Democratic Politics.* Cambridge: Cambridge University Press, 2003.

Alvarez, R. Michael, and John Brehm. *Hard Choices, Easy Answers.* Princeton, N.J.: Princeton University Press, 2002.

Arnold, Peri E. "Bill Clinton and the Institutionalized Presidency: Executive Autonomy and Presidential Leadership." In *The Post-Modern Presidency: Bill Clinton's Legacy in U.S. Politics,* ed. Steven E. Schier, 19–49. Pittsburgh: University of Pittsburgh Press, 2000.

Bailey, Michael, Lee Sigelman, and Clyde Wilcox. "Presidential Persuasion on Social Issues: A Two-Way Street?" *Political Research Quarterly* 56, no. 1 (2003): 49–58.

Baker, William D., and John R. Oneal. "Patriotism or Opinion Leadership?: The Nature of Origins of the 'Rally 'round the Flag' Effect." *Journal of Conflict Resolution* 45, no. 5 (2001): 661–87.

Barabas, Jason. "Presidential Policy Initiatives: How the Public Learns about the State of the Union Proposals from the Mass Media." *Presidential Studies Quarterly* 38, no. 2 (June 2008): 195–222.

Barrett, Andrew W. "Going Public as a Legislative Weapon: Measuring Presidential Appeals Regarding Specific Legislation." *Presidential Studies Quarterly* 35, no. 1 (2005): 1–10.

———. "Gone Public: The Impact of Going Public on Presidential Legislative Success." *American Politics Research* 32, no. 3 (2004): 338–70.

———. "Press Coverage of Legislative Appeals by the President." *Political Research Quarterly* 60, no. 4 (December 2007): 655–68.

Barrett, Andrew W., and Jeffrey S. Peake. "When the President Comes to Town: Examining Local Newspaper Coverage of Domestic Presidential Travel." *American Politics Research* 35, no. 1 (2007): 3–31.

Barrett, David M. *Uncertain Warriors: Lyndon Johnson and His Vietnam Advisors.* Lawrence: University of Kansas Press, 1993.

Baum, Matthew, and Tim Groeling, "What Gets Covered?" In *In the Public Domain,* ed. Lori Cox Han and Diane Heith, 49–72. Albany: State University of New York Press, 2005.

Baum, Matthew A., and Samuel Kernell. "Has Cable Ended the Golden Age of Presidential Television?" *American Political Science Review* 93, no. 1 (1999): 99–114.

Bennett, W. Lance, Regina G. Lawrence, and Steven Livingston. *When the Press Fails: Political Power and the News Media from Iraq to Katrina.* Chicago: University of Chicago Press, 2007.

Berke, Richard L. "Clinton Sounds a Rallying Cry: Security for All." *New York Times,* October 9, 1993, 10.

Berman, Larry. *Looking Back on the Reagan Presidency.* Baltimore: Johns Hopkins University Press, 1990.

———. *Lyndon Johnson's War: The Road to Stalemate in Vietnam.* New York: W.W. Norton, 1991.

———. *No Peace, No Honor: Nixon, Kissinger, and Betrayal in Vietnam.* New York: Free Press, 2002.

———. *Planning a Tragedy: The Americanization of the War in Vietnam.* New York: W. W. Norton, 1983.

Berman, Larry, and Emily O. Goldman. "Clinton's Foreign Policy at Midterm." In *The Clinton Presidency: First Appraisals,* ed. Colin Campbell and Bert A. Rockman, 290–324. Chatham, N.J.: Chatham House, 1996.

Berman, William C. *From the Center to the Edge: The Politics and Policies of the Clinton Presidency.* Lanham, Md.: Rowman and Littlefield, 2001.

Beschloss, Michael R. *Presidential Courage: Brave Leaders and How They Changed America, 1789–1989.* New York: Simon and Schuster, 2007.

Blinder, Scott B. "Going Public, Going to Baghdad: Presidential Agenda-Setting and the Electoral Connection in Congress." In *The Polarized Presidency of George W. Bush,* ed. George C. Edwards and Desmond S. King, 325–50. New York: Oxford University Press, 2007.

Bode, Ken. "Clinton and the Press." In *The Clinton Riddle: Perspectives on the Forty-second President,* ed. Todd G. Shields, Jeannie M. Whayne, and Donald R. Kelley, 23–46. Fayetteville: University of Arkansas Press, 2004.

Bond, Jon R., and Richard Fleisher. "The Limits of Presidential Popularity as a Source of Influence in the U.S. House." *Legislative Studies Quarterly* 5, no. 1 (1980): 69–78.

Bostdorff, Denise M. *The Presidency and the Rhetoric of Foreign Crisis.* Columbia: University of South Carolina, 1994.

Brace, Paul, and Barbara Hinckley. *Follow the Leader: Public Opinion Polls and the Modern Presidents.* New York: Harper Collins, 1992.

———. "Presidential Activities from Truman through Reagan: Timing and Impact." *Journal of Politics* 55, no. 2 (1993): 382–98.

Branigin, William, and Michael D. Shear. "Senate Passes Economic Stimulus Bill." *Washington Post,* February 10, 2009, A1.

Broder, David S. "The Rising Opposition to Reagan . . ." *Washington Post,* September 23, 1981, A27.

Brody, Richard. *Assessing the President: The Media, Elite Opinion, and Public Support.* Palo Alto, Calif.: Stanford University Press, 1991.

———. "Crisis, War, and Public Opinion." In *Taken By Storm: The Media, Public Opinion, and U.S. Foreign Policy in the Gulf War,* ed. W. Lance Bennett and David L. Paletz, 210–27. Chicago: University of Chicago Press, 1994.

Brody, Richard A. "Is the Honeymoon Over? The American People and President Bush." *Polling Report* 17 (2001): 5–7.

Brummer, Alex. "Why the President Still Holds All the Cards." *The Guardian,* January 21, 1985, A1.

Buchanan, Bruce. *The Citizen's Presidency: Standards of Choice and Judgment.* Washington, D.C.: CQ Press, 1987.

Burke, John P., and Fred I. Greenstein. *How Presidents Test Reality: Decisions on Vietnam, 1954 and 1965.* New York: Russell Sage Foundation, 1989.

Burns, James MacGregor. *Presidential Government: The Crucible of Leadership.* Boston: Houghlin Mifflin, 1965.

———. *Running Alone: Presidential Leadership from JFK to Bush II.* New York: Basic Books, 2006.

Callaghan, Karen J., and Simo Virtanen. "Revised Models of the Rally Phenomenon: The Case of the Carter Presidency." *Journal of Politics* 55, no. 3 (1993): 756–64.

Campbell, Colin. "Managing the Presidency or the President? Raising Some Issues Concerning the Bush II Administration's Approach to Executive Leadership." In *The George W. Bush Presidency: Appraisals and Prospects,* ed. Colin Campbell and Bert A. Rockman, 1–15. Washington, D.C.: CQ Press.

Campbell, Donald T., and H. Lawrence Ross. "The Connecticut Crackdown on Speeding: Time-Series Data in Quasi-Experimental Analysis." *Law and Society Review* 3, no. 1 (1968): 33–54.

Campbell, Donald T., and Julian C. Stanley. *Experimental and Quasi-Experimental Designs for Research.* Chicago: Rand McNally, 1963.

Campbell, James E. "Presidential Politics in a Polarized Nation: The Reelection of George W. Bush." In *The George W. Bush Legacy,* ed. Colin Campbell, Bert A. Rockman, and Andrew Rudalevige, 21–44. Washington, D.C.: CQ Press, 2008.

Canes-Wrone, Brandice. "The President's Legislative Influence from Public Appeals." *American Journal of Political Science* 45, no. 2 (2001): 313–29.

———. "The Public Presidency, Personal Approval Ratings, and Policy Making." Presidential Studies Quarterly 34, no. 3 (2004): 477–92.

———. *Who Leads Whom? Presidents, Policy, and the Public.* Chicago: University of Chicago Press, 2006.

Canes-Wrone, Brandice, M. C. Herron, and Kenneth W. Shotts. "Leadership and Pandering: A Theory of Executive Policymaking." *American Journal of Political Science* 45, no. 3 (2001): 690–706.

Canes-Wrone, Brandice, and Kenneth W. Shotts. "The Conditional Nature of Presidential Responsiveness to Public Opinion." *American Journal of Political Science* 48, no. 4 (2004): 690–706.

Cannon, Lou. "Buchanan Urges Speech on Nicaragua." *Washington Post,* April 18, 1985, A1.

———. *President Reagan: The Role of a Lifetime.* New York: Public Affairs, 2000.

Cannon, Lou, and John M. Goshko. "Fight Over Further Aid to 'Contras' Intensifies." *Washington Post,* February 28, 1985, A28.

Carter, Jimmy. *Keeping Faith: Memoirs of a President.* New York: Bantam Books, 1982.

Casey, Steven. *Cautious Crusade: Franklin D. Roosevelt, American Public Opinion, and the War against Nazi Germany.* New York: Oxford University Press, 2001.

Cattani, Richard J. "Public Outcry: 'Don't Touch Our Social Security.'" *Christian Science Monitor,* May 18, 1981, 1.

———. "Reagan Honeymoon Wanes as Congress Stirs on Key Issues." *Christian Science Monitor,* May 27, 1981, 1.

Ceaser, James W. "Demagoguery, Statesmanship, and the American Presidency." *Critical Review* 19, nos. 2–3 (2004): 257–98.

Charnock, Emily Jane, James A. McCann, and Kathryn Dunn Tenpas. "Goin' Mobile: Assessing First-term Presidential Travel from Eisenhower to George W. Bush." Presented at the American Political Science Association annual meetings, Philadelphia, 2006.

Chong, Dennis, and James N. Druckman. "Framing Public Opinion in Competitive Democracies." *American Political Science Review* 101, no. 4 (2007): 637–55.

Clayman, Steven E., and John Heritage. "Questioning Presidents: Journalistic Deference and Adversarialness in the Press Conferences of U.S. Presidents Eisenhower and Reagan." *Journal of Communication* 52, no. 4 (2002): 749–76.

Clayman, Steven E., Marc N. Elliott, John Heritage, and Laurie L. McDonald. "Historical Trends in Questioning Presidents, 1953–2000." *Presidential Studies Quarterly* 36, no. 4 (2006): 561–83.

Clinton, Bill. *My Life.* New York: Alfred A. Knopf, 2004.

Clodfelter, Mark. *The Limits of Air Power: The American Bombing of North Vietnam.* New York: Free Press, 1989.

Cohen, Jeffrey E. *The Presidency in the Era of Twenty-four-Hour News.* Princeton, N.J.: Princeton University Press, 2008.

———. "Presidential Going Public in an Age of New Media." Paper presented at the American Political Science Association Meetings, Washington, D.C., September 1–4, 2005.

———. "Presidential Leadership in an Age of New Media." In *Presidential Leadership: The Vortex of Power,* ed. Bert A. Rockman and Richard W. Waterman, 171–90. New York: Oxford University Press, 2008.

———. *Presidential Responsiveness and Public Policy-Making: The Public and the Policies that Presidents Choose.* Ann Arbor: University of Michigan Press, 1997.

———. "Presidential Rhetoric and the Public Agenda." *American Journal of Political Science* 39, no. 1 (1995): 87–107.

Cohen, Jeffrey E., and John A. Hamman. "The Polls: Can Presidential Rhetoric Affect the Public's Economic Perceptions?" *Presidential Studies Quarterly* 33, no. 2 (2003): 408–22.

Cohen, Jeffrey E., and Richard J. Powell. "Building Public Support from the Grassroots Up: The Impact of Presidential Travel on State-Level Approval." *Presidential Studies Quarterly* 35, no. 1 (2005): 11–27.

Converse, Philip E. "Information Flow and the Stability of Partisan Attitudes." *Public Opinion Quarterly* 26, no. 4 (1961): 578–99.

Coombs, Clyde H., and Lolagene C. Coombs. "'Don't Know': Item Ambiguity or Respondent Uncertainty?" *Public Opinion Quarterly* 40, no. 4 (1976): 497–514.

Cornwell, Elmer E. Jr. *Presidential Leadership of Public Opinion.* Bloomington: Indiana University Press, 1965.

Cox Han, Lori. Governing from Center Stage: White House Communication Strategies during the Television Age of Politics. Kresskill, N.J.: Hampton Press, 2001.

———. "The Rose Garden Strategy Revisited." In *In the Public Domain: Presidents and* the Challenges of Presidential Leadership, ed. Lori Cox Han and Diane J. Heith, 163–78. Albany: State University of New York Press, 2005.

Crain, Rance. "How Gerald Ford's WIN Effort Became a Loser for the Ad Council." *Advertising Age* 78, no. 2 (2007): 14.

Crockett, David A. *The Opposition Presidency: Leadership and the Constraints of History.* College Station: Texas A&M University Press, 2002.

Cunion, William."Second-term Presidents: Free Birds or Lame Ducks?" In *In the Public Domain: Presidents and the Challenges of Public Leadership,* ed. Lori Cox Han and Diane J. Heith, 113–38. Albany: State University of New York Press, 2005.

Dallek, Robert. *Flawed Giant: Lyndon Johnson and His Times.* New York: Oxford University Press, 1998.

———. *Ronald Reagan: The Politics of Symbolism.* Cambridge, Mass.: Harvard University Press, 1984.

———. *An Unfinished Life: John F. Kennedy, 1917–1963.* Boston: Little, Brown, 2003.

Dewar, Helen. "Lugar Says Congress Is Likely to Deny Further 'Contra' Aid." *Washington Post,* January 24, 1985, A1.

———. "Senate Unanimously Rebuffs President on Social Security." *Washington Post,* May 21, 1981, A1.

Dilulio, John J. Jr. "The Hyper-Rhetorical Presidency." *Critical Review* 19, nos. 2–3 (2007): 315–24.

Doherty, Brendan J. "Elections: The Politics of Permanent Campaign: Presidential Travel and the Electoral College, 1977–2004." *Presidential Studies Quarterly* 37, no. 4 (2007): 749–73.

Dowd, Maureen. "Leaders as Followers." *New York Times,* January 12, 1997, A17.

Dreazen, Yochi J. "Bush 9/11 Tour Aims to Bolster Republicans." *Wall Street Journal,* September 9–10, 2006, A4.

Drew, Elizabeth. *On the Edge: The Clinton Presidency.* New York: Simon and Schuster, 1994.

———. *Showdown: The Struggle between the Gingrich Congress and the Clinton White House.* New York: Simon and Schuster, 1996.

Druckman, James N., and Justin W. Holmes. "Does Presidential Rhetoric Matter? Priming and Presidential Approval." *Presidential Studies Quarterly* 34, no. 4 (2004): 755–78.

Edsall, Thomas Byrne. "The Reagan Legacy." In *The Reagan Legacy,* ed. Sidney Blumenthal and Thomas Byrne Edsall, 190–218. New York: Pantheon Books, 1988.

Edel, William. *The Reagan Presidency: An Actor's Finest Performance.* New York: Hippocrene Books, 1992.

Edwards, George C. III. "Changing Their Minds? George W. Bush and Presidential Persuasion." *Extensions,* Spring 2006, 7–13.

———. "Does the Messenger Matter? The Role of Charisma in Public Leadership." *Congress and the Presidency* 29, no. 1 (2002): 25–47.

———. *Governing by Campaigning: The Politics of the Bush Presidency.* New York: Pearson Longman, 2007.

———. *On Deaf Ears: The Limits of the Bully Pulpit.* New Haven, Conn.: Yale University Press, 2003.

———. "Presidential Rhetoric: What Difference Does It Make?" In *Beyond the Rhetorical Presidency,* ed. Martin J. Medhurst, 199–217. College Station: Texas A&M University Press, 1996.

———. *The Public Presidency: The Pursuit of Popular Support.* New York: St. Martin's Press, 1983.

———. "Riding High in the Polls: George W. Bush and Public Opinion." In *The George W. Bush Presidency: Appraisals and Prospects,* ed. Colin Campbell and Bert A. Rockman, 16–45. Washington, D.C.: CQ Press, 2004.

———. *The Strategic President: Persuasion and Opportunity in Presidential Leadership.* Princeton, N.J.: Princeton University Press, 2009.

Edwards, George C. III, and Tami Swenson. "Who Rallies? The Anatomy of a Rally Event." *Journal of Politics* 59, no. 1 (1997): 200–212.

Edwards, George C. III, and B. Dan Wood. "Who Influences Whom? The President, Congress, and the Media." *American Political Science Review* 93, no. 2 (1999): 327–44.

Edwards, Jason A., and Joseph M. Valenzano III. "Bill Clinton's 'New Partnership' Anecdote: Toward a Post–Cold War Foreign Policy Rhetoric." *Journal of Language and Politics* 6, no. 3 (2007): 303–25.

Eisinger, Robert M. *The Evolution of Presidential Polling.* Cambridge: Cambridge University Press, 2003.

Elsea, Jennifer K., and Richard Grimmett. *Declarations of War and Authorizations for the Use of Military Force: Historical Background and Legal Implications.* Washington, D.C.: Congressional Research Service, Library of Congress, 2007.

Entman, Robert M., and Benjamin I. Page. "The News before the Storm: The Iraq War Debate and the Limits to Media Independence." In *Taken By Storm,* ed. W. Lance Bennett and David L. Paletz, 82–101. Chicago: University of Chicago Press, 1994.

Erickson, Paul D. *Reagan Speaks: The Making of an American Myth.* New York: New York University Press, 1985.

Eshbaugh-Soha, Matthew. "Local Newspaper Coverage of the Presidency." *International Journal of Press/Politics* 13, no. 2 (2008): 103–19.

——— "The Political Agendas." *Political Research Quarterly* 58 (June 2005): 257–68.

———. "Presidential Press Conferences Over Time." *American Journal of Political Science* 47, no. 2 (2003): 348–53.

———. *The President's Speeches: Beyond "Going Public."* Boulder, Colo.: Lynne Rienner Publishers, 2006.

Eshbaugh-Soha, Matthew, and Jeffrey S. Peake. "Presidents and the Economic Agenda." *Political Research Quarterly* 58, no. 1 (2005): 127–38.

———. "'Going Local' to Reform Social Security." *Presidential Studies Quarterly* 36, no. 4 (2006): 689–704.

Farnsworth, Stephen J., and Robert Lichter. *The Mediated Presidency: Television News and Presidential Governance.* Lanham, Md.: Rowman and Littlefield, 2006.

Finbow, Robert. "Presidential Leadership or Structural Constraints? The Failure of President Carter's Health Insurance Proposals." *Presidential Studies Quarterly* 28, no. 1 (1998): 169.

Fine, Jeffrey A., and Richard W. Waterman. "A New Model of Presidential Leadership:

Controlling the Bureaucracy." In *Presidential Leadership: The Vortex of Power,* ed. Bert A. Rockman and Richard W. Waterman, 19–44. New York: Oxford University Press, 2008.

Fleischer, Ari. *Taking Heat: The President, the Press, and My Years in the White House.* New York: William Morrow, 2005.

Foley, Michael. "Presidential Leadership and the Presidency." In *The Reagan Years: The Record in Presidential Leadership,* ed. Joseph Hogan, 23–53. Manchester: Manchester University Press, 1990.

Ford, Gerald A. *A Time to Heal.* New York: Harper and Row, 1979.

Fordham, Benjamin. "The Politics of Threat Perception of the Use of Force: A Political Economy Model of U.S. Uses of Force, 1949–1994." *International Studies Quarterly* 43, no. 3 (1998): 68–90.

Foyle, Douglas C. *Counting the Public In: Presidents, Public Opinion, and Foreign Policy.* New York: Columbia University Press, 1999.

———. "The Evolution of Presidential Polling." *Presidential Studies Quarterly* 34, no. 1 (2004): 170–71.

Frisby, Michael K. "Clinton Seeks Strategic Edge with Opinion Polls." *Wall Street Journal,* June 24, 1996, A16.

Gardner, Lloyd C. *Pay Any Price: Lyndon Johnson and the Wars for Vietnam.* Chicago: Ivan R. Dee, 1995.

Geer, John G. *From Tea Leaves to Opinion Polls: A Theory of Democratic Leadership.* New York: Columbia University Press,1996.

Geer, John, and Prateek Goorha. "Declining Uncertainty: Presidents, Polls and Public Opinion." In *Uncertainty in American Politics,* ed. Barry C. Burden, 139–60. Cambridge: Cambridge University Press, 2003.

Genovese, Michael A. "Celebrity in Chief: The President as a Pop Culture Icon." In *In the Public Domain: Presidents and the Challenges of Presidential Leadership,* ed. Lori Cox Han and Diane J. Heith, 13–28. Albany: State University of New York Press, 2005.

———. *Memo to a New President: The Art and Science of Presidential Leadership.* New York: Oxford University Press, 2008.

———. *The Nixon Presidency: Power and Politics in Turbulent Times.* New York: Greenwood Press,1990.

Gergen, David. *Eyewitness to Power: The Essence of Leadership, Nixon to Clinton.* New York: Touchstone, 2000.

Gerring, John. "What Is a Case Study and What Is It Good For?" *American Political Science Review* 98, no. 2 (2004): 341–54.

Giglio, James N. *The Presidency of John F. Kennedy.* Lawrence: University of Kansas Press, 1991.

Gleiber, Dennis W. and Steven A. Shull, "Presidential Influence in the Policymaking Process," *Western Political Quarterly* 45, no. 2 (1992): 441–467.

Goodman, Walter. "The Effect of Images on Government Policy." *New York Times,* October 7, 1993, 28.

Goshko, John M., and Margaret Shapiro. "Speaker O'Neill Assails President for Wanting Nicaragua to Cry 'Uncle.'" *Washington Post,* February 27, 1985, A16.

Greene, John Robert. *The Limits of Power: The Nixon and Ford Administrations.* Bloomington: Indiana University Press, 1992.

———. *The Presidency of George Bush.* Lawrence: University of Kansas Press, 2001.

———. *The Presidency of Gerald Ford.* Lawrence: University of Kansas Press, 1995.

Greenstein, Fred I. *The Presidential Difference: Leadership Style from FDR to George W. Bush.* Princeton, N.J.: Princeton University Press, 2004.

Grossman, Michael Baruch, and Martha Joynt Kumar. *Portraying the President: The White House and the News Media.* Baltimore: Johns Hopkins University Press, 1981.

Gutman, Roy. *Banana Diplomacy: The Making of American Policy in Nicaragua, 1981–1987.* New York: Simon and Schuster, 1988.

Haas, Garland A. *Jimmy Carter and the Politics of Frustration.* Jefferson, N.C.: McFarland, 1992.

Haldeman, H. R. *The Haldeman Diaries: Inside the Nixon White House.* New York: G. P. Putnam's Sons, 1994.

Hamilton, Alexander, James Madison, and John Jay. *The Federalist Papers,* ed. Benjamin Fletcher Wright. Cambridge, Mass.: Harvard University Press, 1787–1788 [1996.]

Hargrove, Erwin C. *The President as Leader: Appealing to the Better Angels of Our Nature.* Lawrence: University of Kansas Press, 1998.

———. *Jimmy Carter as President: Leadership and the Politics of the Public Good.* Baton Rouge: Louisiana State University Press, 1988.

Hart, Roderick. *The Sound of Leadership.* Chicago: University of Chicago Press, 1987.

Heckman, James J. "Sample Selection Bias as a Specification Error." *Econometrica* 41, no. 1 (1979): 153–61.

Heith, Diane J. "One for All: Using Focus Groups and Opinion Polls in the George H. W. Bush White." *Congress and the Presidency* 30, no. 1 (2003): 81–94.

———. *Polling to Govern: Public Opinion and Presidential Leadership.* Palo Alto, Calif.: Stanford University Press, 2004.

Henriksen, Thomas H. *Clinton's Foreign Policy in Somalia, Bosnia, Haiti, and North Korea.* Palo Alto, Calif.: Hoover Institution, 1996.

Herbst, Susan. "The Rhetorical Presidency and the Contemporary Media Environment" *Critical Review* 19, nos. 2–3 (2007): 335–43.

Herring, George C. "The War in Vietnam." In *Exploring the Johnson Years,* ed. Robert A. Divine, 81–94. Austin: University of Texas Press, 1996.

Hess, Gary R. *Presidential Decisions for War: Korea, Vietnam, and the Persian Gulf.* Baltimore: Johns Hopkins University Press, 2001.

Hetherington, Marc J. "The Political Relevance of Political Trust." *American Political Science Review* 92, no. 4 (December 1998): 791–808.

Hetherington, Marc J., and Michael Nelson. "Anatomy of a Rally Effect: George W. Bush and the War on Terrorism." *PS: Political Science and Politics* 36, no. 1 (2003): 37–42.

Hill, Kim Quaile. "The Policy Agendas of the President and the Mass Public: A Research Validation and Extension." *American Journal of Political Science* 42, no. 4 (1998): 1328–34.

Hill, Kim Quaile, and Angela Hinton-Anderson. "Pathways of Representation: A Causal Analysis of Public Opinion-Policy Linkages." *American Journal of Political Science* 39, no. 4 (November 1995): 924–35.

Hill, Michael R. *Archival Strategies and Techniques.* Qualitative Research Methods Series, no. 31. Newbury Park: Sage Publications, 1993.

Hoffman, David. "President Keeps Pushing 'Contra' Aid." *Washington Post,* April 7, 1985, A16.

———. "Reagan to Push 'Contra' Funds Next Month." *Washington Post,* March 9, 1985, A20.

Hogan, J. Michael. "Public Opinion and American Foreign Policy: The Case of Illusory Support for the Panama Canal Treaties." *Quarterly Journal of Speech* 71, no. 3 (1985): 302–18.

———. *Woodrow Wilson's Western Tour: Rhetoric, Public Opinion, and the League of Nations.* College Station: Texas A&M University Press, 2006.

Hogan, J. Michael, George C. Edwards III, Wynton C. Hall, Christin L. Harold, Gerard A. Hazuser, Susan Herbst, Robert Y. Shapiro, and Ted J. Smith III. "Report of the National Task Force on the Presidency and Public Opinion." In *The Prospect of Presidential Rhetoric,* ed. James Arnt Aune and Martin J. Medhurst, 293–316. College Station: Texas A&M University Press, 2008.

Hogan, Joseph. "The Federal Budget in the Reagan Era." In *The Reagan Years: The Record in Presidential Leadership,* ed. Joseph Hogan, 214–36. Manchester: Manchester University Press, 1990.

Holbrook, Thomas M. "Did the Whistle-Stop Campaign Matter?" *PS: Political Science and Politics* 35, no. 1 (2002): 59–66.

Howell, Martha, and Walter Pervenier. *From Reliable Sources: An Introduction to Historical Methods.* Ithaca: Cornell University Press, 2001.

Hyland, William G. *Clinton's World: Remaking American Foreign Policy.* Westport, Conn.: Praeger, 1999.

Ingwerson, Marshall. "Clinton's First 100 Days: It's Been Bumpy Ride." *Christian Science Monitor,* April 22, 1993, 1.

Ivins, Molly. *You Got to Dance with Them What Brung You.* New York: Vintage Books, 1999.

Iyengar, Shanto, and Adam Simon. "News Coverage of the Gulf Crisis and Public Opinion." In *Taken by Storm: The Media, Public Opinion, and U.S. Foreign Policy in the Gulf War,* ed. W. Lance Bennett and David L. Paletz, 167–85. Chicago: University of Chicago Press, 1994.

Jacobs, Lawrence R. *The Health of Nations.* Ithaca, N.Y.: Cornell University Press, 1992.

———. "The Promotional Presidency and the New Institutional Toryism: Public Mobilization, Legislative Dominance, and Squandered Opportunities." In *The Polarized Presidency of George W. Bush,* ed. George C. Edwards and Desmond S. King, 285–324. New York: Oxford University Press, 2007.

Jacobs, Lawrence R., and Melanie Burns. "The Second Face of the Public Presidency: Presidential Polling and the Shift from Policy to Personality Polling." Presidential Studies Quarterly 34, no. 3 (2004): 536–56.

Jacobs, Lawrence R., and Robert Y. Shapiro. *Politicians Don't Pander: Political Manipulation and the Loss of Democratic Responsiveness.* Chicago: University of Chicago Press, 2000.

———. "The Rise of Presidential Polling: The Nixon White House in Historical Perspective." *Public Opinion Quarterly* 59, no.1 (1995): 163–95.

Jacobson, Gary C. *A Divider, Not a Uniter: George W. Bush and the American People.* New York: Longman, 2006.

James, Patrick, and Jean-Sebastian Rioux. "International Crises and Linkage Politics: The Experiences of the United States, 1953–1994." *Political Research Quarterly* 51, no. 3 (1998): 781–812.

Jamieson, Kathleen Hall. *Eloquence in an Electronic Age: The Transformation of Political Speechmaking.* New York: Oxford University Press, 1988.

Jentleson, Bruce W. "The Pretty Prudent Public: Post Post-Vietnam American Opinion on the Use of Military Force." *International Studies Quarterly* 36, no. 1 (1992): 49–73.

Jentleson, Bruce W., and Rebecca L. Britton. "Still Pretty Prudent: Post–Cold War American Public Opinion on the Use of Military Force." *Journal of Conflict Resolution* 42, no. 4 (1998): 395–417.

Jones, Charles O. "Campaigning to Govern: The Clinton Style." In *The Clinton Presidency: First Appraisals,* ed. Colin Campbell and Bert A. Rockman, 15–50. Chatham, N.J.: Chatham House, 1996.

———. *Clinton and Congress, 1993–1996: Risk, Restoration, and Reelection.* Norman: University of Oklahoma Press, 1999.

———. *The Trusteeship Presidency: Jimmy Carter and the United States Congress.* Baton Rouge: Louisiana State University Press, 1988.

———. "The U.S. Congress and Chief Executive George W. Bush." In *The Polarized Presidency of George W. Bush,* ed. George C. Edwards and Desmond S. King, 387–418. Oxford: Oxford University Press, 2007.

Jordan, Donald L., and Benjamin I. Page. "Shaping Foreign Policy Opinion: The Role of TV News." *Journal of Conflict Resolution* 36, no. 2 (1992): 227–41.

Kagan, Robert. *A Twilight Struggle: American Power and Nicaragua, 1977–1990.* New York: Free Press, 1996.

Kaid, Lynda Lee, John C. Tedesco, and Julia A. Spiker. "Media Conflicts Over Clinton Policies: Political Advertising and the Battle for Public Opinion." In *The Clinton Presidency: Images, Issues, and Communication Strategies,* ed. Robert E. Denton Jr. and Rachel L. Holloway, 103–22. Westport, Conn.: Praeger, 1996.

Karnow, Stanley. *Vietnam: A History.* New York: Penguin Books, 1997.

Kaufman, Burton I. *The Presidency of James Earl Carter Jr.* Lawrence: University Press of Kansas, 1993.

Kellerman, Barbara. *The Political Presidency: Practice of Presidential Leadership from Kennedy Through Reagan.* Oxford: Oxford University Press, 1984.

Kernell, Samuel. *Going Public: New Strategies of Presidential Leadership.* Washington, D.C.: CQ Press, 2007.

Kessel, John H. *Presidents, the Presidency, and the Political Environment.* Washington, D.C.: CQ Press, 2001.

Key, V. O. Jr. *Public Opinion and American Democracy.* New York: Alfred A. Knopf, 1961.

Kimball, Jeffrey. *Nixon's Vietnam War.* Lawrence: University of Kansas Press, 1998.

———. *The Vietnam War Files: Uncovering the Secret History of Nixon-Era Strategy.* Lawrence: University Press of Kansas, 2004.

King, Gary, Robert O. Keohane, and Sidney Verba. *Designing Social Inquiry.* Princeton, N.J.: Princeton University Press, 1994.

Kingdon, John W. *Agendas, Alternatives, and Public Policies.* Boston: Little, Brown, 1984.

Klarevas, L. "The Polls-Trends: The United States Peace Operation in Somalia." *Public Opinion Quarterly* 64, no. 4 (2000): 523–40.

Klein, Joe. *The Natural: The Misunderstood Presidency of Bill Clinton.* New York: Doubleday, 2002.

Koch, Jeffrey W. "Political Rhetoric and Political Persuasion: The Changing Structure of Citizens' Preferences on Health Insurance During Policy Debate." *Public Opinion Quarterly* 62, no. 2 (1998): 209–29.

Kornblut, Anne E., and Michael D. Shear. "Obama Says He Erred in Nominations." *Washington Post,* February 4, 2009, A1.

Kneeland, Douglas E. "Reagan Vows to Support Social Security Program." *New York Times,* September 8, 1980, 10.

Kumar, Martha Joynt. *Managing the President's Message: The White House Communications Operation.* Baltimore: Johns Hopkins University Press, 2007.

———. "The Office of the Press Secretary." Presidential Studies Quarterly 31, no. 2 (2001): 296–322.

———. "Presidential Press Conferences: The Importance and Evolution of an Enduring Forum." *Presidential Studies Quarterly* 35, no. 1 (2005): 166–92.

———. "Source Material: 'Does This Constitute a Press Conference?' Defining and Tabulating Modern Presidential Press Conferences." *Presidential Studies Quarterly* 33, no. 1 (2003): 221–37.

Lammers, William W. "Presidential Attention-Focusing Activities." In *The President and the American Public,* ed. Doris A. Graber, 145–71. Philadelphia: Institute for the Study of Human Issues, 1982.

———. "Presidential Press Conference Schedules: Who Hides, and When?" *Political Science Quarterly* 96, no. 2 (1981): 261–78.

Lammers, William W., and Michael A. Genovese. *The Presidency and Domestic Policy: Comparing Leadership Styles, FDR to Clinton.* Washington, D.C.: CQ Press, 2000.

Laracey, Mel. *Presidents and the People: The Partisan Story of Going Public.* College Station: Texas A&M University Press, 2002.

Lee, Francis E. "Dividers, Not Uniters: Presidential Leadership and Senate Partisanship, 1981–2004." *Journal of Politics* 70, no. 4 (October 2008): 914–28.

Levine, Lawrence W., and Cornelia R. Levine. *The People and the President: America's Conversation with FDR.* Boston: Beacon Press, 2002.

Lian, Brad, and John R. Oneal. "Presidents, the Use of Military Force, and Public Opinion." *Journal of Conflict Resolution* 37, no. 2 (1993): 227–300.

Light, Paul C. *The President's Agenda: Domestic Policy Choice from Kennedy to Clinton.* Baltimore: Johns Hopkins University Press, 1999.

Long, J. Scott, and Jeremy Freese. *Regression Models for Categorical Dependent Variables using Stata,* 2nd ed. College Station, Tex.: Stata Press, 2006.

Lowi, Theodore J. *The Personal President: Power Invested, Promise Unfulfilled.* Ithaca, N.Y.: Cornell University Press, 1985.

Maltese, John Anthony. *Spin Control: The White House Office of Communications and the Management of Presidential News.* Chapel Hill: University of North Carolina Press, 1994.

Marra, Robin F., Charles W. Ostrom Jr., and Dennis M. Simon. "Foreign Policy and Presidential Popularity: Creating Windows of Opportunity in the Perpetual Election." *Journal of Conflict Resolution* 34, no. 4 (1990): 588–623.

Mayer, Jeremy D., and Mark J. Rozell. "A Presidency Transformed." In *In the Public Domain: Presidents and the Challenges of Presidential Leadership,* ed. Lori Cox Han and Diane J. Heith, 227–54. Albany: State University of New York Press, 2005.

McCarty, Nolan, Keith T. Poole, and Howard Rosenthall. 2006. *Polarized America: The Dance of Ideology and Unequal Riches.* Cambridge, Mass.: MIT Press, 2006.

McGraw, Kathleen, Samuel Best, and Richard Timpone. "What They Say or What They Do? The Impact of Elite Explanation and Policy Outcomes on Public Opinion." *American Journal of Political Science* 39, no. 1 (February 1995): 53–74.

Medhurst, Martin J. "Eisenhower's Rhetorical Leadership: An Interpretation." In *Eisenhower's War of Words: Rhetoric and Leadership,* ed. Martin J. Medhurst, 285–302. East Lansing: Michigan State University Press, 1994.

Meernik, James, and Michael Ault. "Public Opinion and Support for U.S. President's Foreign Policies." *American Political Research* 29, no. 4 (2001): 352–73.

Mellow, Nicole. *The State of Disunion: Regional Sources of Modern American Partisanship.* Baltimore: Johns Hopkins University Press, 2008.

Miroff, Bruce. *Pragmatic Illusions: The Presidential Politics of John F. Kennedy.* New York: McKay, 1976.

Moffett, George D. III. "Reagan Raises Level of Rhetoric, Pressing for Aid to Contras." *Christian Science Monitor,* February 25, 1985, 1.

Morin, Richard, and Jim VandeHei. "Social Security Plan's Support Dwindling." *Washington Post,* June 9, 2005, A4.

Morris, Dick. *Behind the Oval Office: Getting Reelected Against All Odds.* Los Angeles: Renaissance Books, 1999.

Mueller, John. *Policy and Opinion in the Gulf War.* Chicago: University of Chicago, 1994.

———. *War, Presidents, and Public Opinion.* New York: John Wiley and Sons, 1973.

Murray, Shoon Kathleen, and Peter Howard. "Variation in White House Polling Operations: Carter to Clinton." *Public Opinion Quarterly* 66, no. 4 (2002): 527–58.

Neal, Terry M. "Bush Looks to Rally the Public." *Washington Post,* January 23, 2003. A1.

Neustadt, Richard. *Presidential Power and the Modern Presidents: The Politics of Leadership from Roosevelt to Reagan.* New York: Free Press, 1990.

———. "The Weakening White House." *British Journal of Political Science* 31, no. 1 (2001): 1–11.

———. "What Moves Public Opinion?" *American Political Science Review* 81, no. 1 (1987): 23–44.

Niskanen, William A. *Reaganomics: An Insider's Account of the Policies and the People.* New York: Oxford University Press, 1988.

Nixon, Richard. *The Memoirs of Richard Nixon.* New York: Simon and Schuster, 1990.

Norrander, Barbara, and Clyde Wilcox. "Rallying around the Flag and Partisan Change: The Case of the Persian Gulf War." *Political Research Quarterly* 46, no. 4 (1993): 759–70.

Oneal, John R., and Anna Lillian Bryan. "The Rally 'round the Flag Effect in U.S. Foreign Policy Crises, 1950–1985." *Political Behavior* 17, no. 4 (1995): 379–401.

Ostrom, Charles W. Jr., and Dennis M. Simon. "The Man in the Teflon Suit? The Environmental Political Drama and Popular Support in the Reagan Presidency." *Public Opinion Quarterly* 53 (Spring 1989): 58–82.

Page, Benjamin I. "Democratic Responsiveness? Untangling the Links between Public Opinion and Policy." *PS: Political Science and Politics* 27, no. 1 (1994): 25–29.

Page, Benjamin I., and Robert Y. Shapiro. "Effects of Public Opinion on Policy." *American Political Science Review* 77, no. 1 (1983): 175–90.

———. "Presidents as Opinion Leaders: Some New Evidence." *Policy Studies Journal* 12, no. 4 (1984): 649–61.

———. *The Rational Public: Fifty Years of Trends of Americans' Policy Preferences.* Chicago: University of Chicago Press, 1992.

Page, Benjamin I., Robert Y. Shapiro, and Glenn R. Dempsey. "What Moves Public Opinion?" *American Political Science Review* 81, no. 1 (1987): 23–44.

Palmer, Bruce Jr. *The Twenty-five-Year War: America's Military Role in Vietnam.* Lexington: University of Kentucky Press, 1984.

Parker, Suzanne L. "Toward an Understanding of 'Rally' Effects: Public Opinion in the Persian Gulf War." *Public Opinion Quarterly* 59, no. 4 (1995): 526–46.

Parry-Giles, Shawn J. *The Rhetorical Presidency, Propaganda, and the Cold War, 1945–1955.* Westport, Conn.: Praeger, 2001.

Pastor, Robert A. *Condemned to Repetition: The United States and Nicaragua.* Princeton, N.J.: Princeton University Press, 1987.

———. "The Reagan Administration and Latin America: Eagle Insurgent." In *Eagle Resurgent? The Reagan Era in American Foreign Policy,* ed. Kenneth A. Oye, Robert J. Leiber, and Donald Rothchild, 13–25. Boston: Little, Brown, 1987.

Peake, Jeffrey S. "Presidential Agenda Setting in Foreign Policy." *Political Research Quarterly* 54, no. 1 (2001): 69–86.

Peake, Jeffrey S., and Matthew Eshbaugh-Soha. "The Agenda-Setting Impact of Major Presidential TV Addresses." *Political Communication* 25, no. 2 (2008): 113–37.

Peterson, Mark A. *Legislating Together: The White House and Capitol Hill from Eisenhower to Reagan.* Cambridge, Mass.: Harvard University Press, 1990.

Peterson, Paul E., and Mark Rom. "Lower Taxes, More Spending, and Budget Deficits." In *The Reagan Legacy: Promise and Performance,* ed. Charles O. Jones, 91–106. Chatham, N.J.: Chatham House, 1988.

Petty, Richard E., and John T. Cacioppo. *Communication and Persuasion: Central and Peripheral Routes to Attitude Change.* New York: Springer, 1986.

Pious, Richard M. *The American Presidency.* New York: Basic Books, 1979.

Porter, Roger B. *Presidential Decision Making: The Economic Policy Board.* Cambridge: Cambridge University Press, 1980.

Powlick, Phillip J., and Andrew Z. Katz. "Defining the American Public Opinion/Foreign Policy Nexus." *International Studies Quarterly* 42, no. 1 (1998): 29–62.

Ragsdale, Lyn. *Vital Statistics on the Presidency: Washington to Clinton.* Washington, D.C.: Congressional Quarterly Press, 1996.

Raines, Howell. "White House Learning the Limits to President's Mandate." *New York Times,* May 25, 1981, 9.

Reagan, Ronald. *An American Life.* New York: Simon and Schuster, 1990.

———. *The Reagan Diaries,* ed. Douglas Brinkley. New York: Harper Collins, 2007.

Reeves, Richard. *President Kennedy: Profile of Power.* New York: Simon and Schuster, 1993.

———. *President Nixon: Alone in the White House.* New York: Simon and Schuster, 2001.

Rockman, Bert A. "The Legacy of the George W. Bush Presidency—A Revolutionary Presidency?" In *The George W. Bush Legacy,* ed. Colin Campbell, Bert A. Rockman, and Andrew Rudalevige, 325–48. Washington, D.C.: CQ Press, 2008.

———. "When It Comes to Presidential Leadership, Accentuate the Positive but Don't Forget the Normative." In *Presidential Leadership: The Vortex of Power,* ed. Bert A. Rockman and Richard W. Waterman, 311–30. New York: Oxford University Press, 2008.

Roper, Jon. "The Contemporary Presidency: George W. Bush and the Myth of Heroic Presidential Leadership." Presidential Studies Quarterly 34, no. 1 (2004): 132–42.

Rosen, Corey M. "A Test of Presidential Leadership of Public Opinion: The Split-Ballot Technique." *Polity* 6, no. 2 (1973): 282–90.

Rosenblatt, Alan J. "Aggressive Foreign Policy Marketing: Public Response to Reagan's 1983 Address on Lebanon and Grenada." *Public Behavior* 20, no. 3 (1998): 225–40.

Rottinghaus, Brandon. "Following the Mail Hawks: Alternative Measures of Public Opinion on Vietnam in the Johnson White House." *Public Opinion Quarterly* 71, no. 3: 720–32.

———. "Foreign Policy and the Limits of Crafted Talk." *Political Communication,* 25, no. 2: 138–57.

———. "Reassessing Public Opinion Polling in the Truman Administration." *Presidential Studies Quarterly* 33, no. 2 (2003): 325–32.

———. "Rethinking Presidential Responsiveness: The Public Presidency and Rhetorical Congruency, 1953–2001." *Journal of Politics* 68, no. 3 (2006): 720–32.

Russett, Bruce. *Controlling the Sword: The Democratic Governance of National Security.* Cambridge, Mass.: Harvard University Press, 1990.

Saikowski, Charlotte. "Reagan Moves to Recapture Political Momentum." *Christian Science Monitor,* May 15, 1985, 1.

Sanchez, Maria Elena, and Giovanna Morchio. "Probing 'Don't Know' Answers: Effects of Survey Estimates on Variable Relationships." *Public Opinion Quarterly* 56, no. 4 (1992): 454–74.

Sandlow, Marc. "Bush Claims Mandate, Second-term Goals." *San Francisco Chronicle,* November 5, 2004, A1.

Sanger, David E. "Bush's Road Tour Rolls On in Push to Sell Social Security Changes." *New York Times,* June 3, 2005, 20.

Sartori, Anne E. "An Estimator for Some Binary-Outcome Selection Models without Exclusion Restrictions." *Political Analysis* 11, no. 2 (2003): 111–38.

Schaefer, Todd. "Persuading the Persuaders: Presidential Speeches and Editorial Opinion." *Political Communication* 14, no. 1 (1997): 97–111.

———. "Bill and Hilary's Excellent African Adventure." Paper presented at the annual meeting of the American Political Science Association, Chicago, Ill., August 2, 2004.

Schattschenider, E. E. *The Semisovereign People: A Realist's View of Democracy in America.* New York: Henry Holt, 1960.

Schier, Steven E. *Panorama of a Presidency: How George W. Bush Acquired and Spent His Political Capital.* Armonk, N.Y.: M. E. Sharpe, 2009.

Schlesinger, Arthur M. Jr. *A Thousand Days: John F. Kennedy in the White House.* Boston: Houghton Mifflin, 1965.

Schneider, William. "The Political Legacy of the Reagan Years." In *The Reagan Legacy,* ed. Sidney Blumenthal and Thomas Byrne Edsall, 161–81. New York: Pantheon Books, 1988.

Schubert, James N., Patrick A. Stewart, and Margaret Ann Curran. "A Defining Presidential Moment: 9/11 and the Rally Effect." *Political Psychology* 23, no. 3 (2002): 559–84.

Schutt, Russell K. *Investigating the Social World.* Thousand Oaks, Calif.: Pine Forge Press, 2001.

Shaw, Daron R. "A Study of Presidential Campaign Event Effects from 1952 to 1992." *Journal of Politics* 61, no. 2 (1999): 387–422.

Sheehan, Colleen A. "Madison v. Hamilton: The Battle over Republicanism and the Role of Public Opinion." *American Political Science Review* 98, no. 3 (2004): 405–24.

Shoup, Laurence H. *The Carter Presidency and Beyond: Power and Politics in the 1980s.* Palo Alto, Calif.: Ramparts Press, 1980.

Sigelman, Lee. "Disarming the Opposition: The President, the Public, and the INF Treaty." *Public Opinion Quarterly* 54, no. 1 (1990): 37–47.

———. "Rallying to the President's Support: A Reappraisal of the Evidence." *Polity* 11, no. 4 (1979): 542–61.

Sigelman, Lee, James Lebovic, Clyde Wilcox, and Dee Allsop. "As Time Goes By: Daily Opinion Change during the Persian Gulf Crisis." *Political Communication* 10, no. 2 (1993): 353–67.

Sigelman, Lee, and Alan Rosenblatt. "Mythological Considerations in the Analysis of Presidential Persuasion." In *Political Persuasion and Attitude Change,* ed. Diana C. Mutz, Paul M. Sniderman, and Richard A. Brody, 171–94. Ann Arbor: University of Michigan Press, 1996.

Simon, Dennis M., and Charles W. Ostrom Jr. "The Impact of Televised Speeches and Foreign Travel on Presidential Approval." *Public Opinion Quarterly* 53 (Spring 1989): 58–82.

Skewes, Elizabeth A. *Message Control: How News Is Made on the Presidential Campaign Trail.* Lanham, Md.: Rowman and Littlefield, 2007.

Sloan, John W. "Meeting the Leadership Challenges of the Modern Presidency: The Political Skills and Leadership of Ronald Reagan." *Presidential Studies Quar*terly 26, no. 3 (1996): 795–804.

———. *The Reagan Effect: Economics and Presidential Leadership.* Lawrence: University of Kansas Press, 1999.

Small, Melvin. *The Presidency of Richard Nixon.* Lawrence: University Press of Kansas, 1999.

Smith, Craig Allen. "'Rough Stretches and Honest Disagreements': Is Bill Clinton Refining the Rhetorical Presidency?" In *The Clinton Presidency: Images, Issues, and Communication Strategies,* ed. Robert E. Denton Jr. and Rachel L. Holloway, 225–48. Westport, Conn.: Praeger, 1996.

Smith, Hendrick. "Rebuff for the President." *New York Times,* April 26, 1985, A1.

Smith, Jean Edward. *George Bush's War.* New York: Henry Holt, 1992.

Sobel, Lester A. *Ford and the Economy.* New York: Facts on File, 1976.

Sobel, Richard. *The Impact of Public Opinion on U.S. Foreign Policy since Vietnam: Constraining the Colossus.* New York: Oxford University Press, 2001.

———. "Public Opinion about United States Intervention in El Salvador and Nicaragua." *Public Opinion Quarterly* 53, no. 1 (1989): 114–28.

———. *Public Opinion in U.S. Foreign Policy: The Controversy over Contra Aid.* Lanham, Md.: Rowman and Littlefield, 1993.

Sorensen, Theodore C. *Kennedy.* New York: Harper and Row, 1965.

Stephanopoulos, George. *All Too Human: A Political Education.* Boston: Little, Brown, 1999.

Stimson, James A., Michael B. MacKuen, and Robert S. Erikson. "Dynamic Representation." *American Political Science Review* 89, no. 3 (1995): 543–64.

Stoll, Richard J. "The Guns of November: Presidential Reelections and the Use of Force, 1947–1982." *Journal of Conflict Resolution* 28, no. 2 (1984): 231–46.

Stout, David, and Jeff Zeleny. "Bush Is Firm as Criticism over Iraq Mounts." *New York Times,* July 10, 2007, A1.

Sussman, Barry. "By 3 to 2, Americans Disapprove of Reagan Plan for Social Security." *Washington Post,* May 16, 1981, A8.

Taranto, James, and Leonard Leo, eds. *Presidential Leadership: Rating the Best and Worst in the White House.* New York: Wall Street Books, 2004.

Tenpas, Katherine Dunn. *Presidents as Candidates: Inside the White House for the Presidential Campaign.* New York: Routledge, 2003.

Tolchin, Martin. "Byrd Assails Cuts in Social Security as 'Harsh' and Breach of Promise." *New York Times,* May 16, 1981, section 1, 10.

Tulis, Jeffrey K. *The Rhetorical Presidency.* Princeton, N.J.: Princeton University Press, 1987.

Waterman, Richard W., Robert Wright, and Gilbert St. Clair. *The Image-Is-Everything Presidency: Dilemmas in American Leadership.* Boulder, Colo.: Westview Press, 1999.

Wattenberg, Martin P. "The Changing Presidential Media Environment." *Presidential Studies Quarterly* 34, no. 3 (2004): 557–72.

Weatherford, M. Stephen, and Lorraine M. McDonnell. "Ideology and Economic Policy." In Looking Back on the Reagan Presidency, ed. Larry Berman, 122–55. Baltimore: Johns Hopkins University Press, 1990.

Weber, Arnold R. In Pursuit of Price Stability: The Wage-Price Freeze of 1971. Washington, D.C.: Brookings Institution Press, 1973.

Welch, Reed L. "Presidential Success in Communicating with the Public through Televised Addresses." *Presidential Studies Quarterly* 33, no. 2 (2003): 347–65.

———. "Was Reagan Really a Great Communicator? The Influence of Televised Addresses on Public Opinion." *Presidential Studies Quarterly* 33, no. 4 (2003): 853–76.

Wenger, Andreas, and Marcel Gerber. "John F. Kennedy and the Limited Test Ban Treaty: A Case Study of Presidential Leadership." *Presidential Studies Quarterly* 29, no. 2 (1999): 460–87.

West, Darrell M. "Television and Presidential Popularity in America." *British Journal of Political Science* 21, no. 2 (1991): 199–214.

Western, Jon. *Selling Intervention and War: The Presidency, the Media, and the American Public.* Baltimore: Johns Hopkins University Press, 2005.

———. "The War Over Iraq: Selling War to the American Public." *Security Studies* 14, no. 1 (2005): 106–39.

Wicker, Tom. "Reagan's Real Test." In the Nation, *New York Times,* June 30, 1981, A27.

———. "A Bone in His Throat." In the Nation, *New York Times,* February 22, 1985, A27.

Wildavsky, Aaron. "The Two Presidencies." *Trans Action* 4, no. 4 (1961): 7–14.

Wilson, Woodrow. *Congressional Government: A Study in American Politics.* Boston: Houghton Mifflin, 1901.

———. *Leaders of Men,* ed. by T. H. Vail Motter. Princeton, N.J.: Princeton University Press, 1952.

Wittkopf, Eugene R. *Faces of Internationalism: Public Opinion and American Foreign Policy.* Durham, N.C.: Duke University Press, 1990.

Wittkopf, Eugene R., and James M. McCormick. "The Domestic Politics of Contra Aid: Public Opinion, Congress, and the President." In *Public Opinion in U.S. Foreign Policy: The Controversy over Contra Aid,* ed. Richard Sobel, 36–56. Lanham, Md.: Rowman and Littlefield, 1993.

Wood, B. Dan. *The Politics of Economic Leadership: The Causes and Consequences of Presidential Rhetoric.* Princeton, N.J.: Princeton University Press, 2007.

Wood, B. Dan, and Jeffrey S. Peake. "The Dynamics of Foreign Policy Agenda Setting." *American Political Science Review* 92, no. 1 (1998): 173–84.

Woods, Randall B. "Clinton, Fulbright, and the Legacy of the Cold War." In *The Clinton Riddle: Perspectives on the Forty-second President,* ed. Todd G. Shields, Jeannie M. Whayne, and Donald R. Kelley, 93–110. Fayetteville: University of Arkansas Press, 2004.

Woodward, Bob. *The Commanders.* New York: Simon and Schuster, 1991.

Woolley, John T., and Gerhard Peters. *The American Presidency Project* (online), University of California at Santa Barbara (hosted), Gerhard Peters (database), www.presidency.ucsb.edu.

Yin, Robert K. *Case Study Research: Design and Methods.* Thousand Oaks, Calif.: Sage Publications, 2002.

Young, Garry, and William B. Perkins. "Presidential Rhetoric, the Public Agenda, and the End of Presidential Television's 'Golden Age.'" Journal of Politics 67, no. 4 (2005): 1190–1205.

Zaller, John R. *The Nature and Origins of Mass Opinion.* Cambridge: Cambridge University Press, 1992.

———. "Strategic Politicians, Public Opinion, and the Gulf Crisis." In *Taken By Storm:*

The Media, Public Opinion, and U.S. Foreign Policy in the Gulf War, ed. W. Lance Bennett and David L. Paletz, 250–76. Chicago: University of Chicago Press, 1994.

Zaller, John R., and Stanley Feldman. "A Simple Theory of the Survey Response: Answering Questions versus Revealing Preferences." *American Journal of Political Science* 36, no. 3 (1992): 579–616.

Zarefsky, David. "Presidential Rhetoric and the Power of Definition." Presidential Studies Quarterly 34, no. 3 (2004): 607–19.

Zeleny, Jeff. "Already Back on the Trail, Now to Sell a Stimulus Plan." New York Times, February 8, 2009, A1.

Index

Page numbers in *italic* type indicate tables and figures.

Other Books in the Joseph V. Hughes Jr. and Holly O. Hughes Series on the Presidency and Leadership

The Politics of Shared Power: Congress and the Executive, Louis Fisher
Shaping and Signaling Presidential Policy: The National Security Decision Making of Eisenhower and Kennedy, Meena Bose
Games Advisors Play: Foreign Policy in the Nixon and Carter Administrations, Jean A. Garrison
The Managerial Presidency, James P. Pfiffner
Good Advice: Information and Policy Making in the White House, Daniel E. Ponder
Congressional Abdication on War and Spending, Louis Fisher
Vicious Cycle: Presidential Decision Making in the American Political Economy, Constantine J. Spiliotes
Presidents and the People: The Partisan Story of Going Public, Mel Laracey
The Opposition Presidency: Leadership and the Constraints of History, David A. Crockett
The Presidency, Congress, and Divided Government: A Postwar Assessment, R. S. Conley
The White House World: Transitions, Organization, and Office Operations, Martha Joynt Kumar and Terry Sullivan, eds.
Between Law and Politics: The Solicitor General and the Structuring of Race, Gender, and Reproductive Rights Litigation, Richard Pacelle Jr.
The Presidency and Women: Promise, Performance, and Illusion, Janet M. Martin
Out of Touch: The Presidency and Public Opinion, Michael J. Towle
Power and Prudence: The Presidency of George H. W. Bush, Ryan J. Barilleaux and Mark J. Rozell
The Character Factor: How We Judge America's Presidents, James P. Pfiffner
The Nerve Center: Lessons in Governing from the White House Chiefs of Staff, edited by Terry Sullivan; foreword by James A. Baker III
Nixon's Business: Authority and Power in Presidential Politics, Nigel Bowles
Saving the Reagan Presidency: Trust Is the Coin of the Realm, David M. Abshire
Policy by Other Means: Alternative Adoption by Presidents, Steven A. Shull

Institutionalizing Congress and the Presidency: The U.S. Bureau of Efficiency, 1916–1933, Mordecai Lee

Scripted for Change: The Institutionalization of the American Presidency, Victoria A. Farrar-Myers

The American Campaign: U.S. Presidential Campaigns and the National Vote, Second Edition, James E. Campbell

Running against the Grain: How Opposition Presidents Win the White House, David A. Crockett

Intelligence and National Security Policymaking on Iraq, James P. Pfiffner and Mark Phythian

Honest Broker? The National Security Advisor and Presidential Decision Making, John P. Burke

The Leadership of George Bush: An Insider's View of the Forty-first President, Roman Popadiuk

Bridging the Constitutional Divide: Inside the White House Office of Legislative Affairs, Russell L. Riley

The Unitary Executive and the Modern Presidency, Ryan J. Barilleaux and Christopher S. Kelley